Multilingualism,
Literacy
and Dyslexia

A Challenge for Educators

Edited by Lindsay Peer and Gavin Reid

foreword by
The Rt Hon David Blunkett MP

David Fulton Publishers
London

David Fulton Publishers Ltd,
Ormond House, 26–27 Boswell Street, London WC1N 3JZ

www.fultonpublishers.co.uk

First published in Great Britain by David Fulton Publishers 2000

Note: The right of Lindsay Peer and Gavin Reid to be identified as the editors of this work has been asserted by them in accordance with the Copyright, Designs and Patents Act 1988.

British Library Cataloguing in Publication Data
A catalogue record for this book is available from the British Library

ISBN 1-85346-696-4

The publishers would like to thank Lyn Corson for copy-editing and Sheila Harding for proofreading this book.

Typeset by FiSH Books, London
Printed in Great Britain by The Cromwell Press Ltd, Trowbridge, Wilts.

Contents

Section 3: Policy and Interventions

Section 4: Dyslexia in Adults and University Students

Section 5: Additional Language Learning

Foreword

Being able to read and write well is important to all children. Most take several years to learn these skills and those for whom English is an additional language, or who are learning a foreign language, may take longer. If such children also have dyslexia or other literacy difficulties, they may require additional help. The first step is to identify these children's needs, but this can sometimes be difficult, and there can often be unhelpful delays in identifying the special educational needs of these children.

To find out about the identification and provision for children with English as an additional language (EAL) who may also have special educational needs, my Department recently funded a review of research literature on this topic. This helpful and thorough report, by Tony Cline and Tatheer Shamsi from the University of Luton, was published in March 2000. This confirmed among other things that the identification of special educational needs in children with EAL is complex and often delayed while teachers and other professionals struggle to distinguish between genuine literacy problems – in other words special educational needs – and the difficulties which most children face in learning an additional language.

We have already been able to implement some of the recommendations. For example, the Qualifications and Curriculum Authority has issued assessment guidelines for EAL pupils. These guidelines should be taken into account to ensure that there is compatibility between general EAL assessments and specific assessments to determine whether a child may have learning difficulties. We have also drawn on the findings of this review during our work on the revision of the guidance in the SEN Code of Practice on the Identification and Assessment of Special Educational Needs.

There is no doubt that teachers need to know how to identify children with EAL who also have special educational needs, and also how to provide for such children effectively once they have been identified. Teachers of modern foreign languages also need to be aware of the particular difficulties which pupils with a specific learning difficulty might experience. The difficulty in the past has been that such expertise has not been widely available. The British Dyslexia Association is to be congratulated for taking the initiative in working with practitioners involved in the areas of literacy, multilingualism and dyslexia to bring together current thinking and guidance on assessment and support for practitioners facing the daily challenges of supporting bilingual learners with specific learning difficulties. I look forward to the contribution which this publication will make to spreading awareness of the particular needs of these children, and providing a stimulus for improved, better informed teaching to support their progress.

The Rt Hon David Blunkett MP
Secretary of State for Education and Employment
May 2000

Introduction

Tony Cline, Professor of Educational Psychology,
University of Luton

Over the years researchers and practitioners working in the field of dyslexia, and those working in the field of bilingualism, have had little contact with each other. A conference organised by the British Dyslexia Association in 1999 was, as far as we know, the first such event to be devoted to the single theme – multilingualism and dyslexia. This book grew out of the conference and moves beyond it. The text brings together a multinational group of authors who have lively and stimulating contributions to make. Many of the key features of the conference are reflected here – its international coverage, the diverse professional backgrounds of the presenters, the wide selection of relevant themes, the vitality of the debate and the underlying concern for a central issue of human rights. The aim is to develop and promote a fuller appreciation of the issues and to work towards significant changes in policy and practice.

Most research on dyslexia has focused on monolingual learners, as has most of the work on developing good practice in professional settings. At the same time, in a separate segment of the educational scene, research on bilingual children has generally focused on speakers who do not have special educational needs. Workers in these groups have operated independently of each other but as the work that is reported here shows, there is much to be gained from changing that. This book (along with the 1999 conference and a special issue (2000) of the journal *Dyslexia: An International Journal of Research and Practice* **6**(2) will contribute to achieving the shifts in attitudes and understanding that are required.

The Editors

Lindsay Peer is Education Director of the British Dyslexia Association, and is a widely recognised authority in the field of dyslexia and mainstream education. She appears regularly at national and international events, and has published a considerable body of material, both theoretical and practical. Her field of experience covers teacher training, research, policy and the teaching of both mainstream students and those with specific learning difficulties/dyslexia from preschool through to adult education. She is Vice-Chairman of the Accreditation Board of the British Dyslexia Association, and works closely with higher education institutions. She also has considerable experience of educational needs assessment and counselling. She is particularly interested in the teaching of English as an additional language and specific skills relating to the educational development of bilingual students with learning problems.

Her work involves close liaison with various government departments both in the UK and abroad, including the Department for Education and Employment, the Teacher Training Agency and the Qualifications and Curriculum Authority. Among the committees of which she is a member is the National Literacy and Numeracy Strategy Group. She has lectured internationally in the USA, Israel, India, Sweden, Italy, Belgium, Finland, Iceland and Norway. She was recently honoured with awards for pioneering work on dyslexia in Israel by Bar Ilan University.

Dr Gavin Reid is a senior lecturer in the Department of Equity Studies and Special Education at the University of Edinburgh. An experienced teacher, educational psychologist, university lecturer and researcher, he has made numerous conference and seminar presentations in the UK, Norway, Denmark, Germany, United States, New Zealand, Hong Kong, Poland, Hungary, Bratislava and the Czech Republic.

He has written and edited key course text books for teacher training in the field of dyslexia and literacy – *Dyslexia: A Practitioners Handbook* (published by Wiley, 1998) and *Dimensions of Dyslexia* (vols 1 and 2, published by Moray House, 1996) and is co-author of *Dyslexia in Adults: Education and Employment* (published by Wiley, 2000). He is the co-author of *Learning Styles: A Guide for Teachers and Parents* and *Dyslexia: A Resource Guide for Parents and Teachers* (both published by Red Rose Publications, 1997) and co-author of a group test – *Listening and Literacy Index* (published by Hodder and Stoughton, 2000).

He is a consultant to a number of national and international initiatives in dyslexia and is a member of the Accreditation Board of the British Dyslexia Association.

Notes on the Contributors

Ewan Adams was a research student within the Department of Psychology, University of Surrey, UK, when his study was undertaken.

Carmel Adoram is Coordinator of Evaluation and Research, Jerusalem Education Authority, Israel.

Jenni Beard is the Learning Support Advisor and Welfare Officer/Counsellor at the University of Buckingham, UK. She has worked with dyslexic and mainstream learners.

Awena Carter is a research student in the Department of Linguistics and Modern Foreign Language at Lancaster University, UK. She supports children in primary schools.

Ann Cooke is a member of the Dyslexia Unit, University of Wales, Bangor. A well-known speaker, teacher and researcher, she is a member of the Accreditation Board of the British Dyslexia Association.

Margaret Crombie is Network Support Manager, East Renfrewshire Council, UK, and has researched into the effects of dyslexia on the learning of modern foreign languages.

Pamela Deponio is a lecturer in specific learning difficulties/dyslexia at Moray House Institute, University of Edinburgh, UK.

Rika Deutsch is a teacher trainer and teacher of primary school aged children in the Jerusalem Reading Recovery Program, Israel.

Yota Dimitriadi is a dyslexia teacher and bilingual assessor who is investigating second language acquisition and computers. She gained an award for a presentation on multimedia authoring and dyslexia at the International Conference CAL99.

Nest Tudor Efans is a member of the Dyslexia Unit, University of Wales, Bangor. He works mainly in local education authority schools and has a particular interest in the acquisition of literacy in Welsh and English.

John Everatt is a lecturer within the Department of Psychology, University of Surrey, UK, with a specific research interest in dyslexia.

Tsila Evers, assistant professor at Miami University, USA, has taught courses in Hebrew and educational and social psychology. She is a senior research assistant at the Consortium for Cross-Cultural Research at the University of Michigan, USA.

Stuart Forbes is a senior educational psychologist for the City and County of Swansea, Wales, UK.

Elizabeth Dianne Frost, a native English speaker with interest in bilingual issues has taught in non-English speaking countries for 30 years.

Leonore Ganschow is Professor Emeritus, Department of Educational Psychology, Miami University, OH, USA. She was Vice-President of the International Dyslexia Association from 1992 to 1996. She is a prolific author, researcher and editor in the area of language learning and learning disabilities.

Marjorie Bussman Gillis has a doctorate in special education and works as an educational therapist. She is consultant for the State of Connecticut and Weston School System, USA.

Ted Glynn is Professor of Teacher Education at the University of Waikato in New Zealand. Recent research has focused on bicultural and bilingual issues in New Zealand education.

Sonja Greening works as a resource teacher: learning and behaviour in New Zealand, working with at-risk students.

Louise Miller Guron is conducting comparative research on English and Swedish reading strategies at the Department of Psychology, Goteborg, Sweden. She is author of the English word reading test, *Wordchains* (NFER-Nelson, Windsor).

Marjorie Hall Haley is associate professor in the Graduate School of Education's Center for Multilingual/Multicultural Education at George Mason University in Virginia, USA.

Jane Hutchinson is a research student in the Department of Psychology at the University of Central Lancashire, UK.

Shlomit Ilan has worked for 35 years teaching English as a foreign language in Israel.

Melanie Jameson qualified in French, German and Russian, teaches English for Speakers of Other Languages (ESOL) in Lancaster, UK and is Education Advisor to the Adult Dyslexia Association.

Anne Marie Kidde is an educational psychologist, teacher and consultant working on the assessment of bilingual pupils in Copenhagen, Denmark.

Jane Kirk is a dyslexia advisor and lecturer in the Department of Equity Studies and Special Education at the University of Edinburgh, UK. She was formerly principal teacher of learning support in a secondary school.

John Landon is a senior lecturer in the Department of Equity Studies and Special Education at the University of Edinburgh, UK. He has substantial international experience in multicultural and multilingual issues.

Angus Hikairo Macfarlane is a senior lecturer at the University of Waikato in New Zealand where his research interests include reducing the at-risk status of Maori students.

Hilary McColl, a former French teacher with an interest in special educational needs, is an independent consultant.

David McLoughlin, author and lecturer in the field of dyslexia, is a chartered psychologist working in education and occupational psychology. He is Director of the Adult Dyslexia and Skills Development Centre, London, UK.

Stephanie Miller is a trained and practising Orton Gillingham Educational Therapist. With a background in linguistics, she is a Consultant for the State of Connecticut, USA.

Eleni Morfidi at the time of writing was a researcher at the School of Education, University of Manchester, UK.

Joanna Nijakowska is a teacher of foreign languages in the Foreign Languages Department of Opole University, Poland.

Miriam H. Porter, is assistant professor in the Graduate School of Education's Special Education Program at George Mason University in Virginia, USA.

Robat Powell is a consultant with SCYA/NFER on behalf of the All Wales Reading Test Development Group.

Ian J. Presland works as a resource teacher: learning and behaviour in New Zealand working with at–risk students.

Peter Pumfrey, Emeritus Professor of Education at the University of Manchester, UK, is visiting professor at the Centre for Special Educational Needs, University College Worcester. He is a Vice-President of the British Dyslexia Association and member of the Council of the Dyslexia Institute.

Rea Reason is senior lecturer in education at the University of Manchester, UK. Her work has combined theory and practice in developing methods for identifying and helping children with literacy difficulties.

Theresa Reed works as an educational psychologist for Walsall Metropolitan Borough Council. Born in Hong Kong and ethnically Chinese, she came to the UK as a second language learner at the age of fifteen.

Jean Robertson, senior lecturer at Manchester Metropolitan University, UK, has experience in teaching both dyslexic pupils and the teachers who support them. She is a researcher in the neuropsychology of dyslexia.

Ann Ryan recently retired from the Centre for Applied Language Studies, University of Wales, Swansea, where she was a lecturer in applied linguistics and responsible for the university's dyslexia support courses.

Elke Schneider is a visiting professor of special education in the Department of Educational Psychology at Miami University, OH, USA. She has recently published work on the teaching of modern foreign languages to at-risk students.

Robin L. Schwarz works with learning-disabled English second language students at the English Language Institute, American University, Washington, USA.

Mary Scully is working in the Learning Support Department of Frogmore Community College, Yateley, Hampshire, UK. She teaches French and English.

Susan Secemski is lecturer and teacher trainer, Jerusalem College for Women, David Yellin Teachers' College, Israel. She is supervisor of the Jerusalem Reading Recovery Program.

Chris Smith researches literacy development, expressiveness in reading and the effectiveness and implementation of the Literacy Hour.

Ian Smythe is a researcher within the Department of Psychology, University of Surrey, UK, who has worked in many countries on dyslexia-related issues.

Aglaia Stamboltzis is a graduate of the University of Athens Department of Primary Education, Greece. She holds Masters degrees from the Centre of Special Educational Needs, University of Manchester, UK.

Helen Sunderland works at the London Language and Literacy Unit, South Bank University, UK, where she trains teachers to diagnose and support dyslexic adults.

Martin Turner is a well-known author who worked with three local authorities as an educational psychologist before joining the Dyslexia Institute, UK, in 1991 as Principal Psychologist.

Helen Whiteley has research interests in screening, diagnosis and intervention methods for children with reading difficulties.

Chapter 1

Multilingualism, Literacy and Dyslexia: A Challenge for Educators

Lindsay Peer and Gavin Reid

Challenges

Without question there are many challenges facing education today – teachers, school management, psychologists, politicians, parents and students all have specific needs, and each experience increasing pressures from the changing demands, challenges and priorities of education and society.

The challenges and priorities that face education today are considerable and complex. Financial considerations compete with the desire to provide an equitable education for all students despite the convictions of political will, cutting-edge research and enlightened practices. The needs of multilingual children, their parents and the communities in which they live must be seen as one of those overriding priorities and should not be considered just in financial terms but in terms of equity and best educational practices. Identifying the literacy and communication needs of multilingual children in a culture-fair manner will not only help to ensure the preservation of different cultures but also help to identify the cognitive abilities and communication skills of multilingual children. This must be at the heart of any educational philosophy and innovation in the 21st century.

These challenges and priorities provide the thrust and the purpose for this volume. It is necessary that culture-fair principles and practices are considered in the identification and assessment processes, in classroom practices and provision, the curriculum, in the training of teachers, support assistants and psychologists, in the selection and allocation of resources, in policy and in liaison with parents and the wider community. The need to maximise the potential of dyslexic learners whose first language may not be English is of paramount importance and this must be the priority of identification and assessment procedures.

The last two decades have witnessed great strides in our grasp of dyslexia. Much of this is due to major leaps forward in our understanding of brain function, the evolution of advanced technology, scientific and educational research and the development of effective teaching methodologies. However, there are some areas in the field of dyslexia, such as multilingualism, that, until recently, have not been recognised at all. There are others, such as modern foreign language teaching, that, although recognised, have not had effective methodologies developed. Both of these situations have led to anguish and failure on the part of the learner, the family and the school.

Teachers and psychologists have tended to misdiagnose or ignore dyslexia experienced by multilingual students because of the multiplicity of factors that seem to be causes for failure. Reasons often cited include home background, different or impoverished language skills, inefficient memory competencies, unusual learning profile, emotional stress, imbalanced speech development, restricted vocabulary in one or all languages, leading to reading, spelling and writing weaknesses; sometimes numeracy is affected. However, educators are often aware that these students are very different from others who experience difficulty as they are often bright and able orally or visually. The difference between their abilities and the low level of written work is very obvious. There are similar concerns regarding pupils who have specific difficulties while attempting to acquire a modern foreign language.

What we hope that this book will do, among other things, is suggest the way forward which should be determined by two imperatives:

- what we believe *must* happen on ethical and moral grounds relating to equity and human rights; and
- what our knowledge, skills and understanding tell us *can* happen.

There has been a serious response to these two issues from various government departments in the UK, particularly from the Department for Education and Employment (DfEE), the Qualifications and Curriculum Authority (QCA), the Teacher Training Agency (TTA) and from the Office for Standards in Education (OFSTED) responsible for inspections in schools. In addition it is accepted by the UK government that children with literacy difficulties need to be identified as early as possible if they are to make significant progress.

Following the First International Conference on Multilingualism and Dyslexia held by the British Dyslexia Association (BDA), the DfEE produced a review of research literature on multilingualism and dyslexia (Cline and Shamsi 2000). The intention was to find out what was known about the identification and provision for children who speak an additional language and who also have special educational needs:

The review inevitably focuses on areas of academic weakness in the populations that are studied. It would be very easy for a review of this kind to reinforce negative stereotypes of pupils learning English as an additional language and appear to justify lower expectations of their likely progress in schools where English is the main medium of communication. There are two correctives to that. Firstly there is UK evidence that pupils learning EAL in some LEA areas show substantially improved mean academic achievement by the end of secondary school (Gillborn and Gipps 1996). Secondly there is international evidence that bilingual children do well where the extra intellectual and cultural capital that they bring with them is valued and incorporated in the school curriculum (Collier 1992, 1995a and Cummins 1984). We are focusing on challenges that are overcome by the vast majority of pupils in this population and on exceptional difficulties that are experienced by a minority. That focus should not mislead anyone to expect problems where they need not occur. At the same time if there

is some underachievement because of reading difficulties, we hope to contribute
to identifying the work that is needed to address the problem.

(Cline and Shamsi 2000: 2)

The authors continue: 'The writing process has received less attention from those
concerned with the identification of learning difficulties (Moseley 1997 and Turner
1993, 1997)...We will suggest that some re-balancing would be timely. The goal of
the literacy curriculum is that children should be able to read and write and also that
they should choose to engage with a wide range of text and use their literacy skills
to enhance their understanding and enjoyment of the world and their capacity for
action (Hudelson 1994). For children learning English as an additional language,
biliteracy may offer a particularly rich range of options (Kenner 1998, Wallace
1988). But the wider definition of literacy is rarely mentioned in the literature on
learning difficulties' (Cline and Shamsi 2000: 3).

How do we make students who have both EAL and dyslexic needs more of a
priority for education policy makers? How do we recognise that a system is biased
and then change it? How can we produce and share educational research
internationally? Where can we find tests that differentiate these children and adults
from other groups? What training can be given to teachers who are currently working
with such students? If teachers are unaware of how children acquire language, how
can they recognise those that do not and help them appropriately? How do we
influence initial teacher education so that the next generation of children will be
better off? It is necessary to understand the different learning patterns of multilingual
dyslexic people if teachers are to provide appropriate programmes of learning.

It must be appreciated that this is worldwide problem. Many countries demand
that their students reach a high level of proficiency in a minimum of two languages
before entering vocational or academic higher education. Failure to achieve the
required competence in two languages at this level is a personal tragedy for the
individual but also represents a substantial loss of skills to society which neither
developed, nor underdeveloped nations can afford.

It has long been recognised that dyslexic people have a range of skills, such as
visual-spatial and verbal, that are in great demand. As technology develops, the
specific skills required in literacy in today's world will diminish, changing the needs
of any given society. We need to support the dyslexic community, including those that
speak more than one language. In this ever-changing world it will be people like them
with innovative ideas who will lead the way – it is clearly worth the investment.

The remainder of this opening chapter will discuss some of these key factors, all
of which can influence the outcome of the education process for multilingual learners
who have dyslexic difficulties; we will then provide an overview of this book.

Identification

The identification of dyslexic and other specific literacy difficulties represents a
crucial acknowledgement on the part of education authorities of the importance of
identifying difficulties and strengths as early as possible. It has taken those who
represent the interests of dyslexic people some time to reinforce the message to

education authorities that dyslexia must be diagnosed early if intervention is to be successful. This is also crucial in the case of multilingual learners. It is necessary therefore that culture-fair tests and appropriate strategies for multilingual learners be developed and widely used.

Bolton and M'gadzah (1999) in discussing the training requirements of educational psychologists highlight how one educational psychologist in their study thought that it should be compulsory for all trainees to carry out at least one piece of casework involving the assessment of a multilingual child. This would certainly help to identify the needs of multilingual children and with appropriate training could form a platform for additional training in dyslexia and multilingualism. It should also be noted that the research data published by the Scottish Office Education Department (1991) showed an over-representation of multilingual children assessed as having severe/profound learning difficulties in contrast to their under-representation in moderate/specific learning difficulties. The Commission for Racial Equality (CRE 1992) suggested this uneven distribution was in all likelihood due to lack of clear culture-fair assessment criteria.

Testing

There is much cultural bias in both psychometric testing and particularly in those tests used by teachers to measure gains in literacy – the learning experiences of children may differ from culture to culture. One example of this is the question posed by the Wechsler Intelligence Scale for Children which asks children what they should do if they found a wallet in the street. Children in England or Wales might answer that they would look for the owner's name and, failing that, hand it into the police. When asked the same question in Israel or Ireland, time and again, children would say they would not pick it up as it might explode!

Cultural experiences have a great effect on the way we think, feel and react. Even tests for small children make assumptions about the familiarity of play objects and experiences. Without awareness of the different learning and socialising habits of the particular culture from which the child comes, many unfortunate assumptions may be made about the child's assumed lack of ability. Tests given orally are prone to the same bias and therefore have to be considered with great care and knowledge on the part of the tester.

It is not a viable proposition to trust the use of translation for administration of tests for children whose native language is not the language in which the tests were designed. There are problems of cultural and linguistic bias, differing syntax and structure which would make them unreliable, hence their scores invalid. Cline and Reason (1993) postulate that children who are at risk of dyslexia, due to immature phonological awareness and memory, will face heightened difficulties if the language or dialect adopted in school is different to that spoken at home. Avery and Ehrlich (1987) describe the difficulties for children for whom English has been acquired as a second language in terms of the problems of pronouncing English vowels and consonants which are not in their native tongue. They point out that these children are not used to using relevant mouth muscles in the appropriate way.

The ability to comprehend is also a problem dependent on appropriate word stress, rhythm and intonation. If the specific student's dyslexia is based on weaknesses in auditory processing, clearly the additional strain of another language will exacerbate the difficulties. Cline and Reason (1993) state that 'it seems extraordinary that the research traditions on specific learning difficulties (dyslexia) and on social and cultural differences have remained in different compartments'.

Practice and provision

The selection of resources, and particularly reading material, is of significant importance in the case of multilingual learners. Reading materials can provide stimulation and motivation for learning and enhance the development of literacy skills. It is important therefore that such reading materials acknowledge the diversity of communities and of individuals within these communities. Assessments should be linked to reading material which is seen to be culture-fair and the recommendations from these assessments linked to resources that are culture-appropriate. There is little doubt that reading progress will be accelerated if efforts are made to utilise high interest and age-appropriate reading materials. This applies to all children but it is particularly crucial if there are compounding literacy difficulties. It is also important to consider factors relating to conceptual development; this relates quite strongly to language usage and the learner's own experiences. It is important therefore that the home and community context of multilingual learners are considered in order to facilitate the development of appropriate schema and meaningful concepts. This in itself can aid decoding and literacy skills.

Equal opportunities issues

There is a great need to separate out additional language learners who perform badly due to limited familiarity with the language and cultural differences of the country. For those who demonstrate language and learning disorders that require special education intervention there has been some uncertainty regarding diagnosis which has prevented much work from being carried out. The concerns fall into two groups:

(a) False positive i.e. the risk of labelling a child as having a learning difficulty when one is not present. The Commission for Racial Equality in 1986 drew attention to the fact that pupils whose home language was not 'standard English' were discriminated against in their allocation to special educational provision.
(b) False negative i.e. the risk of failing to identify a learning difficulty early enough. There is much anecdotal evidence from both the UK and USA citing cases of multilingual children who did not receive the appropriate help they required for many years and, as a result, the subsequent difficulties were particularly hard to manage.

Bias

Cline and Reason (1993) cite researchers who have looked at older children and have reached different conclusions. Edwards (1986) investigated perceptions of the language of Afro-Caribbean children. Student teachers and groups of pupils were asked to make a series of judgements on the basis of taped extracts from the speech of four children: a working-class Reading boy, a middle-class boy, a recently arrived Jamaican girl and a British-born Barbadian girl who, unbeknown to the judges, spoke twice: once in a Reading dialect and once in a Began dialect.

A hierarchical situation arose from the judges' evaluations in which the middle-class boy was looked upon most favourably, following by working-class speakers and then by the West Indian speakers. Significantly the same child was evaluated more positively when she spoke with an English accent than when she used a West Indian one. Some of the student teacher judges also considered that West Indian girls would do worse academically and be less interesting members of the class (Edwards 1986; Breinburg 1986; McCormick-Piestrup 1974).

Policy – the school and the community

In order for any of the suggestions in this book to impact on practice there must be sound and enlightened policies. It is interesting to note that a report on the Stephen Lawrence Enquiry (McPherson 1999) suggested that every institution should examine their policies and the outcomes of these policies in order to ensure that any section of the community is not placed at a disadvantage. This should certainly be considered in relation not only to educational practices but also in relation to dyslexia and literacy. It has taken long periods of intensive lobbying, groundbreaking research and wide-scale teacher training programmes to help address the needs of teachers and pupils in relation to dyslexia. It is essential, therefore, that similar pressures and impetus for training is afforded to multilingualism and dyslexia. Furthermore it is essential that these policies consider the needs of the neighbourhood, of communities and of parents.

One vital factor in dyslexia is the need to dispel misleading myths and encourage optimism and cooperation. Information needs to be disseminated and avenues opened for parents and adults with dyslexia in order to allay fears and encourage communication. The parents of multilingual children who have dyslexic difficulties should be encouraged to develop essential skills in self-advocacy and to participate in consultative groups on dyslexia in relation to both practice and policy. This may well require the presence of interpreters for spoken and written English at such meetings.

Essentially only full and effective inclusion education can bring about the desired outcomes in relation to achieving equality for all. Sebba and Ainscow (in a DfEE lecture in 1998) described inclusive education as a process by which a school attempts to respond to all pupils as individuals by reconsidering and restructuring its curricular organisation and provision and allocating resources to enhance equality of opportunity. It is through this process that the school builds its capacity to accept all pupils from the community (adapted from Sebba and Ainscow). This emphasises the need for major and perhaps radical rethinking of the concept of curriculum for all. This concept needs to be directed to the full diversity of cultures, experiences and interests of all children in all communities.

Potential of learners

If the barriers to literacy can be overcome, multilingual learners, as with all dyslexic children, can benefit from a range of learning experiences which can develop language skills and facilitate progress in attainments. It is important that the actual process of learning is understood and highlighted. The development of thinking skills and metacognitive awareness can help achieve this thereby promoting access to the full curriculum for dyslexic children and ensuring that both academic and social learning are considered. Those aspects should also be seen to be important for multilingual dyslexic children. The development of schema and language concepts are fundamental to understanding language in a meaningful context. Once concepts and schema are understood it is easier to apply them to other experiences and other learning contexts.

Cline (1999a) suggests that racism can be conceived as the interaction between an uneven distribution of power and influence, discriminatory practices and the prejudiced belief and attitudes of individuals. It is important that discriminatory practices do not diminish the learning experiences and the potential of multilingual dyslexic learners.

Overview of the book

Section 1: Assessment

All aspects relating to assessment are crucial in the identification of the strengths and difficulties of multilingual learners. It is too easy to misdiagnose any language difficulties they may display. Chapter 2 by Ian Smythe and John Everatt which commences the section on assessment highlights some of these difficulties through cross-linguistic comparisons and particularly the need to understand the language culture and context of different countries. They suggest it is also crucial for a common consensus on the aetiology of dyslexia – clearly a factor which can and has led to the type of misdiagnosis experienced by multilingual children. This point is developed by Martin Turner in Chapter 3 who examines the relationship between multilingualism and learning difficulties. He suggests that multilingual language use is a matter of circumstances while dyslexia is genetically based, but this can result in the double load of multilingual language learning becoming a triple load if dyslexic difficulties are present. It is for that reason that test construction must be pursued in an enlightened manner to take account of language differences. Stuart Forbes and Robat Powell in Chapter 4 provide an excellent example of this crucial test development process in relation to the All Wales Reading Test which takes into account literacy assessment for a population that has exposure to two different languages at levels which may vary widely both within and between home and school. Similarly John Everatt, Ewan Adams and Ian Smythe show in the following chapter (focusing on the London Borough of Tower Hamlets where 25 per cent of the population are multilingual) the range of factors that can influence effective screening for multilingual children. They suggest that most of the existing screening tests were devised for a monolingual population and the multiplicity of factors involved in multilingual students learning development (Peer, from a presentation to Multilingual Forum, BDA 1997) can render some screening methods inappropriate.

In the final chapter of the assessment section Jane Hutchinson, Helen Whiteley and Chris Smith provide a detailed description of the assessments used to measure outcomes in a project involving both EAL and monolingual children. They also attempt to show how language-related difficulties can impact upon literacy development and, importantly, how this should be dealt with in relation to the identification of dyslexia by education authorities. The assessment section therefore highlights the need for appropriate test development, careful consideration of the differences between the language and literacy development of multilingual children and that of dyslexic children to minimise undiagnosed or misdiagnosed dyslexia. It is important, as is suggested in the final chapter in this section, that assessment should provide constructive suggestions for classroom practice and this point is in fact the focus of the next section of this book on approaches and strategies.

Section 2: Approaches and Strategies

As well as considering the link between assessment and teaching, Pamela Deponio, John Landon and Gavin Reid (Chapter 7) suggest some approaches for devising and implementing teaching approaches and emphasise the need for collaboration within the school and with parents. Teaching approaches should be comprehensive and as well as literacy-related activities, such as phonological awareness, other factors involving cognitive, metacognitive and social strategies should also be considered.

In the following chapter Eleni Morfidi and Rea Reason show the beneficial effect of additional phonics intervention for multilingual children. They acknowledge however the range of factors which could have influenced the research outcome, and particularly the need for caution when interpreting test data. In Chapter 9 Agliai Stamboltzis and Peter Pumfrey examine other factors associated with literacy development, in particular the role of text genre, and link this to reading and multilingualism. They also provide practical suggestions for teaching children with dyslexia who have English as an additional language and suggest a range of resource material including internet sources.

It is important to consider the view that literacy is more than reading and spelling and Awena Carter in her chapter on shared writing (Chapter 10) looks beyond the text level and examines the cultural and social influences which can embed the literacy practices of multilingual children. She shows how by supporting children's writing in a collaborative environment a higher level of functioning and thought can be achieved.

This is followed by the chapter by Nest Efans and Ann Cooke who, by examining errors children make in Welsh, make inferences on the generability of such errors in relation to EAL children. This provides some insights into our understanding about children's learning in a multilingual situation in relation to dyslexia.

In Chapter 12 Louise Guron highlights the comparisons in literacy between monolingual and multilingual Swedish speakers and discusses the difficulties in decoding and interpreting second language text. She also describes some current challenges to practitioners in relation to multilingualism and literacy.

Increasingly information and communications technology (ICT) is exerting influence in classroom learning. Yota Dimitriadi in her chapter highlights how the curriculum can be accessed for bilingual children through effective use of ICT – the multisensory nature of the programmes, how connections between two languages can be achieved and the increasing confidence this medium provides to the learner in helping to explore and discuss aspects of the two languages.

Section 3: Policy and Interventions

This section links with the previous one on approaches and strategies but takes a more global overview identifying some of the issues which need to be dealt with by teachers and management. In the first chapter in this section Theresa Reed examines the context of racism and the need for professionals to examine the nature of their procedures. She argues for a 'bilingual-biliterate' curriculum in order to provide real opportunities for all bilingual learners, discusses an intervention framework and shows how we can learn from bilingual research. This is aptly followed by Angus Macfarlane, Ted Glynn, Ian Presland and Sonja Greening who, using the example of Maori culture in New Zealand, show how it is possible for a country to provide an education system which embraces and reflects the culture of, in this case, the Maori group. They emphasise how these practices need to be interwoven through all programmes, initiatives and interventions for cultures such as the Maori. Many lessons can be learnt here for other cultures and for professionals and policy makers in other countries.

This is followed by the chapter by Elizabeth Frost (Chapter 16) who considers the role bilingualism plays in written language difficulties and discusses this with reference to a case study. This examines the effect of early bilingualism on language development as well as the cultural, social and educational implications. This theme is extended in the following chapter when Anne Marie Kidde discusses some key issues in teaching Danish in a multicultural setting and provides comments on best practice. Central to effective practice is teacher training and Marjorie Haley and Miriam Porter in their chapter on rethinking teacher training for linguistically diverse students with dyslexia (Chapter 18) show how it is necessary for professional training to be reconsidered in the light of the increasing number of linguistically diverse students at schools and universities. They provide an outline of a pedagogical framework for such training at both pre- and in-service levels. This emphasises the view that training is a policy consideration and should be an integral component of any policy and intervention.

Section 4: Dyslexia in Adults and University Students

This section highlights the post-school aspects of multilingualism as well as the often unfulfilled potential of multilingual adults. It commences with a chapter by Helen Sunderland who provides a list of critical factors to take into account when assessing multilingual adults and shows how it is possible to identify dyslexia and provide appropriate support following this diagnosis.

University environments are increasingly becoming multicultural and this is highlighted in Chapter 20 with reference to three universities in the UK. In the first example, David McLaughlin and Jenni Beard describe the adjustments that have to be made by overseas students as well as the assessment and support provision within the University of Buckingham. Ann Ryan follows this by examining in detail the similarities in the language processing between dyslexic students and second language learners and describes experimental work in this area at the University of Swansea in Wales. The need to address these issues from a policy and systems perspective is highlighted by Jane Kirk who describes the pioneering work at the University of Edinburgh in this area. She focuses on the training needs of faculty staff and provides examples of both top-down and bottom-up practices.

The following two chapters by Leonore Ganschow, Elke Schneider and Tsila Evers from Miami University in Ohio and Robin Schwarz from the American University in Washington DC describe how the expectation of competence in English is handled by universities in the USA. Ganschow *et al.* suggest a flexible approach to EFL proficiency and provide suggestions for educators to consider. Schwarz describes a learning skills program designed to support ESL students with a learning disability and attempts to answer the question why seemingly bright international students have difficulty with English courses and suggests that a more holistic approach to supporting such students should be encouraged.

It is clear that much has still to be achieved in assessing and supporting international university students so they can fulfil their potential in an academic environment. This section therefore touches on some of these issues which need to be addressed and highlights the existing and potential good practices which can help to achieve equality of opportunity for all students.

Section 5: Additional Language Learning

Additional language learning can present considerable difficulties for children and indeed adults with dyslexia. Certainly at school it is important to ensure that language learning is present and assessed in a dyslexia-friendly manner – all too often it is not! It is for that reason that a substantial section of this book is devoted to that subject. Jean Robertson in her chapter on the neuropsychology of modern foreign language learning (Chapter 23) looks at the role of the cerebral hemispheres in language learning in relation to the task demands and concludes that while both hemispheres need to be involved in the reading process, if material is presented to encourage greater right hemisphere involvement the acquisition of foreign languages is likely to be greater for more students.

This is followed by the chapter by Margaret Crombie and Hilary McColl who examine the notion of 'modern languages for all' and show how the research evidence combined with a firm commitment can minimise the practical obstacles which may prevent the objective of modern languages for all. In Chapter 25, Stephanie Miller and Marjorie Gillis provide a practical example of how this can be achieved and place considerable emphasis on the need to provide language instruction in the native language as well as the foreign language. Melanie Jameson follows this by providing a range of strategies that focus on the strengths of the dyslexic person as well as alternatives and disapplication in relation to the core National Curriculum in England and Wales.

The chapter by Susan Secemski, Rika Deutsch and Carmel Adoram looks at the impact of the Jerusalem Reading Recovery Program on providing the additional skills necessary to help learners return to the mainstream classroom. They suggest that this can have an international appeal and facilitate collaboration between the range of professionals and management who implement policy in this area. Similarly in Chapter 28 Shlomit Ilan provides an example of another specific approach – the global analytical method of teaching the reading of English – and shows how holistic strategies together with structure and repetition can facilitate effective foreign language learning and teaching.

In the penultimate chapter of this book Joanna Nijakowska looks at teacher awareness and attitudes to foreign language teaching in relation to dyslexia in Poland. She emphasises that lack of training and understanding of dyslexic difficulties represent the greatest barriers to second language learning and teaching.

Training is also an issue in the final chapter on using the internet as a multimedia method of teaching a modern foreign language to people with dyslexia. In this chapter Mary Scully shows how the internet has the potential to allow students to be interactive and productive but how careful consideration should be given to dyslexic children to ensure that operation of the internet is fully accessible. For example, Scully found that for the average dyslexic student the speed of delivery of instructions on how to use the internet was too quick, therefore those with language processing problems were not able to process the instructions at the same speed as delivery of the instructions. The result was that the dyslexic student, eager to show the same rate of activity as others, did not seek clarification but instead attempted to copy from peers.

This reinforces the need for all subject teachers to have an understanding of dyslexic difficulties and particularly the most appropriate method of presenting material. This indeed is one of the 'challenges for educators'.

The way forward

There is much still remaining to be achieved if the needs of all dyslexic children and adults are to be fully met. While much has already been achieved within the field of dyslexia, particularly in terms of policies and provision, there is still a great deal of progress yet to be accomplished in the field of multilingualism and literacy.

It is hoped, therefore, that enlightened and adequately funded policies will acknowledge current research and the views of practitioners and parents. It is necessary that current assessment, practice and provision for dyslexic children be extended to meet the literacy and learning needs of dyslexic children whose first language may be other than English. Identification and accurate diagnosis are essential as these can help to identify the most appropriate materials and learning environment for all multilingual learners with dyslexia. It is hoped that the contributions in this volume will help in some way to achieve the means and the motivation for this to become desirable and established practice in every country.

Chapter 2

Dyslexia Diagnosis in Different Languages

Ian Smythe and John Everatt

This chapter includes:

- a discussion of the issues surrounding the definition of dyslexia worldwide
- a discussion of the relationship between cognitive deficits and variations in language/script
- a report of the development of the International Dyslexia Test.

Introduction

There can be little doubt that dyslexia is an international concern (see Table 2.1), although the extent to which it becomes important at the personal, school or legislative level will depend upon a number of factors including the perceived importance of education in the community and the resources available for special educational provisions. Additionally, the awareness and understanding of dyslexia in the local context can play an important part in the recognition of and support for the dyslexic individual. Although the following should not be taken as suggesting that one country has 'got it right' in comparison to another, there are obvious differences in perspectives. To take two examples from those discussed in the following pages. In the UK, it is estimated that there are two million severely dyslexic individuals, including 300,000 school children (Peer 2000). In contrast, there are no such estimates in China. Whether this reflects perceived importance or differences in incidence is as yet unknown; however, it indicates differences in awareness which will naturally lead to variations in provision. Similarly, despite dyslexia being recognised throughout the world (Salter and Smythe 1997), tests to identify the difficulties experienced by individuals with dyslexia exist in relatively few languages. Given the perceived importance of dyslexia assessment and support (Salter and Smythe 1997), there is a need for systematic research that identifies similarities and differences between these contexts which will aid in the development of appropriate diagnostic and remediation tools. This chapter reports the preliminary stages of such a research project and in the process highlights a number of issues which must be addressed by cross-language dyslexia research.

The majority of research seeking to identify the underlying cause(s) of dyslexia has involved studies of English speaking individuals. This research has focused on

Table 2.1: Prevelance of dyslexia as noted by researchers and practitioners in countries around the world (Salter and Smythe 1997)

Belgium	5%	Nigeria	11%
Britain	4%	Norway	3%
Czech Republic	2-3%	Poland	4%
Finland	10%	Russia	10%
Greece	5%	Singapore	3.3%
Italy	1.3-5.0%	Slovakia	1 to 2%
Japan	6%	USA	8.5%

the relationship between dyslexia and poor phonological awareness (Stanovich 1988; Snowling and Nation 1997), with deficits in processing novel letter strings (non-words) often been used as indicators of dyslexia (Rack *et al.* 1992). However, in languages where there may not be the same reliance on phonological awareness (languages which have been described as highly transparent or as logographic, for example), there are still reports of children and adults experiencing similar problems with acquiring reading and writing skills as those experienced by English learners. Other factors such as general speed of processing or visual recognition skills may be more important signifiers of dyslexia in these non-English languages (Wimmer 1993 for German; Ho and Lai in press for Chinese). The development of tests which can be used to diagnose dyslexia in different languages therefore needs to include a broad range of cognitive identifiers.

Any study that attempts to develop tests in different languages must overcome translation problems. This requires experts in both languages to understand what the tests are trying to measure rather than simply changing the wording from one language to a second: a test of rhyming is unlikely to be a test of rhyming across several languages if direct word-for-word translations were implemented.

Definitions

Within the UK, a Working Party of the Division of Educational and Child Psychology of the British Psychology Society was established to consider the assessment of dyslexia. As part of this process, they proposed the following definition of dyslexia (1999: 11):

> Dyslexia is evident when accurate and fluent word reading and/or spelling develops very incompletely or with great difficulty.

If this were the working definition used by the UK-based educational psychologist, then differences would occur between dyslexics in the UK and other countries. In Russia, for example, dyslexia refers only to a reading disorder, while dysgraphia refers to a writing disorder. Dyslexia is manifested in a slower rate of reading and in numerous specific errors which are persistent in nature. In dysgraphia an inappropriate grapheme (letter) may be used, or there may be a syntactical disorder that is persistent in nature (Salter and Smythe 1997). Indeed, many researchers (particularly those writing for the English-based literature) would use the term dysgraphia to be synonymous with spelling difficulties. However, in Italy, dysgraphia is reserved for motor difficulties while disorthographia refers to spelling difficulties. In Poland, motor difficulties specific to writing are referred to by the term dysautographia.

These differences in terminology mean that any study of dyslexia cannot simply rely on local diagnoses to determine commonalities and differences across countries and languages.

A framework for testing

The following model was derived from a review of research into dyslexia and the acquisition of reading, writing and spelling in different orthographies, as well as an analysis of assessment tools available in different countries. The framework incorporates several theoretical perspectives. For example, Fletcher *et al.* (1997) propose a five-process model and, based on cluster analyses, hypothesised sub-types of reading disability. Although the model proposed in the present chapter should be considered as divorced from the sub-type perspective of the Fletcher *et al.* (1997) model, the five-process viewpoint provides a basis with which to compare literacy acquisition across the languages studied. In addition, Wagner and Torgesen (1987) identify three primary 'phonological processing skills': phonological awareness (phonological sensitivity), phonological recoding in lexical access (rapid naming) and verbal short-term memory. The model adopted for this research attempts to distinguish clearly between these (Figure 2.1). Hence, phonological processing in the model refers to the fragmentation and assembly of words, occurring on several different levels (phoneme, syllable, rime/onset) and is separated from the auditory system (which includes auditory discrimination, auditory perception, auditory sequential memory and auditory short-term memory), and speed of processing (indicated by naming speed). Finally, the model includes processes related to the visual system (e.g. visual discrimination, visual perception, visual sequential memory and visual short-term memory) and semantics (the semantic lexicon).

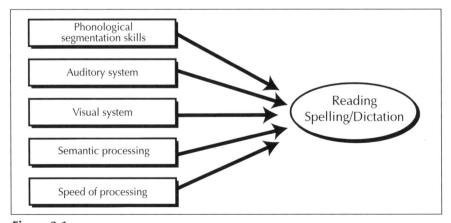

Figure 2.1

Rationale for the proposed model can be seen in the problems presented by learners (particularly those who would be recognised as dyslexic) in English and non-English contexts. Hence while the transparency of the correspondence between spelling and sound has been seen as a key feature of literacy acquisition among English learners, there are additional problems that the dyslexic individual may experience even in highly transparent orthographies. The Hungarian example in Figure 2.2 demonstrates a highly regular writing system which may present problems of visual complexity (diagraphic markers) and auditory short-term memory (its agglutinal nature). Given long enough, the child should be able to translate each of the graphemes into a particular sound, allowing him/her to 'read' this word. However, problems in the visual system or with short-term retention of initial sounds will lead to reading problems. Similarly, slow access of the meaning of the word may lead to poor understanding of vocabulary when placed in continuous text; indeed in more regular orthographies (Wimmer 1993 on German) speed of processing seems a more reliable predictor of reading difficulties. The Hungarian child with reading problems may have few deficits in the area of phonological processing (as defined by the model) yet still present severe problems with acquiring accurate and fluent word reading.

Hungarian has good phoneme-grapheme correspondence. However, there are many difficulties for the dyslexic individual.

'Diszlexiaveszélyeztetettség', the Hungarian for 'at risk of dyslexia', is a very good example of the most difficult points of the Hungarian language. It is difficult for a dyslexic to analyse due to the need to segment the word, and retain in short-term memory all the individual components.

The word consists of two morphemes, the first of which refers to dyslexia. The second part demonstrates the agglutinal nature of the language:

The basic word is 'veszély', a simple noun. It means 'danger'.

'veszélyeztet', is the verb 'to endanger'.

'veszélyeztetett' is 'endangered'.

'veszélyeztetettség' – 'endangeredness', is the noun.

(Thanks to Eva Gyarmathy of the Hungarian Academy of Sciences for the above example.)

Figure 2.2 At risk of dyslexia – in Hungarian

Several types of visual difficulty may lead to poor literacy skills, dependent on the nature of the language and writing system in question. Hence, in the Hungarian example, the use of markers may increase visual confusions. Polish includes a bewildering number of diacritical marks, including acutes, dots, hooks and bars, making even a simple count of the number of letters in the alphabet a complex (subjective) task. Similarly, so called 'logographic' scripts such as Chinese may present problems of potential visual confusions, though equally they could derive from errors of recall given the number of 'logographs' which a child will be required to learn (note that although Chinese is often called a 'logographic' script it may be better described as a morphophonetic script (DeFrancis 1984)).Visual confusion errors can often be found in the writing of Chinese children (see Figure 2.3), though such errors need to be distinguished from grapho-motor deficits.

Although visual errors may be part of the problems presented by the Chinese learner, they are not the whole story (McBride-Chang and Ho in press). Figure 2.3 illustrates some errors that can be found in the results of Chinese dictation tasks. Some errors, such as semantic processing errors, are rare in English (an English learner is unlikely to write 'shoe' when asked to spell 'boot', for example); however, they may be a characteristic of learners of logographic-type scripts. Similar semantic errors have been noted by Yamada (1998) when assessing Japanese schoolchildren's ability to read kanji characters. Semantic processing is incorporated in the model (Figure 2.1) to provide an explanation of these types of errors.

Figure 2.3 Errors in Chinese dictation

The model allows us to speculate on the interrelationship between literacy skills and the separate modules for different languages. Figure 2.4 attempts to show graphically how the hypothesis of the role of orthography and phonology will translate to the five-point model. In English, it is suggested that processes related to phonological awareness will present the major obstacle for children when learning to read/write. This does not mean that other deficits will not be found among English dyslexics, but that the nature of the script being the most likely cause leading to problems related to the phonological system. Conversely, the Chinese dyslexic is more likely to present evidence of deficits in visual areas and the Hungarian dyslexic deficits of speed of processing (see Figure 2.4). These predictions are being assessed in the data collection stage of the research.

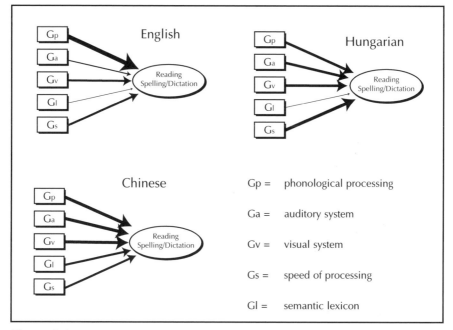

Figure 2.4

About the test

For the data collection phase of the research a series of tests was constructed to assess different literacy and cognitive skills of children from a diverse range of language backgrounds (Table 2.2 for a breakdown of the skills assessed). The combined test incorporates procedures used in a number of screening tools from different countries and languages. It was developed with time and financial constraints in mind, with the aim that it could be used as the basis of a procedure for assessing dyslexia by practitioners around the world.

A vital part of the development of the test has been the need for measures which can be 'translated' across languages. Two types of translation processes are required: those which involve direct word-for-word translation and those which require translation of the test concepts. Hence, in the latter case, tests which measured, for example, rhyme or alliteration required items which assessed these factors, and word-for-word translation was unlikely to produce comparable tests.

When direct word-for-word 'translation' was feasible, many of the measures would be influenced by language or culture-related factors. Digit spans of Chinese speakers, for example, are often larger than those using the English language. This is probably due to differences in articulation rate between Chinese and English digit names. Thus the digit span of a Chinese child that is close to average for his/her English speaking counterparts would be performing at the lower end of the range when compared against his/her Chinese speaking peers. Other measures may be affected by practice, which may be influenced by cultural practices (for example, rhythm tapping). Shape copying among Chinese children may be more advanced due to the need for the Chinese learner to appreciate and produce fine details of the script. These factors lead to problems of cross-country/language comparisons. Identification of deficits was therefore based on performance against local standards.

The tests that are visually based do not require translation as such. They are designed to look at three aspects: visual sequential memory, shape copying and shape drawing from memory. Although the first may be performed in several ways, including on computer, the latter two highlight the continuing need for one-to-one assessment. Shape copying is a measure of visual perception, linked to grapho-motor skills, as it measures the child's ability to copy a simple illustration that is always on view. Shape drawing from memory gives the child a brief time to look at a drawing and then draw it from memory. This may be analogous to copying from a board.

Measurement of the auditory domain attempted to create a distinction between the input stage and the phonological segmentation stage. The auditory components of the test are designed to measure the ability to retain a sound sequence and/or to distinguish between sounds. Different versions (e.g. word versus non-word repetition tasks) allow an assessment of the influence of known versus novel language-based information, providing an indication of the contribution of lexical/semantic information within such processes.

There is increasing evidence that speed of processing is both a significant underlying cognitive factor and identifier of dyslexia. In the present study this factor was assessed by measures of rapid naming of digits and objects (line drawings). Both were included due to the poor correlation between these measures (Smythe and Everatt, in preparation) but neither measure requires translation. However, some tests of rapid naming (e.g. Phonological Assessment Battery (PhAB)) confine items to monosyllabic words. When designing cross-language tests, this restriction is almost impossible to sustain (e.g. in Filipino all digit names are multisyllabic). In the present test material, syllable number was, therefore, also allowed to vary across digit and object names: e.g. a word such as 'elephant' would be recognised internationally, but varies from language to language in terms of the number of syllables comprising its name: in Russian it is the monosyllabic word 'slon'.

Reciting the days of the week has been used not only in English assessments, but also in Russia for screening dyslexic children. However, it was decided to omit this task in Chinese versions of the test since the days of the week are referred to as 'Star day 1, Star day 2, etc.' reducing the task to a simple counting procedure.

Raven's Matrices were also included in the battery of tests. This is a measure of general problem-solving ability, often associated with fluid intelligence (e.g. Carpenter *et al.* 1990), and avoids bias against those with language-related difficulties. The Matrices were included so that groups of children with poor versus average/good scores on literacy tests could be matched on non-verbal reasoning ability in addition to other factors such as age, class and gender. The purpose here was not to equate dyslexia with above-average intelligence, but rather to control a potential confounding factor in group comparisons. Single-case profiling (such as for educational assessment purposes) would treat scores on the Matrices as an additional factor in the profile rather than as a control factor.

Table 2.2 Sub-tests of the International Dyslexia Test

'LITERACY' SKILLS	UNDERLYING SKILLS
Basic knowledge	**Auditory short-term memory**
alphabet and number knowledge	digit span and rhythm
Spelling	**Visual short-term memory**
single word and non-word spelling	visual sequential memory
Reading	**Visual perception**
single word and non-word reading	**Sequencing**
Phonological manipulation	days of week and counting
alliteration and rhyme	**Perception/fine motor skills**
Phonological short-term memory	shape copying
word and non-word repetition	**Maths**
Lexical access - rapid naming	**Visual IQ** – Raven's matrices
Auditory discrimination	**Gross motor skill**

Results

The intention of this chapter was to discuss the underlying philosophy behind the approach, and highlight some of the difficulties when looking at dyslexia in different languages. While the full data analysis is reported elsewhere (Smythe and Everatt, in preparation) two interesting results are worthy of mention.

Figure 2.5 shows the difficulties of two dyslexic Chinese children plotted as a percentage of the average score of the cohort. One shows poor phonological processing (onset and rime), auditory processing and rapid naming. However the difficulties of the second dyslexic child, the most severe case in terms of dictation ability, appear to be in pseudo-character reading. This test consists of a child reading a Chinese character containing two components, one semantic and one phonetic

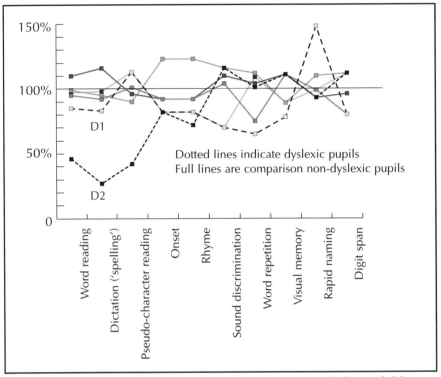

Figure 2.5 Cognitive profile of Chinese dyslexic and non-dyslexic children

radical, which occur in other words, but are shown together in a novel combination (see Ho and Bryant 1997 for more details about Chinese reading). A response that uses the phonetic radical as a cue or a character with the same phonetic radical is considered correct.

Implications for research and practice

This brief review of ongoing work suggests that we need to assess dyslexia from a wider view of the individual than the traditional 'phonological awareness' approach. Dyslexia may be caused by a combination of phonological processing, visual and auditory system deficits. Semantic confusions and speed of processing difficulties may also be present, and it is probable that this is due to a number of possible underlying biological causes. Only by assessing all the cognitive difficulties that affect the acquisition of reading and writing can we hope to understand the underlying cause of difficulties in the dyslexic individual, and find appropriate strategies and alternative learning methods to overcome these. By looking at the whole person (i.e. all their cognitive skills) we can build a profile which helps us identify which skills need strengthening, as well as a possible preferred learning style.

In conclusion, the intention is that this model will provide a method whereby not only can the nature of dyslexia in different languages be understood, but also the dyslexic individual may be identified. Furthermore, only by understanding these issues, and acknowledging similarities and differences between language contexts, will we be able to fully appreciate the complexities presented by the multilingual dyslexic child (Chapter 5).

Acknowledgements

There are too many people to thank for their assistance with this work worldwide, but for material supplied specifically for this chapter we would like to acknowledge Éva Gyarmathy for aspects regarding Hungarian, and Connie Ho of the Chinese University of Hong Kong for development of the Chinese version and assistance with testing in Hong Kong, as well as advice on aspects of the Chinese language and testing. We are also grateful to Suk Han Lee of the Hong Kong Education Department for assistance on choosing miscue analysis errors in Chinese.

Chapter 3

Assessing Varieties of Literacy and English

Martin Turner

This chapter:

- discusses the experiences of international families
- examines the relationship between bilingualism and learning difficulties
- and evaluates practical assessment strategies for teachers and psychologists in relation to dyslexia and bilingualism.

Introduction

Because of experience with the ethnic concentrations in our own cities, the British view of bilingualism tends to exclude South American, Arab, Slav, Oriental and many other important communities. However, this chapter will focus upon the international experience of international families, frequently of mixed race and any and every nationality, all of whom have chosen to speak English and to have their children educated in English.

Languages are not equal (Honey 1997). In particular nowadays English is privileged as the primary international language (78 per cent of Web pages are written in English and no other single language accounts for more than 2.5 per cent according to the OECD). This has little to do with nostalgia for a British empire but much to do with the empire of American language and power, for us an historical accident. Something like two billion people worldwide now use English as a second (or subsequent) language. Accordingly it is rightly seen as a significant commercial asset and a good investment for children (for a sparkling account of the rise of international English see McCrum *et al.* 1992). However language trails culture and values in its wake and there are implications for both rooted and itinerant families who choose to adopt an international medium as the principal language of the family, especially when language is regarded as a *tool of thought*.

Bilingualism would not normally be considered a learning difficulty, but what is the role of learning difficulties within a bilingual repertoire? Are they more common? As yet there are no data that would help us to answer this question. Specifically, can bilingual status contribute to the difficulty with alphabetic learning that is known as dyslexia? Can it perhaps mask it? In what ways do bilingual children present differently to the assessing psychologist? These questions are yielding gradually both to experience and to advances in our understanding of how language skills combine and differentiate.

Finally, what practical assessment strategies commend themselves to teachers and psychologists faced with possible specific learning difficulties (SpLD)? Can existing assessment resources be adapted or converted or are new ones needed?

The international family

The experience of international families has a number of lessons for the psychologist. It is often most difficult to get people to ascribe any importance whatever to the position of English as a second language. Parents may be incredulous at the suggestion that English could have anything but pride of place in their children's repertoire. It is true, too, that children of international families often converse with each other and reply to their parents in English even when addressed in Arabic or other home language. Many gradually seem to unlearn their cultural heritage, especially language.

This is unfortunate. It is always a vital necessity for children to grow up with robust first-hand experience of at least one language. The effect of teaching and school environment on children's language learning, especially that of the peer-group, is of course enormous. Though the social context of learning English, often that of immersion, is a major influence, I am concerned here with L1 – the seedbed of learning that is the child's first or mother-tongue language. The work of Jacques Mehler and others on the astonishingly early development of phonological tuning and selectivity that takes place in the first weeks and months after birth is relevant (e.g. Mehler and Dupoux 1994). We learn to attend to the characteristic sounds and rhythms of our own language within the first few months of life – and to screen out speech sounds that are not important for it. Because of the enormous volume of language learning that goes on early in development, it is correspondingly more difficult for individuals to learn a new language as they get older; after the middle teenage years, such an ability drops precipitately (this development process is vividly described in Pinker 1995).

Where English is the common language of a family, *but is not spoken as a first language by either parent*, the young child is deprived of the vocabulary size, idiomatic flair and rich delta of nuance that accompanies use of a first-hand language. Moreover the heritage associated with a language is absent, thus cutting the child off from both history and identity. We need to know who we are and our language is a store of understandings about our cultural heritage. Language, finally, is a tool of thought and without it a child has no strategy for reflection or problem-solving.

The weakening of language as a tool of thought can be seen in advanced form in families that are both international and of mixed marriage. English is merely the linguistic vapour that hangs around the growing children as a reminder of what is missing. Sami (Box 1) is a boy whose Syrian father and Japanese mother spoke to each other in English. Bobby (Box 2) is a boy whose Swedish father and Malay-speaking Singaporean mother spoke English to their children.

Sami is the youngest of three children of a Japanese mother and an Arabic-speaking Syrian father. The children are spoken to in Japanese by their mother and English by their father. Parents speak each other's languages to a moderate extent. The three children speak English to each other. Facility in Japanese seems to have reduced with each child, so that Sami, though born in Japan, is said to speak it 'like a three year old'. The ten year old spoke hardly little of anything. In assessment, he danced and he drew; he drew and he danced.

Box 1

Bobby is the middle of five children in a family with no known incidence of dyslexia, a specific learning difficulty. His father is Swedish, his mother a Malay-speaking Singaporean. English is the language spoken among the children. Other children in the family have not suffered to the same extent from language deprivation; indeed an older sister has become an accomplished linguist. Bobby showed a discrepancy of 39 points of standard score between his (English) language skills and his spatial ability.

Box 2

Bilingualism and learning difficulty

Bilingualism used to be thought of as a disadvantage: psychologists perhaps thought that a 'clean' trace was necessary for sound first-language learning. It is still acknowledged to be a double load of learning – two words for everything – but subsequently a second language, learned young, has come to be seen as a benefit and a good long-term investment, if only because it is so hard to acquire new languages after the late teens and we live in an increasingly international world with a positive and growing premium on language skills.

How do bilingual children fare in dyslexia assessment? It is possible to quantify the information on cognitive contrasts within each individual profile by means of a Dyslexia Index (the index is described in detail in Turner 1997, Ch. 12). If this is done for the bilingual and total samples, it is apparent that about 10 per cent more of the total sample are attracting a dyslexia diagnosis.

This raises the question of what common phenomenology, if any, there may be between dyslexia and bilingualism. It must, in theory, be virtually impossible to disentangle the two altogether. After all, teachers of modern foreign languages (MFL) usually feel that a gift with *mimicry* is a main predictor of success in learning a foreign language, though the latter in Britain scarcely happens until the secondary years. If by this they mean *phonological skill*, then it stands to reason that dyslexic pupils will not find MFL learning congenial. Sure enough, this is just what we do find. Dyslexic pupils very often say that they prefer German to French, and Spanish to German (in order, presumably, of orthographic transparency) but would much prefer to do none of them. English on its own presents quite enough problems.

The research picture here broadly confirms such observations. The ability to repeat non-words (phonological sensitivity) is a good predictor of vocabulary learning in English (e.g. Gathercole *et al.* 1992, Gathercole and Baddeley 1993). Similarly vocabulary mastery in the first language is the best predictor of vocabulary acquisition in a second or subsequent language (see especially Service 1989, 1992; Service and Craik 1993; Service and Kohonen 1995). A difficulty with learning another, phonologically divergent, language is one of the predictions, therefore, that follows from dyslexia. However bilingualism may to some extent offset the difficulties normally experienced by dyslexic individuals with the acoustic system of any language. Bilingual individuals must be especially attentive to the sounds of language – and the different sounds of different languages – and considerable sensitivity is often to be found in such individuals.

What does seem clear is that bilingual language use is a matter of circumstance – and parentage – while dyslexia is a genetically based specific learning difficulty with non-semantic aspects of language. (Four genes or, more accurately, quantitative trait loci, have been confirmed so far and more need to be discovered.) Although orthography and phonology have been under the research spotlight for two decades, compelling evidence implicates difficulty also with *morphology* – grammar at the level of the individual word (Elbro 1989; Elbro and Arnbak 1996). It may be reasonable to conclude, also, that the double load of bilingual language learning becomes a triple load for the individual who is also dyslexic.

Diagnostic instruments and clinical thinking

If bilingualism and dyslexia, then, flourish in exactly the same linguistic undergrowth, how may we assess the contribution bilingualism is making to an observed dyslexia? Can one assess dyslexia outside the language module, for instance, assuming that the psychologist is not competent in the necessary languages?

It is desirable to make some attempt to assess the contribution (English) language skills are making to general functioning, even if only to be fair to the multiple tasks facing the individual learner, who may be attending classes in English, French and Arabic, for instance, while speaking none of these at home. As in the terms of reference of the Warnock Committee (Department of Education and Science (DES) 1978), bilingual language learning is not to be thought of as a pathology, nor should fallout from this effort be allowed to exaggerate the degree of academic learning difficulty.

The new edition of the British Ability Scales (Elliott *et al.* 1996) does in fact provide a novel piece of technology that allows educational psychologists to address this challenge. The factorial structure of the BAS-II is both novel (it is a three-factor test) and economic in time for the user (core scales measuring general ability take a mere 30 minutes to administer). (Factor analysis permits a sort of controlled generalisation, based on trends, mathematically analysed, in large bodies of data on skilled test performance.) First, let us take a look at the structure of the core scales and the composite (summary) scores that they support, illustrated in Figure 3.1.

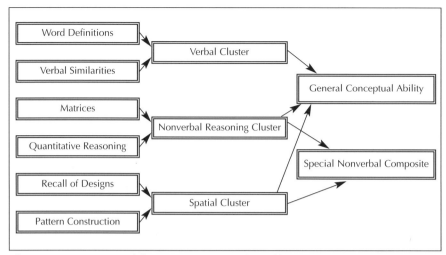

Figure 3.1 Structure of the BAS-II core scales (Elliott *et al.* 1996)

It will be seen that g or the general ability factor (Jensen 1998) is based upon six first-level tests and three second-level composites. It is here called General Conceptual Ability (GCA) and is equivalent to the familiar IQ. The two verbal scales, Word Definitions, an expressive measure of English vocabulary, and Verbal Similarities, an expressive measure of verbal reasoning, thus contribute a third of the scales that make up IQ or index of general cognitive functioning.

However an alternative general composite is provided that omits this pair of English language scales. As can be seen in Figure 3.1, this Special Nonverbal Composite (SNC) is based upon the remaining four scales, those that form the nonverbal reasoning and spatial clusters. The system allows discrepancies among the three clusters to be fully evaluated, but about a standard deviation of difference is required to attain statistical significance between (say) the Verbal and Spatial clusters. This is because of the lower reliability associated with second-level composites (equivalent to Verbal and Performance IQs or Index scores on the Wechsler Intelligence Scale for Children (WISC) Wechsler 1992). The Special Nonverbal Composite, on the other hand, has the peculiar authority associated with the most highly g-loaded measure, including statistical stability and reliability. It also has wider generality than that of a group of merely visuospatial or 'performance' tests. In particular the nonverbal reasoning factor draws on greater symbolic mediation and meaning-making using language.

The system provides for the full evaluation of underachievement in basic skills using a regression apparatus based on the SNC, if wished, instead of the GCA. This is certainly a useful resource for those faced with bilingual children who must be tested in English. However, what is needed is an estimate of the *contribution (English) language skills are making to general cognitive functioning.* The test manual provides only for the less satisfactory evaluation of discrepancies among cluster scores, anyway likely to be more variable. Since the GCA and SNC can be generated from each single set of scores on the six scales, some difference between them is likely to be informative, at least as to the prevalence of bilingual or language-deprived individuals in the standardisation sample. However no apparatus exists to permit such a comparison. Moreover the SNC comprises two-thirds of the GCA, so there is considerable overlap. This makes difficult the calculation of the significance level required for interpretation. Based on the standard error of measurement (SEm) for the two composite scores that *do not overlap*, namely the Verbal Cluster and the Special Nonverbal Composite, it is possible to calculate that 11 points of standard score are required to reach statistical significance at the 5 per cent level of probability (p = 0.05).

Thus a difference between Verbal and SNC of 11 points or more is reliable, and gives you a strong case for using SNC rather than GCA (Colin Elliott, personal communication March 2000).

Next, Table 3.1 gives the actual levels of prevalence observed in the standardisation sample of the BAS-II's predecessor test with the same structure, the Differential Ability Scales (DAS) (Elliott 1990) of differences between SNC and GCA. The differences are absolute differences between GCA and SNC – if you want the numbers for a difference in a given direction, divide the frequency by 2 (Colin Elliott, personal communication March 2000).

Table 3.1 gives in column three the prevalence estimates for a GCA lower than SNC, the likely direction in the assessment of bilingual children with a relative disadvantage on English-language tests. It will be seen that a difference of seven points or more of standard score is exceptional (10 per cent), while a difference of nine or more points is highly unexpected (5 per cent). Column four gives the actual cumulative frequency of such differences as observed in the DAS standardisation sample.

Table 3.1 Differences between CGA and Special Nonverbal Composite on the DAS

Difference	Rounded Frequency (%)	Frequency for difference in a given direction (%)	Actual Cumulative Frequency (%)
13–17	1	0.5	1.1
12	2	1.0	1.7
11	3	1.5	2.7
10	5	2.5	4.6
9	10	5.0	7.5
8	15	7.5	12.5
7	20	10.0	17.3
6	25	12.5	24.5

Discrepancies of this kind enable us to reach several possible conclusions about individuals suspected of showing features of dyslexia:

1. A large difference between English-language skills and other, nonverbal and spatial, abilities suggests that general cognitive functioning should be evaluated independently of language skills and that bilingualism may be compounding this individual's dyslexia to a significant extent.

2. Although there is some disadvantage for the individual on English language tests, language skills are not the major contribution to the variation in his or her general cognitive functioning and the difference is not large enough to cast doubt on the main features of the assessment.
3. Language skills, tested in English, are making a negligible contribution to this individual's learning difficulties.

All these formulations represent a useful step forward in evaluating dyslexia and bilingualism in the same individual. Note that conclusions 2 and 3 make the (reasonable) assumption that language skills in the individual's first language (L1), if unaffected by either bilingualism or dyslexia, would not be excellent.

For teachers, the second edition of the receptive vocabulary test, the British Picture Vocabulary Scale (Dunn *et al.* 1997), helpfully provides an alternative set of norms for 410 pupils aged from 3 years 0 months to 8 years 5 months for whom English is an additional language (EAL). Year 2 norms are interpolated between Years 1 and 3. In general the age-equivalent scores in months obtained by the EAL sample were about three-quarters of their chronological age in months.

Lastly, is it possible to assess dyslexia outside the language module, assuming again that the psychologist or teacher is not competent in the necessary languages? There is still a discrepancy to be observed, that between ability and diagnostic tests, sufficient to identify many specific learning difficulties, including dyslexia (this discrepancy tells us, at least, how dyslexic any individual ought to be). Moreover one field of attainment, that of arithmetic, is fairly international in character. The evaluation of underachievement in written calculation skills is possible using regression methods and is fully provided for using tests such as DAS, WISC and BAS. It is possible, further, to use the One Minute Number Tests (addition and subtraction; Westwood *et al.* 1974), which are open to non-psychologists. This speed-of-processing measure eloquently shows up, not only the inefficiency in both modes, but the relative disadvantage in subtraction. Dyslexic individuals, who often outgrow their initial problems with verbal arithmetic to sail forth upon the wider seas of mathematics, manifest an aversion to subtraction and division that seems to be explicable in terms of the differential requirements placed by these processes upon working memory (Boulton-Lewis 1993). The primary-aged dyslexic individual, therefore, is likely both to be less well automated in routine subtraction and addition of numbers below 20 and to show a selective preference for addition when any similar preference of the age group is taken into account by the norms.

Conclusions

The consideration of practical strategies for evaluating dyslexia and bilingualism concludes our brief look at the most pressing issues in this area. We have seen that varieties of language use are passed off as 'English', especially in international communities and mixed marriages, and that these can compromise language as a tool of thought in the developing child.

Dyslexia is officially a learning difficulty, while bilingualism is not, yet the importance of phonological skills to both makes them impossible to disentangle.

The limited data available suggest that bilingual children are about as likely as monolingual to be identified as dyslexic. In assessment, the responsible strategy is to evaluate the contribution that language skills, tested in English, make to total cognitive functioning. This is now possible for psychologists using the Differential and the British Ability Scales. One teacher-usable test evaluates the disadvantage experienced by the child aged from three to about nine for whom English is an additional language. Another strategy is to assess relative information processing efficiency of the individual by means of *diagnostic tests* that sample skills removed to some extent from the language module, for instance using numbers.

Finally, in many cases one might wish to recommend that schools' usual provision for English as a Second Language (ESL) should be enhanced by means of greater *explicit English language teaching*, so as to promote: pronunciation and vocabulary growth, grammar and sentence structure, educationally significant, rather than just colloquial, communication (see especially Cummins 1984 and Cummins and McNeeley 1987).

Chapter 4

Bilingualism and Literacy Assessment

Stuart Forbes and Robat Powell

This chapter:

- describes some of the language issues encountered when developing literacy assessment measures for a population which has exposure to two different languages at levels which may vary widely both within and between home and school and
- provides a summary of the test development process.

Introduction

The All Wales Reading Test is the first group reading test to be made available with both English and Welsh Medium forms, and was jointly developed by 20 local education authorities (LEAs) in Wales. The project was led by the City and County of Swansea Education Psychology and Formal Assessment Service, which developed and published the test in consultation with the National Foundation for Educational Research (NFER 2000).

Language issues addressed during test development

A number of difficulties specific to the Welsh-language versions of the tests became apparent during the development stage. These were resolved as described below.

Regional dialect

Standard spoken Welsh permits a considerable range of syntactical and lexical variation which derives from its still vigorous regional dialects. Modern written Welsh, too, often reflects a regional flavour, particularly in less formal registers. While such diversity rarely presents difficulty to the educated speaker or even older school pupils, unfamiliar regional vocabulary and idiom can pose problems of comprehension to younger children.

Test materials for young pupils should not therefore contain items which might discriminate against some children because of their unfamiliarity with language forms more prevalent in other parts of Wales, particularly across the North–South dialectal divide. Common nouns in this category include words for 'boy' (SW bachgen/NW hogyn), 'woman' (menyw/dynes), and 'milk' (llaeth/llefrith); adjectives such as 'angry' (crac/blin), 'dirty' (brwnt/budr), and 'ill' (tost/sâl); adverbs such as 'now' (nawr/rwan); and the personal pronoun 'he/him' (e/o). Certain verbal forms also show North–South variation.

A standardised reading test can select only one word where these dual options occur, and two main strategies were adopted to address this. The first was to select the word having greater acceptability in the literary register and being less strikingly dialect. In this way, 'bachgen' (boy) would be chosen rather than 'hogyn'. Where neither word could be considered less dialectal and colloquial than the other, the strategy was to avoid using either. If an item required a liquid in a bottle, it would be 'water' rather than the problematic 'milk'. Where the inclusion of the concept was still felt necessary, it would be expressed through paraphrase. For example, to avoid the term 'angry', an item could read 'Siân was not happy'.

The problem of the masculine personal pronoun 'e/o' was solved by the use of personal names or nouns in place of the pronoun.

Colloquial and library register

All languages differ to some degree between their colloquial and written forms. This difference has been more obvious in Welsh than most, since the written standard was frozen to a large degree in the 1588 bible translation while the colloquial language deviated increasingly from it. However, written Welsh had become far more flexible and closer to spoken forms by the end of the twentieth century.

For the Year 2 All Wales Reading Tests, it was decided to adopt a style close to spoken Welsh, similar to most children's books, e.g. 'maen nhw' (they are) instead of the literary and more concise 'maent'. However, it was felt that the Year 6 materials could include more literary forms, particularly in the more difficult items, e.g. the past passive 'Torrwyd ar eu darllen . . .' (Their reading was interrupted . . .).

Welsh–English comparability

Although the Welsh and English versions of the tests are not translations of each other, some parity of difficulty is implicit since they were developed in parallel, follow similar storylines and include the same illustrations. However, the importance of maintaining a gradation in difficulty as pupils progress through the test affected the design of the two language versions so that items do not always occur in the same order of difficulty.

In the Year 2 Form B test, the first and easiest English item is the picture of a boy. The corresponding Welsh word is 'bachgen', phonetically more complex than 'boy', and trialling revealed this item to be only fourth easiest in the Welsh test. It was therefore placed as Item 4 in the Welsh version.

The difference in syntax between the two languages makes it appropriate to assess certain items in Welsh which simply do not exist in English. For example, the verb 'mae' (is) changes its form to 'bod' in a subordinate clause such as 'I think that John is ill'. The inclusion of 'bod' as a test item proved more difficult than 'is' would be in an English version.

A whole unit in the Year 6 test on choosing a holiday proved more difficult in Welsh, apparently because the English items contained familiar expressions which have almost become clichéd, such as 'glossy brochures', and 'all expenses paid'. The expression of the same concepts in Welsh had to be largely original, more unfamiliar, and was therefore more difficult.

The standardisation sample

The tests were intended to measure the reading performance of first-language pupils, i.e. pupils who speak Welsh or English as their mother tongue. However, the very definition of a first-language Welsh pupil is problematic. By the year 2000, the majority of school pupils fluent in Welsh came from English-speaking homes and had attained fluency through their exposure to Welsh at school, particularly in Welsh-medium schools. Restricting the pupils for whom the All Wales Welsh Medium tests are appropriate to those children speaking the language as their mother tongue would therefore exclude the majority of pupils fluent in Welsh and would make no sense.

The meaning of the term 'mother tongue' in the Welsh context is also far from simple. Where parents are bilingual, schools cannot be sure which of the two languages is the medium of communication in the home. One approach, adopted for some research studies, is to ascertain simply whether the child spoke Welsh before starting school, and most primary or infants schools will have this information. However, the problem described above then arises, that pupils fluent in Welsh but from English-speaking homes are omitted from the target population.

It was therefore decided that the target first-language Welsh population would be pupils receiving their education through the medium of Welsh, regardless of home language. The Welsh-language tests were standardised on pupils receiving their education mainly through the medium of Welsh, and the English-language versions on pupils in English-medium schools. A sub-sample of each population was drawn from pupils being taught through the medium of both Welsh and English, although different pupils were used for the different language versions.

Norm groups

The nature of the standardisation sample's exposure to Welsh, at both seven and eleven years of age, was extremely varied across Wales. In Year 6, the two extremes of the spectrum would be pupils having spoken only Welsh at home during their pre-school years, living in a Welsh-speaking community, and then receiving most or all of their curriculum through Welsh, and pupils having had no preschool contact with Welsh, living in largely English-speaking communities, and being taught through the medium of Welsh for no more than approximately half the curriculum.

Some initial debate took place on the possibility of establishing different Welsh-medium norms, one for mother-tongue pupils and another for those from non Welsh-speaking homes. However, in view of the difficulty of defining just what is a mother-tongue Welsh-speaker, it was decided that this would be too problematic. Even if it could be achieved, the two norms would be largely meaningless anyway since both sub-populations are taught together, follow the same Welsh-medium curriculum, and take the same statutory Welsh assessments at Key Stages 1, 2 and 3.

The tests were therefore standardised on one Welsh-medium population and one single set of norms for Welsh reading was obtained, as for English.

Illustrations

Special illustrations were commissioned to present the tests in the comic format which research had shown to be appealing to pupils of that age. In the Year 2 tests they were an essential part of those items requiring the matching of word and picture and also a number of the easier sentence-completion items where the correct response was represented in the picture. In most of the Year 2 items, however, the illustrations were merely supportive of the meaning contained in the items. In the Year 6 tests, one illustration was included at the beginning of each unit in order to suggest the general context of the unit and make each page more attractive.

Commissioning illustrations made it possible to include a multi-ethnic background element in some storylines and to avoid any particular class or cultural bias in the presentation of the units. However, the correctness of some of the illustrations provoked comment from teachers during the trialling stage. One picture showing children sneakily eating their sandwiches in the bus before the school trip set off was questioned for its inappropriateness!

Summary of the test development process

Key principles

One of the main guiding principles was to produce a test with both English and Welsh medium forms that was 'user friendly' for both children and teachers, and the first step was research carried out in 1993/1994 by Menna Williams, a psychology student. This was published as a dissertation and involved discussion with children and teachers and structured questionnaires sent to a range of publishers and libraries.

During construction of the test the results of the research were taken into account as far as possible, particularly the high ratings given to:

- 'comic' format
- a storyline which involves school
- appropriate print size
- inclusion of as many pictures as possible.

The first forms of the test were developed and used successfully in West Glamorgan and Swansea as part of annual special educational needs and Year 2 reading surveys. In view of the success of the test, the City and County of Swansea were keen for it to be professionally designed and illustrated, and standardised across Wales so that it could be made more widely available. As this was beyond the resources of a single LEA, all the authorities in Wales were approached and asked if they would like to take part in developing the test. Twenty out of the 22 LEAs agreed to contribute funds and the various forms of the test were developed, extensively piloted and standardised. The test was completed in September 2000.

Test form production

The forms of the test for pupils in Years 2 and 3 ('Our Story' Forms A and B/'Ein Stori Ni' Forms A and B) were based on the original format that was originally developed in West Glamorgan during 1993.

The storyline and test items were developed by a team of educational psychologists using a range of resources, including word frequency lists. The English Medium form for Year 5, 6 and 7 pupils ('Our School') was constructed in close collaboration with the Department of English Language and Literature at the University of Birmingham. The original storyline texts, written by a team of educational psychologists, were subjected to a detailed linguistic analysis by applied linguists at the University of Birmingham.

Innovative text analysis techniques drawn from recent advances in the field of computational linguistics were employed for this purpose. Using lexical information gained from the computer analysis of an electronically stored corpus of standard texts for children, the original test texts were analysed for the following features:

- the representativeness of text words in terms of their overall corpus frequency
  i.e. were text words within the 'familiar' range of readers of this age group
- the representativeness of the textual balance of the words of different corpus frequency ranges
  i.e. was the increasing difficult of test texts clearly reflected in a growing proportion of words that occur less frequently in the corpus
- the representativeness of textual collocations
  i.e. were combinations of words used in the text untypical or unusual in any way
- the naturalness of the discourse features of each text
  i.e. did the texts contain typical markers of text cohesion and adequate linkage for textual coherence.

Following the computer-generated analysis, texts were edited to eliminate textual and discourse features unrepresentative of reading materials for the target age group. A rational deletion procedure, based on recent research into item difficulty analysis in cloze tests, was then employed for cloze deletions. Multiple-choice alternatives were chosen with careful reference to the corpus.

As there is currently no similar corpus of text available in electronic format in Welsh Medium, the English Medium version was adapted and translated to provide the Welsh Medium version for older pupils – 'Ein Hysgol Ni'.

Computerised scoring

The forms of the test for Year 5, 6 and 7 pupils were also designed so that they can be mechanically scored by an Optical Mark Reader. A data reading and analysis program was specially written for this purpose and used extensively during the piloting and standardisation process. LEAs in Wales have been made aware of this facility and we are currently awaiting feedback from them about the format in which they would like this to made available and the best ways to fund distribution and technical support.

Piloting

Each test form was piloted extensively in schools across Wales. In addition to the test forms, checklists were also sent to each school for teachers to complete to give their views on the test and any items they felt needed to be altered or excluded.

Rigorous item analysis was then carried out on the results, and the teacher checklist responses were evaluated. This data was then used for redrafting the tests, and each test form underwent internal pilots and at least two external pilots across Wales.

Standardisation

The final test forms were standardised across Wales, and for each form a representative sample of pupils was included where children were taught through both the medium of English and Welsh. In all, 128 schools and 15,000 children took part in the piloting and standardisation of the test.

It is worth noting that the correlations between the Welsh Medium forms of the All Wales Reading Test and other English Medium tests are statistically significant, but tend to be lower than the correlations between All Wales Reading Test Welsh Medium versus other Welsh Medium tests and All Wales Reading Test versus other English Medium tests.

Uses of the test

The All Wales Reading Test is already being used extensively throughout Wales for a variety of purposes, including:

- annual LEA screening and monitoring of progress for pupils with literacy difficulties
- allocation of special educational needs (SEN) resources to schools
- monitoring of school and LEA performance in literacy between Key Stages 1/2 and 2/3
- evaluation of literacy initiatives
- as a research instrument to investigate the relationship between reading performance and language background at home and school.

Implications

This chapter illustrates that with appropriate consideration being given to design, format, language and purpose it is possible to develop an effective user-friendly reading measure suitable for bilingual children. The procedures adopted in this study can be replicated for use in test construction for other communities and languages which have similar exposure to two different languages and at levels which may vary between home and school.

Chapter 5

Bilingual Children's Profiles on Dyslexia Screening Measures

John Everatt, Ewan Adams and Ian Smythe

This chapter:

- considers the range of factors which can influence effective screening for bilingual children
- contains an examination that focuses on the London Borough of Tower Hamlets which has 25 per cent of its population originating from Sylhet in north-eastern Bangladesh.

Introduction

It is generally acknowledged by those working in the field of dyslexia that early identification leads to more effective outcomes in remediation, particularly in the areas of reading and writing. If the dyslexic child's problems are unrecognised, the child can often become anxious or depressed and suffer serious losses in self-esteem, confidence and motivation (Edwards 1994; Miles and Varma 1995; Riddick 1996). Frustration may also arise from problems experienced in skills acquisition, despite an understanding of the task requirements. This frustration may lead to an increase in disruptive behaviour in the classroom or indifference to educational demands. These negative effects often develop further barriers to the process of learning to read and write, producing a spiral of cognitive difficulties and emotional outcomes. Clearly, informed early assessment affording an accurate indication of potential areas of difficulties is of central importance in the effort to meet and treat the specific difficulties faced by the dyslexic individual. Objective assessment procedures and tools are therefore essential to the educational practitioner in both their initial identification of those at risk and their formation of an individual education plan (IEP).

A number of screening/assessment tools have been developed to aid this process: e.g. the Aston Index (Newton and Thomson 1976), the Bangor Dyslexia Test (BDT) (Miles 1993), the Dyslexia Screening Test (DST) (Fawcett and Nicolson 1996) and the Phonological Assessment Battery (PhAB) (Frederickson *et al.* 1997). All were primarily developed to assist in the identification of the needs of the **monolingual** English-speaking child and indeed there is a growing literature on identification and remediation of dyslexia among a monolingual population. Yet very little research has been performed among those from a **multilingual** background. Despite similarities in the descriptions of reading/writing difficulties across languages (e.g. Salter and Smythe 1997) and the lack of evidence suggesting that the incidence of learning difficulties among bilingual children learning the English writing system differs from monolinguals attempting to acquire the same skills, the view has often been expressed that the assessment of the bilingual child is complicated by bilingual-related language problems (Cline and Reason 1993). For example, Peer (1997) points out that the multiplicity of factors involved in bilingual students' learning development poses serious challenges to teachers and psychologists attempting to isolate causal elements in learning difficulty. She identifies home background, cultural differences, impoverished language skills, speech and vocabulary development and inefficient memory competency as factors which may interfere with the child's learning experience and capability to interact and cope in the classroom. These complications may render some screening methods inappropriate among bilinguals, making their evaluation within this context essential. Working with educationalists within the London Borough of Tower Hamlets enabled us to perform an initial assessment of some of these methods of identification. Although the findings reported herein should not be seen as definitive, they can underpin further research and assessment of practices.

London Borough of Tower Hamlets

Tower Hamlets is a multicultural borough in the East End of London with some 25 per cent of the population originating from Sylhet in north-eastern Bangladesh. This Bangladeshi community has been established for most of the twentieth century, its proximity to the docks being indicative of the seamen who arrived in the area via the operations of the East India Company. The UK's industrial boom of the 1950s and 1960s saw an increase in (mainly male) residents from Bangladesh, who were followed in the 1970s and 1980s by wives and children as changes in immigration laws made it difficult to travel freely between Britain and Bangladesh. By the 1990s, when the children in the present study were born, this process was more or less complete and most children educated within Tower Hamlets would have been born in the area (Bose 2000). This process provides a large group of children who, in the main, will be experiencing a bilingual upbringing.

Bilingualism in the Bangladeshi, Sylheti-speaking community of Tower Hamlets has many elements (Bose 2000; James 1995), though the basic ingredients are that Sylheti will form a major part of home life whereas English will be the medium of education at school. Sylheti is a dialect of Bengali and does not possess a written form in its own right, using instead the standard Bengali script. Although these children will be fluent in Sylheti, very few will be able to read Bengali, although most would be expected to read Arabic in Mosque classes since the majority will be brought up as Sunni Muslims. Despite this, many will be unable to write or even understand Arabic outside the context of reading the Qur'an. For most, therefore, English will be the only language for which a set of spelling–sound correspondence rules will be acquired. Although these children may also watch videos made in India in the Hindi language, and hence understand aspects of this language in this context, they will probably be unable to speak, read or write Hindi. Of course, bilingualism is rarely a static state and a speaker's language use will develop according to environment and context. This includes the number of Sylheti speakers in the class and peer group, the linguistic input of the teacher, who may or may not speak Sylheti, and the differing levels of first and second language use in the home. Although many of these children will be exposed to English from preschool age, fluent bilingualism may not come easily to all young Sylheti speakers. This is particularly problematic for early assessment, since exposure to English may not have reached the level hypothesised by those (e.g. Cummins 1984) who suggest that native levels of proficiency in higher order cognitive academic linguistic areas may take five to seven years to develop. A seven-year-old Sylheti-speaking child who has had limited preschool exposure to English may be adversely affected in terms of his/her ability to learn to read and write English.

The primary data presented in this chapter were obtained from Sylheti/English bilinguals whose home language (the language spoken at home) was Sylheti. This group has two main advantages for present purposes. Firstly, a context within which to view the present findings is provided by the work of Frederickson and Frith (1998) which assessed the phonological skills of an older group of Tower Hamlets bilinguals who presented a range of reading/writing skills. Secondly, as indicated above, Sylheti does not have a written form, thereby allowing an assessment of the influence of an additional language independent of the potential effects of having to learn several spelling–sound correspondences.

Child participants

Children whose data are reported in this chapter were selected from 296 Year 3 pupils from five schools. An initial phase involved class-based group testing of Raven's Coloured Progressive Matrices (Raven 1962) and spelling ability (a bespoke English-language test designed for this population – see Smythe and Everatt, in preparation, for details). This was followed by discussions with class teachers and SEN Coordinators about literacy problems and also referral to teachers, children and school records for information on language background. These procedures identified several groups of bilingual children: (i) those who presented no evidence of literacy difficulties (N=7), (ii) those who performed poorly on both the spelling and Raven's tests (N=6), (iii) those who performed poorly on the spelling test and who had a history of sensory (N=1) or schooling problems (N=1), and (iv) those who performed poorly on the spelling test but were average or above average on the Raven's Matrices test and did not present any evidence of schooling, sensory or emotional/behavioural problems (N=9). These bilingual children spoke Sylheti at home and English in school. In addition, monolingual children who spoke English at home and in school were chosen from the same schools and divided into two groups: those who did (N=7) and those who did not (N=7) present evidence of literacy problems. Single word reading performance confirmed differences in literacy skills across the children selected: i.e. those identified as presenting no evidence of literacy problems outperformed those identified as having special needs related to reading/writing on the single word reading measure.

Measures

Measures used in the study were selected to be representative of commonly used dyslexia assessments. Hence, we assessed:

- Phonological skills. Assessed by measures of Non-word Reading, Rhyme and Alliteration. These are common to most dyslexia screening tools (Aston: Newton and Thomson 1976; BDT: Miles 1993; DST: Fawcett and Nicolson 1996; PhAB: Frederickson *et al.*, 1997).
- Lexical access or rapid (automatic) access to output phonology. Rapid naming tasks are also common to most screening tools and are often considered as a measure of phonological ability (Frederickson and Frith 1998) or automaticity (Fawcett and Nicolson 1994).
- Short-term memory or sequencing skills. The most common measure used across the screening tools are Digit and Reverse Spans, with poor performance considered characteristic of dyslexia (Thomson 1990). However, the present study also included measures of sequencing skills which assessed the ability to repeat non-words to compare the children's performance on tasks requiring the storage and repetition of unknown linguistic forms; this has been argued as indicative of poor phonological working memory and may be associated with poor language proficiency (Gathercole and Baddeley 1989). To assess the impact of linguistic material, a further sequence repetition task involved a series of distinct noises (a rhythm tapping task), which retained the sequential and repetitive aspects of the previous measures, but removed the linguistic component.
- Visual and motor skills. These were assessed by two further sequential measures, one involving sequences of abstract shapes (devoid of a previously learnt linguistic label) which the researcher indicated in a set order for the child to repeat, and a second involving a sequence of hand movements for the child to copy. In order to further assess the children's ability to process and retain nonverbal material, a measure of Shape Memory was included which did not require retention of the material in a set order. These measures were developed with reference to the study by Gupta and Garg (1996) and those used in many of the aforementioned screening tools.

Further details on these measures, including the items developed and pilot work performed can be found in Smythe and Everatt (in preparation), which includes a discussion of validity/reliability, or Everatt *et al.* (2000) which includes brief descriptions of the tasks and procedures used.

Results

Group comparisons (excluding those with low Raven's scores or evidence of perceptual or schooling problems) indicated little difference between bilinguals and monolinguals in terms of the ability of different measures to distinguish those with poor reading and spelling scores from those with no evidence of literacy problems. None of the interaction effects between literacy level and language background assessed by a series of two-way analyses of variance were significant at the 5 per cent level. Further details of these group analyses can be found in Everatt *et al.* (2000).

These findings are encouraging in that they suggest that bilingual children may indeed benefit from the early screening procedures devised for monolingual children. In particular, the phonological measures presented consistent findings across bilingual and monolingual groups; findings which are in accord with those of Frederickson and Frith (1998) with an older group of English/Sylheti children. However, these group analyses did not allow an assessment of individual differences between children. Therefore the data were reinterpreted from the point of view of children who showed typical performance across measures and those who were presenting atypical scores. These data are presented in Figures 5.1 to 5.3.

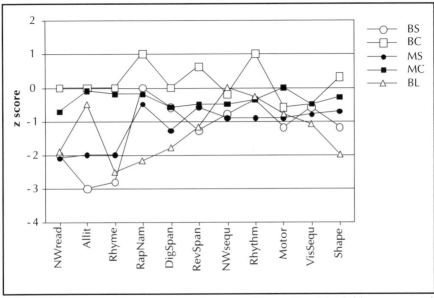

Figure 5.1 Average performance for each group of Tower Hamlets children compared against norms for measures of Non-word Reading (NWread), Alliteration (Allit), Rhyming (Rhyme), Rapid Naming (RapNam), Forward (DigSpan) and Reverse (RevSpan) Digit Span, Non-word Sequence Repetition (NWsequ), Rhythm Repetition (Rhythm), Motor Movement Repetition (Motor), Visuospatial Sequence Repetition (VisSequ) and Shape Memory (Shape)

Each of the figures presents the results of children assessed in Tower Hamlets against norms taken from monolingual English-speaking Year 3 children from other boroughs in the London area. These norms are presented as z scores with 0 indicating average performance and values of 1 and 2 indicating performance which is 1 and 2 standard deviations away from the mean respectively. A negative z score indicates performance worse than average, a positive z value indicates a score better than average.

Figure 5.1 compares the results of each of the groups of children tested in Tower Hamlets. Average performance profiles of bilinguals are represented by lines coded with a B, while monolingual group averages are coded with an M. BS represents those bilingual children who presented evidence of poor literacy despite average or above-average performance on the Raven's Matrices. BC indicates children with average or above-average scores on both literacy measures and the Matrices. MS and MC are equivalent groups to BS and BC but comprise monolingual children. BL represents those children who showed poor scores on the literacy measures and Raven's Matrices.

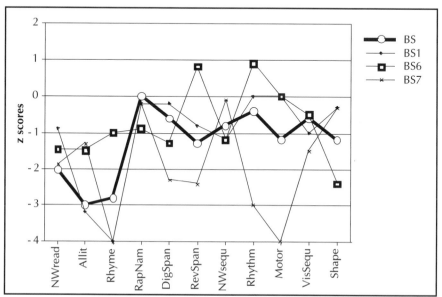

Figure 5.2 Individual profiles of three bilingual children with poor literacy scores but average, or above average, scores on Raven's Matrices compared against norms for measures of Non-word Reading (NWread), Alliteration (Allit), Rhyming (Rhyme), Rapid Naming (RapNam), Forward (DigSpan) and Reverse (RevSpan) Digit Span, Non-word Sequence Repetition (NWsequ), Rhythm Repetition (Rhythm), Motor Movement Repetition (Motor), Visuospatial Sequence Repetition (VisSequ) and Shape Memory (Shape). The average performance profile (indicated by a thicker line) of the group from which they were selected is presented for comparison with Figure 5.1

Figure 5.2 shows the results of the bilingual children who presented evidence of poor literacy despite average or above-average performance on the Raven's Matrices. Three cases are included: case BS1 is representative of the performance of the group in terms of showing deficits mainly on the phonological tasks; BS6 shows evidence of phonological deficits but additional problems in shape memory; BS7 shows a more variable profile, with problems presenting in phonological, digit span and sequencing tasks which require a motor response. Average performance of the whole group is included in this figure for comparison with Figure 5.1.

Figure 5.3 indicates the results of the remainder of the bilingual children who presented evidence of poor literacy skills. However, these children presented additional problems: (i) six children scored poorly on the Raven's Matrices – average performance is presented for comparison with Figure 5.1, as well as case

BL1 who shows a profile of deficits mainly in the sound/phonology measures; (ii) one case (BE1) was recorded as having missed a great deal of school; (iii) one case (BH1) was recorded as having hearing difficulties.

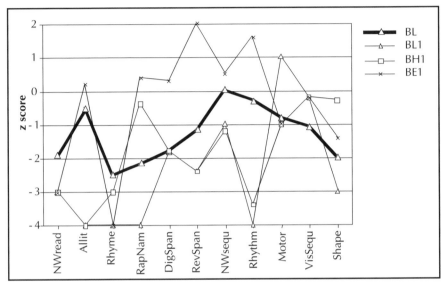

Figure 5.3 Individual profiles of three bilingual children with poor literacy scores and either (i) poor Raven's scores (BL1), (ii) hearing problems (BH1), or (iii) disrupted schooling (BE1) compared against norms for measures of Non-word Reading (NWread), Alliteration (Allit), Rhyming (Rhyme), Rapid Naming (RapNam), Forward (DigSpan) and Reverse (RevSpan) Digit Span, Non-word Sequence Repetition (NWsequ), Rhythm Repetition (Rhythm), Motor Movement Repetition (Motor), Visuo-spatial Sequence Repetition (VisSequ) and Shape Memory (Shape). The average performance profile (indicated by a thicker line) of the group of children with poor literacy and Raven's scores is presented for comparison with Figure 5.1

Discussion

The small number of bilingual children fitting the study's selection criteria, and the fact that the study focused on a specific group of bilinguals (i.e. English/Sylheti speakers), mean that conclusions must be cautious. Whether the findings can be generalised to other populations of bilinguals (those using other languages and/or orthographies) is a question for further research. Nevertheless, similar conclusions to those formed from the present study were derived by Gupta and Garg (1996) from the data of 60 bilingual pupils (average age seven, with half being assessed as dyslexic) living in India, who spoke Hindi as their first language but were educated in English. With these caveats in mind, the findings suggest that young English/Sylheti bilinguals with poor literacy skills (as indicated by poor spelling and reading) can be differentiated from their peers by measures derived from English language dyslexia screening tools. In particular, phonological measures seem to be useful in identifying those with literacy problems regardless of language background, a finding consistent with the general conclusions of Frederickson and Frith (1998) and the view that deficits in phonological processing co-occur with problems in acquiring English reading and writing skills. Such conclusions suggest that bilingual children may indeed benefit from the early screening procedures devised for monolingual children.

In addition to this general conclusion, several other features are worthy of note. Inspection of Figure 5.2 shows the variability in performance among bilingual individuals presenting evidence of literacy problems. For example, although most of these children performed well on the majority of the span and visual/motor tasks, inspection of individual cases identified children with problems in each of these areas. Such findings are consistent with the literature on the assessment of monolingual dyslexics. Hence some studies which have assessed digit span find differences between dyslexics and non-dyslexics whereas others do not (Everatt *et al.* 1999). Similarly, although the findings question the usefulness of visual/spatial and motor measures for identifying all those with literacy acquisition difficulties (at least in the age range assessed), they are consistent with some children possessing poor visual and/or motor skills. Such findings may be consistent with views for a minority visual subtype of dyslexia (e.g. Rack 1997; Watson and Willows 1993).

Another feature worthy of note from the data was the difference between the monolingual and bilingual Tower Hamlets groups on measures that might be expected to favour those with higher levels of language capability, such as rapid naming (Figure 5.1). Here the difference was not, as perhaps might be predicted, in favour of the monolingual group, but showed bilinguals outperforming their monolingual counterparts. Memory span results also point to the possibility of underperformance among the Tower Hamlets monolingual children. In this regard, it is interesting to note that within the schools where testing occurred, a large proportion of children are bilingual, making monolingual children a minority group. Many teachers involved in the study also reported that white, monolingual children, especially boys, were commonly the source of discipline and motivation problems in the class, and that this could be attributed to a lack of emphasis on the importance of school education within the family. In comparison, the Bengali family values tended to be strongly in favour of discipline and hard work. The influence of such socio-cultural factors on the screening measures used in the present study has yet to be fully investigated, but may explain the poor performance of the monolingual Tower Hamlets subjects across a range of different tasks.

The data presented in Figure 5.3 also identify the need to consider the spectrum of factors which can lead to poor literacy skills. A single measure is not enough to identify reasons for difficulties and procedures for support. Hence the boy who had been recorded as missing a great deal of schooling shows specific problems on non-word reading and rhyming tasks (though there are also some problems with visual and motor tasks). These deficits could be interpreted as being responsible for the poor literacy scores produced by this individual; however, they are equally consistent with phoneme processing and rhyming skills developing with the acquisition of literacy (Morais *et al.* 1986). Secondly, the profile of the boy with hearing problems is similar to that of BS7 in Figure 5.1 yet for potentially different reasons. Both boys show deficits in sound/phonological areas and memory span-related tasks, but fewer problems with rapid naming and visual-based measures. Both children are experiencing difficulties with reading and spelling. It is only when considering motor skills which do not require the processing of auditory information that differences between these children (and the potential underlying causes of their problems) emerge. Finally, the similarity of profiles produced by groups of bilingual children irrespective of their ability on the Raven's Matrices is resonant of the views of many authors (see special issue of *Dyslexia* edited by Nicolson and Siegel 1996) that the use of a measure of discrepancy between literacy and general ability (or intelligence) is an inadequate diagnostic tool in the identification of dyslexia. However, again the need to consider individual ability across the measures is suggested, with BL1 being an example of a boy with poor scores across most measures except those involving immediate sequential responses and visual/motor processes.

Conclusion

The present data suggest that bilingual children may indeed benefit from the early screening procedures devised for monolingual children; particularly those related to phonological processing. However, assessment of individual profiles indicates a need to consider differences across a broader range of abilities, requiring several screening indicators. This conclusion regarding bilingual children with problems acquiring literacy skills is consistent with the literature on the identification of monolingual children with reading/writing difficulties. Although caution is needed before these results should be generalised across different populations (language capability, general ability and other socio-linguistic factors need to be more explicitly assessed), they are encouraging and provide directions for further investigations in this area.

Chapter 6

Literacy Development in Emergent Bilingual Children

Jane Hutchinson, Helen Whiteley and Chris Smith

This chapter:

- reviews the literature
- reports on the first stage of a three-year longitudinal study to examine the cognitive-linguistic factors underlying literacy development in bilingual Asian children
- provides a detailed description of the assessments used to measure outcomes and
- discusses the implications of the results for bilingual children.

Introduction

A recent educational and political concern has been the underachievement in the acquisition of literacy skills of ethnic minority children. Pakistani and Bangladeshi pupils are underachieving especially at primary level where attainment is well below national averages. However, the attainment of these children has been found to improve as their fluency in English develops (OFSTED 1999).

Cummins (1984) estimated that ethnic minority children require two years to develop peer-appropriate communicative language, but need between five and seven years to fully develop academic language proficiency. McWilliam (1998) argues that for full academic achievement, bilingual children's command of the English language needs to match that of their monolingual peers and that success in curriculum learning is dependent on children's active involvement in building a complex network of linguistic understanding.

Within mainstream primary schools there are many ethnic minority children for whom English is not their first language. Before they can begin the process of reading acquisition they have to learn spoken English to at least a minimal level. However, because of the lack of research it is difficult to determine whether literacy difficulties experienced by ethnic minority children are the result of a specific deficit (specific learning difficulties (SpLD) or dyslexia), a developmental delay (caused by English language-related difficulties) or a difference (diverse patterns of literacy development in ethnic minority children and their monolingual peers).

The SpLD research has generally focused on white, monolingual, English-speaking children and the link between phonological difficulties and reading difficulties is well documented for this population (Muter *et al.* 1997a): poor phonological awareness leads to difficulties with decoding (the translation of print to sound) which is seen as a critical factor in successful literacy development. The evidence arising from studies of monolingual children, however, does not necessarily help our understanding of the literacy development of children who have English as an additional language (EAL).

Current definitions of SpLD are based on the existence of a discrepancy between reading ability and intelligence (Stanovich 1991). If EAL students require between five and seven years to develop academic language proficiency, then measures of intelligence that rely on language ability are likely to underestimate the general ability of EAL children, thus reducing the likelihood of a diagnosis of SpLD. It follows that a reliance on discrepancy definitions may have contributed to the under-representation of EAL children identified as having SpLD. The proposal of the working definition, 'Dyslexia is evident when accurate and fluent word reading and/or spelling develops very incompletely or with great difficulty' (British Psychological Society (BPS) 1999: 18), with no exclusionary criteria will in the future enable SpLD to be identified in children not previously identified using discrepancy definitions.

Children who have difficulty with decoding skills have been found to rely on contextual information to facilitate word recognition (BPS 1999). However, according to Cline and Reason (1993), children who experience language difficulties may place greater reliance on decoding skills. The implication is that EAL children who experience language-related difficulties and have difficulties with decoding will suffer considerable disadvantage when learning to read, because they will have limited compensatory strategies to facilitate the word recognition process. These difficulties may be further exacerbated as the complexity of the text increases.

The scant research that does exist looking at literacy development in EAL children has revealed some interesting findings. For example, the disparity between the average reading proficiency of Asian pupils and their monolingual peers does not become apparent until about nine years of age, possibly as a consequence of the transition from the single word reading tests used in infant schools to the sentence completion tests used in junior schools (Phillips and Birrell 1990). Sentence completion requires a greater understanding of the meaning of words and thus comprehension skills are critical.

Frederickson and Frith (1998) found that the distribution of phonological skills in EAL children (aged 10–12) mirrored those in monolingual children. However, they found that there were differences in reading accuracy and comprehension. The monolingual children's reading accuracy and reading comprehension were similar while the EAL children's reading comprehension was lower than their reading accuracy. These findings support Phillips and Birrell's suggestion that EAL children experience difficulties beyond single word decoding. Frederickson and Frith suggest that phonological skills cannot be the basis for the EAL children's generally poorer literacy skills and that less well developed reading comprehension, as opposed to accuracy, indicates difficulties with the use of semantic and syntactic cues. They conclude that EAL children may develop competence in decoding while, at the same time, continuing to have difficulties with semantic knowledge.

Comprehension covers a range of complex processes. Perfetti *et al.* (1996) propose six sources of comprehension difficulties categorised into:

Process components

- working memory limitations
- lexical processes
- inference making
- comprehension monitoring.

Knowledge components

- word meanings
- domain knowledge.

Each of these components has the potential to cause comprehension failure. Oakhill *et al.* (1998) argue that comprehension deficits are, in many cases, related to deficits in the processes involved in constructing a representation of the text rather than the knowledge components suggested by Perfetti *et al.* While acknowledging the contribution of components of knowledge, Oakhill and her colleagues have focused on processing skills in their research and, in some cases have ruled out general knowledge deficits as the source of comprehension problems (Cain and Oakhill 1998). This focus on processing components is typical of the expanding literature on comprehension-related skills and arises predominantly from studies of monolingual English-speaking children. Thus, the interpretation of the existing comprehension literature in relation to EAL pupils is confounded by the difficulties they experience with vocabulary and knowledge of subject content (McWilliam 1998).

A number of cognitive-linguistic factors appear to affect the difficulties EAL children have in their acquisition of English literacy. Research supports the use of phonological awareness interventions to increase literacy success with monolingual children, but the findings of Frederickson and Frith (1998) suggest that for EAL children comprehension may be a more critical factor. Reading difficulties may have different causes in different populations and this must be reflected in the appropriate choice of advice and intervention offered with regard to children whose first language is not English. Many questions will need to be answered before EAL children are able to learn to read and make the same developmental progress as children whose first language is English.

The project reported here is a longitudinal study of 50 EAL and 50 monolingual children. In order to capture a period of developmental change while ensuring that children have two years prior experience of the English language, the first stage of testing has been completed with Year 2 children, with 12 and 24 month follow-up. The project examines the development of phonological awareness, short-term memory, listening comprehension, receptive and expressive vocabulary and reception of grammar in relation to the development of reading accuracy, reading comprehension and spelling in both populations. The aims are to:

- advance theoretical knowledge of the development of English literacy in EAL children

- identify how language-related difficulties impact upon that literacy development
- develop recommendations concerning the identification of SpLD in EAL children.

Method

Design

Fifty EAL and 50 monolingual children have been tested on seven literacy outcome measures and 15 measures of underlying cognitive-linguistic skills in the first stage of a longitudinal design. Follow-up testing will be conducted after 12 and 24 months.

Participants

The participants are 50 monolingual and 50 EAL children attending one of ten primary schools in the Preston, Blackburn, Accrington and Haslingden areas of Lancashire. For the monolingual children, English is the only language spoken. The EAL children speak mother tongue, at least some of the time, in the home (27 – Gujerati; 12 – Urdu; 8 – Punjabi; 2 – Bengali; 1 – Pushto). The sample includes the same number of male and female children from each school and the same number of monolingual and EAL children within each class. Each EAL child was matched for gender, age and general ability with a monolingual child.

Materials

A. Measures of outcome
Form One of the Neale Analysis of Reading Ability (2nd edn, Neale 1997) was used to measure accuracy and comprehension of oral reading.

Listening comprehension was measured using Form Two of the *Neale Analysis of Reading Ability* (2nd edn, Neale 1997). The first four passages of the test were recorded onto tape. Children answered orally delivered questions after listening to each passage.

The *Group Reading Test II* (Cornwall and France 1997) was used to measure combined accuracy and comprehension. It involves selecting, from a choice of five, the correct word to complete a given sentence.

The *Wide Range Achievement Test 3* (WRAT3) (Wilkinson 1993) contains tests of spelling, single word reading and arithmetic, which were used to measure coding skills while minimising the influence of comprehension.

B. Measures of underlying cognitive-linguistic ability
Raven's Coloured Matrices (Raven *et al.* 1990) was used to measure nonverbal ability.

The *Test of Reception of Grammar* (TROG) (Bishop 1989) was used to assess the understanding of grammatical contrasts in English.

Letter knowledge was measured using a sub-test of the *Phonological Abilities Test* (Muter *et al.* 1997b).

The *Phonological Assessment Battery* (PhAB) (Frederickson *et al.* 1997) was used to assess various aspects of phonological processing ability and fluency. The battery of tests includes Alliteration, Rhyme, Non-Word Reading, Spoonerisms, Naming Speed and three tests of Fluency (Alliteration, Rhyme and Semantic Category).

The *Test of Word Knowledge* (TOWK) (Wiig and Secord 1992) consists of a number of sub-tests measuring aspects of both receptive and expressive language ability. Scores yield receptive and expressive composites.

Visual discrimination and short-term memory were measured using two sub-tests of the *British Ability Scales* (Elliott *et al.* 1983). These were Rotation of Letter-like Forms to assess group differences arising from the very different visual nature of English and Asian writing systems and Digit Span to assess short-term memory.

The *Language Preference Questionnaire* (LPQ) (based on Beech and Keys 1997) was given to the EAL children to ascertain the name of the language spoken at home and to what extent mother tongue was used for communication and thinking.

Summary of findings

Comparisons of performance levels both within and across the groups of EAL and monolingual children on a variety of reading outcome measures and measures of cognitive-linguistic skills revealed a number of similarities and differences, which can be summarised as follows:

- Similar levels of reading accuracy across groups.
- Lower levels of performance on comprehension-related measures for EAL children.
- Comprehension age below accuracy age for EAL children.
- Comprehension age above accuracy age for monolingual children.
- No differences in letter knowledge, ability to detect small differences in letter-like forms or short-term memory.
- Most phonological skills similar across groups although EAL poorer on rhyme.
- EAL poorer on retrieval from long-term memory when cued by rhyme or semantic category.
- No naming speed deficits for EAL children.
- Performance on measures of grammatical knowledge and vocabulary lower for EAL children.

Do the same factors predict literacy development for both EAL and monolingual children?

While the analysis of similarities and differences in levels of performance between the two groups has provided much useful information, it is also useful to examine relationships between various factors within the groups. For example, what are the key predictors of reading accuracy and comprehension in each of the groups? A series of correlational and regression analyses was used to explore these questions in six areas:

1. Letter knowledge predicted literacy outcome measures for both groups. *A good knowledge of letters is important for the reading success of all children.*
2. For both monolingual and EAL children, the measures of phonological awareness correlated with reading accuracy, which suggests that the *distribution of phonological skills in EAL children (aged 6–7) mirrors that in their monolingual peers*, supporting the findings of Frederickson and Frith (1998).
3. Non-word reading ability was a strong predictor of reading comprehension for both groups of children reflecting the importance of decoding for the comprehension of text. However, the strength of the predictive link was weaker for EAL children. *Thus, despite having adequate decoding skills, many EAL children have difficulties extracting the meaning from text.*
4. Correlations between measures of grammar (TROG) and receptive and expressive vocabulary (TOWK) with the literacy comprehension measures (Neale Reading Comprehension and Sentence Completion) were high for both groups of children. *It is likely, therefore, that the factors underlying the lower levels of achievement for reading comprehension in EAL children are based in poor English language skills, especially vocabulary and grammatical knowledge.*
5. An association between measures of grammar and listening comprehension was also revealed for both EAL and monolingual children, but for monolingual children the predictive association was much stronger. Since listening comprehension does not rely upon decoding skills, it is a purer measure of a child's ability to understand language than is a measure of reading comprehension. A weaker predictive association between grammatical skills and listening comprehension for EAL children suggests that *some factors which contribute to their listening comprehension are not captured by the measures employed here (possibly an aspect of the processing components of comprehension proposed by Perfetti et al.).*
6. Overall, the LPQ indicated that *a preference for speaking and thinking in English was associated with better performance* on most outcome measures and on the measures of underlying cognitive-linguistic ability.

Conclusions

The first stage of this study has highlighted similarities between the EAL and monolingual children on measures of reading accuracy, memory, visual discrimination and most measures of phonological skills. It has also revealed differences (where EAL children perform more poorly than monolingual children) on measures of reading comprehension, listening comprehension, grammatical knowledge and word knowledge.

Similarities in levels of achievement on measures involving reading accuracy (decoding skill) and measures of phonological skills suggest that tests of phonological skills which have been developed for use with monolingual children will also be useful with EAL children. Although tests of rhyme awareness may have a cultural bias, the indications are that measures of phonological awareness may be key determinants in the identification of reading difficulties for both groups of children.

The comprehension difficulties experienced by EAL children mean that those children experiencing difficulties with decoding may not have a sufficient level of understanding to be able to use context as compensation for poor word recognition. As a consequence, EAL children with decoding difficulties are likely to experience a double disadvantage that makes early identification of decoding difficulties especially important.

All measures of language proficiency (grammatical knowledge and word knowledge) revealed lower levels of achievement for EAL children. This suggests that a diagnosis of dyslexia based on a discrepancy between reading accuracy and intelligence (where intelligence tests rely upon language ability for both test performance and the comprehension of test instructions) would not identify the difficulties experienced by EAL children as dyslexia. The adoption of the working definition proposed by the BPS working party (BPS 1999) with a focus on decoding skills, has the potential to remove the cultural bias that has been associated with the identification of dyslexia.

EAL children's lower levels of word knowledge may result in difficulties in understanding both written and orally presented information – the normal modes of curriculum presentation – and may have a negative effect on the attainment of full academic potential (McWilliam 1998). With this in mind, the results presented here highlight the need to introduce measures of language comprehension into infant education.

Most measures revealed a trend for poorer performance in boys than girls. However the greatest gender differences were observed within the monolingual group. These differences will be considered throughout the project.

Overall, the results of this first stage of the project highlight the need to identify phonological difficulties as early as possible in all children, but especially in EAL children where early phonological problems may put them at a double disadvantage in the course of literacy development. The findings suggest that while specific reading difficulties (dyslexia) in EAL and monolingual children may be diagnosed through tests of predominantly phonological skills, EAL children are likely to be prone to more general reading difficulties linked to aspects of comprehension.

Chapter 7

Dyslexia and Bilingualism – Implications for Assessment, Teaching and Learning

Pamela Deponio, John Landon, Gavin Reid

This chapter:

- examines the implications from a Scottish investigation into the nature and processes of identifying dyslexia among the bilingual school population
- examines diagnostic criteria and makes suggestions for appropriate processes and frameworks and
- examines the implications for teaching in relation to language and conceptual understanding, learning styles, metacognitive and social strategies and self-esteem.

Introduction

This chapter arises out of the findings of an investigation carried out in 144 Scottish primary and secondary schools (Deponio *et al.* 2000) of the processes involved in identifying bilingual children who may be dyslexic. The research confirmed the findings of a previous Scottish study (Curnyn *et al.* 1991) that bilingual learners are significantly under-represented among pupils who are assessed as having specific learning difficulties/dyslexia. It also identified a number of possible causes for this level of under-representation, which challenge perceptions, policy and practice governing the support of bilingual learners suspected of being dyslexic.

Children who are coming to terms with the academic and linguistic demands of the curriculum through a language which is not their first language have a major task to close the gap on their English-speaking peer group. Children who are at the same time dyslexic are doubly challenged. Therefore, it is essential to enable teachers to identify such children in the early stages and to provide appropriate support with literacy development which recognises their linguistic, cultural and individual differences. This cannot, however, take place within a context which is conceptualised in terms of a monolingual, monocultural population, and which excludes bilingual children by categorising them in terms of their linguistic and cultural differences alone. In such a context, bilingual children are defined merely in terms of their second language needs. Support is predetermined as English as a second/additional language (ES/AL) support. Approaches which do exist to cover them are considered to be separate and 'specialist' in nature. This has the effect of excluding the mainstream teacher or other professional from grasping the responsibility to cater for the bilingual learner's range of needs alongside, and together with, the needs of monolingual learners. It also excludes bilingual learners and their parents from being considered as an integral and proper part of the diverse school community.

Within the numbers of dyslexic and bilingual children identified in a school or authority there will be a group of children who are both bilingual and dyslexic. Teachers and other professionals need specific guidance on how to identify and support their needs. The Scottish research identified a number of issues which must be addressed. An inter-agency approach is essential, involving in the team a member of the school's senior management, class teacher or year tutor, learning support, ES/AL support, and a professional proficient in the child's first language if possible. The team needs to arrange for the child to be assessed for those indicators which are particularly important signs of dyslexia in bilingual learners.

Because of the possibility of diagnosis of a specific learning difficulty being confused with the normal developmental pattern of second language acquisition, the process of assessment and the establishment of a support strategy tend, according to the Scottish survey, to be lengthy and inconclusive. Therefore, it is important that the inter-agency support team devises at an early stage an individualised educational plan (IEP) which will set targets for both EAL and literacy development and suggest clear and appropriate programmes of support for both, using the L1 where possible and appropriate. Throughout parents should be involved both in the provision of support and in the reporting and decision-making processes. The Scottish research and a number of other studies (Shah 1995; Diniz 1997) have revealed that parents from ethnic minority communities are frequently excluded from involvement because of poor provision of interpreters and stereotypical views of parents' lack of interest in being involved.

Assessment

There are a number of screening and diagnostic tests used to assess dyslexic children (Fawcett and Nicolson 1996; Frederickson et al. 1997; Muter et al. 1997b; Miles 1997). In the main these are directed at the monolingual population of dyslexic children although some have subsequently been standardised using samples of bilingual children (Frederickson and Frith 1997).

Assessment procedures, however, have been developed specifically for the bilingual learner by Sunderland et al. (1997). These focus on checklists, interview guidelines, diagnostic tests, and cultural and linguistic factors which may affect diagnosis. These procedures are extremely useful, not least because they are dedicated to assessing the bilingual learner but also because they provide follow-up guidance for teaching which is a crucial element in all forms of assessment.

It is important, however, as it is in all cases of dyslexia to treat the bilingual dyslexic child as an individual. Many of the blanket approaches can yield informative screening and diagnostic data but these need to be adapted and interpreted for each individual being assessed. The key issues, therefore, in relation to assessing bilingual or multilingual children include the following:

- Screening: when should this take place and what is the nature of, and the criteria for, screening?
- Diagnosis: can adapted formal standardised tests be used successfully? How valid can these be with different populations of children?
- Language: should we be focusing on dynamic rather than static assessment for bilingual children (Usmani 1999; Ogilvy 1992; Meadows 1998)? This takes into account elements of the test situation such as language understanding and links with teaching through scaffolding and developing language concepts.
- Learning style: it is important to view the bilingual child as an individual learner and to take into account the particular learning styles of each individual.

These issues are briefly discussed below in relation to the practicalities of formulating and implementing assessment procedures for bilingual children.

Screening

There are a number of screening tests which can be used for dyslexic children but it is advisable that if these are to be used they are supplemented by a customised interview and observation in the classroom situation. Sunderland *et al.* (1997) provide a checklist which includes:

- Language aspects: this looks at the types of difficulties one would normally associate with dyslexia, for example discrepancies between writing and speech; inconsistencies in spelling such as writing a word a number of different ways without noticing it; sound/symbol relationship; inability to recognise familiar words in print and persistent miscopying.
- Memory: poor short-term memory, for example difficulty in remembering lists, dates, language rules and drills.
- Sequencing: confusion between left and right, up, down, learning the alphabet, days of the week and lists of numbers.

For children who have maintained a high degree of oral competence, and are developing literacy in their first language, similar difficulties discovered through first language assessment in a context where first language is regularly used will act as a confirmation of the above.

- Personal: organisational difficulties, inconsistency in classroom performance. These aspects may be confirmed through interviews with the parents or with teachers employed in the community to provide supplementary first language classes.

Diagnosis

It is important to consider the educational context and the individual child's linguistic, educational and social history when making a diagnosis (Hall 1995). Dewsbury (1999), in discussing the First Steps Literacy Programme, which was devised in Western Australia for early literacy acquisition, emphasised the importance of appreciating that linguistic behaviours do not necessarily represent cognitive development. It is, therefore, important that a diagnosis should not draw conclusions about the child's cognitive abilities on the basis of performance and difficulties in literacy.

In the Scottish research (Deponio *et al.* 2000), it was found that teachers were utilising a wide range of assessment materials but these were not specifically designed for children with a first language which is different from English. It is important that, if such standardised and diagnostic tests are used, they are supplemented by observation criteria which incorporate the child's performance in other curricular areas in different learning contexts. A report by a working party of the Division of Educational and Child Psychology of the British Psychological Society on Dyslexia, Literacy and Psychological Assessment emphasises culture-fair assessment, and that indicators such as phonological difficulties and letter-naming speed can be the focus of a diagnosis in the language of tuition (BPS 1999). Culture-fair assessment may represent the 'holy grail' (Cline 1998), but analysis of test performance within specific cultural and linguistic groups can help to identify those items which consistently lead to cultural confusion or misperception. Poor performance in tests of phonic awareness is an important indicator given the usually enhanced phonological awareness of bilingual learners resulting in good phonic decoding skills at the early stages of learning to read in English. It has also been suggested (Landon 1999) that the failure of a bilingual child who is orally competent in the first language (L1) to respond to pre-reading support in the L1 may be an indicator of a specific learning difficulty.

Language

In view of the need to insure against cultural bias in assessment it is important to consider alternative forms of assessment, such as Dynamic Assessment, to obtain a diagnosis (Usmani 1999). This approach essentially links assessment and teaching and highlights the child's learning process. Usmani (1999) suggests the bilingual, bicultural child may have a broad range of thinking skills which may go undetected if the professional is unaware of the cultural values or fails to understand them in relation to the assessment. Usmani further suggests that the 'big dip' in performance noted in some bilingual children in later primary may be explained by a failure of professionals to understand and appreciate the cultural values and the actual level of competence of the bilingual child in relation to conceptual development and competence in thinking skills. Landon (1999) speculates that teachers may be beguiled by bilingual children's development of good phonic skills in the early stages of literacy development in English into failing to perceive difficulties which they might be having with comprehension. When these difficulties later emerge, they are grouped inappropriately with native-speakers of English who have the more conventional problems with phonic awareness, or their difficulties are assumed to derive from specific perceptual problems rather than from the cultural unfamiliarity of the text.

Procedures

Clearly there are strong opinions on the formulation of an assessment policy which encompasses the needs and abilities of bilingual children. The nature and process of assessment procedures and tests will differ from those suggested for other children. M'gadzah *et al.* (1999) have produced a framework for guidelines, assessment and intervention with implications for all, including the educational psychology services. It is important to note that this framework was suggested following consultation involving school and community. Parents and professionals need to liaise effectively if both perspectives are to be understood and have an impact on practice. A study by Diniz (1997) has shown that such partnerships are all too rare where families from ethnic minority communities are concerned.

The framework suggested by M'gadzah *et al.* includes five steps: background information on the pupil; assessment of classroom environment and school ethos – this includes analysis and differentiation of tasks and the extent to which the classroom meets the cultural and linguistic needs of bilingual learners; and further assessment which should include observations over time, curriculum-based assessment, the use of appropriate tests and the monitoring of teaching approaches. This is followed by the review process and consultation with educational psychologists. This should provide a comprehensive picture of the pupil's strengths and weaknesses and areas of concern. It should also enable a review of targets to take place in the context of seeking the views of parents and the pupils themselves.

This comprehensive process clearly relies on inter-professional cooperation and collaboration between school and community, the availability of resources (including the provision of interpreters) and appropriate training of professionals to work in multilingual and multicultural contexts. It is important, however, to embark on consultation throughout the assessment process and this should be evident at every stage. The views of parents must be considered and cultural factors which can make conventional assessment invalid must be taken into account.

Learning style

There is strong evidence that learning style, both environmental and cognitive, can affect the progress in attainments, particularly in literacy (Dunn and Dunn 1994; Milgram *et al.* 1993; Given and Reid 1999; Riding and Raynor 1998). Dunn and Milgram (1993) examined the learning styles of students in different cultures and noted the diversity of learning styles within, as well as between, cultures. Gregory (1996) has investigated the different approaches to reading and writing taken by biliterate learners and their parents in their various literacies. It is, therefore, important to view the bilingual child as an individual and to attempt to appreciate the learning style of the individual at both input and output stage. This relates to the choice of resources, mode of teaching and learning, environmental factors and classroom ethos and pace of work, mode of assessment and criteria for measuring progress. This underlines the view that assessment is much more than testing; indeed, it should be part of the sharing and learning process between parents, teachers and other professionals.

Teaching approaches

Once assessment has suggested the possibility that a bilingual learner may be dyslexic, consideration must be given to appropriate teaching and learning approaches. It is important that the child's strengths (including competence in languages other than English and cultural experience), motivation and self-esteem, and learning styles are included in these considerations. As teaching approaches are selected and devised, through collaboration between the class or subject teacher, ES/AL and learning support staff, it is important to ensure as far as possible that they are incorporated into the child's daily curricular activities and that a separate programme of work is not offered. The teaching approaches suggested below are appropriate for many monolingual dyslexic learners. Their adaptation, through consultation with ES/AL support staff, can often reduce the need for specialist teaching and offer support to the dyslexic bilingual learner.

Phonological awareness

The phonological delay/deficit hypothesis as an explanation of the difficulties experienced by monolingual dyslexic learners is widely accepted (Snowling 1995; Frith 1997; BPS 1999). Everatt *et al.* (2000) and Frederickson and Frith (1997) have suggested that this may also be the case for bilingual dyslexic learners. It would, therefore, be appropriate for a child to undertake a programme of phonological awareness – including analogical reading. Since such approaches form the basis of the National Literacy Hour (England) and Early Intervention Programmes (Scotland), it is likely that these programmes will be offered routinely, possibly avoiding the need for further intensive work in the form of individual teaching or withdrawal to a support base. However, it should be noted that difficulties which many bilingual learners have with articulating especially English vowels and final consonantal morphemes may impede recognition and production of these sounds. Further, speakers of syllable-timed languages, for example Cantonese, may have difficulty in hearing unstressed syllables in stress-timed English utterances. Previous experience of reading logographic, as opposed to alphabetic, script may also cause difficulties with analogical reading for a literate Chinese pupil (Goswami and Bryant 1990). Therefore, more practice in recognising rhyme and syllable may be necessary for learners from certain language backgrounds.

To compensate for weak auditory processing, other senses can be used to identify sounds and letters. A multisensory approach has been found useful for consolidating learning in monolingual dyslexic learners as it brings into play auditory, visual, oral, kinesthetic and tactile channels of learning. The fact that language is not the primary medium of learning is also likely to be advantageous to bilingual learners.

Automaticity and overlearning

It is necessary for information to be presented to the dyslexic learner on different occasions and in different ways to help the information pass from short-term to long-term memory, thus ensuring automaticity. Spelling, for example, can be taught initially in a multisensory way, leading to overlearning through the use of games, computer activities and word webs. Learning and overlearning will be most effective for monolingual and bilingual learners when words are presented and used in meaningful contexts, and when the need to use the word derives from the pupil and not from the teacher. For bilingual learners this has implications for the creation of culturally sensitive learning environments and tasks.

A dyslexic learner who successfully spells a word during a spelling test will not necessarily spell the same word correctly in a piece of imaginative writing until automaticity has been achieved. This is because the child's full concentration is on the spelling alone in the first case, but is focused on creating a story in the second. While correct spelling is becoming automatic, critical proof-reading is a skill which must be taught. The child, freed from the main task of creating a story, is then likely to self-correct many spelling errors. Process writing, involving collaborative drafting and redrafting of written text in multilingual groups has been found to be a useful approach for bilingual learners in developing compositional and editing skills.

Schema activation, pre-reading discussion and retelling

The awareness of schema is important to the understanding of text. The child who fails to activate the appropriate schema will fail to understand the text; the child who activates the wrong schema will extract the wrong meaning. Consideration of schema is particularly important for dyslexic bilingual learners whose experiences may be socially and culturally different, even in surprising ways, from their monolingual peers (Carrell 1988). Pre-reading discussion using illustrations, titles, captions, topic sentences or keywords as stimuli can help to set the scene and avoid confusion. With children whose English is not sufficiently developed, the discussion can take place in the first language using a parent or bilingual assistant. Texts relating to the cultural experiences of bilingual learners – whether written by fellow-learners or available in published form – will aid schema identification and the activation of short-term memory and visualisation (Steffensen *et al.* 1979).

West (1991) suggests that many dyslexic learners are right-brain dominant and process information in a visual and holistic manner; therefore, it is advantageous to give an overview of a story, situation or task so that a child can have the full picture from the beginning. This approach to learning is also common in many non-literate societies and may well be the preferred learning style of some bilingual learners. Once a text has been read, comprehension can be monitored and language reinforced by encouraging the learner to retell the story with the help of any visuals or word prompts which have used during the original reading. The retelling can lead into writing.

Motivation and self-esteem

A child whose strengths and interests are recognised and used during the process of teaching and learning is more likely to make progress than the child who finds the learning experience alien and self-negating. Bilingual children from culturally different backgrounds from the teacher need, therefore, to be fully engaged in selecting resources and learning approaches which are appropriate and affirming. The teacher should not second-guess pupil choice; the result is likely to reveal more about the teacher's stereotypes than about awareness of pupil interests. In one literacy project in a multilingual class (Landon 1999) bilingual children were encouraged to make free choices from materials on offer in the classroom. The girls chose the same kind of stories as their monolingual peer group; the boys, however, tended to select non-fiction possibly because it was less culturally loaded than the fictional materials and because the topics were more related to conventional male interests.

Clarifying teacher expectations

The teacher may well have a different expectation of the outcome of the reading process from the student. The teacher's aim will be for the reader to comprehend the text and perhaps to apply its message in some way to personal experience or to a learning task. The reader may, however, consider that it is enough merely to read aloud accurately or to finish reading as quickly as possible. For bilingual learners, their different experiences of reading in different cultural contexts may require different outcomes. Confusion arising in this way can be exacerbated in the classroom when the teacher, without notice, seems to veer from an interest in comprehension to an obsession with accurate reading aloud, or when reading or writing rapidly to complete an assignment seems to be more important than the discovery or communication of meaning. It is important that the teacher should make clear the aims and expectations of a task. For children with limited English, this can be communicated by a bilingual assistant via the first language.

Metacognitive, cognitive and social strategies

In order to enable readers to read independently of the teacher, it is important that they develop metacognitive strategies which will allow them to plan, monitor and evaluate their own learning; cognitive strategies which will enable them to manipulate the material to be learnt mentally (through imaging, for example) or physically (through note-taking or grouping items); and social strategies to facilitate interaction with their peer group or the teacher in the purpose of learning (Chamot and O'Malley 1994).

- Metacognitive strategies: these consist of advance organising (for example, skimming, previewing the text), selecting a purpose for reading and scanning to fulfil the purpose, as well as self-monitoring and editing and reviewing the effectiveness of the completed task and the learning experience.
- Cognitive strategies: involve using key visuals or mind-mapping to organise information during reading or as a precursor to writing, inferring from information and applying it to new scenarios or problems.
- Social strategies: using language to collaborate with others during the process of reading or writing.

Conclusion

The Scottish research revealed a great deal of confusion among teachers about the assessment and support of bilingual learners suspected of being dyslexic. There was further a lack of understanding of the processes of literacy development within the context of emerging bilingualism. This suggests that the high level of activity around dyslexia in Scottish schools and authorities in terms of policy making and professional development is excluding the needs of bilingual learners. It is not sufficient merely to create separate policies and staff development programmes to bridge this gap. This approach will only reach the specialist, will tend to be reactive and highlights the exclusion from mainstream provision and planning of this section of the school population. Existing policies and staff development provision need to be reviewed to include bilingualism as an issue. In this way, all teachers will be enabled to address bilingualism and dyslexia with greater confidence and to collaborate with other professionals and parents from a position of understanding. The issues raised by this question will also encourage teachers to view more critically the current orthodoxy surrounding literacy development which has tended to be constructed around a homogeneous and idealised learning community.

Chapter 8

The Effects of Literacy Hour and Phonics Teaching on Poor Readers' Phonological and Literacy Skills: Case Studies of Children with English as an Additional Language

Eleni Morfidi and Rea Reason

This chapter:

- examines the role of phonological processing
- discusses the link between phonological and reading skills of bilingual children in both languages
- describes the method, results and implications of an intervention study based on two different teaching conditions.

Introduction

Research evidence has suggested that a key to the reading difficulties experienced by many children is a problem with phonological processing. Consequently, the learning of phoneme-grapheme correspondences becomes very difficult. According to the phonological representation hypothesis these children have incomplete or inaccurate phonological representations of words in their mental lexicon. This may explain why children with reading difficulties show poor performance on phonological tasks.

The Phonological Assessment Battery (PhAB) (Frederickson *et al.* 1997) is an instrument designed to measure phonological processing. There are norms for children from 6:00 to 14:11 years and it is intended to be used with children whose literacy progress is causing concern. The framework within which it was conceptualised has been provided by Frith (1995). The PhAB includes the following tests:

1. Alliteration
2. Rhyme
3. Spoonerisms
4. Naming Speed: Picture Naming Speed and Digit Naming Speed
5. Fluency: Semantic Fluency, Alliteration Fluency, and Rhyme Fluency
6. Non-word Reading.

As a 'rule of thumb', children who have at least three standard scores below 85 (one standard deviation below the mean) are identified as having phonological weaknesses. The PhAB is regarded as appropriate also for identifying bilingual children who experience difficulties of a phonological nature (Frederickson *et al.* 1997: 106).

A number of studies investigated the link between phonological and reading skills of bilingual children in both languages, and pointed to the potential that phonological assessment presents for the identification of bilingual poor readers (Chiappe and Siegel 1999; Martin *et al.* 1997; Da Fontoura and Siegel 1995). Cummins (1984) suggested that minority students may acquire surface competencies in the second language within two years of arrival in the host country while cognitive/academic skills require exposure to an academic setting for at least five years. Thus it can be claimed that an accurate assessment can be taken once the learner can show competence in oral language to a reasonable level.

Frederickson and Frith (1998) compared 50 Sylheti children (mean age 130 months) with 50 monolingual English-speaking children of similar age (mean age 129 months). The two groups were tested on phonological tasks (using PhAB) and reading (accuracy and comprehension). Differences between the two groups were observed only in the naming speed test, where Sylheti children were faster. They were poorer in reading accuracy and particularly in comprehension, which indicates 'problems in language competence beyond word decoding' (Frederickson and Frith 1998: 126). The percentage of children within the two samples whose performance was at least one standard deviation below the mean was calculated – 18 per cent of each sample obtained three or more scores which were at least one standard deviation below the mean. This suggests a similar phonological profile (i.e. as indicated by the number of PhAB scores below 85) for the two samples.

In a second study the researchers compared monolingual English speaking children who had been identified as having a Specific Learning Difficulty (SpLD) (n = 88, mean age 119 months) with the bilingual Sylheti sample from the former study. The comparison indicated that Sylheti children were better on single word recognition than reading continuous text. The opposite pattern was observed for the SpLD children. The latter group compensated for decoding difficulties using aspects of language (i.e. syntactic, semantic) which allow prediction from text. The authors suggest that the bilingual Sylheti children failed to use semantic/syntactic knowledge because of incomplete acquisition of English language skills.

The evidence suggests that children who have English as an additional language (EAL) do not differ from their monolingual counterparts in phonological processing skills. Consequently, when they show poor phonological processing skills and difficulties in literacy acquisition, they should be treated as their monolingual counterparts with reading difficulties. Some EAL children may show poor reading comprehension while reading connected text. This could be attributed to their competence in a second language and suggests support with higher-order literacy skills (e.g. vocabulary development).

The present intervention study was designed to examine how performance on the PhAB tests may change after application of two teaching conditions with six individual cases of poor EAL readers who were originally identified as having marked phonological weaknesses. The importance of interpreting PhAB with caution in individual cases has been stressed by Frith (1999). Although it is expected that phonological tests do well in discriminating groups, their sensitivity and specificity in individual cases remain to be established (Frith 1999: 207).

Method

The single case approach was followed in which two teaching conditions had been formulated. Teaching Condition 1 involved phonics intervention for ten weeks along with the school's literacy hour. In the second Teaching Condition children participated in the school's literacy hour only. Pre- and post-test measures had been taken from normative tests of phonological processing and literacy and in order to better evaluate progress throughout the study curriculum-based tests were used.

The multiple-baseline design across subjects and behaviours was followed. The design has been widely used in psychology to evaluate the effectiveness of training across subjects, behaviours or settings. The advantage of multiple-baseline design is that it can be used in research areas where the effects of the independent variable cannot be withdrawn or reversed. Three initial probes were administered during the first week of the project to evaluate baseline stability. It was the study's intent to keep the baseline phase to a minimum. Given the relative stability of behaviour the study proceeded to the next step – the introduction of training material. Intervention was introduced to all three subjects in Condition 1 and to all behaviours that required training. A limitation of multiple-baseline designs is the possible covariance of the baselines. Some degree of independence among the dependent variables is required. In the present research the aim of teaching did not allow for considerable independence. It was expected that improvement in one (e.g. letter recognition) would affect ability of another (e.g. letter writing).

In principle, the instruction should be provided in sequential order, while data are collected for the untreated behaviours or subjects however, there are two main disadvantages to this. First, improvement of ability may be extended to baselines still awaiting the intervention and secondly, continuous assessments may lead to sensitisation to the dependent variables. Teaching all of them simultaneously, therefore, rather than individually in sequence was considered the best method. The intention of the study was to give the same amount of intervention to all and address all aspects of training simultaneously with more emphasis on the teaching of letter–sound correspondences. This follows previous research evidence (Hatcher *et al.* 1994).

Subjects

The sample was selected from a larger pool of children, all introduced by the class teachers as poor readers, taken from two classes of English National Curriculum Year 2. Ten children were identified as having marked phonological weaknesses, one child was under medication and a second had a relatively low Raven's Coloured Progressive Matrices (RCPM) score. These latter two were excluded hence eight children participated in the present research of which six had English as an additional language. This chapter reports results from these six individual cases.

Three children participated in Condition 1 (Literacy Hour teaching plus extra phonics training) and three children in Condition 2 (Literacy Hour only). Children in both conditions were at least of average ability as measured using the RCPM, had low reading and spelling scores and at least three PhAB test scores below the standard score of 85. They had similar mean age, RCPM score, and phonological processing skills as measured using PhAB. Control over all variables was not possible (e.g. reading, spelling). The poorest readers were chosen for Condition 1 as the study of these children would give stronger and more reliable results. It was also considered a more ethical decision. The children were followed at Year 3 when the intervention actually started. There were children from both classes in each condition and all children followed formal English education in the same school for at least two years. Details are presented in Tables 8.1 and 8.2.

Table 8.1 Subjects, age (in months), language spoken at home and RCPM scores of children in Conditions 1 and 2

Teaching Condition 1				Teaching Condition 2			
	Language	RCPM raw score	Age (in months)		Language	RCPM raw score	Age (in months)
MA1	(Urdu)	30	81	GU2	(Urdu)	28	89
AD1	(Urdu)	24	84	FU1	(Urdu)	24	87
AM1	(Urdu)	21	84	YA1	(Arabic)	21	93
			M= 83				M= 89.6

Table 8.2 Reading, spelling results and number of PhAB scores below the standard score of 85 (pre-test)

	Pre-Test							
	Teaching Condition 1							
	No. of PhAB scores <85	NARA Accuracy		NARA Comprehension		BAS Word Reading		BAS Word Spelling
		Raw	Std	Raw	Std	Raw	Std	Raw	Std
MA1	5	0	–	1	70	4	–	0	–
AD1	6	0	–	0	–	6	–	3	–
AM1	6	1	–	0	–	8	–	1	–
	Teaching Condition 2							
GU2	6	7	72	1	–	17	61	5	–
FU2	6	3	–	1	–	10	56	2	–
YA2	5	7	–	2	–	13	55	2	–

key: – the raw score is too low for the calculation of a standard score

Tasks

Seven probes (i.e. the assessment of behaviour on particular occasions) were administered in total. These consisted of seven curriculum-based tests from Reason and Boote (1994). These were:

- rhyme recognition (matching rhyming pairs with the aid of pictures)
- auditory sound blending (words were presented orally in bits; the child was asked to give the full word)
- auditory recognition of initial letter sound ('I Spy')
- reading and writing single letter sounds
- reading and writing CV and CVC words.

The normative tests administered before and after each teaching condition were:

- The Phonological Assessment Battery (PhAB)
- Neale Analysis of Reading Ability (NARA) (Prose Reading: Accuracy and Comprehension)
- British Ability Scales (BAS) single word recognition and writing.

The RCPM is a test of nonverbal reasoning ability which was administered once.

Teaching material

Children in Condition 1 received the literacy hour in the class and participated in the phonics training programme for ten weeks. Each one of the children was seen individually in a quiet room three times a week. Teaching activities from Reason and Boote (1994) were used involving rhyme training using pictures, practice in auditory sound blending and alliteration ('Easy Kim's' game and the 'Home' game). The children experienced these activities only when it was shown that they had difficulty with the particular task. These activities took place only three times during the first week of the project and lasted five to ten minutes.

Throughout the project the three Condition 1 children received training in letter recognition and writing ('picture side up' and 'quick flip') (from Reason and Boote 1994) on the letters with which they had difficulty. They were also taught using the Phonological Awareness Training (PAT) programme (Wilson 1997). The PAT is designed to help children to read, spell and write phonically regular words with emphasis in reading words using analogies. These sessions lasted approximately 15 minutes.

Children in Condition 2 had the literacy hour in the class only. The school voluntarily participated in the National Literacy Project in 1997 when the study took place. The teachers followed the literacy hour framework which is now part of the National Literacy Strategy (DfEE 1998). The National Literacy Strategy (NLS) consists of a curricular framework for reading and an organisational framework for planning the teaching in the classroom. This is described as the 'Literacy Hour'. The teaching framework involves work at the level of **text**, **sentence** and **word**. The importance of systematic teaching of phonics and spelling is underlined and is addressed in the teaching framework. The class should have one hour of dedicated literacy teaching each day, the focus being on reading and writing instruction with approximately 50/50 balance of whole-class and group teaching. The two class teachers coordinated to a great extent.

The overall structure of the literacy hour should have:

(a) 15 minute whole-class reading or writing session working with a shared text e.g. a 'big book';
(b) 15 minute whole-class session on word level (phonics, spelling, word recognition, vocabulary extension);
(c) 20 minutes of directed group activities;
(d) a plenary session at the end of the lesson (approximately 10 minutes) for pupils to present prepared work, reflect on what they have learnt, plan follow-up activities etc.

The children with reading difficulties had 30 minutes per week to work with the teacher on the shared text. During this time, working at the word level, poor readers focused on simple words and took part in linguistic games involving **word patterns, alliteration, rhyme, segmentation** and **blending**.

Results

There are two terms used that have to be defined before examining children's results. *Teaching Phase I*: the first four teaching weeks taking into account the half-term break. During Teaching Phase I the children in Condition 1 had 11 teaching sessions. For each child, performance is shown with the mean percentage of the scores before and after the half term. *Teaching Phase II*: the last six teaching weeks. During Teaching Phase II, Condition 1 children had 19 more sessions. At the end of Teaching Phase II a final probe was administered and all the scores were converted into percentages. The results reported here involve the four most important tests (letter recognition, letter writing, word recognition, word writing).

• Mean Baseline Performance:

Condition 1 children: performance ranged from 12 per cent (word writing) to 61 per cent (letter recognition) on average. Condition 2 children: they achieved higher levels with performances ranging from 61 per cent (word recognition) to 78 per cent (letter recognition and writing) on average.

• At the end of Teaching Phase I:

Condition 1 children: they showed progress which ranged from 54 per cent (word recognition) to 90 per cent (letter recognition) on average. Condition 2 children: their performance ranged from 74 per cent (word writing) to 92 per cent (letter writing) on average.

• At the end of Teaching Phase II:

Condition 1 children: they reached high levels of performance, which ranged from 82 per cent (word writing) to 97 per cent (letter recognition) on average. Condition 2 children: they achieved accuracy in their performance, which ranged from 82 per cent in both word recognition and writing to 91 per cent in letter writing on average.

• Follow-up:

Condition 1 children: their scores ranged from 87 per cent (word writing) to 99 per cent (letter recognition). Condition 2 children: they showed a range of 83 per cent (word writing) to 96 per cent (letter writing) on average.

Children in Condition 1, although originally poorer, showed considerable improvement in their performance in all tests. The magnitude of their improvement and the rapidity of change once the intervention was applied, indicates the influential role of phonics intervention in children's performance in the particular tests. The effects of training were replicable across all behaviours (i.e. tests) and across all subjects. The design established a strong case of verification and replication. Children in both teaching conditions made progress – however, progress was more evident with children in Condition 1. Although these children were originally poorer, they were performing at the same level with Condition 2 children at the end of intervention.

Teaching Condition 1 was more effective in promoting writing skills. This finding may be explained from the content of the intervention provided – PAT material includes a good deal of writing activities. Phonological skills may be even more important for spelling (Goswami and Bryant 1990).

All six children showed improvement in the PhAB test scores regardless of teaching condition. As can be seen in Table 8.3, GU2 showed the smaller change (two less highlighted scores in the post-test). YA2 had three less highlighted scores in the second time, while AD1 and MA1 had four less. Five less highlighted scores appeared in the PhAB profiles of AM1 and FU2. These two children also showed the maximum gains in the curriculum-based tests. All of them also showed progress to some extent in both the curriculum-based tests and the normative literacy measures. What seems to be evident from children's scores is that literacy and phonological skills have both progressed with age and instruction.

Table 8.3 Reading, spelling results and number of PhAB scores below the standard score of 85 (post-test)

	No. of PhAB scores <85	NARA Accuracy		NARA Comprehension		BAS Word Reading		BAS Word Spelling	
Post-Test									
Teaching Condition 1									
		Raw	Std	Raw	Std	Raw	Std	Raw	Std
MA1	1	5	–	2	70	11	55	5	–
AD1	2	6	–	1	–	16	57	5	–
AM1	1	7	–	1	–	13	56	6	–
Teaching Condition 2									
GU2	4	13	75	2	–	22	55	4	–
FU2	1	13	78	1	–	22	57	5	–
YA2	2	19	81	2	–	24	55	4	–

key: – the raw score is too low for the calculation of a standard score

The children in Condition 1 originally had 17 standard scores below 85 but at the end of intervention they had 4. Condition 2 children had 17 at the pre-test and 7 at the post-test. Eleven highlighted scores (i.e. standard scores below 85) remained unchanged indicating persistent difficulties. In total 23 highlighted scores changed. It could be argued that scores which exceed the cut-off point of 85 (one standard deviation below the mean) approach normal rates. It also suggests that phonological processing ability is not a binary variable but a skill which develops and can be amenable to instruction. Although change was observed and this could be attributed to the effects of instruction, control subjects should be included to allow for more precise measurement of the effects of either teaching condition.

Discussion and implications

Other possible influential factors may explain part of the change. The children in the present sample came from low-income families. The beneficial role of phonological training on the reading abilities of children who come from low-income families has been stressed previously (Morais *et al.* 1998; Morais 1991). Such pupils are at risk of reading failure especially if they are taught with a whole-language approach (Nicholson 1997). It could be argued that children who come from a minority group and speak a different language at home may not have experienced linguistic games prior to school. They may come to school with different affective and cognitive characteristics. EAL children have different linguistic backgrounds and receive the same classroom instruction as children who come from English-speaking families. Adult–child interaction in school and educational treatment factors may provide some help but it may not be sufficient to bring them to the same level of competence as native English-speakers at the early school years. They may be able to catch up later or they may still lag behind at later grades.

Age and the severity of the problem also need to be considered. Children who have not played 'I Spy' at a younger age or heard stories before they go to bed, may develop reading and phonological skills at a slower rate. Children with phonologically based reading difficulties may take even longer to develop phonological representations (Goswami 1999a). If the phonological skills of the children in the present sample were still developing, a highlighted score on PhAB would not reflect persistent and enduring phonological difficulties. The children in this research presented weaknesses which did not show the severity that prohibits teaching effects to be observed. These children cannot be considered as treatment resisters and they can benefit from inclusion of word-level work and extra phonics teaching. The more they get the better. A follow-up could more clearly show whether the effects on PhAB are still evident.

Cautious interpretation of PhAB scores is needed which takes full account of the learning opportunities available to the children. An interaction of many factors needs to be considered when interpreting performance. Influences from age, gender, socio-economic status, ethnicity, exposure to the language of instruction, literacy concepts, type and severity of the observed weaknesses, response to teaching, the number of years the child has failed in reading and the learning opportunities available to the child may interact and explain test scores. Some of them may be more influential than others. According to Adams (1990) the key to phonemic awareness seems to lie more in training than in age or maturation, and the activities that seem to lead most strongly to the development of phonemic awareness are these involved in learning how to read and spell.

As indicated by the tests' raw scores (Table 8.3), all six children showed that although there was some progress in normative tests of literacy, they were still below the expected level of performance for their age. Although most of the children (five out of six) did not continue to have enough highlighted scores on PhAB to suggest marked phonological weaknesses, their reading ability was still below expected levels. Progress in terms of phonological skills was not readily generalised to the normative literacy tests.

Lyon and Moats (1997) suggested that children with reading difficulties who eventually master phonics concepts cannot automatically transfer these concepts to real-word and text-reading situations. This could be achieved by providing training time in explicitly integrating learned phonological concepts into word and text reading tasks. In the present intervention study the component of text reading was not addressed. The results are in line with previous research which has shown insensitivity of standardised measures to treatment changes. Normative tests are considered poor measures of progress following remedial teaching (Nicholson 1997; Lovett *et al.* 1990). Moreover, 'Matthew effects' (Stanovich 1986) need to be considered when attempting to evaluate the effects of interventions. Slow development of phonological processing skills leads to delayed early literacy skills. The reading failure that these children experience in their first steps interacts with poor motivation, thus reading becomes a difficult and less pleasurable task. In addition, these readers are usually expected to read material which exceeds their capability and progressively they are exposed to less text than their peers. Motivational side effects are considered just as important as the cognitive consequences of reading failure (Stanovich 1986).

Conclusion

The number of highlighted PhAB scores is not necessarily indicative of the child's persistent weaknesses – the particular PhAB tests on which the children show weaknesses may illustrate more clearly the source of the reading difficulty. Some of the PhAB tests are more closely connected with processes involved in reading (Solity 1996). The PhAB manual stresses the importance of interpreting children's scores in the light of their learning experiences and this is demonstrated in the present study with a small number of EAL children.

Chapter 9

Text Genre, Miscue Analysis, Bilingualism and Dyslexia: Teaching Strategies with Junior School Pupils

Aglaia Stamboltzis and Peter Pumfrey

This chapter:

- briefly outlines the existing literature on genre theory, miscue analysis (the analysis of children's oral reading errors)
- briefly outlines the literature on bilingualism and dyslexia and
- links the major theoretical ideas with practical suggestions for the teaching of children who have English as an additional language (including those with dyslexia).

Introduction

In a multicultural society like Britain, there is concern over the acquisition of reading and writing of children who speak a language other than English at home. Given that reading is one of the most complex and important skills the child must acquire in school, reading in a second language may present extra difficulties for these children who are not familiar with the phonological, syntactic and semantic aspects of the target language. Such problems are exacerbated when the learner is also unfamiliar with the cultural mores of the society whose language is to be acquired. If a child is also dyslexic, the difficulties are exacerbated.

In the last decades, the idea of genre has begun to loom larger in thinking about literacy development. Genre is defined in the dictionary as 'a particular type or style of literature, art or music'. In relation to textual material it refers to different types of texts. Genre theory provides a view of language in which words and sentences are seen to be patterned and organised to achieve different purposes and meanings. The aim is to raise pupils' awareness about the variety of language meanings and the purposes for which different written forms are used. Genre theory is a method of teaching reading and writing in close relation to language activities (Kress 1994).

Research in dyslexia and research in bilingualism have generally inhabited different worlds. Dyslexia refers to a difficulty relating to the analysis of words in print. Research on bilingual children and good practice in their education has generally focused on speakers who do not experience learning difficulties in literacy. It seems likely that these groups could learn much from each other (Cline 1999b). The aim of this chapter is to present and discuss teaching strategies, techniques and materials which may benefit both bilingual learners and pupils with dyslexia.

Aspects of genre theory

The term 'genre' is used to refer almost exclusively to different types of writing. Ideas about genre have resulted mainly from the seminal work of Halliday (1978) who described the relationship between language and its social context. He emphasised that the language we speak and write is the result of the social situation in which we are communicating. Individuals express meaning through language and, as they do so, they change social reality. In particular, there is great discussion about the different types of language we use for different purposes. The relationship between our cultural environment, our communicative purpose and the genres we use forms the basis of genre theory.

Littlefair (1991, 1992) proposes a linguistic definition of genre which is much wider than one which refers simply to a category of texts. She outlines 'genre' in relation to 'register'. We can think of genre as a text's framework of meaning and register as the details within that framework. Register represents *what is being spoken or written about, who is being spoken or written to and how the message is being communicated.* These three aspects of a situation are termed by linguists *field, mode* and *tenor* and they are expressed through language. Writers use language which is appropriate to their purposes and therefore to the form of genre they have chosen. Table 9.1 illustrates the relationship of genre, register and language.

Table 9.1 The relationship of genre, register and language (adapted from Littlefair 1992: 5)

GENRE (writers' or speakers' purposes)
GENRE STRUCTURES (forms)
REGISTER
Reflected by field, mode and tenor
expressed through
LANGUAGE (choices of vocabulary, grammar, syntax etc.)

A complementary definition is given by Kirk and Pearson (1996). They consider genre to include two aspects. The first is the purpose for which the text is written. For example, authors of detective stories have the purpose of writing a story which is about creating mystery and solving a crime. Authors of science text books have the purpose of explaining natural phenomena to pupils of particular ages. Such different intentions have an effect upon the second aspect – the structure of the text;

that is the way the words and sentences are chosen and organised. Both the intention of the author and the structural framework of the text are considered to define particular genres.

Miscue analysis: definitions, methodological and practical considerations

Miscue analysis represents one of the most important developments in reading assessment and teaching in recent years. It has become popular in research, instruction and evaluation. It involves children reading a text aloud while the teacher (or the researcher) makes notes on a second copy of the text of the ways in which the child reads, paying attention to the deviations from the printed text. The most commonly used miscue categories are: refusals, substitutions, omissions, insertions, reversals and self-corrections. Children's oral reading errors are construed as providing 'a window on the reading process' (Goodman *et al.* 1987).

Miscue analysis has been plagued by several methodological weaknesses. For example, miscues in oral reading do not necessarily reflect what happens in silent reading and there are inconsistencies in miscue definitions in different studies. Nonetheless, it remains an effective way of studying the strategies employed by readers when trying to read aloud words in print. Miscue analysis has been extensively used in comparing children who differ in reading ability, but it has rarely been used as a tool for investigating the reading strategies of bilingual learners (Cline 1999b).

Research on genre theory, reading and bilingualism

There has been a large amount of research into children's reading, including how reading develops and the nature of differences between effective and ineffective readers. However, research on the effect of text genre on children's reading miscues and comprehension is relatively scarce.

A pilot study was designed by Kirk and Pearson (1996) to find out which text is the most effective in teaching children to read. Four genres (*story, reading scheme, poetry, informational text*) were presented to 20 children from Years 1 and 2. Not unsurprisingly, this investigation demonstrated that no one genre holds all qualities required for helping children learn to read. Although *story* proved to be the most immediately attractive genre, the other genres had also something to offer the developing reader. The authors suggest that teachers must capitalise on the various genres' qualities in order to develop particular aspects of children's reading.

A similar study was conducted in a primary school by Morfidi and Pumfrey (1998). It examined whether backward (older) and normal (younger) children (of the same reading level), reading *narrative, autobiographical* and *informational texts* will produce different miscue patterns in terms of their use of grapho-phonic, syntactic and semantic systems. This study revealed that normal readers, although at the same reading level, read more fluently and were less affected by text genre. On the other hand, backward readers had not yet reached automaticity. They appeared to be more constrained by the graphic similarity of words showing redundancy of context cues and they were more affected by the text genre than normal readers.

Within the context of genre theory, Stamboltzis (1997) compared the reading miscues and comprehension patterns of younger versus older pupils (of the same reading level) and monolingual versus bilingual pupils. Texts of three different genres (narrative, autobiographical and informational) were given to pupils to read aloud and retell. This study suggests that the narrative genre affected substantially the reading performances of younger and bilingual pupils. The autobiographical genre evoked the highest number of reading errors and raised comprehension problems for the bilingual readers. Finally, the informational genre proved to be the easiest one and it seemed to enhance reading for pleasure and understanding.

Cline and Cozens (1998) investigated the effect of text and content area on children's reading miscues and comprehension. The miscue analysis showed that the bilingual and monolingual groups drew upon grapho-phonic and syntactic cues to a similar extent in both narrative and informational text. Furthermore, it was found that after 4–6 years in English-medium schools, the bilingual children did have a broad grasp of the cultural scope of the texts but, in many cases, lacked the specific culturally related knowledge or vocabulary that would facilitate detailed recall and retelling (see Table 9.2).

Bringing together the findings of the above studies, it can be concluded that children read genres in different ways and no single genre has all the qualities required for helping children learning to read. Textual features such as text difficulty, layout and presentation may affect in different ways pupils' reading performance. There is also evidence indicating that miscue patterns vary as a function of the interaction among the readers' background knowledge, the nature of the written material and the conditions surrounding its presentation.

Emphasis should be given to Cline and Cozens' (1998) observation that some bilingual children, after struggling to read culturally unfamiliar material with a limited English vocabulary in the early stages, become habitual users of the surface cues in print and, in effect, learn not to read for meaning. Background knowledge is necessary if full comprehension of a text is to occur; however, this type of knowledge is culture specific. Readers in a second language must develop a large vocabulary, basic syntactic structures and higher level interpreting strategies if they are to cope with different types of text (Beech and Keys 1997).

Dyslexia: current definition, theories and practice

Dyslexia has been described as a combination of abilities and difficulties which affects the learning processes in one or more of reading, spelling, writing and/or numeracy. Accompanying weaknesses may be identified in areas of speed of information processing, short-term memory, sequencing, auditory and/or visual perception, spoken language and motor skills (British Dyslexia Association 2000).

A recent definition proposed by the British Psychological Society (1999: 11) reads: 'Dyslexia is evident when accurate and fluent word reading and/or spelling develops very incompletely or with great difficulty'. This definition focuses on literacy learning at the 'word level' and implies that the problem is severe and

Table 9.2 Profile of studies investigating the relationship between reading and text genre

Author	Sample	Genre	Findings
Kirk and Pearson (1996)	N = 20 Years 1 & 2	Story, Reading scheme, Poetry, Information text	Story: the most immediately attractive genre. Reading scheme: encourages reading accuracy. Poetry: encourages reading with intonation. Information text: engages the readers in its meaning.
Morfidi and Pumfrey (1998)	N = 20 Years 3 & 5 (normal versus backward readers matched for reading ages)	Narrative, Autobiographical, Informational	Normal readers read more fluently and were less affected by text genre than backward readers.
Stamboltzis (1997)	N = 81 Years 3 & 5, Monolingual versus bilingual (matched for reading ages)	Narrative, Autobiographical, Informational	The narrative genre affected the reading accuracy and comprehension of younger and bilingual pupils. The autobiographical genre affected the reading comprehension of bilingual pupils.
Cline and Cozens (1998)	N = 52 Key stage 2 Monolingual versus bilingual	Narrative, Informational	All children made more use of grapho-phonic cues. Bilingual children did less well than their monolingual peers in retelling in the informational text.

persistent despite appropriate learning opportunities. It must be remembered that word reading is but one facet of learning to become literate.

Dyslexia is increasingly described as a 'difference in learning' rather than a 'learning disability'. Neurological research shows that the brains of dyslexic people often differ in varied ways from those of non-dyslexics both in structure and in function; it is therefore hardly surprising that learning is acquired and expressed in a different way (Jameson 1999). Most of the research reported in the literature focused on the English language. Research on the weaknesses of dyslexics in other languages is now growing, and people of different countries are now collaborating with each other to see how dyslexia manifests itself in languages other than English.

Miles and Miles (1999) report the findings from a comparison among transparent languages (Italian, Spanish, German, Czech, Welsh), more opaque languages (French, Greek) and languages with morphemic scripts (Chinese, Japanese). The authors were interested to see whether the predominance of phonological weaknesses, a feature of dyslexic patterns of difficulties in English, would also be apparent in other languages. It was found that 'even in transparent languages there were problems if the beginnings of words changed, if the internal structure varied, or if other words, such as pronouns, were added on the end, thus blurring the clear perception of the word. In languages with a morphemic script there still proved to be a few phonological elements which might prove particularly important in the early stages of learning the written language' (Miles and Miles 1999: 56). As a conclusion, the area of phonology including a weakness in the processing of speech sounds provides an important clue for the understanding of dyslexia in all languages.

The question of sub-types and the Balance Model of reading

The division of dyslexia into sub-types has implications with respect to aetiology and remediation. One of the most influential attempt at sub-typing is that of Boder (1973) who analysed dyslexic children's reading and spelling errors and classified them as 'dysphonetic', 'dyseidetic' or 'mixed'. The first group was said to have a primary deficit in symbol–sound (grapheme–phoneme) integration, resulting in inability to learn phonetically. The second group was said to comprise children whose reading–spelling pattern reflects primary deficit in the ability to perceive letters and whole words as configurations or visual gestalts. The third group includes children who have mixed difficulties of the auditory and visual kind.

Bakker (1990) adopted a neuropsychological approach to reading and dyslexia. According to the Balance Model, during the initial stages of reading when perceptual analysis of the text predominates, the right hemisphere appears to mediate reading. As reading becomes more advanced and the analysis of semantic and syntactic features increases, the 'balance' of hemispheric control seems to shift from the right to the left hemisphere. Two sub-types of dyslexia can result if the pattern of normal development does not take place. The resultant sub-types are the P-type (perceptual) and the L-type (linguistic). Identification is based on analysis of the pupil's oral reading errors and reading style.

The P-type pupil relies heavily on perceptual features of the text which results in slow and fragmented reading. Words may be sounded out according to their grapho-phonic properties almost on a word-by-word basis. For this sub-type the greatest impact may be on rate of reading and comprehension. In contrast the L-type pupil neglects the initial involvement with the perceptual features of the text and begins to read inappropriately by using linguistic strategies. Reading here is fast, perceptually careless, and reveals many inaccurate responses to text. Sub-type identification is made partly on the basis of observed miscue patterns in reading behaviour and it is estimated that 60 per cent of subjects can reliably be classified according to this model (Robertson and Bakker 1999).

In conclusion, sub-type theories may have useful implications for the remediation of reading problems. They may inform the challenge of finding the optimum method of teaching pupils according to their individual pattern of strengths and weaknesses at a given stage of literacy development. The search for Aptitude X Instruction Interactions can be useful in informing teaching decisions for all pupils (Pumfrey 1996; Robertson 2000).

An overview of teaching strategies and materials for bilingual learners with dyslexia

Various methods and teaching strategies have been tried out to alleviate learning difficulties. Many of them seem to be promising but, given that dyslexia is not a unitary condition, no single method can be effective for all pupils with dyslexia.

The intervention programmes for dyslexic pupils derived from Bakker's Balance Model are based on the assumption that the normal developmental process of literacy acquisition (either in the first or in a subsequent language) begins with greater involvement of the right cerebral hemisphere and subsequently transfers to the left hemisphere. Bakker argues for the stimulation of the underused hemispheric functions. He has developed two interventions. The first is Hemispheric Alluding Stimulation (HAS) based on the presentation of perceptually modified text; the second is called Hemispheric Specific Stimulation (HSS). This involves flashing words to the right or left visual fields, dependent on the type of dyslexia (Bakker 1990).

Several researchers (Goldberg and Costa 1981; Paulesu *et al.* 1996) present experimental evidence on the dual hemisphere involvement in reading. When the task demands of learning a second language are considered, it becomes apparent that many of the challenges presented are similar to those in acquiring a first language. Bakker's neuropsychological model can be implemented for dyslexic pupils who have English as an additional language. Robertson (in press) summarises some practical implications for teaching. Bakker's work in developing intervention programmes provides one of the better examples of a theoretically based identification of potentially important Aptitude X Instruction Interactions (Pumfrey 1996).

Another promising type of intervention for dyslexic pupils is the multisensory teaching method originated by Samuel Orton in the mid-1920s. Multisensory teaching is simultaneously visual, auditory, and kinaesthetic to enhance memory and learning. Children with dyslexia often exhibit weaknesses in auditory and/or visual processing. They may have weak phonemic awareness which means they are unaware of the role sounds play in words. In general, they do not pick up the alphabetic code or system without explicit instruction. When taught by a multisensory approach, learners have the advantage of learning alphabetic patterns and words by utilising all three pathways (visual, auditory and kinaesthetic). Orton (1937) suggested that teaching the 'fundamentals of phonic association with letter forms both visually presented and reproduced in writing, until the correct associations were built up' would benefit learners of all ages. All multisensory teaching programmes contribute to the same purpose, namely that of remediating the phonological weaknesses of children by the systematic building up of associations between speech sounds and their representations in writing (Thomson 1990).

The Multisensory Structured Language (MSL) approach is recommended for teaching first language skills to dyslexic pupils. Grammar, syntax and phonology are taught through a programme which emphasises hearing, seeing, speaking and writing. Methods should explicitly teach correspondence between written aspects and the sounds they make. Ganschow *et al.* (1995) have provided details of a wide range of strategies which are helpful in teaching dyslexic pupils in general and may also be helpful for pupils who have English as an additional language. There are many other aids and books aimed at promoting multisensory teaching. For an excellent review, consult Miles and Miles (1999).

Another major source of information on how to teach bilingual pupils comes from genre-based approaches to literacy. Genre-based ideas have implications for the selection of reading materials and the adaptation of reading instruction for the various groups of pupils. The following considerations are suggested as worthy of the class teacher's attention:

- Genre theory suggests that pictures, captions and labels can enhance the decoding and comprehension of text for bilingual pupils who learn to read. Extensive use of visual material is recommended.
- Story reading can be a powerful language development tool for all pupils in general and bilingual pupils in particular. Listening to stories can help children develop vocabulary, concepts, oral fluency and sense of story.
- Listening activities and role-playing provide exposure to natural English-speaking situations.
- Any curriculum task presented to the bilingual child needs considering for the cognitive demands inherent in the task.
- Reading instruction for bilingual learners should foster natural, meaningful language opportunities. The Language Experience Approach (LEA) is perhaps the best alternative for teaching reading to bilingual learners.
- Children from similar language background might discuss in their native language what they have read in English.
- Genre theory suggests that teachers should carefully monitor the reading materials to ensure that they are predictable enough and of a suitable difficulty level.
- Children should be briefed in advance about texts with culture-specific vocabulary. New and culturally unfamiliar material should be linked directly and explicitly with the child's present knowledge and understanding.

- Miscue analysis can identify patterns of strengths and weaknesses of bilingual pupils in general and of dyslexic bilingual pupils in particular.
- Clearly structured teaching makes learning much more comprehensible to the dyslexic bilingual pupil.

Finally, we present two examples of specific teaching methods for bilingual pupils with learning difficulties in the UK. The first one is a valuable resource pack for teachers in multicultural classrooms by Cline and Frederickson (1991), *Bilingual pupils and the National Curriculum: Overcoming difficulties in teaching and learning*. This set of learning materials aims to help teachers and educational psychologists improve their knowledge and understanding in relation to work with bilingual children in general and with those considered to have learning difficulties in particular.

The materials come in a 'user-friendly' ring folder. They comprise an introductory chapter, plus a 'menu' of six substantial units on:

- language and community
- language development
- cognitive development and learning difficulties
- the National Curriculum in multilingual schools
- multi-professional assessment of special educational needs and
- additional resources.

The materials focus on an important series of issues. The structure is clear and the contents coherently presented. Suggestions are made for group and individual activities plus group exercises (Pumfrey 1994).

Another method which offers specific help for bilingual pupils with learning difficulties is *Peer tutoring – Integrating 'bilingual' pupils into the mainstream classroom* (Curtis 1990). This method suggests structured peer-tutoring techniques to support children with limited proficiency in English. It has been argued that the collaborative work of children in pairs has positive outcome if teachers are able to organise and monitor this activity carefully. Structured pair work is advocated for children of differing ability in which a fluent English-speaking child helps a less fluent English-speaking child in a cooperative learning environment.

These are only two examples of methods that offer specific help for bilingual pupils in the UK. As more families move around Europe and beyond, more children with learning difficulties are in need of a supportive education. Their parents cannot always afford private tuition, and language barriers can make integration into local schools difficult. Fortunately, an increasing amount of information concerning second language learning, multilingualism and dyslexia has started to appear on the internet.

Access to Information on Multicultural Education Resources (AIMER) and European Children In Crisis (ECIC)

Access to Information on Multicultural Education Resources (otherwise known as AIMER, University of Reading, UK) is a database of great importance to those concerned with cultural diversity and the curriculum. It is a national database which offers students, teachers and advisers information on multicultural anti-racist teaching materials. It includes about 3,000 resources on all areas of the National Curriculum (including English, mathematics, history, geography, technology, life sciences, music, arts etc.), as well as English-language support materials and materials in community languages.

European Children in Crisis (ECIC, Brussels, Belgium) is a non-profit organisation which intends to develop, promote or undertake concrete actions in favour of personal and scholastic development of children with learning difficulties whose families move around Europe. ECIC acts on behalf of these children by organising training sessions to bring parents and teachers together with experts, providing information and raising awareness of the issues involved for individual children in crisis. ECIC has produced a multimedia training pack on the effect of dyslexia across cultures. A 30-minute video explores the experience of learners with dyslexia having to cope with new languages and new cultures The video is accompanied by a guide which informs learners, parents, teachers and schools where to go for help on assessment, training and resources.

Conclusion

At present, the fields of genre theory, multilingualism and dyslexia are fruitful and promising areas for research. A major challenge in development work on teaching strategies for bilingual children will be to evaluate the impact on their progress of varying the balance between addressing their needs as second language learners and addressing the specific needs that relate to dyslexia. One of the challenges for teachers of bilingual children with dyslexia is to find effective strategies for supporting families to play an active role in the children's progress towards literacy (Cline 1999b). We are confident that the new millennium will see dyslexia and multilingualism being recognised as professional challenges that can, in co-operation with parents and carers, be increasingly successfully understood and alleviated.

Chapter 10

Shared Writing in the Support of Dyslexic Children from Different Cultural Backgrounds

Awena Carter

This chapter:

- explores the concept of situated literacy
- examines the divide which some dyslexic children find between the cultures of home and school
- highlights aspects of purposeful writing
- describes the benefits of shared writing.

Introduction

Situated literacy

Literacy is acquired in cultural and social settings, of which school is only one. This means that literacy is to do with far more than texts: it is embedded in the cultural attitudes of the settings in which it is both acquired and used, as Taylor's (1983) seminal work *Family Literacy* makes clear. These cultural attitudes will be responsible for the views of a family or community about issues such as education, behaviour, leisure, power, gender – which in turn determine the nature and uses of literacies by that family in the community.

Dyslexic children and the literacy of home

It is often thought that dyslexic children tend to avoid all literacy events: their parents might recount a reluctance on the child's part to open a book or to write a greeting in a birthday card, for example. But as Barton (1994: 4) points out 'literacy impinges on people in their daily lives, whether or not they regularly read books or do much writing'. As an illustration of this he describes a person being woken in the morning by the news on a radio alarm, 'a written text which is being spoken' (1994: 3) who then goes on to read the newspaper or the mail. It is easy to think of the chaos of many breakfast times where different literacy events are part of the routine – reading or writing school notes, shopping lists, reminders, a last-minute greetings card, checking the day's engagements in a diary or calendar. Whether or not the dyslexic child takes part in the often unremarkable literacy events of home, their particular nature and mix will determine his/her understanding of the uses of literacy.

Literacy practices embedded in a family's culture are transmitted to the child through the process of socialisation. Weinreich (1978: 20f) observes in this respect that '(s)ocialisation is the means by which culture ... is transmitted' to the child by the adults in his family and community and that, as a result of this socialisation, '(children) actively seek to structure the world, to make sense and order of the environment'. Or, as Kress (1997: 59) points out, 'making sense of the world happens in a world already laden with sense' so that even children from the same ethnic background come to school from a variety of different cultural contexts.

School is not the only literacy domain

Children bring their own understanding of the uses of literacy to school where they have to become proficient in school-based literacy. Some children start school with an understanding of the uses of literacy which sits well with school-based literacy. Heath (1983: 262) shows the ways in which this cultural capital is likely to ensure the child's success in school and later in work. Other children may find that the literacy practices of home will be ignored and discounted in the interests of school-based literacy. If these children are dyslexic this cultural divide is likely to compound their difficulties: they are being expected to become proficient in a literacy which may make little sense to them and their resulting frustrations are likely to lead to feelings of inadequacy. In addition most school-based literacy tasks are in the form of exercises rather than what may be termed the 'purposeful' literacy practices of the world outside school.

Guided writing

Guided writing, which is likely to be encountered by British schoolchildren in the literacy hour, can serve as an illustration of the nature and aim of school-based literacy. In this method the teacher may write a sample sentence for a class or group of children. She uses this to talk about one of the secretarial aspects of writing like spelling, punctuation or formatting and the children are then expected to generalise what they have been shown into their own writing exercises. The teacher can then use these exercises to assess progress and to plan interventions. In this model the power is firmly with the teacher and the subtext is, 'Do it like this and you will be able to write as well as I'. While it serves the majority of children well, this sort of demonstration by itself is of little use to the dyslexic child who is likely to become confused and to find that his/her feelings of inadequacy are confirmed.

How people write

Out-of-school writing (or 'purposeful writing') tends to be very different: it involves choices and decisions which are constrained by the purpose as well as by the secretarial aspects of what is to be written. The final version may be the result of more than one draft and there is often some collaboration from family members or colleagues – in contrast to in-school writing tasks which are usually exercises set to assess individual work.

Decisions and choices in purposeful writing

An examination of some of the likely processes involved in writing a letter of complaint about a late train and missed connections will serve to exemplify the ways in which people write.

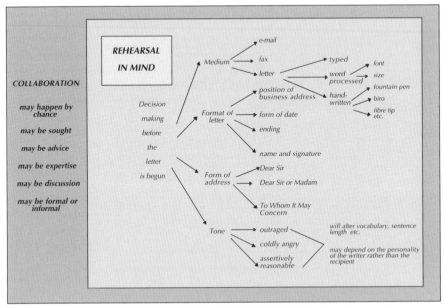

Figure 10.1a Some processes involved in planning a letter of complaint

Figure 10.1a illustrates some of the choices which might be made both before and during the actual writing of the letter and shows the complexity of decision making involved in purposeful writing. 'Mental rehearsal', for example, leads to decisions about both the secretarial and compositional aspects of the letter before it is even begun, each decision leading to other possible choices, only some of which are listed in the diagram. Not all of these choices may be made in the writing task of the moment: some previous choices and experience will be invisibly part of this writing event in the same way as corrections and rephrasing are invisibly part of a finished word-processed document.

There are more choices to be made as a result of beginning to write and the final copy may be typed or written by someone else, illustrating the relatively greater importance of the compositional stage of the writing process (see Figure 10.1b).

Dyslexic children's difficulties with decision making

Dyslexic children are often too preoccupied with the secretarial aspects of writing to have any spare capacity for making choices about form or content – their decisions tend to be concerned with orthography rather than with style. The shared writing approach which will be described is one way of helping dyslexic children to be aware that there are choices which they can make and supports them in decision making.

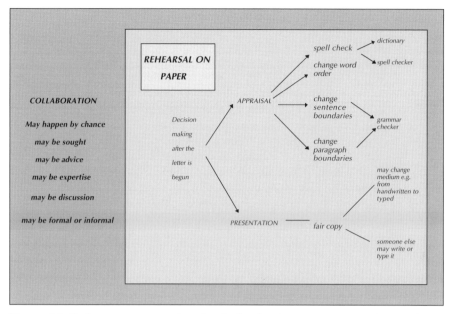

Figure 10.1b Some processes involved after beginning to write a letter of complaint

Shared writing

Supporting dyslexic children's writing involves scribing, accepting approximate spellings and little or no punctuation. This not only provides diagnostic material for intervention but also replicates the ways in which 'successful' writers develop written literacy. Shared writing becomes purposeful writing when authentic settings are used for real purposes: stories are 'published' to be read by other children; letters are sent to other children or to adults in the expectation of a reply; magazines are written and circulated. And allowing the child to situate this sort of writing in his own cultural context uses the strength of his own model of literacy.

The case for collaboration

Sharing and supporting writing in this way makes it possible for the child to achieve more than he/she could by themselves and this is often a criticism directed towards this sort of approach by those who believe that the only test of a child's ability is in independent work. Bruner (1986: 73), however, in his exploration of the work of Vygotsky, explains Vygotsky's Zone of Proximal Development (or zoped) as 'an account of how the more competent assist the young and the less competent to reach…higher ground'. That its aim is progression is made clear by Vygotsky (quoted by Bruner 1986: 73) 'the nature of the zone of proximal development enables us to propound a new formula, namely that the only "good learning" is that which is in advance of development'. Children, operating 'in advance of development' are enabled to develop, as may be seen from evidence of progression in their written work.

Sharing writing tasks with children is a way of replicating the confirmatory collaboration with family, friends or colleagues which is such an important feature of purposeful writing and it is worth examining how it finds expression in this zoped. The teacher is, in Bruner's phrase 'more competent' and the dyslexic pupil 'less competent' in written literacy. The teacher in supporting the pupil provides the scaffolding which enables the child to operate at a higher level than he/she would otherwise find possible. But this does not necessitate a power stance on the part of the teacher so appearing to be imparting knowledge and understanding to an inferior: this would only tend to confirm a dyslexic child in his/her low idea of themselves. On the contrary, the approach which underpins this method involves treating children as though they are literate and therefore equal. They are expected to think about what they are going to write, to make choices and decisions, to take control of the work they are going to produce. The teacher is sometimes an amanuensis, sometimes suggests a possible way forward, sometimes demonstrates correct practice – but she always does this in a manner which suggests that the pupil is equal in effort and commitment if not yet in achievement.

How power is shared in shared writing

Children usually have to learn how to respond to this approach because it tends to overturn their perceptions of where the power should lie in school. Power usually resides in teachers because of their superior knowledge and therefore dyslexic children are often very resistant to efforts to enable them to take and exercise power over their own work. But although this collaboration presupposes a sharing of power, in practice the teacher retains power over the choice of interventions and the pupil retains power over the choice of subject matter.

Cultural content in children's writing

This approach to extending written literacy depends on the non-critical acceptance of the subject matter which the child chooses to write and read about. In this sense the teacher must accept the child's culture and seek to celebrate it, building on what the child brings with him/her however this may confront the teacher's own chosen ways of looking at the world. This does not, however, embrace cultural attitudes which may inhibit learning.

How progression results from using children's own cultural contexts

In this chapter I have discussed a shared writing approach which may be used with children from different cultures. By supporting their writing, by scribing where necessary and encouraging mental and oral rehearsal, as well as drafting and redrafting, it is possible to enable them to replicate successful literacy practices. This is particularly the case in a collaborative environment where children are empowered to take responsibility for their own work. The approach does not depend for its success on a formal knowledge of the rules of English spelling and grammar but on enabling children to operate at a level in advance of their development. When supported in this way they can attain a higher level of functioning and of thought which enables them to work more independently.

Chapter 11

Children's Spelling Errors in Welsh and English Writing

Nest Tudor Efans and Ann Cooke

This chapter:

- will present a brief overview of some characteristics of written Welsh, pointing out those most likely to cause difficulty
- examines mistakes that Welsh children make when writing in Welsh
- shows spelling and linguistic differences between English and Welsh which are likely to be troublesome for all learners and for dyslexic learners in particular
- offers some suggestions about how this contributes to our understanding about children's learning in a bilingual situation and about the identification of dyslexia and its associated learning difficulties.

Introduction

The linguistic pattern in Wales is one of considerable regional diversity. In some areas little Welsh is spoken as the mother tongue and children begin to learn Welsh mostly as a completely new language. In other areas, particularly in North and West Wales, there is a high proportion of first language Welsh speakers and here Welsh is often the language of the whole school environment. By National Assembly (and formerly Welsh Office) policy, Welsh is a core subject in the National Curriculum through all key stages. (That is, it is an obligatory subject right through the school years from reception to Year 11.) It can be taken as a first or second language. A number of schools throughout Wales are designated as Welsh language schools – Ysgolion Cymraeg; in these schools, Welsh is the medium of the whole curriculum.

Within this broad context, local authority policy on language education varies from one part of Wales to another. In North West and West Wales the objective is for all children to become bilingual orally, and for basic literacy to be established in Welsh and English by the time children are 11. In these areas Welsh is the language of the classroom in the first years and children begin reading and writing in Welsh. English is introduced formally at Year 2 or 3. Children therefore start learning Welsh as a second language at school entry or in nursery school (Ysgol Feithrin). Monoglot English children coming into these areas after starting school elsewhere spend a term in a language unit learning Welsh. Most young children from non-Welsh-speaking homes – dyslexic children among them – learn to speak the language without undue difficulty when it is introduced as part of the medium of communication in school.

Welsh has a very regular writing system. This has led to an assumption that children taught in Welsh would be less likely to experience dyslexia-type difficulties, and it has tended to hinder the early identification of dyslexia, especially among first-language Welsh children. It is not unusual for children who make a good start to encounter difficulties when reading and writing are introduced in English. When this happens, it has sometimes been assumed that the difficulties have been caused by the linguistic situation and that, with time, they will disappear.

Written Welsh and Welsh grammar

Welsh has a highly consistent writing system with few exceptions to one-to-one sound-to-spelling regularity. Irregular spellings are rare.

Alphabet

The Welsh alphabet has 28 letters including 8 consonant digraphs, 7 vowels (a, e, i, o, u, w, y: i and w can be vowels or consonants). j is used in borrowed English words and si is used as an additional consonant digraph. There are only two exceptions to regularity: y, which has two sounds (obscure and clear) and ng, which in a very few words stands for a sound different from the normal.

Spelling

The length of vowels is not always shown in writing. Accents such as ^ or ¨ may be used to reflect length distinction of vowels or to denote stress. Short vowels may also be marked by doubling the n or r following the vowel. There are five irregular dipthongs, each one involving the use of either y or e: ae, oe, wy, yw, ey. All vowel combinations in Welsh are pronounced as distinct sounds.

The letter y, when used in combination with other vowels in dipthongs, has five variations of sound (llwy, gwyn, byw, llyw, gwŷdd). Consonant digraphs and clusters can cause difficulty, especially the voiced/unvoiced pairs:

dd – th   f – ff

r – rh   ch – ll

(While the last pair are not phonetically identical they cause similar difficulties.) These sounds can be persistently difficult for dyslexic children.

However, the relative simplicity of the Welsh spelling system means that once initial mastery of the alphabet has been achieved, words are intelligible. The only possible alternative symbol always represents the required sound.

Grammar

On the other hand, Welsh grammar is complex. Difficulties can arise because spoken Welsh is less formal than the written language, and affect first-language Welsh speakers as well as learners.

Mutations

Welsh – like other Celtic languages – uses mutations, which means that initial consonants are changed according to various rules of grammar and spelling when words are formed into sentences. Though some mutations occur almost as natural products of adjacent sounds, others are complex, particularly the nasal mutations.

There are three kinds of initial mutations and nine consonants which are mutable. They are an essential feature of Welsh syntax. For example, the case of a noun may be denoted by mutation or non-mutation.

Clywodd ci – A dog heard (using radical form)

Clywodd gi – He heard a dog (soft mutation)

Mutations can be difficult to hear and to pronounce even for Welsh children learning their mother tongue – especially those who are dyslexic.

The effect of mutations is to produce a change of word identity (sometimes also of meaning) with consequent difficulties of recognition and comprehension. In reading, dyslexic children's lack of language awareness prevents them making the connections between the original word, which they might know, and the modified version. Some examples can be seen in Figure 11.1.

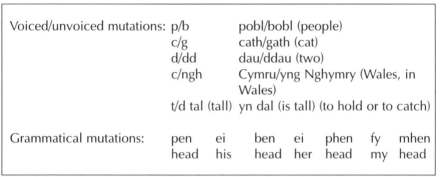

Figure 11.1 Mutations in Welsh grammar

Verbs

Verb forms are conjugated. Problems seem to come from the diversity of forms used in formal and informal writing and from differences between spoken and literary Welsh. Some verbs have diverse ways of forming tenses. For instance 'we ran' has 18 acceptable forms in Welsh, even without examples of spoken Welsh which use auxiliary verbs.

Words for the different persons of a single verb can be dissimilar, for instance,

canu (to sing)   canaf   canwn

ceni   cenwch

can   canant

Where mutations are also found there can be added difficulties, for instance:

cerdded a cherddais i gerdded (to walk)

Nouns

All nouns have gender. Plurals of nouns are formed in seven different ways. These include internal vowel changes, adding various plural endings, and a combination of both. Other plural forms are shorter than the singular, for instance:

gwraig gwragedd (wife/wives)

plentyn plant (child/children)

aderyn adar (bird/birds)

Adjectives
Some also have gender mutations for instance:

cap gwyn/cot wen (white cap/white coat)

Prepositions are conjugated.

Errors in written Welsh

Both Welsh dyslexic individuals writing in their first language, and learners of Welsh as a second language, make relatively few spelling mistakes because of the regular spelling system of the language. They are to be seen particularly in the wrong choice of vowel and failure to observe correct mutations. Mistakes also occur because children who have particularly severe difficulties lack the necessary phonemic skills for correct spelling, but most do not arise from the spelling itself. 'Bizarre' spelling mistakes are rare in Welsh.

Grammatical mistakes might be expected to occur more often and examination of children's written work in Welsh shows that this is indeed the case. These include mistakes which would be unlikely to occur in spoken language, for instance, failure to make agreements and use of the wrong gender of an adjective. They can be found in the writing of dyslexic adults as well as that of Welsh children and learners (see Figure 11.2).

	Errors: spelling	grammar	word total
E aged 10 yrs	4	14	110
M adult (graduate)	5	14	125

Figure 11.2 Number of spelling and grammatical mistakes in writing by two Welsh first-language speakers

The number of spelling errors made by E should be compared with the same child's writing in his second language, shown in Example 3 (see page 91).

Introduction of written English

When English is introduced the learner is confronted by a different writing system. Difficulties now arise from phonology and spelling. The greatest percentage of errors in English spellings have been shown to occur in vowel spellings (Kibel and Miles 1994) not merely because of the irregularities but as a result of the large number of alternative spellings for each vowel. For the Welsh/English bilingual learner there is an additional complication: while some spelling-to-sound correspondences are identical in both languages (b, d, h, l, m, n, r, s, t) many are different. Some examples of these differences are shown in Figure 11.3.

It can be seen that English spelling is much more complex than Welsh. English has many more alternative spellings and such irregularities as the multiple sound–spelling correspondences of 'ough' are absent from Welsh. This is due, of course, to the way that the two languages have developed along very different linguistic routes. Other instances where letters and sounds differ between English and Welsh are shown in Figures 11.4 and 11.5.

Welsh spelling	Nearest English spellings
* i, y	ee, ea, e-e, ei etc.
ai, ae, au	i-e, y, igh etc.
ei	a-e, ai, ay etc.
aw	ou, ow
or	or, au, aw
oe	oi, oy
y	i,
y	u
w	oo, u-e, ew

* In some part of Wales, children refer to this letter as 'e dot' to distinguish it from y and u, the alternative spellings for this vowel.

Figure 11.3 Different vowel values of Welsh and English

Welsh vowel sounds not found in English:

    u as in cul (narrow) sounds more like the /u/ of French
    ei as in eistedd
    e as in mel (honey) sounds more like a lengthened short vowel e

Examples of English vowel sounds not found in Welsh

    o-e as in broke
    aw as in paw
    a-e as in make

Figure 11. 4 Examples of different vowel sounds in Welsh and English

So it is understandable that children who rely on strategies of phonological segmentation and letter by letter word-building that have worked in Welsh run into difficulties, even with regular spellings, when they begin to read and, particularly, to write in English. The samples of work that follow show typical errors and error patterns made by children who have all begun their reading and writing work in Welsh, and have started learning to write in English in Year 3.

Consonant letters and spellings

k, q, x, z are not found in Welsh.
Welsh has no 'soft c' or 'soft g' spelling.
Silent letters do not occur in Welsh except where consonants are doubled.

Some consonant digraphs are found in Welsh and English but have
different sounds, while others are specific to Welsh:

Welsh sound English sound

ch	chwarae (guttural) chair – different sounds
dd	ddau (as in them) d (add)
ll	llyn Specific to Welsh l (full)
ff (unvoiced)	ffrind f (fluff)
f (voiced)	fy v (van)
rh	rhaw Specific to Welsh. r (rheumatic) Irregular spelling

Figure 11.5 Differences between Welsh and English consonant letters and
consonant digraphs

Example 1 K, Boy, 11 years (First language English)

Dyslexic. Statement of Special Educational Needs (SSEN)

> The name of my school is could Ysgol D. The stuf I like in scool is Maths. Miss
> W takes ys I bont like ythyr Subjecs because I bont like lsining, riding and raiting.
> In the holeday I playd my playsteishon.

Comments

could	This may be a confusion with recently learnt could, or an attempted phonic spelling.
because	Successful writing of a new word.
ys, ythyr	y is the Welsh spelling for the English vowel u.

playsteishon ⎫
riding (reading) ⎬ All the incorrect vowels would give the
raiting (writing) ⎭ correct sound in Welsh.
bont   A (typical) b/d confusion.

Example 2 A, Girl, 11 years (First language English) Statement of Special Educational Needs (SSEN)

Errors made in a piece of writing about her family.

> hi (he) i would give the correct sound in Welsh.
> (There might also be a confusion of meaning here, as hi means 'she'.)
> tyes serives (Tyre Service) ⎫
> Ifro (name Ifor) ⎬ Confusion of letter order.
> Brid (bird) ⎭

celdyn ygr than my (children younger than me). The confusion of Welsh and English spellings added to phonological difficulties results in spelling errors that border on the bizarre.

Example 3 E, Boy, 9 years (First language Welsh)

Teenis

Ior havt o sorve in first short in evrie game this worek wil help **uou** cut ior tous sgrach ior back and hit the bool and **y**try in the box cros cort. **Iou** goto to do ffo hand **io** gto go **you** make surcl with yo right arm. Bacand **yo** goto mak the same thing but with the left hand foli **uo** must hit a deep bol then punch and ame wer **iu** ned the bool to land. smas **io** must do te same thing surf hut in the net this time

Translation
You have to serve in (the) first shot in every game. This work will help you: touch your toes, scratch your back and hit the ball. And you try (to hit the ball) in the box cross-court. You've got to do forehand. You've got to make a circle with your right arm. Backhand, you've got to make the same thing but with the left hand. Volley: you must hit a deep ball, then punch and aim where you need the ball to land. Smash: you must do the same thing. Serve: hit in the net this time.

Comments
All the attempted spellings of 'you' are printed **in bold**. It is correct once, and there are nine incorrect versions, most of which show E trying out different combinations of Welsh and English vowel spellings (ior, uou, y, iuo, io, you, yo, uo, iu, io).

ior (your)	He has been more successful here.
teenis (tennis)	The wrong letter is doubled.
foli (volley)	This would be correct in Welsh spelling.
ffo (forehand)	Shortened word but ff would be correct in Welsh.
sgrach (scratch)	Voiced/unvoiced consonant error.
surcl (circle)	Soft c error and the Welsh spelling of /ur/.

He has used the Welsh phonic system almost all through, though there are some surprising correct words: first, right, game, same, punch.

English–Welsh confusions

There is some evidence that confusions in the reverse direction take place, English spellings being used in Welsh, for example use of 'magic -e'. In general, however, there seems to be less confusion over new conventions where the Welsh/English distinction is clear, for example magic -e, ch and sh sounds.

Conclusions

Is it possible to draw any conclusions from these examples about language learning in the bilingual situation, and about teaching and assessment of dyslexic children learning Welsh and English?

Phonology

The regularity of Welsh spelling allows children to utilise an alphabetic-phonic strategy for reading and spelling from the outset. Phonic strategies are emphasised for beginning readers; with such a regular language these are very reliable. But Welsh children can get stuck on phonic sounding-out, and can have difficulty in establishing the habit of reading whole words.

Teachers in infant classrooms display words around the room which encourages whole-word reading:

> drws – door
> ffenestr – window
> bwrdd – table
> llyfrau – books

There is no tension between visual and phonic factors here so the practice is doubly helpful. Consistent mapping of sound to symbol encourages the development of phonological skills as the child interacts with reading.

However, for those cases where severe dyslexic difficulties are observed in Welsh first-language speakers, an approach which brings explicit phonic structure to the process of learning Welsh has been found to be essential: teaching of the less familiar spelling patterns in groups, a progressive introduction of more difficult sound-spellings, and teaching and practice of alternative spellings.

Practice with the segmentation of words into onset and rime does not seem so significant for Welsh-speaking children, and the structure of the language makes these strategies less appropriate. Development of a visual strategy for word and spelling learning is necessary for severely dyslexic children from the outset. When the learner starts English this strategy becomes even more essential and needs to be taught.

Language structure

It can be seen that the difficulties for dyslexic children learning to write Welsh as a first as well as a second language arise more from the grammatical structure of the language than from difficulties of a phonological kind. When words mutate they may become difficult to recognise and this may affect comprehension when children are reading. Comprehension may be impaired when this leads to difficulties with word recognition. The pattern of mutations may not be remembered, which will affect both spelling and grammar. In spelling, phonological difficulties occur particularly over choices between voiced and unvoiced consonants. For instance, in the example shown in 'Tennis' above, sc is represented as sg, which is an acceptable spelling in Welsh.

'Simplest spelling' strategy

It might be expected that children would generalise their spelling by resorting to the simplest form they know when they meet a difficulty. It could also happen that children whose mastery of Welsh spelling is developing, generalise this to their more recently started English writing, as in fwtbol. English sounds which have no

Welsh equivalent (for instance /ch/ as in chat) may be easier to remember, and words whose spelling is unusual may be recalled as wholes (water, could, because) but these may also reflect hard work by a teacher!

Practical applications

Observations from this study, and from the experience of teachers of dyslexic children, suggest that looking for early difficulties with reading and writing is not a reliable way to identify dyslexia in children learning in Welsh. This is particularly true of those whose first language is Welsh. In assessment of children for dyslexia, tests of spelling will not be very informative about difficulties. Grammatical errors and phonological difficulties – shown by mutation errors – are more likely to reveal difficulties, and these can only be seen in free writing. Explicit teaching of the phonic system of written Welsh and of Welsh phonology may help children to separate Welsh and English spelling when English is introduced.

Chapter 12

Multilingualism and Literacy in Sweden – Multiple Sources of Reading Difficulty

Louise Miller Guron

This chapter includes:

- comparative literacy data for monolingual and multilingual Swedish speakers
- an overview of Swedish literary culture
- an examination of influences on second language reading proficiency
- a discussion of specific difficulties in decoding and interpreting second language text.

Introduction

Sweden's location on the northern periphery of Europe and its most popular exports in music and industry easily give the impression of a relatively isolated, homogenous, monolingual nation enjoying high standards of living and universal literacy. Indeed, cultural and linguistic homogeneity is strong among those Swedes whose families have been resident for many generations. However, for the Swedish minority groups, many of whom arrived as refugees in the last 25 years, linguistic and cultural backgrounds are diverse and levels of Swedish literacy are far lower than those of the indigenous population.

When referring to multilingual speakers learning to read Swedish it is important to specify to whom we are referring. The term non-native speaker is useful as a language-neutral term when examining the global issue of majority language reading proficiency among immigrant groups of various countries, or when comparing international literacy data. However, the rather inappropriately called second-generation immigrants, whose first language is other than the majority language, are of course by definition native citizens though they would nonetheless be classed as non-native speakers of the language in question. This terminology thus threatens the important distinction between nationality or citizenship and first language and should only be used in general international comparisons. When referring specifically to those for whom Swedish is an additional language the term SAL speakers will be used, and those for whom Swedish is the first language will be referred to as S1 speakers.

In Sweden, the National Agency for Education maintains a database of children who have at least one parent whose first language is other than Swedish and who use this language on a daily basis with the child. By this definition, the overall national percentage of SAL speakers in Swedish schools has remained fairly stable for the past seven years, with numbers rising steadily in larger towns. However, there is considerable variation in the percentage of SAL speakers in different parts of the country. For example, in 1999 the proportion of SAL pupils was 38 per cent in Malmo in the south, while the proportion in the smaller southern towns was around 13–17 per cent and towns in the northern half of Sweden had a proportion of just 2–9 per cent.

Swedish literacy data in an international context

The various levels of literacy among adult SAL speakers are well reflected in a recent report from the Swedish branch of the International Adult Literacy Survey (IALS) (Myrberg *et al.* 2000). By 1999, IALS reports were available from 12 participating countries (Australia, Belgium, Canada, Germany, Holland, Ireland, New Zealand, Poland, Sweden, Switzerland, UK and US) allowing for cross-national comparisons of non-native literacy status and of discrepancies between native and non-native literacy levels in various countries.

The first overall international IALS report identified four groups that did not reach higher than literacy levels 1 or 2. These were: first-generation immigrants (born outside the country and having lived in-country for at least one year), people who had not concluded their compulsory school studies, people diagnosed as dyslexic and the elderly. The discrepancy in literacy scores between immigrant participants and native speakers was greatest in German-speaking Switzerland, where almost 60 per cent of immigrants achieved combined scores at level 1 compared with less than 10 per cent of native Swiss residents. In Sweden the proportion of people who only achieved level 2 literacy scores or lower was twice as great among SAL speakers as it was among S1 speakers. The majority of SAL speakers tested in Sweden did not reach level 3, while 75 per cent of S1 speakers achieved level 3 or higher.

Levels of literacy among SAL speakers differ considerably according to the age of migration to Sweden. Those who immigrated to Sweden as children read and wrote at the same level as S1 speakers. However, one in five of those SAL speakers aged 16–20 who arrived during their teenage years read at the lowest level on the IALS scale, while only one in a hundred S1 speakers of the same age group read at this level. Nonetheless, participation in SAL classes per se does not seem to have the positive influence on Swedish reading that one might expect. While four out of five of those studying SAL expressed satisfaction with their courses, four out of ten achieved only level 1 literacy. Ironically, those SAL speakers who achieved the lowest IALS test scores were those who had most frequently attended SAL classes (Myrberg *et al.* 2000).

However, there is no reason to suggest that the presence of a large number of multilingual speakers in the population should necessarily bring down the national average score on literacy tests. The Swedish overall adult literacy scores in the IALS survey are the highest of the 12 participating countries and in Canada there was a higher number of immigrant participants performing at literacy levels 4 and 5 than native speakers. Nonetheless, the discrepancy in scores between native and non-native speakers in Sweden was second highest of all participating countries, with the greatest discrepancy being in New Zealand (Elley 1992). The discrepancy in Norway was almost as high as in Sweden, while in contrast, non-native language speakers in Cyprus, Venezuela, Spain and Indonesia were found to read almost as well as native speakers of those countries. An explanation offered for the high discrepancy in New Zealand is that the multilingual speakers were mostly Pacific Island students who do not have strong literacy traditions. Multilingual speakers in Sweden and Norway, however, come from a much broader spectrum of cultures, so the discrepancy in reading scores must be considered with reference to a number of other background factors.

There is some debate as to whether it may be detrimental for children to start their reading instruction in a language other than their mother tongue. There is a tradition in Sweden which holds that SAL children should first establish elementary reading skills in their home language before attempting to read Swedish. A popular response to the discrepancy in literacy levels between SAL and S1 speakers then, is that improvements should be made in Swedish instruction for SAL speakers and that more time should be spent in SAL lessons. However, results from Singapore (Moore 1982) demonstrate that early explicit reading instruction in the majority language can result in high literacy scores at age nine, regardless of whether children have received first language reading instruction. A study of Berber-speaking children in Morocco who learn to read in Arabic has also shown that it is quite possible to learn to read in a language other than the mother tongue (Wagner *et al.* 1989).

It may be argued that learning to read in, say, Swahili or Arabic before embarking on explicit instruction in reading Swedish requires unnecessary segregation in school and subjects the SAL child to an undesirable delay in establishing a good foundation in literacy in the majority language, which could have negative consequences for subsequent Swedish reading development. The most important factors likely to improve literacy among SAL speakers (Myrberg *et al.* 2000), lie beyond the classroom, above all in the number of daily contacts with Swedish texts and in the level of integration with majority language literary culture.

Swedish literary culture

The written word and the ability to read are very highly valued in Sweden; this has roots in culture and history as well as the Swedish climate and demography. In 1684 a royal decree was announced requiring that all inhabitants of Sweden and Finland (then part of the Swedish kingdom) should be able to read the holy scriptures independently. The head of each household was held responsible for ensuring that all members of the household learnt to read. Failure to read was punished by public disgrace and loss of civil rights; illiterates were not permitted to marry or provide witness in court. Needless to say this campaign was very successful! By 1720 each household possessed an average of two or three books and when the first compulsory school system was established in 1842 the vast majority of the population was able to pass the annual church examination conducted by the parish vicar, which included both oral reading and comprehension of religious texts (Lundberg 1999a).

Sweden's sparse population and cold climate have also contributed to a culture which, in the absence of regular face-to-face contact values the written word very highly. Social historical development since the 1700s led to the dispersion of farms away from villages over large tracts of land where human communication depended to a large extent on written texts. The current value placed on the written word in Sweden was reflected in the IEA study, where panels of officials from nine participating countries were asked to estimate the demands placed on reading skills for various sub-groups of the adult population. The Swedish and Finnish panels rated their countries' demands on literacy as the highest.

Influences on L2 reading proficiency

When approaching any text, in either the first or a subsequent language, there are a number of mental facilities or central cognitive prerequisites that are necessary if we are to gain maximum benefit from the reading experience. One might argue that all such facilities are to some extent influenced by the cultural and linguistic experience from which they have developed, including visual-motor acuity and aural sensitivities. However, the research to date converges on two key functions that most directly predict reading skill and which are influenced most critically by L1 background and familiarity with L2; these are, the grapheme–phoneme translation skills and text-processing skills that enable the reader to decode and interpret the words on the page.

Figure 12.1 presents a simplistic model outlining the influence of L1 background and L2 familiarity on the central prerequisites for reading, which in turn predict L2 reading proficiency. Both L1 culture and the L1 writing system are likely to influence methods of word reading and text processing in L2. For a non-native speaker, mental representations of textual references to, say, family occasions may well result in inferences and plot predictions much at odds with those of the text. A child whose only L1 reading experience is based on reading the Koran is unlikely to have developed the text-processing skills taken for granted in western comprehension exercises, which include literary criticism, questions of authorial intention, multiple choice and so on.

The influence of L1 background on the approach to L2 text is compromised or counterbalanced by the level of familiarity with L2 culture and daily requirements to work with L2 texts. Explicit instruction in L2 language skills and L2 reading is clearly of critical importance, but, ironically, increased time spent in classrooms with other non-native speakers inevitably reduces the contact with native speakers that is probably equally important to the development of fluent reading skills. Textbook instruction may also reduce the frequency with which non-native speakers meet 'real life' literary demands in L2, which are critical for building the confidence needed to combat unfamiliar text.

Before the second language reader can bring themselves to open the second language book or carry out the comprehension exercise they must be motivated to reap the benefits that are to be had from the text. One can say that motivation should ideally consist of three aspects. The first aspect is instrumental or centred on the text; the reader should be goal oriented and interested to absorb what the text can reveal. Secondly, motivation should be integrative or centred on the L2 culture; the reader should have some interest in knowing something about or participating in the second language culture. Third, motivation should be intrinsic to the task; the reader should experience some enjoyment of second language literacy activities for their own sake. Reading comprehension exercises should be fun to do. Even where L1 background lies close to L2 and familiarity with L2 is optimal, these motivational aspects are essential to L2 reading fluency.

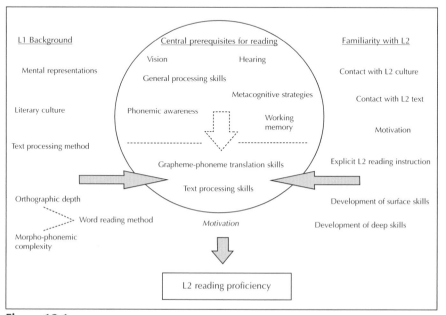

Figure 12.1

Decoding L2 text

It is now well established that if we are to gain fluent access to a text, our word decoding should be both accurate and automatic, for which we need a 'robust, well structured and finely grained representation of the phonological units' that make up those words (Goswami 1999b). There is also evidence that the experience of reading in alphabetic scripts reinforces phonological awareness (Oney *et al.* 1997; Liow 1999; Akamatsu 1999) and that reading in non-alphabetic languages such as Chinese may bypass this conditioning process. Even reading alphabetic writing systems such as English and French, which have less transparent correspondences between grapheme and phoneme, is thought to have a reduced conditioning effect (Wimmer and Goswami 1994). In contrast, there are studies suggesting that reading highly transparent orthographies such as Finnish, Italian or vowelled Hebrew provides a consistent feedback of the grapheme/phoneme relations resulting in very distinct phonological representations (Cossu *et al.* 1988). It therefore seems likely that the phonological experience and orthographic coding mechanisms habitually employed by an SAL speaker who is already literate in L1 may influence his/her word reading strategy when reading L2.

Habitual reading methods developed in non-alphabetic or non-transparent writing systems include a great deal of rote learning or 'sight-word' reading and whole word reading. An SAL reader already literate in a non-alphabetic or non-transparent L1 writing system may then experience difficulty in translating the relatively shallow grapheme–phoneme correspondence rules of the Swedish writing system as a result of the transfer of these word reading strategies. Furthermore, without a good level of awareness of the specific sounds that make up the second language, the necessary translation of written graphemes into their phonological forms will also be considerably impaired. The development of so-called 'surface skills' in Swedish, including awareness of which sounds are likely to occur at the beginning and end of words or which blends of sounds are most probable in the language, is also likely to contribute to word reading proficiency.

However, a number of studies confirm that, given adequate phonological skills word decoding skills can be developed rapidly in L2 regardless of L1 origin. A study by Frederickson and Frith (1998) compared phonological skills, reading accuracy and reading comprehension in bilingual Sylheti (EAL) speakers and in English monolingual (E1) children aged 10–12. The two groups showed no differences in phonological awareness, but the comprehension skills of the EAL speakers were much poorer than their reading accuracy. The same group of EAL speakers were compared with a group of younger dyslexic children on single word reading and text reading. Here, in spite of the age difference, the younger dyslexic children gained higher scores on their text reading while the EAL speakers performed better on single word reading. This indicates that the children with the phonological difficulties compensated for their dyslexia by predicting from context. The EAL speakers, however, while having no difficulty identifying the words on the page lacked the necessary semantic and syntactic knowledge or cultural familiarity with the text and this resulted in significantly poorer reading.

Collins (1999) compared E1 and EAL pupils from 60 schools in the UK defined as 'hard to teach'. This study also found no significant differences between E1 and EAL speakers on phonological awareness and letter identification tests, but there were significant differences in concepts about print and on a sentence-based reading test, even when the test was delivered in the bilingual speaker's first language. The study also found a significant variation in the number of books and other reading materials in the children's homes, and teachers were seen to correct EAL readers' mistakes more frequently, thus denying these students the chance to correct themselves. Furthermore, EAL readers' mistakes were more likely to result from neglecting semantic or context cues rather than from specific word identification difficulties and EAL readers were more likely than E1 speakers to improve their comprehension of the text when teachers provided an introduction or orientation to the text first, or provided visual information or aids to text structure.

These findings suggest that the reading difficulties of the 'hard to teach' EAL speakers were not difficulties of phonological awareness or decoding, but were rather centred around reading comprehension, and were more likely to be the result of economic or cultural disadvantage. Similar findings have been seen in Sweden.

In the IEA study of nine-year-olds, in spite of clear differences in reading comprehension scores, the SAL and S1 pupils showed only very slight differences in Swedish word reading skills. When word reading scores were controlled to take account for differences in standards of living, the results were almost equal (Taube 1995). The same decoding/comprehension disparity was found in a recent study of Swedish juveniles detained in custody, where SAL and S1 boys of the same age were found to have the same levels of word reading and spelling proficiency but the SAL boys had much lower scores on a prose reading test (Svensson *et al.* in press).

From the studies cited above there seems to be a consistent pattern that the specific difficulties of multilingual students do not lie in phonology or single word decoding (dyslexia) but are centred around the interpretation of the L2 text. Investigations of reading difficulties among individuals for whom the additional language is also the language of the majority culture should then focus on factors underlying such difficulties of interpretation.

Interpreting L2 text

Where persistent reading failure is evident in an SAL speaker it is always possible that he or she may be suffering from dyslexia. However, in order to comprehend what has been decoded the reader must be able to integrate the new information into an established framework of cultural references. As seen above, reading comprehension tests often elicit a poor response from multilingual pupils in spite of good word recognition skills and these difficulties may be explained by specific difficulties in lexical inferencing, plot prediction and mental imagery as a direct result of alienation from the culture of the text.

Studies by Yuill and Oakhill (1988) and Oakhill and Patel (1991) showed that monolingual poor comprehenders over the age of about nine years were able to improve significantly their reading comprehension skills by remediation training that encouraged children to apply processing strategies as they read. This included encouraging inferencing (where the children say what they can work out about a story from each of the individual words), asking children to practise question generation for different passages, and covering over pieces of text and asking children to guess what was missing, then to reveal the missing text and discuss the prediction. Imagery training was also studied, which encouraged the children to generate the mental images of events in a text and then to answer questions relating to factual events that had occurred as well as information that could only be inferred from the story and descriptions of details that may have been imagined when 'picturing the story'.

In the first of these studies, Yuill and Oakhill found that poor comprehenders benefited more from inference training than skilled comprehenders, but also that those poor comprehenders who had received inference training made very significantly more progress than those poor comprehenders who had received training in speed and accuracy of word decoding. In the second study, Oakhill and Patel found that the imagery training was also especially beneficial for poor comprehenders, probably because they were integrating the information in the text in a way that they didn't normally do. Training programmes such as these could be designed for non-native speakers with reading comprehension difficulties where phonological skills and word decoding skills per se are known to be good.

A further factor contributing to reading comprehension difficulties is that the reader meets the second language in a decontextualised form (Lundberg 1999b). Verbal communication in a second language is embedded in a spatial and temporal framework supported by extra-linguistic cues such as facial expression, gesture, intonation and so on. Comprehension uncertainties in contextualised communication can usually be disambiguated by negotiation with the interlocutor and by an increased reliance on exophoric references (this, that, here, now, etc.) within the shared context. This support is not available in comprehending text, where words used are more abstract, lower frequency and more phonologically complex, often derived from a different etymology to that of spoken vocabulary (Corson 1995).

Conclusion

Sweden represents an interesting case study of a country that is still coming to terms with an increasing population of multilingual minority groups and a parallel increase in the social and economic divide between highly literate native speakers and the large numbers of effectively reading-disabled individuals for whom Swedish is an additional language. Probably the greatest current challenge to practitioners is to resist simplistic analyses or short-cut solutions to the social divisions now evident as a result of differing levels of literacy. However, Sweden's strong literacy traditions, the exceptionally high overall national literacy scores and a well-established reading research base should provide an opportunity to produce leading research in multilingualism and literacy and good practice in multilingual classrooms. It will be interesting to watch the development of the Swedish example in the coming decade.

Chapter 13

Using Information and Communications Technology (ICT) to Support Bilingual Dyslexic Learners

Yota Dimitriadi

This chapter:

- raises issues about the use of new technologies to assist bilingual learners with their second or first language literacy skills
- highlights some of the difficulties such learners face with the use of ICT
- discusses the potential of technology to improve specific linguistic skills
- attempts to consider a more 'dynamic' approach to the educational process by focusing on the potential of standard content-free packages.

Introduction

The increasing cultural and linguistic diversity found in the school population has started raising a number of considerations among practitioners regarding the ways they could approach learners with bilingual experiences in the classroom setting. The issue becomes more complex when the educational profile of some bilingual children, resulting from thorough and long-term assessment, seems to present characteristics of dyslexia-type difficulties.

Even though research has indicated that the pattern of difficulties dyslexia presents is exemplified differently in every language, technology could provide a useful diagnostic tool for some of the learners' educational strengths and weaknesses in non-language specific problems that accompany dyslexia, e.g. sequential memory, concentration span. Technology could also facilitate access to the curriculum by providing alternative ways of processing and illustrating information (McKeown 2000) through a variety of representational media such as sounds, images and text. At the same time equipment and programs that could support simultaneous input from different languages in oral, written or visual format (Edwards 1998) provide bilingual learners with the opportunity to enrich the curriculum with their diverse cultural experiences. Features such as objectivity, adaptability to the user's needs and learning pace and multisensory approach to the learning tasks not only coincide with the methodological principles advocated in the field of dyslexia but also bridge the gap between community and school languages. In this way language is seen in its holistic view, as a medium to communicate ideas to an audience with different interests and styles, prioritising meaning over solely partial structural considerations such as handwriting or mechanical spelling and grammatical rules.

Information and Communications Technology (ICT) has transformed our educational experience by offering skills that enhance conceptualisation and expression of ideas and can be used both as a means to approach regional culture and to claim membership into a wider international community. Technology has managed to promote the differentiation in learning styles as a norm in the educational process (Dimitriadi 1999). Originally the deification of linear script excluded those with learning difficulties. However, the innovative media (computers, videos) and resources (talking word processors, multimedia packages, the internet) have now empowered users to access curriculum content. Interaction with the media enables them to share ideas and experiences with people from all over the world which will help them extend the possibilities offered to them.

Current practice on using technology in education relies on uncritical use of commercial subject-specific CD-ROMs. However, a key point is the need to utilise the facilities offered by standard content-free packages that can be adapted to the needs of the individual dyslexic learner.

Bilingual dyslexic learners

It has to be emphasised that bilingual dyslexic learners, like their monolingual dyslexic peers, consist of a heterogeneous group. They carry a range of productive and receptive skills in reading, writing, speaking, listening and thinking (Baker 1996) that stretches in a continuum from balanced proficiency of all skills in both languages involved to partly developed competences or underdeveloped skills in one or both of these languages. Constructing a profile of their educational strengths and weaknesses in both languages, as well as gathering background information about the socio-cultural and religious context in which they belong, will help in the setting up of a teaching programme. The morphological and phonological structure of the languages themselves and the approach the child has developed towards them are important issues as they define the typology of problems the learners might exemplify in the other language. This educational profile will determine the appropriateness of incorporating the technical resources in the learning process.

The following section focuses on the pattern of difficulties associated with dyslexia and describes possible ways of employing ICT to support bilingual dyslexic learners developing their literacy skills.

Reinforcing alphabet skills

The aim here is first to help the users establish correspondence between phonemes and graphemes in one language; in addition, connections need to be made between the way in which apparently similar graphemes have different sounds in other languages. Pointing to the letters of the keyboard provides a visual and kinaesthetic approach to practising the correspondence between letters and sounds. A talking word processor provides the learner with immediate aural feedback through typing of individual graphemes.

Similarly, a range of touch-type programs, designed to help users type quickly and accurately, can be used to assist learners acquire autonomy in keyboarding and character recognition. It also 'enables older students to revisit phonics without loss of face' (McKeown 2000).

Spelling problems

If users' oral skills in the second language are sufficiently developed to allow them to construct simple sentences, then a voice recognition system, programmed to understand regional accents and problematic utterance, will encourage the input of speech and translate it into script. If users lack the skills to self-check the transcribed passage, other resources can be used to read the script back to them and help with minor corrections.

Spellcheckers with phonically constructed wordbanks facilitate the writing process by generating lists of possible alternatives. Some programs provide additional aural feedback, a feature that is particularly useful to novice learners of a foreign or a second language who need to practise their pronunciation skills in addition to their spelling skills.

Spreadsheets and word-processing packages can be used to devise matching tasks using words in two languages, combining sounds, words and images. Spelling rules can be presented in a dynamic and colourful way by using a presentational package such as *PowerPoint*. It is possible to include simultaneously an oral and written translation of the rule into another language.

Improving reading comprehension and accuracy

Talking word processors with pre-recorded wordbanks provide immediate aural feedback to the users by repeating each word or sentence typed. Listeners are prompted to self-correct the sentence they typed by seeing their spelling mistakes in the form of highlighted words. Users can also open a passage from the internet or other sources, saved in text format, into the program, highlight the whole document or parts of it and listen to it. This facility assists them with deciphering new or unknown words. It also helps them move on to analysing the content of the passage instead of spending all their time trying to unravel the phonological aspect of the script.

Enhancing auditory processing and discrimination

Talking word processors can be programmed to repeat each phoneme typed. This facility provides the users with constant practice of exploring the relationships between graphemes and phonemes in the target language.

In addition, language-learning CD-ROMs that offer visual waveforms, pitch curves and recordable input with pronunciation error detection (Caldwell 1999) provide a visual version of aural patterns. This feature assists learners in constructing a multisensory picture of the integral aspects of the production of speech. Currently these programs are not content-free but run on a pre-recorded bank of phrases and words.

Improving visual processing and discrimination

Learners can explore the facilities found in the 'Accessibility Options' of the 'Control Panel' menu in Windows (or the equivalent controls in other window environments) and slow down the pace of the mouse and can even set it up to leave a visual trail on the screen. Users with visual difficulties will be enabled to follow the path it leaves. Fonts on the desktop, and even the icons in frequently used packages can be enlarged to facilitate access to program facilities for those learners who find it hard to read small size fonts. It may also be useful to change the default type and size of fonts appearing in the programs to one more appropriate to the learner (for instance, bigger round shaped characters).

Some dyslexic learners have been reported as feeling more confident in approaching script when looking through coloured acetate. There is the possibility of replacing the white colour of the page background with another one more friendly to the user's eyes to create a contrast with the colour of the fonts.

Exercising memory

A 'Slide Show' program can be used to set up a list of words, asking learners to repeat them in the order they appear. Users can then be asked to repeat the procedure followed by employing the basic functions of the programs; for instance opening, saving, printing and exiting a program.

Helping with directional difficulties

Some difficulties may be connected to the directional flow of the learner's written language structure. For example in Cantonese Chinese or in Arabic scripts the characters follow a different course to that of European languages. In such cases, a multimedia computer allows learners to record their voices instead of typing the information and temporarily they overcome the burden a new script might pose. In addition, the set-up of mainstream European word-processing packages follows the left to right direction, prompting users to the direction the words need to have in the specific language.

If problems in orientation are not a direct result of differences in the language structure, then other activities such as sorting word lists into two columns (practise between 'left' and 'right') or asking the users to set up the header and the footer of a document (reinforcement of 'up' and 'down') are useful tasks. Devising activities using the left and the right buttons of the mouse might also reinforce the learner's directional skills.

Dealing with possible speech and language difficulties

Programs with speech output (either synthesised or recorded) can be beneficial for learners with speech and language processing difficulties. The pace in which words or sentences are heard can be controlled to be slower than natural speech, giving the opportunity to users to listen more clearly to every syllable of the word, something that is not always straightforward when speaking. The programs also translate the space between the words and offer help with pronunciation pattern, even though sometimes they might not provide accurate interpretations of the words.

Moreover, using a multimedia computer learners can experiment by recording their own voice and hearing it back. This will give them the opportunity to process and analyse the way they pronounce words and establish connections between the input, lexical representation and output (Stackhouse and Wells 1997) of the oral patterns and their relationship to the written equivalent.

Ameliorating poor concentration

One way of prompting the user's attention might be by reducing the waiting time for the appearance of the screensaver, providing a discrete stimulus for going back to the task. Another option is the use of 'Screen Mates'. They are a family of programs coming under the category of 'Desktop Enhancement' and consist of several types of characters that perform tasks or remain motionless on the desktop. Usually they follow the mouse pointer around providing an entertaining facilitator for children who also have poor visual skills.

Focusing on problems with fine motor coordination

If users find the ordinary mouse difficult to control, it is possible to adjust its sensitivity or to use an alternative type such as a tracker ball or a joystick. The graphic pen can also replace the mouse and provide a kinaesthetic approach to the forming of individual letters especially since different scripts might necessitate different approaches to the art of writing.

Practising study skills

Some word-processing programs have the facility to provide a 'document map' which helps the learner to see the key points of a passage and gain an overview of its content. At the same time the internet is considered as a great source of information. It offers endless possibilities of finding passages in different languages and topics related to the interests and cultural experiences of the learners, using them as a reference point to improve their literacy skills. This activity helps them explore what key words are in order to use them in their search, in looking for key points in the passage, reading between the lines, and then synthesising their own passages. In that final stage of the process Mind Mapping (iANSYST) is a useful activity in helping them to identify the main points of their work. Computerised versions of Mind Mapping (iANSYST) offer flexibility in readjusting points dynamically, something that is more difficult on the restricted size and space of a paper version.

Case studies

Two case studies are described below to show how some of the technical features described were incorporated in the teaching programme of bilingual dyslexic learners. The degree of language acquisition in each language and the profiling of their needs determined the resources chosen.

Mateo

Mateo is eight years old. His mother is English and his father is Greek. He recently came to England and attends an English-speaking school. In Greece he used to go to an English language school but he did not seem to have acquired autonomy over the English script. The only person that speaks to him in Greek now is his father or his grandparents when they come over for a visit. His mother has been talking to him in English a lot since he was very young and Mateo has developed a very rich expressive oral vocabulary in English. Before he came to England Mateo had been assessed as having dyslexic difficulties. His knowledge of spelling rules is limited in both languages. He has problems with basic skills such as recognising the letters of the alphabet or putting them in order, especially in English. His reading skills are also weak in English. In addition, he seems to have some articulatory problems and his handwriting is poor and sometimes illegible.

The aim of the project was to help Mateo develop alphabet skills in both languages: knowledge of the sequence they follow, distinction between vowels and consonants and then move on to the establishment of phoneme–grapheme correspondence. Since he is a newcomer in England it was felt that if he improved these skills he would be able to move on to more advanced spelling patterns while the discourse developed during the project would help him establish some connections between the two alphabets.

Mateo's experience with computers was limited to his home computer games. The first step was to initiate him into the basic processes (switch on and off the computer, open and close a document) and help him familiarise himself with the keyboard. Some tasks involved Mateo listening to the sounds or the names of the letters and trying to point to them on the keyboard. Punctuation markers, use of capital and lower case letters helped him realise the two functions that some of the keys play. Mateo learnt how to enlarge the size of fonts and then he was shown how to use a graphic pen to trace over those letters on the screen. He was also asked to try to copy them in different colours on the screen. This activity helped him develop a feel for the letter shapes and their directional layout. At the same time he practised his fine motor skills by trying to follow the line patterns of the letters he typed.

He was also introduced to touch-type programs in an attempt to improve his fine motor coordination and practise more with identifying the letters. When presented with a Greek keyboard these initial skills helped him compare the structure and phonology of the letters in both languages. He also realised basic differences in the punctuation markers in Greek and English. The motion of the pointer was slowed down to help him pay attention to various reference points on the screen.

A multimedia authoring package (a program able to incorporate text, sounds, animation and images) was used to produce a multisensory project on the alphabet. Mateo decided that a dictionary would be an appropriate idea as he would be able to put in the letters of the Greek alphabet and incorporate words that started with each one of these letters. He chose words from his home and school environment, words he felt confident enough to spell in Greek. He also thought that translating these words into English and recording them could provide easier access to those who needed to read his work. Mateo was shown how to record his voice in a passage and incorporate it in the finished product. Being enthusiastic about this novelty he kept clicking on the soundwave object and listening to his voice. Slowly his articulation in some of the repetitive word patterns improved.

Mateo was also very careful in choosing the background pattern and colour for each part of the project. He spent time deciding on the size, style and colour of the fonts bearing in mind the message he wanted to put across. For instance, when he put the word 'hand' (χέρι), he chose a type of font that resembled fully cursive handwriting.

As his receptive and expressive oral vocabulary in English was good, the internet was also used as a source of information. Mateo was shown how to copy and paste a passage in a talking word-processing program, highlight and listen to it. He sometimes commented on the way the words were pronounced by the program and he selected the parts of the passage he thought would be interesting to include in his work. We also practised grapheme–phoneme correspondence with the assistance of the same package. Mateo was asked to look at the letter, say its sound and then check whether the system pronounced it 'properly'. This activity and the discussion that took place around it helped him improve his awareness of the correspondence between sounds and letters in English.

Danae

Danae is nine-year-old third generation Greek. She was born in England and attends a local English-speaking primary school. Her first language is English even though both her parents are Greek. She speaks English in her home and school environment. There is a small circle of relatives and friends that talk to her in Greek. Danae seems to understand most parts of the discourse in Greek but when asked she tends to answer in English. She can speak fragmental words and everyday expressions in Greek but not sustain a conversation. She has been attending a heritage language school once a week for the last four years. Danae has been recently assessed and statemented as being dyslexic. Her developmental history shows that she has been having problems with her hearing. In practical terms, she shows poor knowledge of orthographic rules in English and does not seem to know any reading strategies to assist her to cope with long words. Danae has a poor concentration span and sequential memory. Her alphabet skills are above average in English and she recognises most of the letters in Greek. She seems to be aware of the morphic correspondence letters in both languages might present. For instance the English letter 'p' looks similar to the Greek letter that corresponds to the English sound 'r'.

The aim of the project was to assist Danae improve her expressive oral vocabulary in Greek using everyday words from the home environment (relatives, objects and pets) and standard expressions (How are you? It is cold and rainy today etc.). Danae is able to recognise some of these words and phrases when she listens to a conversation but not automatically produce them when she speaks. Danae would be shown how to spell those words that follow a simple CVCV (Consonant-Vowel-Consonant-Vowel) pattern in Greek. Danae was already a confident computer user as her father had been showing her how to work with standard office programs.

To prompt Danae's attention a 'Screen Mate' was selected. It appeared in random positions on the screen making a sound. That proved helpful as Danae did not feel any pressure from the teacher to go back to the task. We also used the 'Accessibility Options' to set up 'Togglekeys' and alert Danae to use capital letters when necessary.

It is difficult sometimes for Danae to stay still for a long time. To help her concentrate more when reading we used the 'Split' facility found under the 'Window' toolbar option in *Word*. She felt more confident as she did not have to stay still all the time or be reminded to do so. We also arranged for the screensaver to appear when the computer stayed idle for two minutes. This worked well as Danae used the computer for small tasks and not to write a lengthy story that would necessitate her to stop typing in order to think.

The 'Autocorrect' option was used to build a list of regularly used words in Greek. This process helped Danae to analyse the words into the constituent graphemes and decide which part she would use as a reminder. In addition, it gave us the opportunity to talk about suffixes and the morphology of Greek words (for instance, genders).

Danae built up a file of Greek spelling points incorporating animation and sound in *PowerPoint*. This helped her take ownership of the rules, explore the facilities the program offered and come up with ideas of how to construct the rules so that her friends would like them. In a written spelling test that was administered to her at the end of the project she seemed to remember the rules as part of the structured activity. She learnt to shift between English and Greek fonts on the English keyboard and to match the similar sounds to the different letters of the two alphabets.

To help her build a sight vocabulary we also used the 'Display' option from the 'Control Panel' menu and Danae learnt how to change the 'Background' of the screen. Each week Danae used 'Paint' to write one of the words of the list in Greek and either draw a matching image or insert a clip art picture. For instance she wrote 'κότα' 'hen' and drew a picture of it. The file was chosen to be the background theme for that week and so Danae had the chance to see the word and its spelling very frequently. Furthermore, we set up lists of key words in *Word* and used the 'Document Map' option to highlight and revise them.

We decided to make up small dialogues to use the words and phrases she had been practising. This resulted in a small multimedia project in which words in both languages were heard and were shown in written format. Pictures accompanied the dialogues and some animated images popped up to reinforce the passage. Danae used the digital camera to take pictures for the illustrations of some of the words and she imitated different characters during her recordings of the dialogues. At the end of the project we invited her family to have a look and Danae explained the project and the way she constructed it to them.

Conclusion

The examples above have been described in order to demonstrate the effective use of technology in working with two individual bilingual dyslexic learners. The outcome of both case studies was positive, not only because the learners developed some specific language skills but also as they established connections between the first and the second language. In both cases, the learners compared the two linguistic systems finding similarities and differences in their structure. They became more confident in exploring the notation of both languages and in discussing the problems they have. At a more advanced level, the multisensory nature of the programs enabled them to overcome difficulties with traditional ways of learning and led them towards higher levels of abstract thinking. These two learners began to realise that language is not only a collection of fixed symbols and rules but also, and more importantly, a system of negotiating meanings. They were able to use the technical facilities of the various programs to express their creative thoughts. In their projects they showed consideration for the style of the presentation and for the needs of the audience. The novelty of working with a range of different media was probably a significant contributor to the success of the projects. Furthermore, the awareness raised during the process regarding linguistic diversity encouraged the learners to recognise the strength of their cognitive abilities and provided them with metacognitive strategies to cope with their educational difficulties.

Acknowledgement

The practical part of the research was supported by a grant from the Greek Institute of the National Scholarships (IKY).

Chapter 14

The Literacy Acquisition of Black and Asian 'English-as-Additional-Language' (EAL) Learners: Anti-Racist Assessment and Intervention Challenges

Theresa Reed

This chapter critically examines:

- the context of racism and the need for professionals to examine the nature of their procedures
- the validity of assessment and interpretations of assessment
- the misleading use of simplistic and restrictive labels
- the need for a comprehensive, contextualised assessment framework
- and the need to avoid self-serving agendas in promoting bilingual development.

Learning from the Lawrence Inquiry: the need to establish anti-racist practice to avoid institutional racism

In Britain, all academic and professional development must now be guided by the 'Macpherson (Lawrence) Report' (Macpherson 1999) as well as by new amendments to the 1976 Race Relations Act (which emphasise the 'enforcible duties of public bodies and institutions to positively pursue and achieve Race Equality outcomes'). This means that the rights and entitlements of Black and Asian ethnic groups must be protected at all costs, that there can be no justification for woolly thinking that might lead to gaps in services/inappropriate provision and that complacent/exaggerated views can no longer be excused or tolerated. The essence of anti-racist practice is the acceptance by professionals that they are duty-bound to be vigilant at all times in case their behaviour, even momentary lapses, should impinge on those groups that are most vulnerable to discriminatory actions. It demands, then, that constant checks be made, following closely the definitions in the Macpherson (Lawrence) Report, to ensure that professionals' responses conform precisely to the requirements set down in the text:

- 'Racism' in general terms consists of conduct or words or practices which advantage or disadvantage people because of their colour, culture or ethnic origin. In its more subtle form it is as damaging as in its overt form (Macpherson 1999: 6.4).
- 'Institutional racism' consists of the collective failure of an organisation to provide an appropriate and professional service to people because of their colour, culture or ethnic origin. It can be seen or detected in processes, attitudes and behaviour which amount to discrimination through unwitting prejudice, ignorance, thoughtlessness, and racist stereotyping which disadvantage minority ethnic people (Macpherson 1999: 6.4).

The onus is now on professionals (including researchers) to examine the nature of their practices as well as to be accountable at the process level, so that the risks of inadequate/inappropriate actions which may disadvantage or damage the long-term interests of Black and Asian groups are not overlooked or excused on grounds of professional expediency, unavoidable 'ignorance' or mere 'thoughtlessness'. Hence it is vital for professionals to question the process involved as well as to examine closely the areas of 'ignorance' and 'thoughtlessness' for themselves, to save being challenged. Institutional racism is maintained when powerful professionals seek to defend/influence ways of doing things that suit white agendas, in spite of the cost/risks to which minority groups are subjected. Thus professionals have to bear in mind that proposals they are keen to put forward, such as seeking to link dyslexia with multilingualism, may not turn out to be the universal panacea they are assumed to be. In fact, it may be naive ('ignorant') to believe that monocultural views apply equally in a multicultural context, and it would be 'thoughtless' of professionals if the risks associated with the simple wish of extending the monolingual definition and assessment rationale developed for dyslexia to a multilingual context have not been carefully weighed up before the first step is undertaken, since the concern was originally defined in relation to 'white monolingual English-speakers' whose literacy skills in their first language (L1) were judged not to be commensurate with other areas of functioning.

The context of racism

The history of racism should have warned us that it is ill-advised to force western practices (i.e. often developed purely with the white person's needs in mind) onto Black and Asian groups when their interests have not featured in the thinking or development process at the outset. Therefore time must be given to take stock, instead of railroading questionable notions (e.g. it is a good thing to donate white monolingual ideas to Black and Asian multilingual groups), which can be fraught with danger if these ideas are driven through with enthusiasm, but without initial clarification of the nature of diverse needs or a questioning of the legitimacy of putting the Black and Asian multilingual groups on the spot for the sake of having a 'white agenda' more widely endorsed.

Ironically, even if there is a genuine wish to share a good thing with the Black and Asian groups, there is often a serious long-term cost attached, which may well outweigh limited, short-term benefits. If white professionals are not even aware (in their 'ignorance') of the need or have failed (through their 'thoughtlessness') to assess the risks (e.g. those attached to 'labelling') to which Black and Asian groups are vulnerable (i.e. the risk that pejorative views/negative stereotypes are likely to be reinforced, even in cases where 'labels' bring positive benefits for the majority group), then the interests of Black and Asian groups are ill-served through 'labels' becoming exploited to affirm existing prejudices and raise anxiety/fear. Thus, in an uncanny way, what suits the white majority tends to make things much worse for Black and Asian groups.

The fact is that the 'ignorance' and 'thoughtlessness' displayed by western psychologists (e.g. in extending the application of psychometric tests before considering the question of their validity for Black and Asian groups) have cost the latter dearly. If the same blunders of misassessment and misplacement continue (as documented in Coard 1971; Fish 1985; Carter and Coussins 1986; Tomlinson 1989; CRE 1996), then 'ignorance' has been allowed to prevail, as psychometric testing is being carried out regardless of its consequences (CRE 1996). Professionals are clearly 'thoughtless' if they choose to gloss over the inherent cultural-linguistic bias that invalidates the use of such tools/discriminatory data (Usmani 1999).

It is equally problematic if organisations/professionals seek to push through a white agenda in blind faith (even if the belief is that the 'dyslexia' label can, for instance, ensure a share of the benefits for minority-language groups, hence offering a way out of the fundamental inequity in resourcing), since they are thereby ignoring the real risk of misassessment, especially at a time when the distinction between EAL needs and special needs continues to confuse many professionals, and the momentum that could drive development of valid assessment practice (that takes cultural, linguistic and religious contexts properly into account) is perpetually sapped by energies being diverted to a white agenda.

The marginalising process

It is always risky to extend favoured white models across all cultural-linguistic groups unless there is strong evidence of fit and proven benefit. The process should involve appropriate, specific research development and curb white presumptions, until valid conclusions can be drawn and all sides are well satisfied with the balance of the ongoing debate. It is vital that such a process should never be shortened or neglected, otherwise it is indicative of a double standard (i.e. matters to do with Black and Asian interests can be disregarded as being straightforward, and can therefore be considered at the general level).

The reality is far more complex whenever Black and Asian interests have to be taken into account, so that a great deal more should be done to create collaborative partnerships with Black and Asian bilingual professionals/communities in such endeavours. This means issues must not surface in a way that takes them by surprise (by being based on white concerns and brought up by the white group). It also means they must feel at ease, when airing issues, to consider and formulate their own views properly. Thus the due process of consultation would entail respecting the reservations and different wishes of Black and Asian communities, including their need to explore the pros and cons without time restrictions or pressure, and to have the confidence to adopt whatever stance or perspective they feel to be right, without the risk of being ridiculed, ostracised or becoming enticed/resigned to going along with the flow of majority wishes.

In order to participate properly, the Black and Asian groups must have access to sound evidence data, which are best drawn from independent, quality research. Research validity is more likely to be safeguarded when it is conducted by professionals who have appropriate cultural-linguistic expertise and can offer different ways of viewing difficulties encountered by Black and Asian groups so that their complex needs, together with any disadvantages, constraints and barriers they face, are properly understood and addressed in a holistic manner. Otherwise, there is a 'thoughtless' tendency on the part of professionals to overgeneralise: e.g. they may quote as evidence of dyslexia research that has been designed for a different purpose/population sample; they may bring under the umbrella of dyslexia, as if this were the underlying reason, all learners who underperform: (a) 'monolingual English-speakers' who struggle with literacy skills of their first language (L1); (b) 'foreign-language (L2) learners' who fall behind in L2-class, though their L1 may be faring well, (c) 'Black and Asian EAL-learners' perceived as struggling insofar as the pace/standard is set by L1-English peers, their situation being made worse by the unnecessary barrier of a 'subtractive' learning environment. Since such indiscriminate classification is bound to mislead and confuse people, it will be useful at this point to clarify the situational difference between the three groups: Baker (1996: 66) defines an 'additive' bilingual situation (i.e. groups 'a' and 'b') as one 'where the addition of a second language and culture is unlikely to replace or displace the first language and culture (Lambert 1974)', and a 'subtractive' bilingual situation (i.e. group 'c') as one where 'the learning of a majority second language may undermine a person's minority first language and culture'.

Anti-racist assessment for Black and Asian bilingual pupils: the validity of process and interpretation

Professional expectations and assessment criteria based on unfounded assumptions are racist in effect if they damage or disadvantage Black and Asian bilingual pupils' educational opportunities and career prospects, or if they favour white monolingual pupils as a result. The danger is obvious if the presumptions about the rate of acquisition of EAL and associated literacy proficiency are that these pupils should quickly catch up with first-language (L1) English speakers. Such a premise is unsupported by the evidence: the process took eight years (Hakuta and D'Andrea 1992) among a group of Mexican-Americans, and Cummins (1984) estimated that it would take at least five to seven years before EAL-Canadian children could cope with cognitively demanding tasks in a context-reduced environment (English classroom). Thomas and Collier (1997) further confirm, through their large-scale longitudinal bilingual study, that it takes pupils starting with no English at least seven to ten years to reach average level in English reading, if they are educated in a 'subtractive' context, though progress can be accelerated (four to seven years) if they are taught in an 'additive' bilingual setting.

While dyslexia may offer a way of assessing children who encounter specific difficulties, it offers too restricted a view for bilingual learners whose learning experience is dependent on many contexts (family, institution and society) as well as interacting effects (e.g. physical/psychological problems, socio-economic/refugee status, degree of acculturisation). A narrow assessment approach risks condoning the 'thoughtless' dismissal of a whole range of crucial factors that need to be understood as well as encouraging 'ignorance' by viewing Black and Asian EAL pupils as having learning difficulties on account of attainment gaps. Quality teaching, that is teaching which promotes 'additive' bilingual development, ensures appropriate language/literacy scaffolds and effective aids. It adopts an 'assessment-through-teaching' approach in all curricular areas and facilitates interaction in two-way bilingual exchanges. A conducive learning environment is one that is free from racism, motivated by engineering success through a 'cooperative learning' culture and through taking community mentors as role-models. Such environments have not been provided well enough or for long enough to raise achievement. Therefore the primary task should be to address these problems immediately, since they are the root cause of low achievement, as opposed to resorting to labelling.

Equally the emotional dimension must also be considered. Ellis (1997) cites studies (Horwitz 1987; Wenden 1987) which have examined how 'individual learner differences' (e.g. learners' beliefs about their own language learning) affect second-language acquisition and found evidence that such feelings may facilitate or inhibit learning. He also reports studies which showed some students feeling fearful and anxious at having to learn or compete in L2: for instance, Horwitz and Young (1991) highlighted the issue of 'language anxiety'; Ellis (1989) himself found some learners were frightened by teachers' questions, feeling stupid and helpless in class; Oxford (1992) listed alienation as one source of anxiety, akin to 'culture shock'. Ellis and Rathbone's (1987) finding that learners were unable to focus on the learning task when troubled by emotional stress, was supported by MacIntyre and Gardner's (1991) studies review, substantiating the claim that anxiety not only has negative effects on performance in the second language but also bears a high correlation to achievement. Even though many of these studies are based on white learners acquiring foreign languages, it is easy to imagine Black and Asian bilingual pupils suffering a similar situation-specific anxiety when functioning in a monolingual 'subtractive' environment, especially in a predominately white school-setting. Thus the issue of comparing Black and Asian EAL performance with that of L1-English speakers is not as straightforward and as fair as we sometimes tend to presume.

The accountability involved in assessment

Athough assessment is usually justified on the grounds that professionals require information for decision making, the process of gathering the necessary data and how judgements are made should be subjected to tighter scrutiny than at present, if institutional racism is to be challenged effectively. As long as the risks of 'process-bias' and 'misjudgement' continue to go unchecked (statistical data reviewed in Reed 1999: 94), then professionals must be held to account. However, racist practices will be perpetuated if professional training remains inadequate, with the result that there will be little leadership or direction for stringent anti-racist assessment. If the will to examine professional practice stops short of anti-discriminatory considerations, this will in effect risk marginalising racial equality issues because of an imprecise focus. Priority action is to engage expertise and independent mechanisms for objective process-monitoring. This should always involve Black and Asian bilingual professionals who have the relevant skills and are given the legitimacy to lead on practice, in order to end the kind of 'inappropriate' assessment which uses labels simplistically while ignoring crucial bilingual/cultural contexts. If there exists confusion/disagreement over the label's definition, then it should not be used for Black and Asian bilingual learners, who are particularly vulnerable to 'false-positive' judgement errors, the effects of confused assessment being much more damaging in their particular case. Similarly, labels which endorse unrealistic expectations are dangerous (easily fostering the view that 'learning disability' can be judged by the attainment gap in EAL-related skills): that alone would cause irreparable damage to the life chances of such pupils. When professionals continue to accept this state of affairs or the risk of misjudgement as an inevitable 'margin of error', institutional racism then occurs.

The validity of the assessment, judged in terms of 'best outcomes', without being compromised by 'false-positive' errors or questionable assumptions

The only way to avoid the risk of confused and restrictive assessment practices and their racist effects is to develop a comprehensive contextual assessment framework, by thoroughly exploring 'enriched cultural' and 'language-transfer' strengths and constraints imposed by the socio-cultural context in education/experience of racism. The quality data will help professionals to see that the 'thoughtless' pursuit of simplistic answers and convenient short-cuts, while useful for meeting report deadlines, is too superficial to constitute a meaningful exercise. The improved outcomes will also open the eyes of professionals to the inappropriateness of generalising white models/paradigms and the inadequacy of white tools for Black and Asian EAL-assessment, raise their awareness of the importance of valid psychological research into Black and Asian bilingual needs and, hopefully, allow them to clarify for themselves the misconceptions they have as monolingual 'majority' professionals.

'Comprehensive contextual assessment' encourages professionals to make careful checks so that the information used is verifiable/can be validated. Misinterpretation is further minimised if assessment is done over time and fully involves the family (an involvement which need not be constrained by the 'language/communication barrier', if bilingual professionals are available). However, the demands placed on the professionals are clear: they must have sufficient competence to appreciate the interplay between complex linguistic/cultural/racist contexts and academic achievement. It is also essential to bear in mind that institutionalised racist practice will prevail as long as white views and white thinking are allowed to dominate; misinterpretation and negative expectations will also persist. But as long as changes in professional practice are made on an ad-hoc basis, led by perpetual swings between professional 'complacency'/'anxiety', 'ignorance'/'thoughtlessness', then misinterpretation and negative expectations will persist.

More valid assessment practices will result in improved outcomes, bringing satisfaction to Black and Asian professionals and bilingual pupils alike. Institutional racism is divisive and disenfranchises partnerships, maintaining barriers which severely restrict Black and Asian families' access to information, communication and entitlement to quality services. Furthermore, these families are left in no position to protest or complain, either being kept ignorant of the cost/risks they might bear if their participation in the decision-making process is ineffectual or being forced to rely on 'helpful advocates' to take up issues on their behalf.

Intervention framework: learning from bilingual research

Access to valid, large-scale, longitudinal bilingual data reduces the risk of misleading or misdirecting professional practice. One such study (Thomas and Collier 1997) is worthy of attention because its findings dispel many unhelpful myths and misassumptions about bilingual development, and rightly puts the focus on 'institutional practice' and 'programme deficiencies'. Their recommendations could form a basis for 'best practice' when considering EAL-intervention because they are based on the 'best achievement' quality bilingual educational programmes can effect. The message is this: if raised achievement has not been realised, then professionals must focus on the provision of bilingual input first (apart from tangible physical problems). Indeed, this line of thinking is substantiated by the central message in the most recent DfEE guidance: *Removing the Barriers* (DfEE 2000) advises professionals to adopt a 'positive approach to expectations', aided by 'ethnic monitoring' of academic attainment/level of EAL (which dispenses with the need to rely on 'standardised test' data/labels): 'Look at the results in terms of shortcomings in provision rather than as problems with the pupils themselves' (DfEE 2000: 26).

Professor Tim Brighouse (Chief Education Officer for Birmingham) also emphasised the need for 'positive attitudes' and to 'avoid deficiency models' in the same DfEE Conference (Birmingham, February 2000), reflecting the sentiments expressed by one primary head teacher, quoted in the conference document (DfEE 2000):

> I think we've moved on. We don't talk so much about faults lying with the child. We are looking much more closely at our teaching. (DfEE 2000: 26)

The key to efficient intervention is to nurture bilingual development. This calls for a thorough understanding of the 'second language acquisition' process (Ellis 1997). Monolingual professionals have to accept the fact that proficient EAL acquisition is bound to take time (in terms of years), that it cannot be rushed merely on the basis of needs generated by curricular demands or consideration of 'attainment league-tables'. In fact, monolingual professionals have also to realise that their own anxieties could form the basis of institutional racism: the risk is that Black and Asian EAL learners might be judged unfairly when subjected to the common but erroneous expectation that the nursery–reception phase is quite adequate for EAL preparation, and that it is evidence of failure if they struggle with L2-literacy from then on, when white yardsticks (e.g. based on L1-language/literacy skills norms) form the basis for judging learning progress (particularly damning when applied to the 'Infant baseline'). The fact that these same pupils may excel in home-language/L1 literacy and numeracy is rarely perceived as a noteworthy achievement, neither does such success help to dispel the suspicion of 'learning difficulties'/an associated 'condition', or to tilt the balance if 'negative-expectations' hold sway.

The 'proof of the pudding' for effective intervention is when 'institutional racism' can be dismantled in a way that will bring real opportunities to all bilingual learners, which is first and foremost the realisation of a 'bilingual-biliterate' curriculum. To provide anything less is a poor substitute which will limit opportunities and undermine the chance of success. The fundamental message that comes out of Thomas and Collier's research adds weight to the familiar wisdom from the study of 'bilingualism', which is that Black and Asian bilingual pupils (even those born here) will be best served if they can use their dominant language (i.e. home language), because this will enable them to operate at their highest cognitive level, thus allowing them to exploit their life-experience and cultural learning in a dynamic way. Conversely, being made to use a less familiar language-medium (EAL) is bound to be restrictive, needlessly disadvantaging them during the primary years, especially when they are required to deal with complex, cognitively challenging tasks that are set in a culturally alien context.

Being wise and joining forces to make a difference

Unequal educational outcomes have arisen as a result of totally neglecting to promote a bilingual and biliterate heritage. Professionals would do well to heed the wisdom gained in the field of bilingual research: 'children learning to read in their home language...are not just developing home language skills. They are also developing higher-order cognitive and linguistic skills that will help with the future development of reading in the majority language as well as with general intellectual development' (Baker 1996: 155). Many monolingual countries invest a great deal in order to develop into 'bilingual' nations, and countries that are fortunate enough to possess language diversity in their population have wisely nurtured 'bilingualism' in an 'additive' manner, 'bilingual' classes no longer being provided by subsidising a 'voluntary community effort' or being viewed as 'additional luxuries'. They have thus been receptive to the overwhelming evidence that 'integrated-bilingual' provision offers a 'first-class' education for every pupil.

Not surprisingly, many governments maintain first-language teaching for their nationals abroad (including British English schools) as a priority, and some minority languages are successfully revived through political negotiations (e.g. French in Canada, Spanish in the US, Welsh in Britain). The cost of 'thoughtless' action (e.g. employing monolingual support with bilingual-funding, and failing to exploit 'home-language'/associated literacy in the academic curriculum) is to court failure, a failure which not only depresses Black and Asian bilingual achievement but also reduces our country's global prospects. Thus professionals must join forces to press for more appropriate resources to match the distinctive needs of Black and Asian language minority groups (rather than sweeping them onto a majority agenda), and they can indeed make a difference by pooling energy/influence to improve the state of Black and Asian bilingual education (Thomas and Collier 1997: 77–9): by addressing the wider context of developing the 'home-language' through academic work which would aid EAL acquisition, by fostering interactive discovery-learning and peer-tutoring, in an 'anti-racist, additive-bilingual' socio-cultural context that all effective schools can offer. Professionals have to accept that an anti-racist perspective demands a clear vision that focuses exclusively on the interests of the Black and Asian communities, which cannot sit with other self-serving agendas.

Chapter 15

Maori Culture and Literacy Learning: Bicultural Approaches

Angus Hikario Macfarlane, Ted Glynn, Ian J. Presland and Sonja Greening

This chapter:

- addresses the relationship between Maori culture and literacy learning
- focuses on the importance of embracing bicultural approaches to respond to the learning needs of the indigenous Maori of New Zealand
- outlines some of the issues involved in literacy development for children and
- provides models of good practice.

Introduction

Over the last two hundred years, Maori have endured sustained and systematic cultural belittlement leading to the widespread acceptance of the perception within the dominant European (Pakeha) society that Maori language and culture are inferior, subordinate, insignificant and irrelevant. This institutionalised perception and belief system was instrumental in the near demise of the Maori language and culture and has marginalised Maori as a people. This alienation has resulted in disproportionate representation by Maori in such areas as poor health, low socio-economic status, higher rates of offending and incarceration, poor housing conditions and low educational achievement. Within mainstream education a disproportionate number of Maori children have been diagnosed as having language difficulties which in some cases may be classified as dyslexia. For these children, acknowledgement of the importance of Maori learning styles is a critical factor in any intervention programme.

If real and purposeful change is to be effected in the area of Maori literacy learning, New Zealand educationalists need to implement an ongoing commitment to the development and delivery of sound bicultural classroom practices. This practice must embrace and reflect the holistic nature of Maori culture and learning, and be interwoven through all programmes, initiatives and interventions.

The cultural partnership

Changes in special education must be viewed in the context of change in education in general, these in turn reflecting a changing society. Major social and demographic changes have occurred in New Zealand in recent years. The population has become culturally and ethnically more diverse as new migrant groups have been absorbed into the country. There have been major social and economic shifts which have widened the gap between rich and poor, and there has been a growing recognition of the unique position of Maori in New Zealand society and attempts to implement the Treaty of Waitangi more effectively.

The Treaty of Waitangi defines the relationship between Maori and non-Maori, a relationship arising from their status as joint partners in founding the nation in 1840. Many non-Maori New Zealanders have come to regard the Treaty of Waitangi as an expression of principles such as partnership and equity. Maori have regarded the Treaty as a charter for power sharing in the decision-making processes of government, for self-determination as an indigenous people and as a guide to intercultural relations in New Zealand (Durie 1995). The Treaty now occupies an important position of providing guiding principles for subsequent legislation, government policy and administrative practices. It has particular significance for educational professionals (Glynn *et al.* 1997; Macfarlane 1998).

Article Two (a) of the Treaty of Waitangi implies that the Crown and its agencies must recognise the right of Maori to continue to define, protect, promote and control all of their treasures and resources. Included among those treasures and resources are all those things to do with language, epistemology and pedagogy – what counts as knowledge, and how that knowledge is to be preserved, transmitted, used and evaluated.

Towards inclusion

In another change, which has had far-reaching social implications, 1990 saw New Zealand undergo a major educational restructuring designed to separate policy from operations and schools from central control. The policy documents associated with these changes clearly recognise the diversity of New Zealand society and give direction towards an inclusive system of education.

Every school in New Zealand is now a self-managing entity governed by an elected Board of Trustees. This board enters into a contractual arrangement with the Crown. The National Education Guidelines (Ministry of Education 1997) form a major part of these contractual arrangements and a basis for audit and review. They are part of every school charter by law and are therefore key indicators of the way in which education is delivered and managed in New Zealand.

The National Education Guidelines stipulate national goals, administrative processes and a curriculum framework which individual schools are required to incorporate in their aims, policies and practices. These guidelines are based on the premise that a school's fundamental purpose is to provide optimal learning opportunities for all students (Ministry of Education 1993). The National Education Goals (Ministry of Education 1997) establish an official commitment to equity requiring schools to 'recognise the importance of educational opportunities for all' (1997: 6) and to pay 'particular attention to those with special needs' (1997: 7).

The National Administration Guidelines (Ministry of Education 1997) specify processes by which schools can ensure their goals and aims are met. They include the analysis of barriers to learning and achievement and the development of strategies to overcome these barriers. Attention to a wide range of environmental influences is advocated including 'administrative structures and teacher behaviours' (Ministry of Education 1997: 17), which may impinge upon student learning and behaviour.

The New Zealand Curriculum Framework (Ministry of Education 1993), the official policy for teaching and learning in New Zealand schools, sets out the essential learning areas and skills for all students. It is also quite explicit in stating that it applies to all students 'irrespective of gender, ethnicity, belief, ability or disability, social or cultural background or geographical area' (Ministry of Education 1993: 3).

Current educational philosophy, policies and practices

Although most New Zealand children do well in reading, writing and mathematics, there is evidence that some do not. Of special concern is the wide discrepancy between the highest and lowest levels of reading achievement and significant differences in performance in all areas between particular groups of children. The New Zealand government is cognisant of this widening gap in academic achievement, especially the gap as it applies to many Maori children. In attempting to address these educational concerns, the government has adopted the following goal: 'By 2005, every child turning nine will be able to read, write and do maths for success' (Ministry of Education 1999: 5).

A report, prepared by the Literacy Taskforce (Ministry of Education 1999), made it clear that student achievement is influenced by personal, cultural, family, and school factors. The taskforce was adamant that the expectations of the achievement of all children should be the same, regardless of the language of instruction or their ethnicity. This group also agreed that although the goal is relevant and appropriate to children in Maori medium education, the procedures and approaches for achieving the goal may well be different from those in English medium education. There are many general features of learning to read and write that apply across countries, but others are specific to New Zealand. For example, our cultural context includes recognition of the educational and language needs of both Maori and non-Maori deriving from obligations of the Treaty of Waitangi and such official policies as the recognition of both English and Te Reo Maori as official languages. The Literacy Taskforce endorsed eleven principles of best practice of instruction, significant among which is the one that refers to teaching that takes account of children's linguistic and cultural backgrounds.

Bishop and Glynn (1999) adamantly declare that classrooms are places where learners can bring 'who they are' to the learning interactions in complete safety, and their knowledges (including languages and language patterns) are 'acceptable' and 'legitimate'. Ashman and Elkins (1998) refer to the overlapping of disorders of oral language and written language, adding to the complexity of the human communication phenomenon. This complexity is sometimes demonstrated by Maori children who may have been assessed as experiencing literacy difficulties, yet can excel in reciting intricate and lengthy waiata moteatea (ancient song and verse), whaikorero (speech-making), and karakia (incantations). In addition, while communication can operate through verbal units of sounds, syllables, words, sentences and discourses, there are also non-verbal behaviours, which have a cultural basis. Non-verbal signals include facial expression, eye contact, proximity, tone of voice, pitch of voice, gestures, body movements, speech pace, and pausing (Jones, cited in Charles 1999; Ashman and Elkins 1998). An example of this is the following identical statement uttered by a Maori child:

'Haere atu koe.' Leave now please.
'Haere atu koe!' Get out of my space!

Learning programmes and projects

The availability of speech and literacy services varies throughout New Zealand. As with all services – such as the Specialist Education Services (SES), a national organisation, and Resource Teachers of Learning and Behaviour (RTLB) an initiative of 750 teachers nationwide to provide inclusive services to schools – a set of priorities is applied which is periodically reviewed and changed. It is difficult to predict just what services might be available at any point in time or place. However, there are projects and initiatives constantly being developed and commissioned. One such activity in New Zealand was the two-year exploratory project called School Community Iwi Liaison (SCIL). The Curriculum Division of the Ministry of Education commissioned SES, Poutama Pounamu Education Research and Development Centre based in Tauranga as the contractor to develop a professional development contract called 'Pause Prompt Praise' (PPP). The programme was designed to raise Maori student literacy achievement in mainstream settings. This group focused on improving the teaching and learning of reading and literacy as well as strengthening links between the school, the community and local Iwi groups. The SCIL project was in no doubt that adult tutoring as a teaching-learning strategy to help children read, does work.

Two additional programmes, Tatari Tautoko Tauawhi (TTT), and Kia Puawai ai te Reo (the blossoming of the language) have also achieved significant outcomes at the Poutama Pounamu Centre.

Maori learning styles

A Maori view of learning is an important issue in the provision of special education service. Maori people acknowledge that learning is lifelong, a natural consequence of one's interaction with people and the environment (Walker 1990). Theirs is an oral tradition and the notion of the written counterpart is a relatively recent phenomenon. Allowances must be made for different learning styles and teaching styles must ensure that the student's mana (integrity) is not devalued. It is not uncommon for Maori to declare that all children are special, hence they are ascribed an element of tapu (sacredness). Macfarlane and Glynn (1998) contend that it is the right of Maori students to see their language, cultural knowledge and preferred learning styles legitimated within the classroom.

Several proponents of preferred Maori learning styles have identified Maori ways of teaching and learning. However, Joan Metge (1984) outlines five primary interactions which have significance for education practitioners. The first of these is ako, which refers to the unified cooperation of learner and teacher in a single enterprise. The second of these is learning through exposure or modelling: a process Metge describes as informal, sometimes semi-continuous but embedded in the life of the community.

Glynn and Bishop (1995) maintain that this strategy covers a wide range of applications from listening without any expectation to perform to natural antecedents to imitate behaviour. The third style, that of group learning, has implications for socialising children into literacy and oracy practices as these activities (such as waiata and kapa haka) build social and cultural identities. The final Maori preferred learning styles are learning 'by the heart' and 'story-telling', which Glynn (1998) describes as deceptively simple narrative approaches to learning and teaching. Students from different ethnic and cultural groups can expect to have their language and cultural values and practices acknowledged and affirmed in inclusive schools, both through the curriculum and through culturally sensitive teaching styles and strategies. This participation is intended to maximise their opportunity for educational achievement. Paradoxically, participation in mainstream education in New Zealand has come for Maori at the cost of their own language and culture. However, consistent with an ecological paradigm, responsibility for developing inclusive assessment teaching strategies that will benefit Maori students does not rest with Maori teachers and Maori consultants alone. These responsibilities are shared with all classroom teachers, principals, school trustees and social agencies (Moore *et al.* 1999).

Dyslexia: cultural implications

The majority of definitions of developmental dyslexia assume that an individual should be reading or spelling at a level predicted by either his or her measured intelligence, chronological age, or grade placement (Wright *et al.* 1996). There appears to be little evidence that dyslexia is more or less prevalent among Maori than in any other ethnic group in New Zealand. However, it is possible that some Maori have been wrongly labelled 'dyslexic' when there is present a learning difficulty that could be better ascribed to other sources. According to Spreen (1988) it is important to stress that movement in and out of the dyslexic group is due to a large number of variables which can potentially affect reading development: family background, behaviour variables and cognitive variables. In addition, socialisation values are reflected in how well the participation structures match those that children are familiar with in their home culture (McNaughton 1995). Maori socialisation patterns identify older siblings and extended family as being expected to take immediate responsibility for the needs of the younger siblings. Taking into consideration McNaughton's contentions, attention needs to be directed toward continued research being carried out at the Poutama Pounamu Centre for Excellence.

Classroom culture and learning environment

This has to be viewed as pivotal and fundamental in providing the strong foundation which is necessary to support the successful implementation of appropriate and effective strategies. Classroom culture needs to embrace the true wairua (spirit) of the Treaty of Waitangi, this country's founding document, including those of tino rangitiratanga (self-determination), participation and cultural identity.

The following principles should be interwoven throughout classroom programmes and practices:

- Taha wairua: spiritual well-being of the students and the learning environment.
- Taha tinana: physical – the body.
- Taha whanau: family – the need to include the family in all aspects of, and decisions regarding, learning.
- Whakapapa: cultural identity – including the whanau (family), hapu (sub-tribe), and iwi (tribe), how they connect together, and how the student fits into them.

In order to implement these principles, the class first needs to establish itself and operate as a 'team', which can then be regarded, and referred to, as a whanau (family). This process includes establishing the 'culture' of the classroom, deciding on the rules, outlining the routines and expectations and creating a 'warm' physical environment. Children should have ongoing opportunities to assist and help here; they need to be able to contribute in areas of decision making and the establishing and maintenance of the classroom kawa (protocols, rules, systems).

Tino rangitiratanga (self-determination) can be encouraged by way of goal setting, monitoring and evaluation, recognising the importance of making good choices; and thus achieving positive consequences.

Taha wairua (spiritual well-being) is able to be established through teaching the importance of respect and manners, valuing differences, beliefs, others' ideas and contributions, encouraging and supporting others, promoting a quiet and calm environment, and the use of timely and sincere positive reinforcement. Teachers need to ensure that they model these behaviours in all interactions in the classroom.

Taha whanau recognises that children's families should be encouraged and allowed to participate in all areas of learning and be communicated to and with at every opportunity.

Whakapapa (cultural identity) recognises that preferred learning styles must be valued and catered for. Learning activities need to allow some degree of choice, and provide options, which best suit the preferred learning styles of children when responding to learning opportunities, activities and lessons. Cooperative learning and peer-tutoring, those preferred by Maori children, are excellent strategies which encourage supportive learning and team cooperation, and are proven to minimise 'failure' for many less able children, while enhancing the learning of the more able.

Finally, a safe environment; one free of verbal and physical abuse, one with clearly set and consistently applied boundaries and routines, and one which encourages problems and concerns to be addressed and dealt with openly, needs to be established.

Teaching and learning strategies

In order to enhance the learning of Maori students identified as having specific learning difficulties (dyslexia), strategies best employed are those which accept and acknowledge the tikanga (values) and kawa (protocols) of Maori culture.

Many of the teaching approaches for use with dyslexic children (Reid 1998) are consistent with the preferred Maori learning styles outlined by Metge (1984). They include such approaches as:

- Adopting a holistic perspective when working with a child who may be diagnosed as dyslexic. This would include knowing about and accommodating the child's preferred learning style.
- Implementing assisted learning techniques which can include programmes involving peer or adult support and incorporate the important principles of modelling.
- Overlearning or rote learning (e.g. chants) are important aspects of a multisensory approach (oral, visual, auditory, tactile, and kinaesthetic) to learning, in particular the opportunity to be exposed to a wide variety of oral literature.
- Use of rhymes, alliterations and patterning are important components for children acquiring knowledge and skills about sounds. This then lays the foundations for confident transmission of oral knowledge. Such oral knowledge acquired through rote learning strategies is not superficial learning but rather learning that is as complex as it is deep (Glynn and Bishop 1995).
- Strong family links where every member of the whanau has a contribution to make in the belief that people learn from each other and that learning is an ongoing, lifelong process.
- Taped assisted reading is a highly structured and sequential step method of teaching reading where the student moves to the next level once mastery (or criteria) has been reached.
- Paired reading structures where children of similar reading abilities read to each other in turn. One child reads and the other listens. Topping (1996) suggests the strategy of paired reading can reduce the anxieties of reading for dyslexic children, reduce their all-consuming fear of failure and encourage reading practice.

While there are a number of similarities between recognised and adopted approaches to the teaching of dyslexic children and many of the principles by which Maori children best learn, there is one significant difference in teaching and learning approaches. Many individual programmes (e.g. Letterland) are a common strategy when working with dyslexic children. However this strategy is not appropriate when working with Maori children who may be experiencing specific learning difficulties (including dyslexia), as their preferred learning medium is to be part of a group. Withdrawal or exclusion from the group or class does present additional barriers to Maori learning in that such an approach can heighten a sense of inadequacy or failure on the part of the child.

Therefore cooperative learning structures and peer-tutoring (especially reciprocal peer-tutor–tutee situations) learning environments form an essential part of a holistic approach to learning. Also for Maori children the relationship between the teacher and the learner may be more critical than the quality of the programmes devised and implemented. Rei (cited in Tapine and Waiti 1997) links teacher interaction with children and the encouragement of participation to the overall self-motivation and happiness of children. The teacher must promote the individual and encourage communication within the classroom environment, allowing learners to express their ideas freely, and valuing their contributions so that they become part of the learning process.

Conclusion

In conclusion, when working with Maori children from bicultural backgrounds in Aotearoa, who are experiencing specific learning difficulties (dyslexia), the required approach in terms of responding to their needs, is more a holistic one rather than one employing specific strategies targeted at remediation and/or addressing deficit. The approach needs to encompass a range of components, and must embrace the cultural dimensions of Maoridom. Failure by teachers to apply these practices is tantamount to doing a disservice to Maori children, as it fails to acknowledge the importance and value of culture.

A holistic approach to lifelong learning is best encapsulated in the following Maori proverb:

Ehara taku toa I te toa takitahi
Engari taku toa I te toa takitini
My strength does not lie in working alone
Rather my strength lies in working with others.

Glossary of terms

Aotearoa	New Zealand
ako	to learn as well as teach
aroha	love
awhina	help, assist, support
hapu	sub-tribe
hui	gathering, meeting, workshop
iwi	tribe, race, people
kaiawhina	support tutor
kapa haka	team performing dance
karakia	prayer, incantation
kaumatua	older person
kaupapa	strategy, purpose
kawa	protocol
kohikohinga	word grouping
Kohanga Reo	nursery, preschool
koroua	old man
kuia	old woman
Maori	native New Zealander
mana	integrity, respect
mihimihi	greeting
pakeha	non-Maori European

pakiwaitara	story-telling
powhiri	formal greeting, ritual of encounter
raranga	weaving
tapu	sacred, restricted
tauparapara	chants
teina	tutee
te reo	language
te reo maori	Maori language
tikanga	protocol, values, customs
tinana	oneself, body, physical
tinorangatiratanga	self-determination
tuakana	tutor
tukutuku	weaving
tuhi ata tuhi mai	written feedback
waiata	song
waiata moteatea	ancient song, verse
wairua	spirit, intent
whakairo	carving
whanau	family, team
whakapapa	genealogy, cultural identity
whakaputa whakaaro	brainstorming
whakatauki	proverb
whakawhanaungatanga	forming relationships, networking

Chapter 16

Bilingualism or Dyslexia – Language Difference or Language Disorder?

Elizabeth Dianne Frost

This chapter:

- deals with some key issues regarding diagnosis and misdiagnosis of bilingual dyslexic children
- ascertains the role bilingualism may play in written language difficulties and
- relates these findings to a relevant study.

Introduction

Bilingualism

As far back as 1977 Hornby defined bilingualism in the following way: 'Bilingualism is an individual characteristic that may exist to varying degrees from minimum ability to complete fluency in more than one language' (Hornsby 1977).

In 1984 Hornsby defined dyslexia as: 'difficulty in learning to read and write – particularly in learning to spell correctly and to express your thoughts on paper – which affects those who have had normal schooling and do not show backwardness in other subjects' (Hornsby 1996).

The case that follows highlights the issues that are inherent in the above definitions.

Summary of case

The case concerns a girl born in Switzerland in 1973 to a Norwegian father and English mother. The language spoken in the home was English and the language outside the home Swiss German. By the age of six, when the family moved to Norway, she spoke both languages fluently. In Norway, English continued to be the home language, but Swiss German was replaced by Norwegian outside the home.

During her first year in Norway the girl attended preschool, and the following year, at the age of seven, started primary school. Her language difficulties, particularly with written language, were first registered when she was nine years old and persist today. At the age of 25 she attained a reading age of 12.6 on the Schonell reading test and a spelling age of 10.8 on the Schonell spelling test. Some errors taken from essays she wrote at the age of 17 will help to illustrate the nature of her difficulties:

her, hear	for 'here'
bee, by, bye	for 'be'
nezt, neckst	for 'next'
soccocicetyk	for 'society'

We see here errors typical of dyslexia: an example of homophone confusion, various attempts at spelling the simple word 'be' (she said she often tries spelling this in five or six different ways in an essay hoping that one may be right), a reliance on phonics in attempts to spell 'next', and finally a rather bizarre spelling for 'society'.

The assessment and case study brought to light other characteristics of dyslexia, examples of which follow. A poor visual memory causes the young woman to rely heavily on memory tricks to recall spellings. She has difficulty with memorising basic words, unusual spellings and rules for the use of punctuation and capital letters. In addition, she experiences problems with sequencing, including the alphabet, and is slow when using a dictionary. She also exhibits some confusion with phonics, for example, certain consonant clusters such as the difference between the /kj/ and /skj/ sounds in Norwegian. Moreover, she experiences right/left confusion, difficulty when trying to read maps and has a poor concept of time.

Her attitude to writing is best summed up in her own words:

I dare not write notes to people.
I only write letters to people I know very well.
I write unclearly so that letters may not be identified.
I am always nervous when I have to communicate something in writing.

This fear of writing is exemplified by a situation which arose when the girl was 18 and had a holiday job in a department store. Asked to put a notice on the lift saying it was out of order she did not dare write it for fear of making mistakes. The purpose of the following literature study was to ascertain whether such a cluster of difficulties could be attributable to bilingualism rather than to a specific learning difficulty.

The effects of early bilingualism on language development

As the child was born and grew up in a bilingual situation, it was important to examine the effects of early bilingualism on language skills. Theories concerning the effects of early bilingualism on language development can be divided according to whether they suggest negative or positive consequences. Many early studies, carried out from around 1920 to 1960, indicated that bilingualism exerted a negative influence on children's academic development. A study carried out by Pinter and Keller (1922), for example, reported 'a linguistic handicap' in bilingual children. Such studies led to the widespread belief that bilinguals suffered from some sort of deficit as a result of having to learn two languages. Indeed, bilingualism was regarded 'almost as a disease' (Cummins 1984) by many teachers.

From about 1960 onwards, results of studies have taken a more positive view and indicated that there may be cognitive advantages associated with bilingualism. As young children are the best learners of foreign languages, it is assumed that bilingualism is positive. Cummins (1984) indicates that:

> Bilinguals mature earlier than monolinguals both in terms of cerebral lateralisation for language and in acquiring skills for linguistic abstraction. Bilinguals have better developed auditory language skills than monolinguals but there is no clear evidence that they differ from monolinguals in written skills.
>
> (Cummins 1984)

An attempt to explain these contradictory findings was made by Cummins (1976, 1979, 1981b). He propounded the *developmental interdependence hypothesis*. This suggests that children can attain high levels of competence in their second language (L2) if their mother tongue (L1) is well developed. On the other hand, if skills in L1 are not well developed, and early education takes place entirely in L2, then further development of the mother tongue will be delayed, and this, in turn, will exert a limiting effect on the acquisition of L2. In addition, he suggested the *threshold hypothesis*. This suggests that a certain minimum or threshold of competence must be attained in both L1 and L2, before the aspects of bilingualism which may positively influence cognitive growth may be effective. If a child's two languages are both definitely underdeveloped, there may be cognitive disadvantages for the bilingual child.

The opinion that bilingualism has no major effect, either positive or negative, on the development of children is becoming more widespread. This position is summed up by McLaughlin (1978):

> almost no general statements are warranted by research on the effects of bilingualism. It has not been demonstrated that bilingualism has positive or negative consequences for intelligence, linguistic skills, educational attainment, emotional adjustment or cognitive functioning.
>
> (McLaughlin 1978)

While early research therefore emphasised the negative effects of bilingualism on the academic development of children, most recent research findings seem to refute the assumption that bilingualism per se is a cause of academic difficulties. Disadvantages, however, resulting from being below the minimum threshold level in two or more languages could make the learning situation more difficult, particularly for a child with a degree of dyslexia.

Cultural and social aspects of bilingualism

As bilingualism is inextricably woven into the cultural and social environment in which it is found, any attempt to discover the effects of bilingualism on learning must take such factors into consideration.

The relative social status of languages may affect attitudes towards them and their users and the type of bilingualism resulting from their use. Lambert (1974, 1977) distinguishes between *additive* and *subtractive* forms of bilinguality. *Additive bilinguality* occurs where the community, family and the child attribute positive values to the two languages concerned. Here, the learning of the second language will not threaten the mother tongue. *Subtractive bilinguality* occurs when the new language is more prestigious than the mother tongue. In this case L2 will tend to replace L1 in the child's repertoire. The danger involved here is that children whose mother tongue is not sufficiently developed are likely to be disadvantaged in acquiring their second language.

While it is important to develop the mother tongue, it is also essential that the child should acquire the majority language as quickly as possible in order to avoid possible social isolation and rejection. During the initial stages of learning, the child's possibility for contact with his/her peers will be limited because of limited language possibilities, and s/he may be thought of as uninteresting, or even stupid. When such an opinion is formed it is often difficult to change and may persist with that group of acquaintances (Hvenekilde 1994). This can lead to the development of low esteem on the part of the newcomer with accompanying educational, psychological and social problems.

Thus where learning difficulties are present, cultural and social factors related to bilingualism, such as negative attitudes towards language and possible social isolation, may well make an already difficult educational situation more stressful and impede language acquisition.

Bilingualism and schooling (with particular reference to Norway)

When considering the consequences educational factors may have for bilingual learners, the following issues are of interest in the context of this case: academically related aspects of language proficiency, the importance of mother tongue teaching, and factors concerning schooling in Norway. As an education system reflects the political environment in which it exists, relevant political attitudes will also be considered.

Academically related aspects of language proficiency

Immigrant children often learn to communicate effectively in their new language in everyday situations within a relatively short time. The development of language necessary for the development of academic language skills, however, takes much longer. These two types of language skills were termed *basic interpersonal communication skills* (BICS) and *cognitive academic language proficiency* (CALP) by Cummins (1984). While a child may acquire surface fluency fairly rapidly and thus appear to have a good command of the language, Cummin's research (1981b) has shown that it takes five to seven years for children starting school in a second language to reach a level of academic language proficiency equivalent to native speakers. Bilingual children may thus be disadvantaged throughout this period.

Mother tongue teaching

As the development of the child's mother tongue is directly related to competence in a second language, it is important that this development be furthered in school. Hall (1995), in her guide to teachers working in multilingual schools, recommends that schools encourage use of the mother tongue in the classroom. Both this language and the child's culture should be given high status by the school, and not only valued but developed and utilised. She emphasises that children whose home language is not well established before starting school are likely to be at a disadvantage, as their underlying conceptual and linguistic proficiency will be insufficiently developed to aid transfer to their second language. Mother tongue instruction will help them develop adequate cognitive language skills.

Reference to Norway
In Norway, an attempt to meet the needs of bilingual pupils has been the provision of mother tongue teaching. This provision has varied in accordance with changing political attitudes towards immigrants, attitudes which have varied from a *melting pot* attitude, aiming to assimilate foreigners into Norwegian society, to a *salad bowl* attitude, favouring integration of newcomers into a pluralistic society.

Until very recently Norwegian society has been homogeneous. When non-Norwegian speaking pupils first began to arrive in numbers in the 1970s, the aim was to assimilate them into Norwegian society as quickly as possible: they were to learn Norwegian and become Norwegian (Hvenekilde 1994). As results of research into multiculturalism and bilingualism began to be known, attitudes began to change and in 1978 it was recommended that immigrant pupils should be offered mother tongue teaching. Provision of this varied throughout the country, and teaching was, and still is, usually offered out of school hours and at a venue outside the child's regular school. By not integrating L1 teachers in the school system and giving them instead a peripheral position, Jakobsen (1997), claims that the authorities are reinforcing the minority, low status both of the teachers themselves and of the languages they teach.

Political attitudes and their reflection on the education system may therefore have repercussions for the bilingual learner. Possible consequences of neglect of mother tongue teaching are that the development of the first language and, as a consequence, learning in a second may suffer. This could again aggravate an already difficult situation for a child with specific learning difficulties.

Identification and assessment of learning difficulties in a bilingual child

The problem here is to distinguish between second language learners who perform poorly at school due to limited knowledge of their new language and/or cultural differences, and those who have specific learning difficulties requiring special educational intervention. If the bilingual child has a written language problem, is it a consequence of difficulty with L2, or is it due to a dyslexic learning difficulty?

Assessment involves avoiding two errors (Hall 1995). The first is the danger of diagnosing a dyslexic type of learning difficulty where none is present – this is termed *false positive labelling*. The second is failing to diagnose a learning difficulty where one exists and therefore failing to give appropriate help at an early stage. The result of this is that difficulties may become more entrenched and difficult to manage. Children may be left for years without proper assessment and help on the assumption that, because of their bilingualism, they just need more time. This is termed *false negative labelling*.

Another difficulty involved in assessing bilingual children is the linguistic and cultural bias of standardised tests which are very often given in the majority language and based on the culture of the dominant group. According to Hall (1995: 13), there is 'no test which serves to answer the question of whether or not a bilingual child has learning difficulties'. If this is so, how then may a bilingual child who is experiencing language problems be assessed? Ann Robson, an educational psychologist, states that she is unable to make a decision about a bilingual child without checking a certain amount of 'crucial' information. This includes details of the child's family, medical, linguistic and educational history, in addition to a comprehensive picture of the child's situation at the time, including community and classroom context, family status and evidence from other professionals involved. Without such a full examination, she maintains, there is a risk that wrong assumptions may be made.

The language in which children are assessed is also significant as the risk of misidentification is greater when children are assessed in a language they have not mastered. Language disorders or difficulties may be more reliably identified if children are evaluated by persons fluent both in L2 and the child's native language. This is important, as true disabilities are usually unrelated to a particular language, and a commonly cited indicator of disability in second language learners is that the disability expresses itself across languages.

The adequacy of school and classroom practice is also important. Where bilingual pupils are found to have difficulties of a dyslexic nature, a collaborative approach is desirable. Bilingual, special needs, and class teachers and parents should work as a team to formulate a suitable response to the child's needs. Schools should try to establish reliable systems for recording and reporting so that pupils are neither wrongly labelled or overlooked. In this context, reference to Norway in the 1970s is again relevant. According to Vik (1976), the education system of that time lacked systematic testing and evaluation tools. She claims that harm and injustice were done to children due to the lack of ongoing evaluation and diagnostic information.

It is clear that difficulties involved in identification and assessment of learning difficulties in bilingual children mean that there is a greater risk of misidentification and a thorough examination of the case is therefore necessary to ensure that wrong assumptions are not made.

Implications from the literature for case study

In 1979, when the child moved to Norway, the influence of early, more negative theories about bilingualism was still prevalent there, as was the melting pot or assimilation attitude towards immigrant children. On starting preschool the child was able to speak very little Norwegian and was rejected by her peers because she spoke 'funny'. She was to remain with this same peer group throughout her nine years of compulsory schooling and the wounds caused by the rejection she experienced during this early period never healed. Repercussions of this, both social and educational, were to affect her into adulthood. Socially, she experienced problems because she was never included in the group of girls who lived close by her and with whom it would have been natural to socialise, and educationally, because the situation caused her to allow social rather than academic considerations to influence her choice of school and subjects at upper secondary level. This resulted in her later having to spend greater time and effort in achieving her academic goals.

The social rejection experienced led to the development of a form of *subtractive bilingualism*. Although the child's native language, English, may be considered a high status language internationally, to her peers it was simply unknown and different. To them, the child was a stranger to Norwegian ways, could not speak their language properly, and it seemed, an object of rejection. Their treatment of her affected her attitude towards her mother tongue and she in turn began to reject English. A *subtractive bilingual* situation developed with Norwegian tending to replace English in the child's repertoire.

By the time she started school the child was well on the way to mastering *basic interpersonal communication skills* in her new language, but her development of *cognitive academic language proficiency* would have been at an elementary stage. Unfortunately, her mother tongue, which could have aided the development of cognitive language skills, was not utilised in the classroom. This is perhaps not surprising considering the pervading attitudes concerning bilingualism and assimilation at the time.

Repeatedly, in her third to sixth years at school, the child was reported to be struggling with reading and writing in Norwegian. She received extra help from a speech therapist for a short period at the age of 11, but, as she was generally bright, it was considered that her problems were due to bilingualism and would disappear with time. At this age she began to learn English as a foreign language at school. Here, similar problems manifested themselves and it was reported that her written work was not up to the standard of her oral. (Such problems also affected her learning of German, which she started at the age of 13.) The girl remembers the English lessons as being torturous as the teacher presumed that being able to speak the language she would also be able to spell it, and often asked her to write words on the blackboard.

Despite the fact that problems manifested themselves in English, no assessment was carried out in that language. A thorough investigation of the child's background and situation at that time might have helped compensate for this, but only a limited picture of the child's circumstances was obtained by the school. While there was communication between the class teacher and the speech therapist, there was none between the speech therapist and the parents. Knowing little about dyslexia, the parents believed that their child's problems were due to her language situation, as the school said, and would disappear with time.

In addition to English lessons at school, the child started to attend extra-curricular English mother-tongue classes. Unfortunately, she disliked going to these lessons intensely and stopped after a very short period. The reasons for this were threefold: firstly, she said that she was expected to write and hated having to do that; secondly, she did not want to be different from the other children and wished to concentrate on being Norwegian; and thirdly, classes were held after school at a rather inaccessible venue. As she was experiencing such social problems, her parents, not realising the importance of mother tongue development, thought it best to allow her to discontinue the lessons. Had there been communication between the mother tongue teacher, the school and the parents this may have been avoided. Here, Cummin's *developmental interdependence hypothesis* springs to mind. The lack of development of her L1 would have negatively affected the development of L2. In this context it should be remembered that the child's language situation was further complicated by her having had a third language, German, as L2 until the age of six.

The level of her L1 development was therefore lower than it would have been had she spent her early years in a monolingual environment. The question which then arises is whether her two languages, English and Norwegian, could have been underdeveloped to a level below that of Cummin's lower threshold of bilingual proficiency when she started school with concomitant negative affects.

Interviews with teachers

Two interviews were carried out. The first was held with the class teacher who taught the child during her first three years at school. She said that the language mistakes made by the pupil were not unusual for children of that age, but that they continued to be made was disturbing. As the child was quick in other subjects it was thought that her mixed language background was to blame, but in the light of the problems having persisted the teacher would now query the conclusion reached at that time.

The second interview was held with the English mother tongue teacher. She remembered the child being a weak speller, having a weak visual memory and lacking in confidence. Had she known more about the problems she said she would have done more to try to help. Communication between the school and mother tongue teacher would have been advantageous here.

Conclusion

The findings of this study concern bilingual children who exhibit difficulties with written language. While bilingualism per se has not been found to be the cause of written language disorders, it has been seen that associated factors – in particular social, cultural, political and/or educational attitudes and practices – may make an already difficult learning situation more stressful, and thus exacerbate problems and impede progress. Correct identification and assessment of language disorders/difficulties is of utmost importance in a bilingual child as incorrect labelling may result in the lack of, or giving of inappropriate support. The case in question here would appear to be one of false negative labelling. That is, of failing to diagnose a dyslexic type of difficulty where one is present. This being the case, early identification and the giving of appropriate support might have helped avoid some of the academic struggle and embarrassment experienced by this young woman in connection with her language skills throughout both her private life and academic career.

Given the attitudes and knowledge available in Norway during the early 1980s, it is perhaps not surprising that this child's written language difficulties were attributed to bilingualism. Had the difficulties been of a more extreme nature, they would not have been misinterpreted. It is children whose difficulties are relatively mild who are likely to be falsely labelled. A full and careful examination of the factors which may be causing difficulty, including adequacy of classroom practice, is necessary if the bilingual child's real needs are to be assessed at a sufficiently early stage.

We have seen that complex contributory factors may easily blur the picture of the learning situation of bilingual children making it difficult to pinpoint the root of problems. Internal factors within the child, such as possible learning disorders, are interlinked with the nature of the bilingualism and external dimensions in the place of domicile. Some children will master such a situation and thrive, while others may flounder. What is vital is that each individual case should be analysed on its multiple levels so that a correct analysis may be made and suitable help given.

Fortunately, as knowledge resulting from research is being applied, teachers are becoming better informed and there should be less occurrence of false labelling situations. The establishment of improved routines in schools will, hopefully, enable better informed decisions to be made about the difference between the problems arising from lack of L2 language acquisition, and those resulting from language disorders of a dyslexic nature.

Chapter 17

Special Education or Second Language Training: What do Bilingual Children Need?

Anne Marie Kidde

This chapter:

- describes a developmental project in two mainstream schools in Copenhagen – Danish in mainstream classes, the DMK project 92-95
- focuses on assessment materials and methods of teaching Danish
- describes collaborative methods between bilingual pupils and parents
- provides an evaluation of the validity of tests
- and provides suggestions for good pedagogical test practice in relation to bilingual children.

Bilingual children in Denmark

Bilingual families have mainly settled in and around Copenhagen, the capital of Denmark, and in the larger cities. A variety of different ethnic groups are represented but the largest groups are Turkish, Pakistani and Arab-speaking pupils of whom many will be of second, third or fourth generation.

The Danish school system

According to Danish legislation all children between 7 and 16 who are domiciled in Denmark are entitled to compulsory education. Most pupils attend folkeskolen which means 'the school for all' and which comprises both normal and special education.

Special education falls within the same legislation and has the same educational goals as teaching in the normal schools. It is given as remedial instruction and is not organised on the basis of fixed categories but is flexible in order to meet the requirements of pupils whose development and function require special consideration and support. All pupils who attend school are entitled to education and remedial instruction according to their special needs.

Two central principles for special education in Denmark are:

- minimal intervention and
- inclusion.

Remedial instruction is offered to bilingual children as to all children with special needs following the structure used for Danish pupils. The latest pedagogical debate and descriptions from special schools have pointed out that the tools and measurements used in the assessment procedure need clarification and adjustment in relation to bilingual pupils. All assessments for special education involve educational psychologists and speech therapists. Other specialists can be called on to give supplementary information of varying aspects of children's functioning if required.

Mother tongue lessons

According to Danish legislation bilingual pupils are entitled to instruction in their own language. A prerequisite for setting up mother tongue lessons is that a minimum of 12 pupils enrol. This tuition is free and voluntary and is given in addition to the timetable, but there are attempts to provide coherence between mother tongue teaching and the content of the curriculum.

Bilingual teachers

In schools with a high percentage of bilingual pupils, bilingual teachers teach the mother tongue and take part in daily teaching. They also cooperate with Danish teachers in order to serve as educational/language/cultural mediators within the lessons and consult with parents, other teachers, psychologists and health staff. Mother tongue teaching has been viewed as essential to the language development of the bilingual child.

How do you teach the subject Danish in a multicultural class?

The DMK project

The developmental project 'Danish in multicultural classes' focused on materials and methods of teaching Danish. Six hundred pupils in two mainstream schools were monitored according to their attainments in literacy during this three-year period. The classes comprised of 7 to 12 ethnic groups. No special arrangements were made. The aim of the developmental project was to look at the multicultural population as a whole and describe central aspects in teaching the subject Danish in a multicultural setting.

The project focused on two aspects:

a) Teachers' evaluation of their own teaching practice

Teachers in Danish were asked to reflect on the suitability of their teaching, the material and methods regarding the whole multicultural group. The teachers presented a detailed teaching plan for the year and described detailed themes or subjects they had worked on commenting on specific considerations that had been taken to meet the needs of the whole group, including bilingual children. This material has been presented in three books which provide ideas for teaching reading, writing and literature in Danish. (Kidde 1997a, 1997b, 1999).

b) Diagnostic criteria

Screening tests in reading, comprehension and spelling were used to measure attainments of bilingual children. An evaluation of the validity of the tests was considered and aspects of test construction and administration were also evaluated. Instructions needed to be clear, understandable and short. In addition to oral instructions the tester had to create illustrations on the blackboard to ensure that bilingual children had a clear understanding of the task.

It is a long-standing issue as to whether standard reading tests for groups developed in a western society will be reliable in relation to a multicultural group. Interest has mainly been placed on the test material itself and the use of test standard results. It has been pointed out that it would not be a proper task to ask a bilingual child to read and identify pictures which were unfamiliar to him/her. For instance churches (instead of minarets) would be words belonging to a context which would be remote from some children's reality.

Other investigators have pointed out that the purpose of testing is also to get an impression of the reading qualifications of the child in relation to the schools system and teaching in which the child is actually being taught. All readers need:

- good and relevant pre-comprehension
- good decoding skills
- linguistic competence
- rich vocabulary
- an active attitude towards reading.

Miscue analysis

Bilingual children often score significantly lower than their monolingual peers in normative tests with the result that special education is suggested in cases where some other form of support is needed. During the working process with the outcomes from the tests, differentiation in categories concerning good and more insecure readers was subject to investigation as well as the diagonal dimension. As the material was fairly substantial it was possible to identify specific tasks in the test material where a drawing or a particular word proved to be difficult to a majority of bilingual pupils. These observations were also taken into account when deciding the kind of support the child would need. The teacher should bear in mind this aspect when interpreting results and before deciding which measurements for support are needed.

Structure of testing

Younger children (grades 1–2) had their language sensibility pre-reading understanding, reading development and reading skills examined to see whether they were able to decode letters and syllables and transform it to reading.

The middle group (grades 3–6) were tested regarding their reading accuracy 'technical reading skills'. Furthermore their reading comprehension was measured. Writing skills were also tested with different spelling and orthographic tests.

The eldest group (grades 7–10) were examined to study their reading capability concerning text understanding. Also the orthographic skills in writing were tested so as to ensure the understanding of written instructions as well as oral instruction.

Intervention

The study revealed that children in kindergarten classes needed concrete, well-structured and activity-filled teaching. Phonological awareness, work with rhymes and telling fairytales are important parts of kindergarten activities. Teachers do not find these activities useful in a multicultural setting because it is difficult for a bilingual child with a limited understanding of Danish to concentrate and be an active listener. Therefore pictures, videos, slides and other material presented along with reading aloud can help to create a peaceful working atmosphere while at the same time stimulating the language and concepts of bilingual pupils. Kindergarten class teachers reported it to be effective to support small groups of bilingual children who had equal linguistic competence in Danish whereas it did not seem to matter so much whether the children belonged to the same ethnic group.

Younger children (grades 1–2)

Parallel reading development was found with bilingual and Danish monolingual children acquiring reading skills. However bilingual children tended to learn at a slower pace and the quality of their reading development depended on the simultaneous development of language and concepts in their second language (Danish).

The teachers' evaluation of their teaching showed that a variety of different presentations of material improved both learning and reading. Visualisation in combination with oral presentation and use of mimics, gestures and singing help children to acquire reading skills. All the teachers reported that it was important that a variety of different methods were employed during the first stages of reading instruction. A multisensory system must be employed – phonological awareness must be developed at the same time as children look at cards or overheads with letters and illustrations of objects to develop language and concepts. The letters should be drawn, cut out, painted and formed from different materials. The most important activity is to use words alongside activities which make children verbalise.

Recently another developmental project in Denmark (Nielsen 1997) has proved that bilingual children learn to read and acquire decoding skills at the same levels as Danish children, but highlighted that it is important to ensure that reading comprehension develops satisfactorily.

The middle group (grades 3–6)

Bilingual children in grades 3–6 generally had a technical reading capacity that matched their Danish peers but at the same time some of the bilingual children had comprehension difficulties. Bilingual readers had difficulties other than decoding that prevented them from fulfilling the task. They often lacked knowledge of prepositions and inflectional endings. Miscue analysis would highlight this and comprehension tests would demonstrate more clearly the child's reading ability. It should be borne in mind that even though the bilingual child has failed a particular task, this should not necessarily be taken as evidence of reading disabilities. Teachers recommended that all children should be introduced to a great variety of materials and themes during lessons. It is emphasised that this will improve bilingual children's communication and comprehension skills.

The eldest group (grades 7–10)

Tests on this group showed that if their schooling had been unbroken they would be able to read technically without problems to the same standard as their Danish peers. It was shown that many bilingual pupils had difficulties in understanding the contextual meaning and they would have difficulties in comparing and contrasting several pieces of information. Close analysis showed that bilingual pupils had difficulties with adverbs, prepositions and pronouns, which are very important for the understanding of nuances in texts. Failure in solving these tasks in relation to bilingual children may not be an indication of dyslexia but must be taken as an indicator that the pupils need help to improve their comprehension skills in the second language. Teachers' awareness is critical because linguistic skills in this area are important in test situations and in examinations where the pupils will have to be able to decode questions and understand the structure of exercises.

The results of the study revealed that many bilingual children had expressive language difficulties in relation to their reading capacity. In cases where all questions were multiple choice and the child had to decide which answer was correct, it was clearly easier for bilingual pupils to cope even with difficult subjects which needed consideration. Many bilingual children seem to have difficulties expressing themselves. They get stuck with the words used in the original text and have difficulties finding their own words. Corresponding comprehension difficulties were only seen with Danish children with severe reading difficulties

Teachers found it important to urge bilingual pupils to have a more positive attitude towards reading and to support them with their second language development. This should not take place within the framework of special education. Support should be given both through discussion with the class teacher and related to subjects taught in class. The bilingual child should be prepared in advance for new subjects and themes so that s/he will already have an understanding of the subject which will be very useful in class.

Orthographic skills

In order to assess writing and spelling skills, a pedagogical analysis of the different kinds of errors was used. An analysis of the results found within bilingual and monolingual pupils showed that even competent bilingual spellers had difficulties with sound differentiation in vowels and consonants whereas they had good skills in orthographic areas which could be built on rules, i.e. grammatical rules or rules about 'hidden' letters which pronunciation would not identify.

Comments on best practice

Tests

In relation to bilingual children, normative tests and screening tests should be used with extra care. Picture material in tests will often require some cultural understanding. A bilingual child will have a double task both to 'read the word', 'understand the picture' and relate the picture to their own frame of reference.

When using individual reading test material it is very important, that the tester is sensitive with regard to pronunciation and intonation. Many bilingual children who use another language at home will speak with an accent which is different from native speakers, and when reading aloud teachers and psychologists who have limited experience of bilingual pupils will mistakenly identify failure as signs of dyslexia. It would be a good idea to have an overview of alphabets and phonological rules belonging to the predominant ethnic groups you meet in school. An analysis between the first and second language can come in useful. It is also advisable to consult a bilingual teacher if possible to obtain a detailed understanding of the specific disabilities found in bilingual children.

Qualitative test material is found to be very useful to bilingual children because it can be used to control reading comprehension. Results from these tests can be used both as an indicator of the kind of remedial instruction the bilingual child needs and can also be used in the educational planning for the whole class. Special educational assessment must include individual detailed tests including details of linguistic aspects of the bilingual child's mother tongue and length of stay in the present country of residence.

Reading and spelling errors, as we see them on the basis of tests, can appear similar with bilingual and with monolingual children but it is important to be aware of the fact that they should be treated differently. Special education should be chosen explicitly for pupils with severe decoding problems.

In both mainstream and special schools teachers must update their knowledge of how bilingual children acquire second language skills. Discussion between school, educational psychologist, the bilingual teacher and parents on the development of the child's reading capacity is very important and the best way to provide fruitful stimulation for the bilingual child.

Chapter 18

Rethinking Teacher Training Programmes for Linguistically Diverse Students with Dyslexia

Marjorie Hall Haley and Miriam H. Porter

This chapter:

- discusses the need to rethink pre- and in-service training programmes for general and special educators who teach linguistically diverse students with dyslexia
- provides an overview of existing teacher training programmes
- describes specific effective instructional strategies and practices for teachers of English to speakers of other languages (TESOL) and special education teachers
- provides a paradigm for teacher training programmes for teachers of linguistically diverse students with dyslexia and
- looks at the impact and influence of demographics and federal legislation.

Introduction

With projections that one in every three Americans in the United States will be Black, Hispanic, or Asian by the first few years of the new millennium, greater attention must be given to ensuring that multilingual/multicultural populations succeed in mainstream education. Those involved in decision-making processes need to understand how language, culture and other background characteristics influence performance. Changing demographics in the United States have often been cited as reasons to mandate training in multicultural and multilingualism for pre-service and in-service teachers (e.g. Garcia and Pugh 1992; Dunn 1993; Banks 1997). Bruder (1992) indicated that by the year 2010, California, Florida, Texas, and New York will contain one-third of all United States youth. In Texas and California, 57 per cent of those youth will be non-white and in New York and Florida, 53 per cent will be non-white. Linguistically diverse students should be served by general and special educators who have been effectively trained in how language and culture influence learning. Teacher preparation plays a vital role in providing both pre- and in-service educators with an understanding of linguistic, cultural, socio-economic and related variables, and their effects on the teaching-learning process. Additionally, training must include methods of using assessment data to plan instruction and to select, adapt, and/or develop curricula to meet the needs of linguistically diverse students with dyslexia.

Statement of the problem – building the case

Teacher training programmes are faced with the challenge of providing excellent teacher preparation. In the United States, the teaching force is facing an increasing number of linguistically diverse children, some of whom have multiple forms of dyslexia. This teaching force is not well equipped to help these children adjust to school and succeed. There are far too many teachers who do not share or know about their students' cultural or linguistic backgrounds and too few have had the professional preparation to work well with linguistically diverse students with dyslexia.

A large number of cases of dyslexic linguistically diverse students are classified as having learning disabilities and mental retardation. They are all too frequently taught by teachers with minimal training, if any, in both second language acquisition and special education. Most of the provision of special education services for these students takes place in self-contained and resource room classrooms. Due to the shortage of teachers in both bilingual and special education, most bilingual exceptional students receive instruction solely in English. Many problems may occur as a consequence of these students not receiving instruction in both their native language (L1) and their second language (L2). Some of the major issues are: (a) language delay in both the native language and second language, (b) delay in the acquisition of reading skills in both the native and second language, (c) learning problems related to the lack of instruction and appropriate transition from the native language to the second language, (d) behaviour problems associated with experiences of failure either in regular or special education, (e) increasing numbers of at-risk and drop-out students due to the lack of appropriate instruction in the L1 and L2, (f) cultural identity problems, and (g) poor self-esteem problems associated with cultural factors (Omark and Erickson 1983).

The impact of demographics

Prior to 1960, the majority of immigrants in the United States came from Europe. Since then, and most notably in the past ten years, the majority of immigrants have come from Asia, Central America, and the Caribbean. In addition, a number of non-immigrant groups such as Puerto Ricans and Mexican-Americans, are among the fastest growing ethnic/racial groups in the nation. By the year 2050, descendants of these groups – all non-white, and many, non-native speakers of English – are expected to represent 40 per cent of this country's population. According to the US Department of Education's Office for Educational Research and Improvement, in the ten-year period between 1979 and 1989, the total number of children aged 8 to 15 years enrolled in US schools who spoke a language other than English 'increased by 41 per cent' (Pallas *et al.* 1989: 22). This statistic is particularly noteworthy when one considers that during the same time period, overall school enrolment declined by 4 per cent (Pallas *et al.* 1989: 22). It is evident that the number of limited English proficient (LEP) students is growing. School officials who never before had to instruct these students are now finding they must meet this need. Additionally, the number of linguistically-diverse *and* special education trained personnel in these areas is limited, if not non-existent. Furthermore, in those districts that do offer English as a second language (ESL) special education classes for LEP students, there is little or no support services for these teachers. Similarly, there is a lack of specialised training for the classroom teachers who attempt to instruct these students for most of the school day. In addition to increased in-service training, as Sleeter (1992) postulated, there must be appropriate components relevant to this need included in pre-service teacher education programmes.

The demographic characteristics of today's classrooms are very different than they were 20 years ago and according to Banks (1997: 5) by the year 2020 'Whites will make up only 54.5 per cent of the nation's population' and students of colour will comprise 45.5 per cent of that population. This change in population brings new challenges for teachers. Not only do today's teachers work with 'regular' education children, but they must also educate the culturally and linguistically diverse, and address students with special needs. The Council for Exceptional Children (CEC) has recognised the need for training to include multicultural and multilingual components.

The CEC recognises the changing demographics stated above and that cultural and linguistic diversity will continue to increase while the number of culturally and linguistically different professionals entering the field of special education continues to decline. According to the CEC,

> Given the pervasive nature of diversity, professional standards are needed that guide professional practice in ways that are relevant to the multicultural populations served in special education. Specifically, these standards reflect the premise that, to design effective interventions, special educators must understand the characteristics of their learners, including factors such as culture, language, gender, religion, and sexuality.   (CEC 1996: 13)

States such as California, Texas, Florida, New York, Massachusetts, Connecticut, Michigan, Illinois, and Ohio, in which the population of linguistically diverse students has increased significantly, have initiated Bilingual Special Education programmes (Ortiz and Ramirez 1988). As a result, there has been a push to combine both bilingual education and special education to meet the needs of linguistically diverse exceptional students across the nation.

Although literature on culturally and linguistically diverse (CLD) students with disabilities is now more generally available, research on dyslexia and literacy occurring concomitantly with linguistic and cultural differences is virtually nonexistent. What is even scarcer is the amount of information on educating teachers to work in school settings with this ever-increasing population of students. The available literature calls attention to such issues as the disproportionate representation of language minority students in special education and the need for better prepared and trained teachers. There is also a great deal of attention paid to federal legislative compliance with regard to educating special needs students.

The influence of Federal Legislation

In the United States during the past ten years many empirical and legal issues related to the education of linguistically diverse students with disabilities have received special attention and litigation. According to Duran (1988) the right for appropriate special education services to linguistically diverse handicapped students was specifically established with the passage of Public Law 93-112, the Rehabilitation Act of 1973. As a direct result of the implementation of Public Law 94-142 in 1975, the Education Act for all Handicapped (EAH), and the Rehabilitation Act of 1973, Section 504, the individual needs of exceptional bilingual (linguistically diverse) students have received much needed attention (Ortiz and Ramirez 1988). Consequently, a process for providing special education to meet the individual needs of each student with disabilities was started. Since then, more than four million students have been identified as having some type of disability (Ortiz and Ramirez 1988). Individuals with Disabilities Education Act (IDEA) of 1997 strengthens the concept of least restrictive environment for children with disabilities. It can be argued that the provision of this environment, in the case of linguistically diverse students with dyslexia, requires teachers appropriately and effectively trained in both special education and English as a second language.

In spite of these federal laws, the majority of special education programmes as presently structured do not meet the needs of limited English proficiency dyslexic students. IDEA does not address the training or preparedness of teachers or the language of instruction issues. As a consequence, most special education programmes are staffed by teachers with little to no training for working with linguistically diverse student populations.

Overview of existing teacher training programmes and effective instructional strategies and practices for TESOL and special education teachers

The UTEEM (Unified Transformative Early Education Model) at George Mason University, Fairfax, Virginia, is the only one of its kind in the United States. This programme provides a triple endorsement: Early Childhood Education – PK-3; Early Childhood Special Education – Birth to Age 5; and, English as a Second Language – PK-12. This programme includes a Master of Education Degree. According to the programme's handbook, 'UTEEM is an innovative model for preparing graduate students to work with diverse young children and their families in inclusive early childhood settings. Teaching, learning activities and experiences integrate the perspective of three specializations...' (p. 1). Emphasis in this programme focuses on culturally diverse children with special needs who are second language learners. This is a component that should be a part of all training programmes, especially where there is a large culturally and linguistically diverse population.

Teachers working in culturally and linguistically diverse school settings must receive adequate training to better accommodate the needs of their dyslexic students. Appropriate identification and diagnosis are too often mishandled as teachers grapple with determining if a student is language different or language disordered.

Roseberry-McKibbin (1995) provides a checklist of 16 items to be used in determining if a student is language different or language disordered:

- Nonverbal aspects of language are culturally inappropriate.
- Student does not express basic needs adequately.
- Student rarely initiates verbal interaction with peers.
- When peers initiate interaction, student responds sporadically/inappropriately.
- Student replaces speech with gestures, communicates nonverbally when talking would be appropriate and expected.
- Peers give indications that they have difficulty understanding the student.
- Student often gives inappropriate responses.
- Student has difficulty conveying thoughts in an organized, sequential manner that is understandable to listeners.
- Student shows poor topic maintenance ('skips around').
- Student has word-finding difficulties that go beyond second language acquisition patterns.
- Student fails to provide significant information to the listener, leaving the listener confused.
- Student has difficulty with conversational turn-taking skills (may be too passive, or may interrupt inappropriately).
- Student perseverates (remains too long) on a topic even after the topic has changed.
- Student fails to ask and answer questions inappropriately.
- Student needs to hear things repeated, even when they are stated simply and comprehensibly.
- Student often echoes what she or he hears.

'If a linguistically and culturally diverse (LCD) student manifests a number of the above behaviors, even in comparison to similar peers, then there is a good chance that the student has an underlying language-learning disability and will need a referral to special education' (Roseberry-McKibbin 1995: 79). Currently, only special education teachers are provided with this information as a part of their course work in assessment for special education. Certainly this is information that needs to be shared with all teachers who work with this population of students.

Garcia (1991) reported the results of descriptive studies done in preschool, elementary and high schools where the culturally and linguistically diverse were found to be successful. The commonalities found among those classroom were as follows:

- Emphasis on functional communication between teachers and students and among students.
- Instruction was organized around thematic units.
- Instruction was organized so that students interacted with each other in cooperative learning situations.
- Students moved systematically from writing in their native language to writing in English with no pressure from the teacher.
- Teachers were highly committed to the success of the students.
- Principals were highly supportive of teachers while keeping aware of the need to conform to district policies.
- Parents from all cultures were involved in parent support activities and expressed satisfaction and appreciation for their children's experiences in school.

From the above findings, the following set of guidelines were suggested (Garcia 1991):

(1) curriculum, including that for diverse populations, should be intellectually challenging;
(2) academic content must be related to the experiences and environment of the culturally and linguistically different child;
(3) content areas and language learning should be centred around a single theme;
(4) students should be involved in active rather than passive activities;
(5) opportunities should be provided for children to apply what they have learnt in meaningful contexts.

The National Association for Bilingual Education (NABE) has created 'Portraits of Success' – a joint project that involved NABE, Boston College, and the Northeast and Islands Regional Educational Laboratory at Brown University. This is a continuing project which identifies characteristics of successful bilingual education programmes and promotes the implementation of quality bilingual education. One of the programmes identified was Greenway Middle School in Arizona. This Spanish transitional bilingual and ESL programme offered content area subjects in Spanish and sheltered-English and teachers were certified in a content area as well as in bilingual education and/or ESL.

Another model programme cited is Rachel Carson Elementary School – called Transitional Bilingual Education. Ninety-two per cent of the students at this school come from Spanish-speaking backgrounds. The school has a traditional bilingual Spanish programme and a dual language preschool programme. The principal and a number of the staff are bilingual (Brisk 2000). These are two of five model programmes described in the Brown University website. Programme nominations are continually accepted and must meet the following criteria: be within the pre-K-12 grade range; use two languages for academic instruction; have been in existence for at least three years; and, can show evidence of success for at least two years (portraits@lab.brown.edu).

Anstrom (1996) offers the following characteristics of effective instructional programmes for language minority students:

- Provide LEP students the opportunity for at least five years of special services before moving them to mainstream programmes.
- Avoid mainstreaming LEP students before they have acquired the necessary English language proficiency as this puts them at a disadvantage in developing academic skills.
- Allow students more time in special programmes in order to promote students' academic and social growth and adjustment.
- Include native language instruction to develop both academic proficiency and English language ability.
- Select native language instructional approach based on student characteristics, such as level of oral proficiency.
- Actively involve students in peer instruction to help them gain self-esteem, increase achievement, and develop new goals.
- Incorporate prior knowledge, skills, and abilities of students into the overall school curriculum.

- Focus on complex meaningful problems, embed basic skills instruction into the context of global tasks, and make connections with the students' out of school experiences and culture.
- Emphasise reading, language arts, and content-area instruction.
- Offer sheltered English as a Second Language class to provide content instruction.
- Organise and deliver instruction that engages students in academic learning.
- Monitor student progress and provide immediate feedback.
- Integrate English language development with academic skills development.
- Vary instructional delivery to include teacher-directed, individual and small-group activities.
- Build self-esteem and improve academic achievement by incorporating the students' cultures into classroom instruction.
- Encourage parent participation in school activities and goals.
- Build lessons from resources that exist within students' experience and backgrounds in order to promote more active student engagement and increased student learning.

The National Clearinghouse for Bilingual Education (NCBE) (1996) discusses the characteristics that define those schools that have been successful in educating highly diverse populations. Many of these characteristics have been noted above but bear repeating. For example, culturally and linguistically different students need to be included in 'challenging, core, academic classes'. Curriculum should be arranged in thematic units to allow students to see the relationships across academic disciplines. Additionally, the students' cultures should be incorporated into the curriculum. Other characteristics involve allowing students to study subjects that are relevant to their lives and organising students into cooperative learning groups.

Finally, parents are involved and communicated with on a regular basis. Berman et al. (1995) list seven lessons about exemplary practices and schools serving LEP students:

- A comprehensive school-wide vision provided an essential foundation for developing outstanding education for LEP students.
- Effective language development strategies were adapted to different local conditions in order to ensure LEP students access to the core curriculum.
- High quality learning environments for LEP students involved curricular strategies that engaged students in meaningful, in-depth learning across content areas led by trained and qualified staff.
- Innovative instructional strategies which emphasise collaboration and hands-on activities engaged LEP students in the learning process.
- A school-wide approach to restructuring schools' units of teaching, use of time, decision making, and external relations enhanced the teaching/learning environment and fostered the academic achievement of LEP students.
- External partners had a direct influence on improving the educational programme for LEP students.
- Districts played a critical role in supporting quality education for LEP students.

All of the above is supported by the study done by Thomas and Collier (1997) in which they, too, discuss the characteristics of effective programmes for culturally and linguistically different students. These researchers support allowing students to do their academic work, on grade level, in their first language. According to Thomas and Collier (1997) this will allow students to be more successful in the second language. They also suggest that these students must be provided a 'socio-culturally supportive environment' that is 'interactive with discovery learning' that allows students to work cooperatively (Thomas and Collier 1997: 50).

Case study

Liu Ha is a special education ESL mathematics teacher in a large, urban high school in Virginia in the United States. She is in her third year of teaching and complains that she is often very frustrated that general educators are extremely uninformed about working with dyslexic ESL students. Ms Ha was very quick to point out that there is a desperate need for crossover training between general educators and special education. 'Theoretically, inclusion works. But the training is not there. The course work in teacher training programmes needs to be very specific. Special education is the law and general education teachers need to know and understand that. Staff development and in-service workshops are important but training needs to take place at the pre-service, university level.'

Recommended paradigm for teachers of linguistically diverse students with dyslexia

Special educators and ESL educators need crossover training to deliver integrated services that account for children's second language and disability characteristics. Currently, a paucity of TESOL (Teachers of English to Speakers of Other Languages) programmes provide crossover training in special education, and few special education programmes encourage specialisations in TESOL. Professionals are left to find their own training opportunities at conferences and workshops and from these haphazard events to piece together the elements that formulate appropriate practice. Responsive Special Education/TESOL teacher training programmes would create a well-formulated and comprehensive sequence of new course offerings that would cover both the theoretical and practical issues in serving LEP students with disabilities.

A pedagogical framework for special and ESL education teacher training should require a minimum of 30 hours in course work and a full year student teaching internship. Basically, this programme would not differ from most general education or interdisciplinary graduate programmes. The following represent core courses which should be required for both special and ESL education training:

- Introduction to special education.
- Strategies and practices in teaming.
- Teaching reading and writing in multilingual/multicultural settings.
- Foundations of multilingual/multicultural education and pluralism.

- Second language acquisition and language learning.
- Standards-based teaching and learning.
- Curriculum development and instruction.
- Developmental psychology.
- Assessment.
- Educational technology.

Conclusion

It is estimated that in the United States 15 per cent of the general population has a learning disability (Monarez 1992: F3). It is possible that many of the ESL students whom we view as poor language learners are struggling because they too have a learning disability. Given changing demographics in the United States, all educators must face the reality of culturally and linguistically diverse students in today's classrooms. School districts which never before had to instruct these students are now finding they must address and meet this need. Frequently, the number of linguistically diverse and special education-trained personnel is limited. We must include training components relevant to this need in all teacher training programmes.

It is safe to say that there is an abundant need to diversify the education profession at practitioner, administrative, and personnel preparation levels in order to better serve culturally and linguistically diverse students with dyslexia. Furthermore, there is an urgency to rethink pre- and in-service training programmes for general and special educators who teach linguistically diverse students with dyslexia. As clearly evidenced in the changing demographics, this population will continue to grow and teachers must be adequately trained to meet the needs of these students.

Chapter 19

Diagnosing Multilingual Adults

Helen Sunderland

This chapter:

- looks at the question of whether or not it is possible to assess adult learners for dyslexia when they are still at the stage of learning English
- examines two case studies to highlight how far the above factors restrict and obstruct assessment and
- provides a list of critical factors to take into account when assessing dyslexia in multilingual learners.

Introduction

Multilingual dyslexic adults in the UK find themselves in a 'Catch 22' position. Their specific learning difficulties are impeding their progress in acquiring accurate written and spoken English and yet in many cases their educational providers say it is not possible to assess them for dyslexia because they have not yet acquired these English language skills. The inability of providers to assess such students for dyslexia means learners are denied the specialist support they need in order to progress. As Cline (Cline and Reason 1993) has said, it is an equal opportunities issue.

What are the difficulties in assessing multilingual learners for dyslexia? There are several factors that could be confusing. First, is it possible to tell whether students' difficulties are due to dyslexia or to the fact that they are learning English? Is knowledge of their own languages influencing how they use English? Then what about students' prior learning? If, for instance, students have had very little schooling, surely that will influence their ability to perform on the assessment. How far is cultural bias contributing to difficulties in understanding text?

Case studies

The two students in the case studies were assessed using a methodology for diagnosing adults derived from consultations with teachers and educational psychologists and subsequently developed by the London Language and Literacy Unit (Klein 1993; Sunderland *et al.* 1997). This involves an in-depth diagnostic interview; tests of short-term memory, phonological awareness, and sequencing; reading of whole text, single words and non-words and analysis of miscues; spelling error analysis and analysis of a piece of free writing. The names of the students have been changed.

Hawa

Hawa came to England in 1982 from Iran where she was a lawyer. In 1987 she tried and failed to follow the 'CPE', a course and examination that allows overseas trained lawyers to practise in this country. She then started and ran her own businesses. Now she wants to return to law.

Hawa's mother tongue is Baluchi though all her education was in Farsi. She remembers having difficulty when starting primary school as she could not understand what the teacher was saying. According to Collier (1995a), learning in a second language could account for some of her difficulties, as research showed that students who did not have a certain amount of schooling in their mother tongue were behind their peers in learning a second language.

Hawa was slower than her classmates in learning to read and has always had problems with writing – in Farsi as well as in English. Her particular problems have always been spelling, handwriting and grammar.

> I did have a problem with reading and writing (pause) maybe the sound you know, I never know the sounds.

At 15 she started to learn English formally and had difficulty with it from the start. However, Hawa felt that in Iran her problems with writing were discounted because she had a very good memory and could learn quickly. She was an 'A' student in maths and science and got the equivalent of an upper second in her degree. At the time of assessment Hawa is in an advanced ESOL class, having attended a GCSE course the previous year. She speaks English fluently with a wide vocabulary but she has particular difficulties with writing English and the level of her written English is far below that of her spoken English. Our interview was conducted at normal speed, and Hawa appeared to have no problems in understanding my questions and I was able to understand her without difficulty.

Hawa's reading in English is now at an advanced level; she reads *The Times*, particularly the law reports and the business news, but she has to reread several times in order to make sense of the article. As part of the diagnosis Hawa read an advanced piece about the ascent of Everest. She read fluently, though without much use of punctuation and her recall was poor. Analysis of her miscues suggests both difficulties with visual recognition, for instance reading *muskell* for *muscle* (a word she knows in English) and phonological processing, for instance reading *promoting* for *promptings*. On the Snowling graded non-word reading test (Snowling *et al.* 1996), Hawa managed most of the one-syllable words, having problems mainly with vowel sounds, a reasonable error considering that vowel sounds are different in Farsi. For instance she read *hast* for *hust*, a common error for Farsi speakers, according to Swan and Smith (1987). However, she did not manage to get any of the two syllable items right, and missed out or mis-sequenced consonants as well as vowels, for instance reading *molmosemet* for *molsmit*, or *tomekt* for *twamket*. This, together with her inability to 'sound out' words from the text that she read, would indicate a problem with the sound/symbol relationship and an auditory language processing difficulty.

Hawa reports a lot of difficulties with spelling, in Farsi as well as English. In her dictation, many of her mistakes were due to sounds being mis-sequenced or misheard, for instance writing *emergnices* for *emergencies*, and *solider* for *soldier*. As with the misreading of non-words (see above) these errors would indicate a problem with the sound/symbol relationship and holding the sequence of sounds in her memory. Hawa also had spelling errors that indicated a lack of absorption of English spelling rules or an inability to remember what words look like, such as writing *deafeated* for *defeated*, and *sadest* for *saddest*. Interestingly, considering that this is a word she has probably written many times, she repeatedly spelt her homeland *Baluchistan* incorrectly, writing *Baluchastin*. In her spelling, Hawa has more difficulty with the types of spelling errors just described than with the 'common' difficulties that Farsi writers have with English as described in Swan and Smith (1987); for instance, errors with vowels or consonant clusters. As Farsi spelling is 'invariably phonetic...and students' written English tends to be the same' (Swan and Smith 1987: 133) it might be expected that Hawa would try to spell English phonetically, and yet, as has been shown, this is not the case.

Hawa also reported having problems where her hand appeared to act independently of her:

I know the spelling but when I write it down it gets wrong
I know you write opinion o-p-i-n-i-o-n you know
Yes
Sometimes I put i-o-n-i-n.

This would indicate a problem with motor integration.

Hawa wrote two short pieces about law. Though she managed to convey the main points of her argument, her difficulty with grammatical construction, untidy writing, poor spelling and lack of punctuation made the pieces difficult to follow. Even when told she has made errors, she has difficulty in identifying them. Her writing was in stark contrast with her obvious understanding of the legal concepts which she was able to explain to me orally. Hawa's handwriting is irregular, leaning both ways and of varying size. Hawa says her handwriting in Farsi is untidy and has always been poor.

and my handwriting you know, I tried hard to be tidy and that but it never comes Helen (laughs) never comes naturally. For a little while I can do it, but afterwards I get all untidy again.

Together with some of her spelling difficulties (see above) this is symptomatic of motor integration problems.

Hawa has problems with her grammar making mistakes of tense, singular/plural agreement, articles, and prepositions. The latter two are described in Swan and Smith (1987) as being particularly difficult for Farsi speakers. However Hawa can demonstrate that she knows the rules; she has problems in applying them and this is the same when she writes Farsi.

Tell me a little bit about how, what the difficulties were?
It was the grammar, in Farsi too, I couldn't apply the rules.

Difficulty in generalising and applying rules is a common feature of the dyslexic learning style (Krupska and Klein 1995).

Hawa has other features that indicate poor visual-motor integration. She was a clumsy child, could never catch a ball and still has problems bumping into things, tying shoelaces and recognising right and left. She often gets lost, even if she has visited the place before. She could say the months of the year forwards, but when asked to say them backwards, she was only able to say 'December, November', then gave up. Hawa has problems copying, saying she forgets what words look like, even after a short time.

Hawa also has features that indicate poor auditory processing. She has problems with word retrieval, in English, Farsi and Baluchi. She says she has difficulty remembering sounds in her head. Although highly educated and in an advanced ESOL class, she cannot make sense of the phonetic alphabet (something that is commonly used by students at this level of language learning). She is distracted by background noise. She also has problems with articulation, for instance with dyslexia, pronouncing it more like dyxlexia. She reports she has articulation problems with long words in Baluchi and Farsi too. This latter could be a problem with input (i.e. auditory processing) or output (i.e. motor integration).

There is a discrepancy between Hawa's obvious intelligence, her determination to succeed, her ability to speak English and her written English. In Iran she obtained a good degree and started a professional career. She perceived herself as a good student, in spite of problems with reading, writing and spelling.

> Did it actually count against you the fact that you couldn't spell and everything at primary school, I mean…you never got kept down or anything?
> Because I was so good for history science and the maths
> And you didn't have problems passing your exams?
> No because of my knowledge the amount…I know.

Hawa's spoken English is fluent and expressive and contrasts strongly with the standard of her written English. When opening her pizza business at home, she successfully persuaded a reluctant council official to grant her a licence:

> I asked the council to if I could make a pizza from home and the delivery, and the council was surprised and they said I can't let you, and I said you have to let me because I can't pay it the one thousand pound mortgage, and in the end I convinced the lady I can do it and she said she give me certificate and make a commercial kitchen in my house.

Though she does not speak standard English, she has no problem making herself understood or, as is shown above, in persuading people of her point of view. This view of herself is reinforced by her GCSE teacher assessment, in which she got a 'C' for speaking and listening, but only an E overall because her writing dragged the mark down. It is also reinforced by her ESOL tutor:

> There was also a big discrepancy between her ability to um er discuss things and explain things in quite idiomatic though not always accurate English and how glaringly disjointed her grammar appeared to be when seen in print.

Comment

It could be argued that Hawa's difficulty in written English is merely due to the fact that she has picked up 'basic interpersonal communication skills' (Cummins 1984) but not yet developed her 'cognitive academic language proficiency'. However, she was educated to degree level in Iran, and as part of this study had to write an academic thesis, this would suggest that she has these skills, just needs to transfer them to English. Cummins' iceberg theory (1981c) suggests that when these skills are developed in mother tongue, it is much easier to transfer them to an additional language.

In favour of a diagnosis of dyslexia is Hawa's continued difficulties in writing, particularly spelling, grammar and handwriting. These occur in English and, according to Hawa, in Farsi. They occur in spite of an academic background in Farsi, tuition in English, fluency in spoken English, ability in other subjects and in spite of efforts to improve. Also in favour is Hawa's difficulty with relating sound to symbol, demonstrated in her difficulties 'sounding out' new words and non-words when reading, and in her non-phonetic spelling when writing. The fact that she always had difficulty learning a foreign language also points to the same conclusion (Ganschow and Sparks 1995). Her inability to proof-read and copy, and her need to reread frequently in order to access meaning, also point to dyslexia, this time of a visual nature. Finally, her difficulties with handwriting, the problems she has with being clumsy and with ball games, plus the tendency she reports of her hand 'taking over' when writing, all point to dyslexia associated with motor integration difficulties.

Possible confusing factors are the fact that even Farsi is her second language; she did not learn her mother tongue, Baluchi, at school. Another possible explanation for her poor written English (though not for her problems in Farsi) is the fact that she had only been attending ESOL classes for about 15 weeks at the time of the first interview. Though she had been to GCSE classes the year before, this was only once a week. So it could be argued that she had not been exposed to much academic English in this country. However, she had studied English at school, mainly reading and writing activities, and had always found it difficult. Finally, it may be that some of her difficulties with grammar are due to language transfer, though this factor does not appear to explain her problems with spelling.

On balance, in spite of the fact that she is reading and writing in her third language, Hawa shows strong indications of dyslexia, with auditory, visual and motor organisational problems. Her educational level and general intelligence are such that there is a discrepancy between her general ability and the difficulties she has with writing. Her problems in English are mirrored by similar difficulties in Farsi and some in Baluchi (though she has never used this language for academic purposes). There are other indicators, not connected with her academic efforts that, taken with her problems with reading and writing, would also indicate dyslexia.

Halima

Halima referred herself after seeing a TV programme on dyslexia and recognising characteristics of dyslexia in herself. She was born and went to school in Somalia. Her mother tongue was Swahili, but she spoke Somali at school and with friends.

She came to England, spending some time in Kenya first, when she was 29 years old in 1990. She very much wants to be able to read and write.

Aged five, Halima was very eager to go to school and was looking forward to learning. However she had problems right from the start with reading and writing. Her teachers accused her of laziness, and she became unhappy and started to miss school.

It wasn't easy for me from the first time, that's why they say OK maybe she's stupid, or she's lazy she doesn't want to learn.

She did not receive any extra help, and became progressively more behind the other children. Neither Halima nor her family could understand what the problem was; she has a brother and a sister who were less keen on school than her and who truanted but who, nevertheless, learnt to read and write. Halima left school at the age of 12. She never did understand why other children could learn to read and write but she could not. Somali is a phonetic language, and Halima is aware of this, and tells me that it should be easy to learn to read and write it because it is written as it sounds.

Somali is easy to learn because the sounds and writing ... it's just going the same, the way you know you talking and the way you writing it's just the same, and everybody can learn ...
But you found that difficult?
Difficult yea.

As Halima got older, she tried again to learn to read and write, first at college in Somalia, then at college in Kenya. She left both after a few months, because she was having so many difficulties. Again, she told me she could not understand what the problem was.

When I left the school ... was the campaign they was doing, you know for the Somali people, everybody they have, everyone have to learn Somali writing and reading ...
The people they was living in the countryside and doesn't know how to write and read, and they was making that campaign how to writing and read (pause) then after that I can see like ... someone who has just you know (pause) his life was just the countryside just look for the sheep and the camels and something like that and he doesn't know anything about education? and just after a few weeks (not) even ... for a few months, just for a few weeks you can see he's writing and reading.
And after that I say yea, there's something wrong for myself.

At the age of 29 Halima came to England. She tried again, attempting four different ESOL classes, but never staying more than a few months because she found the reading and writing so difficult. When she asked the teachers about the reason for her difficulties she was told they were because she could not speak English. However, she could see other students who spoke much less English than her who were learning to read and write. Again, she could not understand why she was different. Finally, watching a TV programme about dyslexia and recognising many features in herself, she referred herself for assessment.

Halima speaks English extremely fluently and had no problems getting across her point to me, or in understanding what I said to her. The interview was conducted in English, and though I spoke slightly slower than normal speed I did not have to restrict my vocabulary in order to make myself understood. Halima does not read Somali, though it is written in the same script as English. As it is a phonetic language, the fact that she cannot sound it out indicates that she has problems with the sound/symbol system. She has said as much herself – when asked if she 'sounds out' words, she replied 'If I can do this I can read Somali'. She can read some English, for instance she can understand letters of appointment, and details of time, place etc.

Halima read two short beginner level passages to me. Because of her low level of literacy we chose traditional tales of a kind she was likely to be familiar with (Sunderland *et al.* 1997). She made over 10 per cent of errors in each one. She also attempted a list of 'non-words' (Snowling *et al.* 1996). The analysis of her reading supports the suggestion that Halima has auditory processing problems, and that she uses a visual approach in reading (Klein 1993). She read with confidence and expression and her use of punctuation was good. She appeared to rely on visual cues, finding it difficult to decode words she did not recognise. This was the case even when the word was phonically regular, such as *Nasreddin*. Analysis of Halima's miscues shows quite high semantic matches, indicating that she was engaging with the meaning. She did not use the syntactic system as much, for instance reading *dead* for *died*. However it is worth noting that the syntactic system is not likely to be helpful to her because, although she speaks English fluently, her use of syntax is not that of Standard English. Her recall was good; though unable to read several key words, she understood the main points and the underlying moral of the texts. Her good comprehension indicates that she was comfortable with the chosen texts and that cultural unfamiliarity cannot be blamed for her miscues. Her ability to read 'non-words' was poor, only reading 5 out of 20 words correctly. When asked about her strategy for reading unfamiliar words she said that she missed them out which again indicates an inability to 'sound out'. Halima also showed some indications of visual difficulties, with problems tracking print.

Halima cannot write at all in Somali. She took 15 minutes to write the beginnings of three sentences about herself in English. She could not complete any of them. The level of her writing is in stark contrast with her very fluent and expressive spoken English. Her handwriting is immature and irregular and she does not use cursive script.

Halima was given a 100-word dictation, adapted to make the content familiar to adult English learners (Sunderland *et al.* 1997). It took her 20 minutes to do half, then she became very tired and gave up. Again, Halima used a mainly visual approach, with many of her spellings visually similar; for instance, she spelt *offics* for *office* – she had remembered the *c* – or *tal* for *talk*, *youg* for *young*, *wsa* for *was*. Almost all of her errors indicated difficulties with sound/symbol relationship. For instance she wrote *airpotn* for *airport*, *haubn* for *husband*, *bua* for *bus*. On six occasions she could not make an attempt at the word, even write the initial sound.

On Halima's form she spelt her address wrong – *huose* for *house*, *Huhges* for *Hughes*, indicating sequencing difficulties, and she could not remember more than the first two letters of her town, which is a phonetically regular spelling. Halima says that if she writes her address more frequently then she begins to remember it, but if she does not write it for, say, three weeks, then she forgets and has to copy it, thus also indicating weak visual memory. In her interview, Halima explained how she has difficulty remembering sequencing in spelling:

> I couldn't catch the spelling for the 'girl' (pause) you see I remember 'g'? I remember it's got the 'l'? I remember it's got the 'i'? I remember it's got the 'r'?
> Yes
> But I can't remember how? (pause) You know?
> Which order?
> Which one he's going to put first and which one is going to go last.

Halima had difficulty with a number of phonological awareness tests. Though she could pick two out of three rhymes when they were said to her, she could not produce words to rhyme with *pan*, *well* or *sun*. She also had to think very hard before deciding whether two words were the same or different and only got two out of four right. She found blending sounds to make words difficult, giving 'c-a-n' as *car*, 't-ell-y' as *tell*. Finally, she had trouble identifying extra sounds in words e.g. in *rap/trap* – she identified the extra sound as *b*. She has several other problems with language that indicate auditory processing difficulties such as difficulty concentrating with background noise, and has problems following an argument when there are several people talking or with following oral instructions and directions. She has pronunciation difficulties, for instance with *Coronation Street*, and *Thursday*; and word retrieval problems. All of these occur in Somali and Swahili as well as in English.

Halima has a very poor short-term memory. She could not repeat a telephone number, and normally has to write them down. She cannot remember lists of instructions, directions or names. Halima took three tries before reciting the months of the year in order. Twice she got stuck at April, then at the third try she said all 12 in the correct order, thus demonstrating that she does know them in English. Halima also has problems reading an analogue clock, and has to use a digital one at home.

As Halima has not had the kind of education as Hawa, it is not so easy to find a discrepancy. However, her spoken English is very fluent, and her understanding is good. She has learnt this almost alone in the eight years she has been in London, having stayed only a few months in her ESOL classes, and mixed mainly with other Somali families and friends. She has also picked up some functional reading. In contrast, she has learnt almost no writing, and not managed to learn to spell her address, despite having tried to teach herself. On the other hand, she is also not literate in Somali, and so could be expected to have a great deal of difficulty in writing English. However, there is a strong contrast between the amount of effort she has put in, plus her determination to learn, and the skills of reading and writing she has actually picked up. Three times in the interview she refers to having a 'broken heart' because of her problems, and as an adult she went back to try to learn to read and write six times, plus the time she came to see me.

When asked about her other school subjects she said that she did not manage to learn these because she missed so much schooling due to her problems with reading and writing.

My mind wasn't in the school
My heart is broken and I never learn.

Comment
It can be argued that Halima shows enough positive indicators for dyslexia to be sure of a diagnosis. These indicators are her lack of progress in reading and writing despite attempts and determination to learn. They also include her poor auditory abilities, demonstrated in her inability to 'sound out' in reading, either in Somali or in English; her spellings; and her difficulties with the phonological tests. Then there is the discrepancy between her fluent and expressive oral English and the level of her literacy skills. These are combined with indicators for dyslexia not associated with educational attainment, such as poor memory for instructions and sequence.

Alternatively it might be said that Halima has a low level of education and thus her inability to learn to read and write is not remarkable. She went to school for only seven years, and for much of that time her attendance was poor. Though she attended six different classes as an adult, she stayed only a few months in each, and it takes a long time to learn to read and write. Furthermore, in most of these she was trying to learn to read and write in a language with which she was not very familiar. Her phonological difficulties could be attributed to the fact that she has never successfully learnt to read and write. However, she herself has pointed out that in all cases she had more difficulty than her peers in learning literacy skills. This was so even when those learning had similar attendance patterns or knew less of the language than she did (see above). Morais *et al.* (1979) have shown that adults with only a small amount of tuition in reading, such as Halima has had, improved their ability to perform phonological tasks, and so it might be expected that Halima would also be able to do so.

Conclusions

It would seem that, in spite of her low level of education and her low level of literacy in English making a diagnosis difficult, Halima shows enough indicators of dyslexia to make a positive diagnosis. It is the conjunction of her continued inability to learn despite repeated efforts, her phonological difficulties and the other indicators not connected with her educational background that make a positive diagnosis likely.

I would argue that these case studies show it is possible to diagnose adult students for dyslexia even when they are still in the process of learning English. However, there are certain questions that must be asked and certain factors that must be taken into account before drawing conclusions about dyslexia. First of all, it is essential that students are asked about difficulties in their own languages as well as in English. The fact that Halima and Hawa had problems with reading and writing and other difficulties, such as articulation or following oral instructions, in their own languages as well as in English demonstrate that their problems are not just a result of operating in a foreign language. Secondly, the structure of their own languages needs to be taken into account. Hawa's spelling difficulties were inconsistent with transfer from phonetically regular Farsi. Halima could never learn to read Somali, despite it being a phonetically regular language. Both of these back up diagnoses of phonological processing difficulties. The student's educational background also needs to be considered. For instance Hawa is educated to degree level in Iran and so she might be expected to be able to transfer academic literacy skills from Farsi to English. Halima, however, has had little previous schooling and this makes the diagnosis more difficult. Diagnosis needs to take into account the length of time the student has been in England, the amount of study in English s/he has undertaken and the student's level of English. For instance, Hawa has studied English in Iran and had been in England for 16 years at the time of diagnosis. Her spoken English is fluent and persuasive. This makes the discrepancy with her written English all the more surprising. Halima too has been in England some time (eight years) speaks quite fluently and is able to understand almost all of the interview, despite not having studied English for an extended period. Because her written English is so very poor the discrepancy with speaking skills is still evident, though it is much less obvious than in Hawa's case. Finally, assessments such as reading passages, need to be carefully chosen to ensure that they are culturally familiar to the student.

Thus the difficulties the students have in their own languages, the structure of these languages, the educational and language background of the students, the length of time they have been learning English, their level of spoken English compared with their reading and writing skills, are all crucial factors for consideration when diagnosing dyslexia in multilingual students. If they are considered along with other evidence when drawing conclusions, then it should be possible to give multilingual adult students access to the same dyslexia diagnosis and support that their English peers receive.

Chapter 20

Dyslexia Support in a Multilingual University Environment

University of Buckingham, England –
  David McLoughlin and Jenni Beard
University of Wales, Swansea – Ann Ryan
University of Edinburgh, Scotland – Jane Kirk

University of Buckingham, England

This section:

- examines the adjustments which have to be made by overseas students
- describes the role of the learning support service
- describes the screening and assessment process and provides detailed analysis of specific tests and their implications for identifying dyslexic students and
- describes examination accommodations.

Introduction

Entry to higher education represents a significant transition for any young person. They face new demands on their literacy and learning skills, need to become more independent in terms of organising their daily lives and usually have to develop new social networks. Some students find it difficult to make the necessary adjustments and this can be exacerbated when they have left the security of their family, their home country and are working in a second language in an unfamiliar cultural setting. Difficulties with adjustment can be even worse when the student has either diagnosed or undiagnosed specific difficulties with learning and literacy.

Some of the varied problems encountered by foreign students include:

- Adjusting to a new culture.
- Encountering a different education system requiring different study skills.
- Living up to expectations of family and friends back home.
- Racial discrimination.
- Dealing with new found freedom. (Khoo *et al.* 1994)

The multilingual student is therefore at risk of failing to adjust to the experience of higher education. Learning support resources within universities need to be adapted to the specific problems faced by overseas students.

The context

The University of Buckingham is a small international university catering for students from the United Kingdom and for students from up to 80 other countries worldwide and is the only independent university in the United Kingdom. Best known for its courses in Law and Business Studies, it also has Humanities and Science Schools. Overseas students can be found pursuing all courses. The size of the university allows easy access for students to their lecturers and tutors on a one-to-one basis if they are struggling. They also benefit from a tutorial system, with tutor groups being no larger than ten students. Although this does have advantages some overseas students find it quite different to what they are used to, and for some it is intimidating. At the same time a high level of personal tuition allows for lecturers and tutors to identify discrepancies between a student's performance in tutorials and his/her written work generally, as well as in examinations. Over a period of years a systematic referral, screening and assessment procedure has been developed. The population of dyslexic students identified at the University of Buckingham is 5 per cent, which is substantially higher than the 1.2 per cent to 1.5 per cent identified within the total population of higher education students in the United Kingdom (National Working Party on Dyslexia in Higher Education 1999).

Reasons for presenting/referral

Overseas students may not have heard of dyslexia but, like their fellow students from the UK, they know they have underachieved. The possibility that they have a learning problem is in their mind even if they do not know what the reason might be.

When a learning support service was established at Buckingham there was a reluctance to tell students about the possibility of dyslexia in the early stages of their university career because some academic staff feared that there would be a flood of bogus candidates. This has proved to be false as most overseas students find it difficult enough to accept that they are dyslexic without making it up when they are not. Furthermore, it is important to identify students as early in their career as possible. A student seeking help six weeks before his final examinations, because a dyslexic friend had recognised similar traits, proved to be dyslexic, but had not come forward before as he was unaware of the condition. Dyslexia is now explained to 'Freshers' during the first few days of their time at the university. Explanatory literature is placed in their 'Welcome Pack' and each new student is expected to fill out a questionnaire which lists important indicators.

Providing information is not foolproof and many students slip through the net or deliberately do not come forward for help. The next source of referral is the tutor. First essays can show up discrepancies between their verbal performance in tutorials and their written work. However, because a student's problem could be one of language rather than dyslexia it is sometimes much later in the course before tutors begin to worry. By this time the student may well have completed an examination and problems will show up more clearly, or the student themselves will realise they are still underperforming and will seek help.

Informal referral is facilitated by the fact that Buckingham is a small university and has a good 'grapevine' system. Students have become proficient at recognising other dyslexic students. Dyslexics tend to group together and often attract other undiagnosed dyslexics to their group, and peers will recommend that they seek the assistance of the learning support adviser. Some cultural groups, however, continue to be unwilling to ask for help. As is the case in many UK universities there is quite a large Eastern European group but 'apparently' there are no dyslexics. Perhaps when one is willing to come forward then there will be others. As there has been a learning support service at Buckingham for a long time some students seek help because past students have suggested it.

Overseas students sometimes present late in their course as their problems have been attributed to 'language'. It is noticeable that dyslexic students take longer to learn English than non-dyslexic students. They may get by very well with a level of English that is not accurate but descriptive. Many students are international in that they speak several languages and can pick up another one very easily. However, they cannot write in any of their spoken languages adequately. Most overseas students have a similar learning curve pattern and come to good workable English at about the same point, but dyslexics take longer and this is something academic staff have learnt to recognise.

Screening

Overseas students usually find it very difficult to summon up the courage to approach a counsellor as in a lot of cultures this would be seen as a weakness. Africans for example perceive asking for help about personal problems as 'letting down their family' (Idowu 1985). They usually seek help because they are desperate, they have failed exams or are underachieving badly. Students are allowed to take their own time and set the pace of the sessions. Sometimes students will eventually say they think they could be dyslexic, or the list of problems they describe indicates that they might be dyslexic. When it seems appropriate the subject is broached. There have been occasions when students have been provided with dyslexia support without the word 'dyslexia' being mentioned.

A student will be provided with an explanation of what dyslexia is. That it does not mean a 'lack of intelligence' is emphasised. They are asked questions in the form of a checklist about their childhood and background. The checklist is not very formal and is a means of allowing students to talk about themselves. Inevitably some students are more honest than others, and often answers refer to comparisons with the people they were at school with rather than intrinsic difficulties. It is here that some understanding of the cultural context is important. Many African students, for example, have been taught in a very formal manner using traditional teaching methods and their principal difficulties are in organisational skills and not necessarily in reading and writing.

If there are a reasonable number of indicators that the student has some learning problems a screening test is undertaken. Initially this involves measures of auditory and visual memory, spelling, writing and reading. More recently the Dyslexia Adult Screening Test (DAST) developed by Fawcett and Nicholson (1998) has been used.

Thus far 20 students have been tested using the DAST, the majority of them being from overseas. The DAST includes 11 sub-tests:

Rapid Naming	Backwards Digit Span
One Minute Reading	Nonsense Passage Reading
Posture/Stability	Nonverbal Reasoning
Phonemic Segmentation	One Minute Writing
Two Minute Spelling	Verbal Fluency
	Semantic Fluency

On the basis of experience so far thoughts on using the DAST with overseas students are as follows:

Rapid Naming

It is important to allow students to look at this test and make sure that they are at ease with the English word for each of the images, and explain that it is not their knowledge of English but the speed at which they give the names which is being tested. Otherwise working in a second language would not seem to be a problem.

One Minute Reading

Many overseas students have been taught to read English in a very formal manner. They are able to read quickly and with few errors. University students have to have a reasonable level of reading ability otherwise they would not contemplate attempting a degree. Reading at speed does not, however, necessarily mean the student understands the words.

Posture/Stability

This test is not affected by language.

Phonemic Segmentation

This test is useful with students working in a second language. It is very important to tell students to listen and carry out the instructions. It is not necessary for them to understand the words although in the main they do. 'Wigwam' causes some confused looks. It is difficult also to explain spoonerisms but with some demonstration using other words students seem to get the idea.

Two Minute Spelling

The spelling test as with the reading test is rarely a problem as most of the words used will have been learnt and can be remembered by the student. Some of the characteristic dyslexic errors are present but not significantly more than for a monolingual English-speaking student.

Backwards Digit Span

Overseas students are usually confident in their use of the names for numbers and only have problems with remembering digits if their working memory is poor.

Nonsense Passage Reading

Some bilingual students find this test easier than those whose first language is English. They do not have preconceived ideas of English words and do not necessarily see the nonsense words as different.

Nonverbal Reasoning

This test does not raise language problems.

One Minute Writing

The only difficulties found are those expected for a dyslexic.

Verbal Fluency and Semantic Fluency

These tests are obviously language based and if the student has to 'hunt' for English words it would not be a true reflection of their ability. Allowing a student to name words in his/her own language has proved helpful.

In general it would seem that the DAST can usefully be used with students whose first language is not English. There is however a risk of dyslexia being identified when in fact there is a spoken language problem. It is essential therefore to combine the results with a comprehensive interview and to take into account the student's history, particularly as this relates to education and language experience. The screening procedure is sufficient to identify those who are 'at risk' and indicate that the provision of study-skills lessons is in order. External validation of the procedure is provided by referral to an educational psychologist for a full assessment. This is also an essential requirement if accommodations are to be made for students when they take examinations.

Formal assessment

Students referred for further evaluation are assessed using the procedure typically employed by educational psychologists when attempting to diagnose dyslexia. The following tests are administered:

- Wechsler Adult Intelligence Scales (Revised)
- Wechsler Memory Scales (Third Edition) Digit Span Test
- British Ability Scales Test of Immediate Visual Recall
- Spadafore Diagnostic Reading Test
- The Wide Range Achievement Spelling Test (Third Edition)
- A free writing task.

Comments on how overseas students cope with the above procedure are as follows.

Wechsler Adult Intelligence Scale (WAIS)

Although it does provide measures of verbal and nonverbal intelligence, in the diagnosis of dyslexia the WAIS is at its least useful when used as an IQ test. Diagnostically it is helpful because of the contrasts it can show between some abilities and others. In particular, when assessing university students suspected of being dyslexic one is interested in the difference between language ability and working memory skills. The verbal ability of adults with learning difficulties has been demonstrated to be highly predictive of success academically and in employment (Faas and D'Alonzo 1990). An inefficiency in working memory has been described as the 'core deficit' in dyslexia (McLoughlin *et al.* 1994).

Table 20.1 shows the profile of verbal sub-test scores, plus digit symbol, for 41 overseas students selected at random from the records. Their countries of origin included Nigeria, Gambia, Germany, Israel, India, Pakistan and several Scandinavian countries.

Table 20.1

		Informa-tion	Digit Span	Vocabul-ary	Arith-metic	Compre-hension	Similar-ities	Digit Symbol	
	WAIS (R) PROFILE for 41 overseas students								
H	19								19
I	18								18
G	17								17
H	16								16
	15								15
	14								14
A	13								13
V	12					X	X		12
E	11								11
R	10								10
A	9			X					9
G	8	X					X		8
E	7		X		X				7
	6								6
	5								5
	4								4
L	3								3
O	2								2
W	1								1
		Mean 8.88	Mean 7.44	Mean 9.9	Mean 7.76	Mean 12.07	Mean 12.24	Mean 8.20	
		Sd 2.35	Sd 1.76	Sd 20.6	Sd 1.99	Sd 1.62	Sd 1.50	Sd 2.86	
		Range 4–23	Range 4–13	Range 6–14	Range 5–13	Range 10–18	Range 10–15	Range 4–19	

Although within the sample there was enormous variation as demonstrated by the range for sub-test scores it can be seen that overseas students achieve a similar profile to that often associated with dyslexia, with the lowest scores being on the ACID sub-tests, that is, those on which dyslexic people have been shown to score less well, viz. A (Arithmetic), C (Coding or Digit Symbol), I (Information), D (Digit Span).

Digit span and digit symbol (coding) can be regarded as 'culture-free'. This can also be assumed for arithmetic provided the student understands the language. There is a cultural bias to the information sub-test but there are a number of items which can be considered as 'universals'. Students from anywhere should for example know where the sun sets and how many weeks there are in a year. In considering these students' performance on the 'information' sub-test it is therefore important to conduct an item analysis.

As mentioned above comprehension and verbal reasoning are regarded as the best predictors of academic success and the mean score on both for the sample is above average. The main difference between the profile of overseas students and that encountered among students from the United Kingdom is on the vocabulary sub-test. This is perhaps inevitable given that students are asked to define some fairly sophisticated words . The word 'ponder' has been variously defined as 'think', 'a place where you keep fish' and 'a kind of car (Fiat Panda)'. It should be noted that there was considerable variation, the range of sub-test scores being between 6 and 14. Although some overseas students do have a limited vocabulary they can deal effectively with sub-tests such as similarities which require one or two word answers and the comprehension sub-test which requires 'common sense' responses.

Memory skills

Repeating numbers backwards is regarded as one of the more accurate measures of working memory. The digit span sub-test in the WAIS does not give separate scores for digits forward and digits reversed. However, this is provided by the same test from the Wechsler Memory Scales.

The British Abilities Scales Test of Immediate Visual Recall is also administered as a way of establishing how students can recall visually presented material.

Reading

In assessing reading among university students there are three important components; accuracy when reading prose, silent reading comprehension and silent reading fluency. To measure each of these the Spadafore Diagnostic Reading Test is used. This allows one to rate reading accuracy and comprehension according to whether they are at professional, technical, vocational or functional levels. The professional level is that expected of a university student. The overwhelming majority (92.7 per cent) of the sample read accurately at the professional level. Essentially the students in the sample are good readers. However, only 34.1 per cent scored at the professional level on a test of silent reading comprehension, which is arguably the more important reading skill when studying at an advanced level. This could be a function of working in a second language but suggests that developing effective reading comprehension strategies is an important area for tutors to address. Furthermore, the mean silent reading speed was 135 words per minute, whereas one would ordinarily expect an undergraduate to be able to read and comprehend at 250 words per minute.

Spelling

The mean centile ranking for performance on the WRAT-3 Spelling Test was 32.35. There was considerable variation, the range being from the 1st to the 79th centile. Many overseas students who have learned English formally can do quite well on a single word spelling test. They do however have particular difficulty with homophones.

Writing fluency

The mean writing speed for the sample was 19.03 with a standard deviation of 3.96. There was considerable variation, actual writing speeds ranging from 10 to 27 words per minute. One could normally expect an adult in full time education to be able to write at 25 words per minute.

In summary, the cognitive profiles, literacy and learning difficulties manifested by dyslexic students from overseas are not vastly different from those of students whose first language is English. That is, they have trouble with:

• working memory skills
• weak reading comprehension
• slow reading
• slow writing
• problems with written expression
• weak spelling.

Explaining test results and the nature of dyslexia is essential with any student as it is this which empowers them. It is even more important when dealing with a student from a different cultural background where dyslexia is not understood, and where there is a stigma associated with 'having something wrong with you'. Those of us who are used to finding clients to be pleased and relieved when told they are dyslexic need to be very careful. The image of the African student with tears rolling down her cheeks after being told she is dyslexic had quite an impact.

Follow up

In addressing the needs of overseas students learning support tutors will be teaching many of the same skills that they introduce to UK students. At Buckingham the programme for students is derived from a book on basic study skills written for UK students (Beard 1994). One major area of difference is however likely to be in the development of a student's spoken language, particularly his/her vocabulary. The extent to which students whose spoken English is quite poor can develop a 'technical vocabulary' which relates specifically to their course is very impressive. A need for counselling dyslexic students has been recognised because they can be angry about and confused by the late identification of their difficulties.

Accommodations in examinations

All students at Buckingham are examined in the same way and no concessions are made for the language problems of overseas students. If a student wishes to have special provision in examinations, they have to have a current educational psychologist's assessment. Dyslexics are examined in a separate room from the other students and are allowed an extra ten minutes for each hour of written examinations. No allowances are made for poor written English in assessed coursework.

University of Swansea, Wales
This section:

- explores the idea that there may be similarities between the language processing of known dyslexics and of second language learners
- describes the support system in place for dyslexic students at the University of Wales, Swansea
- addresses the difficulty of distinguishing between these two categories and
- outlines experimental work in progress at Swansea in this field.

Introduction

One of the more interesting challenges for a modern university arises from the presence of students whose first language is not English. Such students may have been educated in Britain and come from ethnic minority groups, while others arrive from Europe for university exchange courses. Many come as postgraduates from the Middle East. Occasionally, however, any of these groups may contain students who seem to take longer than their peers to develop basic skills in the second language and it is tempting to ascribe their slow development to the fact that these are people who do not learn languages easily. In reality, it may be that they suffer from undiagnosed dyslexia and it might be useful to the individual student to have some early confirmation of this before proceeding to the more formal stage of identification by an educational psychologist.

Links between dyslexia and second language acquisition

Since Marshall and Newcombe's seminal paper in 1973, there have been many studies which compare the performance of dyslexic and age-matched subjects. The findings indicate with considerable consistency that dyslexic readers perform in a manner very like that of younger subjects whose reading age is the same as that of the dyslexic subjects. Whether this is due to a phonological deficit in the dyslexic subjects or to a developmental lag is still a matter for debate.

Masterson (1983) provides an example of an early study of this type. She used stimuli developed by Coltheart *et al.* (1979) for a range of reading and spelling tasks. Masterson's findings showed that the group of four developmental dyslexic children in her study performed in a manner very like a control group of 13 seven-year-old subjects who were just beginning to learn to read.

It has been argued that the slow development of reading skills which can be observed in dyslexic children and in younger children matched for reading age, can also be observed in adult, non-native speakers learning a second language. To test this hypothesis, Al-Sulaimani (1990) conducted a replication of Masterson's 1983 experiment but used a group of Arabic speakers who were learning English and studying for further degrees in London. The results showed this group of adult second language learners to share many of the processing difficulties Masterson found with her dyslexic subjects and her control group of seven-year-olds. Ryan (1993) showed that even if the stimuli in lexical decision tasks were controlled for frequency to a greater extent than had been the case in Masterson and Al-Sulaimani's studies, second language learners still showed dyslexia-like tendencies in a range of tasks which involved reading aloud, spelling and homophone choice.

Studies of second language learners also indicate that the acquisition processes follow steps very like those of young native speakers, both in terms of phonology (e.g. Milton 1985) and the decoding and encoding skills needed for reading and writing (e.g. Coady 1979; Ryan 1997). In particular, there is a stage in the development of these skills where the learner, like the young native speaker, is highly dependent on 'bottom-up' processing, and where higher-level processing will be hampered by a lack of automaticity, particularly in reading continuous text (Yang and Givon 1993). This leads to the proposition, not that non-native speakers are dyslexic, but that certain features of learning to read may be present in beginning readers, non-native learners and cases of developmental dyslexia.

It could be argued that there is sufficient similarity between native speaker dyslexic and non-native speaker language learners to ask whether the teaching systems used for English as a foreign language (EFL) might provide a good foundation for teaching adult dyslexic students. As a sign of the confidence in this similarity, the syllabus developed for use with the dyslexic support classes at University of Wales, Swansea is based on study-skills material designed for non-native students and also on some fundamental preconceptions about the nature of second language learning:

- a recognition that 'bottom-up' processing continues in early stages of adult reading
- there is a lack of automaticity in non-native speaker language use
- there is a need for visual support of all taught material
- the students need reassurance
- relaxed learning is likely to be more successful
- 'multi-sense' learning is more likely to be more successful
- it is wise to attack on all four skills (speaking, listening, reading and writing) simultaneously
- these students have slower reading and organisation skills than most.

For a more detailed discussion of second language learning and teaching, see, for example Harmer (1987) for practical ideas, Cook (1991) for an overview of EFL teaching methods or Spolsky (1989) for a theoretical assessment of the necessary conditions for successful learning.

Dyslexia at university

It is now considered perfectly normal to find dyslexic students admitted to university, whether they have arrived in higher education straight from school, or have spent some time outside formal education and have only recently followed an 'access' course. The latter group have possibly had some advantages in that their tutors will have deliberately taught them the rudiments of practical study skills for life in a university setting. Those who come directly from school will have worked hard and been allowed extra time for their A-level examinations, but will probably not have had any tuition in the survival-cum-study skills which most undergraduates pick up as they go along.

The University of Wales, Swansea is typical of many institutions of further and higher education in recent years, in having a declared admissions policy concerning students with dyslexia (National Working Party on Dyslexia in Higher Education 1999). Indeed this has been outlined in the national working party report in higher education for assessment and support. One of the support mechanisms to which it is committed is a regular series of classes on study skills which are available to dyslexic undergraduates, in conjunction with one-to-one tutorial classes available by individual arrangement.

The use of the term 'undergraduate' is not accidental. Government funding is currently available for support classes for any undergraduate who is dyslexic, and provided that the classes are of a general 'study skills' nature, rather than extra tuition in a particular subject. This assistance, like the money for technical support (e.g., computers, printers and tape recorders) comes from central government funds and is no longer means tested. Postgraduate students are not, however, included in this provision. Their numbers may be small at present, but the very success of the dyslexic undergraduate programme must inevitably ensure that the numbers of dyslexic postgraduates will rise with time and will force universities to consider how best to finance their support. There is evidence at some universities that postgraduate students can access the university support provision in the same manner as undergraduates (Kirk 2000).

Dyslexic students who have been accepted for university admission have already achieved that position by considerable personal effort. They have succeeded in passing A-levels, perhaps with extra time allowances and perhaps with the use of personal computers, and almost certainly with a great deal of determination. These students have already developed strategies for study which have got them thus far. What do they need that is new? Not the concept of working alone and being responsible for their own learning; this aspect of university study is something they already understand very well as this is precisely what they are good at. Without this, they would not have got over the school hurdles. Many will have learnt how to spell acceptably and the arrival of the personal computer has already solved the problems of handwriting. All these individual methods come into their own in the university setting. What is likely to be missing is a structured approach in study skills, and this is what the regular class provides.

The Swansea syllabus

In the development of a structured syllabus for these support classes it has been valuable to examine the provision offered elsewhere. We have looked at two other sources, one in University of Wales, Bangor (Cooke 1994), and one in Haifa, Israel (Bensoussan 1993) where many of the courses are in English. However, the most practical source of ideas, materials and methods has come from our understanding of the development of study skills among second language learners.

The courses at the University of Wales, Swansea are offered in the Centre for Applied Language Studies, a department whose main function is to provide English language support classes for postgraduate, overseas students. The evidence quoted above, however, suggests that the language decoding problems of dyslexic readers are very similar to those met by foreign learners and, if this is so, teachers who have been trained specifically to work as teachers of English as a foreign language are ideally placed to understand the difficulties of the dyslexic native speaker. The assistance offered to all foreign, postgraduate students by the Centre is largely in the field of study-skills classes to help them make full use of the method of teaching employed in British universities. These classes focus on note-taking from lectures to large groups of students and on the techniques of essay writing. These are skills which have to be developed and for many foreign students cause an initial barrier to their learning. It has been argued (Gilroy and Miles 1986) that dyslexic students need the same kind of help with study skills. This involves a focus on reading, writing, note-taking and seminar presentations as well as the accurate use of library catalogues, which are often computer-based, and the use of computers for writing essays. Many non-native speakers welcome information about the use of time in examination conditions, the distinctive British and American method of compiling a bibliography and the British method of writing essays. It is, of course, difficult to distinguish features from the above list which are specific to dyslexic students rather than to the student body in general. The biggest difference between the dyslexic and the 'normal' student is probably in the speed with which all study takes place, and in the lack of confidence in their abilities which dogs so many dyslexics.

One of the features of the Swansea support for dyslexic students is a series of regular study-skills classes for those students who already know that they are dyslexic; this is in addition to a 'drop-in' service for individuals. We have found that a class has several merits. Firstly, the students meet each other and often exchange their coping strategies as well as gaining moral support from each other. Secondly, the students are in a normal classroom or seminar situation where they can usually make practical advances in study skills. By contrast, the one-to-one help is often a response to a crisis in trying to meet the deadline for academic work and by its nature can carry an atmosphere of alarm, panic and often tears which the tutor has to handle as sensitively as possible. The class, however, contributes to confidence building and allows the students to get away from the concept that 'dyslexia spells trouble'.

Developing a test for language dysfunction

Because the Centre for Applied Language Studies sees both dyslexic and non-native speaker students, our interests have been aroused in trying to find a way of discriminating between these two categories. There is increasing interest in the plight of the non-native speaker who is also dyslexic. Universities in Britain see numbers of European students with varying degrees of competence in English, and occasionally students who have been helped through their dyslexia at school, as happens in Britain. But sometimes, a student is dyslexic without being fully aware of the help available, and sometimes nobody thinks to offer assistance because the student is written off as simply being a poor language learner. It can be very difficult to distinguish between someone whose problems stem from dyslexia and someone who is simply taking longer than usual to express themselves in a foreign language.

There is a small amount of evidence that suggests it is possible to be dyslexic in some languages without this causing any serious impairment of the ability to process text. The evidence comes from the study of a Spanish student of English who showed no signs of any learning difficulty in his native language, but who had considerable difficulty with accurate spelling in English. The analysis of his case (Masterson *et al.* 1985) suggested that the problem was caused by his difficulty with the irregular orthography of English, while the condition went almost unnoticed in Spanish where the spelling is phonologically regular. The authors of the paper suggest that dyslexia may go unnoticed in certain languages. In addition, there is no evidence that dyslexia is impossible in either Arabic or Hebrew, but it seems likely that students whose first language is Semitic may find increased difficulty with English where the irregular orthography is known to create barriers to learning in both writing and reading the language (Ryan 1997).

Identifying those non-native speakers in need of dyslexia support

In establishing a design for this test, we have chosen to make the following assumptions about dyslexia.

- Dyslexia is a lifelong language disorder whose symptoms can often be alleviated, but which is present even in adults.
- Phonological processing plays a critical role. It seems extremely likely that the core cognitive deficit is phonological and there are several family studies now in progress to support the hypothesis that the condition is genetic in origin.
- Visual processing is involved, but at a level of individual differences. Stanovich *et al.* (1997: 122) suggest 'that the reading behaviour of the majority of dyslexic children is within the normal range but that these children show greater differences in phonological awareness tasks than children who display a surface dyslexia pattern'. Orthography of the target language plays a part (Goswami 1997). Certain types of teaching may provide the classroom intervention which will prevent the development of differences for the dyslexic child.

In the studies underway at Swansea we have focused on using this phonological deficit in our test design. We wanted to create a simple instrument which could be used to guide language tutors, not to diagnose dyslexia which is the job of an educational psychologist, but to identify students whose language difficulties might be caused by more deeply seated processing failures rather than by simple second language acquisition problems. The tutor would then be in a position to provide additional help with spelling and word recognition. At school and university levels, if dyslexia could then be confirmed formally by the normal identification process used by that institution, the student would have access to whatever support funds were current at that time. We claim nothing more for it than an early warning system.

The test

The test consists of two pages, each containing 24 non-words and printed back to back so that the first page cannot be read until the subject follows the instruction to turn the page over. These non-words are designed on the pattern CVCVCV (for example, 'gipola') and are designed with two ideas in mind: firstly that it should be possible to say the word aloud or imagine a pronunciation for the word, and secondly, the word should not have any known equivalent in any real language known to us. This means that real words such as 'potato' or 'tomato' are excluded, and we did our best to avoid such words from the Romance languages, for example, 'harina' (Spanish for flour). Side one contains 16 target words of this type and 8 distracters of the same type; side two contains the same 16 target words with 8 different distracters. The task given to the subjects is to read over the first side for two minutes and then when instructed, to turn over and mark any words they recognise on the second side.

The subjects consisted of students at the University of Wales, Swansea from a variety of language backgrounds, native speakers and a small number of known dyslexics. So far, we have conducted only 'norming' trials to get an idea of the likely range of scores among a random student population. What has emerged from the trials is that language background does not seem to affect the scores, but it looks as if known dyslexia does. In other words, we have a design capable of being developed which can be used with speakers of a wide range of languages and which appears not be affected by the language spoken by the subject. We cannot make extravagant claims on the basis of such small numbers (around 200 subjects), but it points a way forward in helping to identify non-native speakers whose language difficulties may prove greater than normal.

There are several caveats to be expressed here. Firstly, we have to ask ourselves what we are testing. We make no claims that this is a test for anything except short-term recall and visual processing of text, what we might call language dysfunction. In any presentation of the test we make this very clear. Although such difficulties are often aspects of dyslexia, they could also appear with subjects who were excessively tired, very nervous, suffering from vision problems, etc. Secondly, there were small numbers of Hebrew speakers in one group and their scores were all surprisingly low, which raises the question as to whether the Semitic languages are resistant to assessment in this way. Earlier studies of Arabic speakers (Ryan 1997) suggest that there may be fundamental differences between European and Semitic languages which unconsciously affect language processing in a second language. Thirdly, not all the dyslexic scores were low, and this clearly shows the power of compensatory strategies in reading as well as quite marked individual differences.

University of Edinburgh, Scotland

This section:

- highlights the role of the dyslexia advisor
- describes the assessment and support provision
- emphasises the cross-university role of supporting students with dyslexia from overseas, including staff development and
- provides examples of the assessment and support process with reference to two case studies.

Introduction

Of the 20,000 students currently studying at the University of Edinburgh, around 3,000 are from overseas. There are several reasons for the high numbers of overseas students choosing to study in Edinburgh. Edinburgh is a capital city and, therefore, has all the cultural attractions associated with a major tourist and business centre. The university has built up its links with the city and is justifiably proud of its 'town and gown' reputation. It has worked hard at achieving international standing: it offers a wide range of programmes at both undergraduate and postgraduate level; it attracts major grants for research purposes; and is committed to the progressive enhancement of its teaching and learning strategies.

Role of Disability Office and Dyslexia Advisor

In addition to providing extensive support for students whose first language is not English, the University of Edinburgh offers a range of support for students who have specific learning difficulties (dyslexia and other related conditions). The Disability Office is situated at the centre of the university and is easily accessible to all students. One of the aims of the Disability Office is to work very closely with other departments, administrative and academic. The Dyslexia Advisor is responsible for supporting over 400 students with dyslexia. This support covers a range of activities including: one-to-one interviews; group tutorials; meetings with the Director of Studies and the student to discuss any potential processing difficulties that may be encountered on the course; and the delivering of staff development courses to raise awareness of dyslexia within the university. The staff development courses are offered either as part of a whole university initiative or, more specifically, to a single department. The university aims to establish an ethos where appropriate support is the responsibility of all members of staff.

However, for students with dyslexia, there does need to be one-to-one sessions with the Dyslexia Advisor in order to put support in place. At this initial interview the Dyslexia Advisor gives students information about their entitlement to that support. This information should give them confidence to raise issues associated with dyslexia and study with all their tutors, including prior sight of lecture notes; focused reading lists; and specific assessment arrangements. At this first meeting it will be established whether or not the student has an up-to-date report of an assessment by an educational psychologist. If the student comes from overseas often the report is written by a physician and requires to be translated to allow it to be scrutinised by the University Psychologist so that a Personal Learning Profile can be compiled. If the student shows no evidence of dyslexia, or has never been formally assessed, then the university procedures for identifying students with dyslexia are put in place.

The university identification and assessment procedures have been developed in consultation with a dyslexia sub-group, which reports to Senatus through the Disability Committee. This sub-group includes members from all nine faculties as well as representatives from Registry and the Students' Association.

The first step is the screening interview. The Dyslexia Advisor carries out tests to establish whether or not the student has indicators of dyslexia. The tests used are QuickScan Screening Test, British Spelling Test, Series 5 and the Spadafore Reading Test, and a ten-minute test of free writing. In addition, a semi-structured interview questionnaire is completed. If the results of the tests indicate specific difficulties then the student is referred to the University Psychologist, who formally assesses using the WAIS to establish a cognitive profile and other measures of reading and writing. After the assessment has been completed the Dyslexia Advisor and the University Psychologist jointly compile the Learning Profile. In this profile, in addition to the results of the assessment, there are three important sections: firstly, there is a section giving the dyslexic profile of the student: secondly, there is a section giving the implications for study; and, finally, there is a section on IT and other forms of support. The profile is then discussed at a meeting between the Director of Studies, the student and the Dyslexia Advisor.

The support arrangements are similar whether the student is from the UK or overseas. The difference is the involvement of the Institute of Applied Language Studies (IALS) at an early stage in the procedure. For overseas students the decision to offer a place at the University of Edinburgh is based on an internationally recognised test, normally IELTS or TOEFL, which most prospective students take in their own country. After admission, IALS offers a second test, TEAM (Test of English at Matriculation), which is used for diagnostic purposes. This test is intended to assess whether the student is likely to need to take any of the additional English language courses run by IALS. TEAM tests three areas of academic English: vocabulary, listening and writing. It takes less than an hour. If the score of the student for the test is less than 50 per cent the university requires that student to take appropriate English Language Testing and Tuition (ELTT) courses. At this early stage IALS and the Dyslexia Advisor work together to ensure that specific examination and support arrangements are put in place so that all students can demonstrate their true potential. Among the specific examination arrangements offered are: extra time; examiners alerted to a processing difficulty; use of word processor; and the provision of a scribe.

Immediately after entry, and early in their courses, the Dyslexia Advisor will work with the individual students to ensure that support strategies are in place for effective learning. It is important that strategies which have been successful in their first language are transferred, and used, in their studies in English. In order to ensure that transfer takes place their learning style must be identified. If their strength is in spatial awareness then they should be advised to use diagrammatic strategies to plan written work and as a strategy for revision. If their strength is in aural perception then they should be encouraged to use recording equipment in lectures and tutorials and dictaphones to record their thoughts before committing them to paper. Whatever the first language, or preferred language for study, the appropriate use of the correct learning style is essential. The Dyslexia Advisor will work with students to identify their strengths and weaknesses and encourage them to adopt appropriate strategies.

Another important feature of the university support provision is advice and provision of IT equipment for students with dyslexia. The university has a Disabled Students' Support Fund that is used to buy equipment for students whose needs are not covered by the UK government-sponsored, Disabled Students' Allowance. After consultation with the Dyslexia Advisor appropriate equipment is purchased and lent to the student for the duration of the course. In addition, the Fund can be used to provide note-takers, scribes and for specific study-skills tuition. Study-skills tutorials are arranged for all students with dyslexia. Among the topics covered at these sessions are essay writing, revision strategies and exam techniques. A hidden advantage of the small group tutorial is that students from overseas and home students can work together. Very often students whose first language is not English can feel doubly insecure if they also have dyslexia. Finding that they have the same difficulties as home-based students can raise their self-esteem, particularly when they are encouraged to share their effective strategies for learning.

The use of the library can be problematic for students with dyslexia. It can be even worse for those studying in a second language. The process of reading can be extremely slow and laborious and, if time restrictions are imposed on the lending of books, can be very stressful. The Dyslexia Advisor, in collaboration with the University Library, offers specific arrangements for the use of the library to students with dyslexia. Among the range of strategies offered are: double-time loan on reserve books; weekend borrowing on short-loan books; access to individual study rooms in the library; and staff assistance with locating texts. In these ways it is hoped that the library experience of students with dyslexia can be made more productive and less stressful.

The Dyslexia Advisor takes part in staff development sessions throughout the university. Some sessions last for a whole morning, while others involve a short awareness-raising talk in an induction programme for new Directors of Studies. Wherever the staff development is provided, matters relating to specific learning difficulties in a language other than English are discussed and advice offered on how to support all our students. In addition, every member of staff has been issued with an aide-memoire card which, on one side, describes the difficulties encountered by students with dyslexia and, on the other side, offers some advice on marking and supporting these students. This bookmark, which was produced by the dyslexia sub-group, covers only the minimum amount of information on dyslexia but has proved useful in raising awareness. Another initiative currently on the agenda of the sub-group is the production of a staff handbook on dyslexia. This handbook, which contains a section on multilingualism, will offer more in-depth information and advice on identification and support of students with dyslexia. The contents of this handbook are also on the university website.

Although a very thorough report on Dyslexia in Higher Education was published in 1999 (National Working Party on Dyslexia in Higher Education 1999) no guidance was given, or reference made, to multilingual students with dyslexia. However, the report suggests that 'There are many difficulties encountered in higher education by students with dyslexia, but simply to list them fails to give any insight into the whole experience of any individual'.

The remainder of this section, therefore, provides two case studies which embody the general principles and aims of the university in identifying and supporting students from overseas.

Sami

Sami is 22 and in the second year of his Computing Studies course. He was admitted to this university in 1998 and came with a report of an assessment carried out by a chartered educational psychologist in 1996. Sami is trilingual in French, Arabic and English. This report recommended that he be given extra time to complete his examinations for entry to university.

Sami's school education was in Beirut and at the Lycée Francais Charles de Gaulle in London. He was observed to have a learning difficulty when at school in Beirut pre-1984 although specific difficulties were not mentioned. During his first five years at the Lycée he was given extensive specialist tuition and was assessed in 1994 by a chartered psychologist. Full account was taken in the assessment of the fact that he is trilingual in French, English and Arabic. Among the difficulties noted was his extremely slow pace of processing. The results of the WAIS (R) indicated that Sami was of average Verbal Ability (Verbal Scale IQ 101) and of superior Performance Ability (Performance Scale IQ 122). In the test of free writing his pace was very slow (18 words per minute) and his spelling was weak in relation to ability.

Very shortly after he started his computer science course he began to struggle, not because he had any difficulty understanding the material, but because he could not get access to a computer for long enough in order for him to complete programming tasks. The pace at which he works is extremely slow; he is very easily distracted by what is going on around him; and, when he is writing a computer program, he cannot interrupt the process to save to disk or he loses his train of thought and has to start again. He says he must complete the process at one sitting. The university, through the Disabled Students' Support Fund, provided Sami with a computer loaded with the same software and programs used by his department. He works very long hours but is successful in producing his coursework. He also needs extra time in the library and extra time to complete examinations. During his first term at university Sami became very stressed about his situation. A number of his tutors related his poor results in course work to his first language not being English rather than trying to support his dyslexic difficulties. However, now that he has the extra time to process all his assessed work he is achieving much better grades and is on track to get a 2.1 Honours degree.

Enrique

Enrique is an undergraduate from Spain. Shortly after he started his course in Biological Sciences he made an appointment to see the Dyslexia Advisor because he was concerned about his progress. He reported how hard he worked and how disappointed he was with his results. He thought his lack of achievement was due to English being his second language. However, he was concerned that he had additional processing difficulties.

He was screened for dyslexia using the QuickScan Screening Test. This computerised test takes account of the first language of the student. The results showed that Enrique had some of the indicators normally associated with dyslexia and that his learning style is visual/kinaesthetic. In addition, during a semi-structured interview, Enrique confirmed that he had certain other characteristics that are associated with dyslexia, for example, poor organisational skills and poor aural perception. He was referred to the University Psychologist for further assessment. The psychometric testing confirmed that Enrique was significantly dyslexic. He has good language comprehension but difficulties with short-term memory and speed of processing. His pace of reading is extremely slow. In addition, his time management organisation is poor. Specific examination arrangements were put in place for him and all his tutors were alerted to his processing difficulties. His IT needs were assessed in the light of his dyslexia and he obtained a desktop computer, loaded with relevant software, to complete his work in his own room. In order to help his organisation a Psion 5 was purchased. He uses this to take notes in lectures as well as an aide-memoire. Because of his slow pace of reading and writing along with his poor aural perception the main difficulty he encountered with his course was in practicals. He fell behind and was not able to access the relevant information and acquire the practical skills necessary to complete his course work. The university employed a postgraduate student to work alongside Enrique in the laboratories and he is now achieving success in this area.

In addition to the academic problems that Enrique had to deal with he also had concerns about disclosing his newly diagnosed dyslexia to his parents in Spain. At this stage they were blaming his lack of achievement on laziness! However, when he was able to show them the report from the psychologist they became supportive and sympathetic to his difficulties. This, in turn, made Enrique less stressed and more positive about his studies.

Although procedures for support of students with dyslexia must be based on a clear commitment and adequately resourced by the institution, each individual student has to be considered in the light of their own specific difficulties and chosen programme of study. The cases above demonstrate that support for multilingual students with dyslexia must be suited to their individual needs.

Chapter 21

Difficulties of English as a Foreign Language (EFL) for Students with Language-Learning Disabilities (Dyslexia)

Leonore Ganschow, Elke Schneider and Tsila Evers

This chapter:

- explains why students with language-learning difficulties in other countries may find the university requirement of proficiency in EFL a daunting, if not insurmountable task
- explains how universities in the United States handle the expectation of foreign language study for these students
- focuses on issues of legal protection, advocacy, eligibility, and accommodations
- suggests a flexible approach to a university's expectation for EFL proficiency and
- presents questions and suggestions for educators to consider in examining the necessity of EFL and in developing diagnostic criteria and reasonable accommodations that address a 'continuum' of severity.

Introduction

In a number of non-English speaking countries, students who wish to enter or remain at a university are expected to demonstrate proficiency in English. They often must pass a proficiency test. Preliminary results of a recent international pilot survey on English as a foreign language (hereafter referred to as EFL) indicated that expectations for English proficiency at the university level are high (Schneider *et al.* 1999). Survey responses from Language Development educators/researchers in 13 countries in Europe, 5 in South America, and 8 in Asia (including Israel) showed that over two-thirds of the respondents said EFL was 'highly necessary' in a student's everyday life at the university. Close to one-third reported that students are prohibited from entering higher education or are dismissed after entry because of inability to fulfil the English requirement. In Israel, for example, students must take English at the university to complete the general entrance requirement; if they continue to fail, they may not continue their college education. Students in Germany are screened in grades 4–6, at which time they are placed in different school 'tracks' based on their abilities. Each track requires learning English at increasing levels of difficulty. Students with language-learning difficulties may be screened out of university preparatory schools because of their inability to pass EFL requirements. The English proficiency requirement is especially difficult for students with language-based learning disabilities; it essentially eliminates many who otherwise would be able to master the content of university-level courses.

In the United States educators at colleges and universities have been working on expectations of study of a foreign language for students with language-based learning disabilities for over 24 years. Close to 3 per cent of all students who enter US universities have classified learning disabilities (including dyslexia) (Henderson 1995). A number of these students who graduate from the university go on to complete graduate and/or professional school training (Ganschow *et al.* 1999). Given the history of support in higher education for students with language-learning disabilities, it might be helpful for educators in other countries to find out how universities in the United States handle the foreign language requirement.

Why EFL may be difficult for students with language learning disabilities

Extensive research indicates that individuals with language-learning disabilities have difficulties with tasks involving listening to, speaking, reading, and/or writing their native language (Catts 1989). These problems have a genetic and neural basis (Duane 1991); there are individual differences in severity of the language disability (National Joint Committee on Learning Disabilities 1997); and it is a lifelong disability, not outgrown with age and maturity (Vogel 1998). Students who have problems learning their native language are almost certain to exhibit similar and often greater difficulties learning a foreign language (Ganschow and Sparks, in press; Ganschow *et al.* 1998a).

Most individuals with language-learning disabilities initially have difficulty grasping the phonological (sound)/orthographic (symbol) and morphological (roots, prefixes, suffixes) rule systems of their native language (Brady and Shankweiler 1991; Feldman 1995). Many also lack awareness of grammatical structures (such as sentence patterns or tense markers) (Vogel 1975). These basic language problems are often compounded by difficulties remembering and/or retrieving words and difficulties processing language quickly and efficiently (Wolf 1999). Individuals with phonological/orthographic and naming-speed deficits generally have severe problems learning to read, write, and spell (Bowers and Wolf 1993). Those who fail to acquire adequate word reading skills and automaticity develop increasingly greater failure in reading over time, e.g., negative attitudes, reduced vocabulary, less practice reading, and fewer opportunities to learn good comprehension strategies (Stanovich 1986). Those who fail to develop adequate writing skills early on develop a fear of writing and tend to write primarily simple sentences using words they know, and their writing is filled with spelling and grammatical errors (Bain *et al.* 1991).

Research on foreign language study in the United States has also shown that the sound/symbol rule system of the foreign language poses considerable difficulty for most students who struggle to learn a foreign language (Ganschow *et al.* 1998a). Poor understanding of grammatical structures and the morphology of a foreign language cause problems for many (Schneider 1999). Findings indicate that poor foreign language learners need systematic instruction on the structure of the foreign language (Schneider 1999). Whereas many students find learning a new language challenging, those who have relatively weaker language skills face greater hurdles.

In the case of non-English speaking countries, students learning EFL have their own unique sets of problems because of structural differences between their native language and the foreign language. Figures 21.1 and 21.2 show two examples, the first of a student whose native language is Hebrew and who is learning English; the second, of a student whose native language is German and who is learning English.

The examples in Figures 21.1 and 21.2 illustrate important differences between languages that students with language-learning disabilities may fail to recognise. Research has shown that students who receive explicit instruction in the rule systems of the native and/or foreign language do progress (Ganschow *et al.* 1998a). Yet, they do not catch up with their peers who do not have language-learning disabilities. EFL presents one of the biggest academic challenges these students are likely to face in college.

Phonology
In Hebrew there is no equivalent sound for /th/ as in this or these. Hebrew speakers may say /dzis/ or /dzees/, respectively.

Grammar/Sentence Structure
1) In Hebrew the adjective FOLLOWS the noun, and the DEFINITE ARTICLE is repeated.
Example: 'HABAIT HAADOM' means (literally) 'The house the red'. Hebrew speakers might use the Hebrew syntactic rule in English and say: 'The house the red' instead of 'The red house'.

2) In Hebrew questions are formed by adding a question mark at the end of a sentence and ending on a high pitch.
Example: In Hebrew, the sentence: 'Did you come?' is 'ATA BATA?' Hebrew speakers might apply the same rule to English and say: 'You come?' *instead of* 'Did you come?'

Figure 21.1 Structural differences between Hebrew and English that may pose problems for students with dyslexia

Phonology
The English sound /v/ is spelled {v} in English but {f} in German.
Example: The van is very voluminous.

The German student with language-learning disabilities may say the above sentence as follows: The fan is fery foluminous.

Grammar/Sentence Structure
In German the conjugated verb moves to 1st position when a question is formed.
Example: 'Er besitzt einen Hund' *changes to* 'Besitzt er einen Hund?'

English uses 'do-forms' to form a question and the main verb remains after the subject.
Example: 'He owns a dog' *changes to* 'Does he own a dog?'

The German student with language-learning disabilities may say the above sentence as follows: 'Owns he a dog?'

Vocabulary/Spelling
In German, often three or more words from different parts of speech are put together to form a new word; connectives (s) are added between the two last words; and though nouns are capitalised in German, they lose their capital letters within compound words.
Example: Sonnen + unter + gang + Spektakel = Sonnenuntergangsspektakel or 'spectacular sunset'.

In English one seldom sees more than two words put together to form compound words; English generally does not make use of connectives and English rules for capitalisation differ from German.

The German student with language-learning disabilities might find it difficult to identify the individual words in 'Sonnenuntergangspektakel', forget to include the connective 's' between the last two words, and capitalise both nouns. Pronunciation of this word is likely to be very difficult because of failure to recognise the four words within the compound word.

Figure 21.2 Structural differences between German and English that may pose problems for students with dyslexia

Support for students with language learning disabilities at US universities

A review of policies and procedures at US universities for students with language-learning disabilities may be helpful to educators. In this section the authors describe three areas related to these students that have been addressed in the United States: (1) laws, policies and advocacy; (2) eligibility; and (3) services.

Laws, policies and advocacy

Laws such as Section 504 of the Rehabilitation Act of 1973 and the Individuals with Disabilities Act protect individuals with learning disabilities from birth through adult life (Heyward 1992; Tucker 1996). Most of the learning disabilities services at universities in the United States were established in the 1980s (Vogel *et al.* 1998). At the university level, educators, service providers, and administrators generally provide their own interpretation of these laws. Compliance with the laws is a matter resolved by mutual agreement of the institution, the disabilities service provider, and the student. Sometimes, however, differences have to be handled by the courts. Two recent lawsuits provide a case in point. In one case (Guckenberger v. Boston University, 1997) the issue involved claims from students (plaintiffs) that Boston University had instituted an across-the-board policy precluding course substitutions in foreign language and mathematics. The judge initially ruled that the university (defendant) was responsible for demonstrating that course substitutions would fundamentally alter the nature of the university's liberal arts degree. After the university provided that evidence, the judge ruled in favour of Boston University. The ruling clarified the rights of universities to determine their own curriculum, and as a result, students who attend Boston University are required to fulfil the foreign language requirement.

A second case (Bartlett v. New York State Board of Law Examiners, 1997) involved a law school student who sought accommodations in taking the licensure exam. The State Board's expert witness determined that she did not have dyslexia, based on cut-off scores on a standardised reading test. Yet, she had a long history of dyslexia and had received accommodations while in law school. The court declared that clinical judgment is required in the case of adults, who have spent years learning compensatory skills, and ruled in favour of the student based on the severity of her disability in the context of the bar exam. The judge reminded the courts that 'one cannot look to whether an individual is disabled without considering in what context the individual might be "substantially limited"' (p. 52). This position also is supported by the National Joint Committee on Learning Disabilities (NJCLD), a group of experts in the field who have stated in a position paper that 'severity of disability differs and varies in different contexts and with the demands of different life stages' (NJCLD 1997). These cases demonstrate that the courts play an important role in decisions involving students with language-learning disabilities at university.

University educators and administrators have been addressing the issue of foreign language accommodations for students with learning disabilities for over 20 years. Each university has its own procedures for the foreign language requirement. Some require a foreign language in select majors only (Ganschow *et al.* 1989). Some require a foreign language prior to entering the university or students must make up the deficiency in the first two years (Philips *et al.* 1991). In the United States, then, there is flexibility for students with dyslexia to select a university or a programme of study that does not include a foreign language. For an even greater flexibility of options, many universities have procedures for course substitutions for students with classified learning disabilities who demonstrate severe difficulties completing the foreign language requirement (Philips *et al.* 1991). Students may select language, literature, and/or culture courses related to a specific language as course substitutions. Some universities accept American sign language and computer programming as substitutes. In a few universities, foreign language faculties in consultation with learning disabilities staff offer special classes for students who self-identify as (or are determined to be) at risk for learning a foreign language (Hill *et al.* 1995).

In the United States there are a number of national/international professional organisations that advocate for students with learning disabilities. They include organisations that specialise in policies, procedures, and services specifically related to disabilities in higher education (e.g., Association on Higher Education and Disability); organisations that specialise in learning disabilities with interest groups on university issues (e.g., International Dyslexia Association and Learning Disabilities Association of America); and an umbrella organisation that focuses on disabilities that includes learning disabilities (Council for Exceptional Children).

Eligibility

Until recently universities were inconsistent in their criteria for eligibility for accommodations and on assessment instruments for determination of a learning disability. In 1997, however, the Association on Higher Education and Disability (AHEAD) published a document that established professional standards for diagnosticians, criteria to use in identifying a learning disability, assessment instruments appropriate for university students, and qualifications for diagnosticians. The guidelines include the use of clinical judgment by competent certified diagnosticians. Sometimes students are evaluated prior to entering the university. In other cases the student pays for a private diagnostic evaluation after entering the university. A few universities stipulate that entering students be reassessed by their diagnostician prior to consideration for special accommodations.

Educators in the United States have also made suggestions specifically for diagnosis of foreign language-learning problems. In general, the diagnostician should use both formal and informal assessment approaches and assess both native and foreign language-learning performance. Suggestions for the diagnosis of a foreign language-learning problem include: (a) an informal interview with the student to determine early history of difficulties learning to read, write, and spell as well as evidence of history of problems learning a foreign language, such as reports from teachers and tutors, foreign language grades, and evidence of struggle despite tutoring assistance; (b) formal assessments in the native language that include indicators of slower-than-normal reading rate, poor spelling, and poor decoding, especially of nonsense words; (c) an assessment of written language, including paragraphs in narrative and essay formats; and (d) a description of specific problems in the foreign language classroom, obtained through interview with the student, teacher, and/or tutor and through samples of daily work (Sparks and Ganschow 1993a).

Services

By law students classified as learning disabled are entitled to accommodations that do not compromise essential requirements of a course or programme; thus, concern is taken not to lower academic standards or alter programmes substantially. The issue of compromising programme standards, for example, formed the basis for the foreign language decision in the aforementioned Guckenberger v. Boston University case, where the judge ruled in favour of the university because Boston University presented evidence that a course substitution for the foreign language would compromise its Arts and Sciences programme.

Colleges and universities differ greatly in the extent of their services for students with learning disabilities. These services exist on a continuum ranging from minimal legal compliance at some universities to specialised two-year colleges designed specifically for students with learning disabilities. There is also a continuum of services at graduate and professional schools, ranging from minimal compliance to model graduate training programmes designed to help students attain degrees from dental, medical, and law schools (Ganschow *et al.* 1999). According to federal legislation, universities must make 'reasonable' accommodations that might include, but are not limited to, extending the length of time for completion of a degree; allowing course substitutions; providing auxiliary aids, such as taped texts, readers, note-takers, and automated spellers and dictionaries; allowing for part-time rather than full-time study; and modifying examination procedures. Special accommodations are available for university and graduate entrance exams.

The Technology-Related Assistance Act of 1988 provides legislative support for the use of assistive technology. For writing difficulties, the laptop computer has been useful for editing, note-taking in class, and typing instead of hand-writing essay exams. With new dictation capabilities, students with language-learning disabilities can dictate writing to avoid the interference of problems with transcription processes, such as spelling, capitalisation, punctuation, and usage – which interfere with the composing processes of students with dyslexia. Students who are working specifically on reading comprehension in the foreign language are likely to find a combination of reading and listening to text helpful (Higgins and Raskin 1997). Here assistive technological support includes speech-control tape recorders, reading machines with optical character recognition, listening aids that use a microphone and headset, and voice output systems that read back text displayed on a computer screen (Day and Edwards 1996).

The above accommodations are sufficient for many students with language-learning disabilities. Some, however, need more intensive intervention. A few universities have developed special courses specifically designed to help struggling foreign language learners. The University of Colorado, for example, has a modified foreign language programme for students who have extreme difficulties (Hill *et al.* 1995). Students must apply and be assessed to substantiate their problem. Once approved for the modified instruction, students may sign up for Latin, Spanish, or Italian. They are told that they must spend a minimum of two hours of foreign language study daily outside of their classes; they are advised to take a reduced course load and to avail themselves of tutoring assistance; and they sign a contract of attendance and commitment. Students receive full credit for the modified course work and are expected to return to the mainstreamed class after two to three semesters to complete the two-year requirement. Findings to date indicate that most who complete the course work have been able to handle the final semester in the regular classroom.

A flexible approach to EFL for students with language-learning disabilities

The authors recommend a flexible approach to expectations of proficiency in EFL. Three areas to consider are (1) the impact and need for EFL proficiency; (b) diagnosis and (c) compensatory options. Figures 21.3, 21.4 and 21.5 present ideas to consider in developing a flexible approach to EFL.

The impact and need for EFL proficiency

If educators in the university system plan to encourage individuals with disabilities, including dyslexia, to consider higher education as an option, it would be helpful to examine the impact of EFL on their students and on the university system. Educators should also examine the necessity of the requirement. The authors recommend starting with the questions in Figure 21.3. By answering these questions, the university staff will be in a better position to make decisions on policies regarding EFL.

Diagnosis

If educators at the university decide to develop services, their planning should include an assessment of the prospective student's language-learning difficulties. The assessment might be implemented by a staff member in the institution; alternatively, the service provider might refer the student to an outside independent diagnostician and/or agency. To clarify the diagnostic process, university educators might ask themselves the questions presented in Figure 21.4. Once the student has a diagnostic profile of language strengths and weaknesses, the service provider and the student can select options that are available from the university.

Compensatory options

If educators at the university decide to develop options regarding EFL requirements, they should consider a continuum of support. Some students might only need extended time to take an English proficiency test; others might need a taped version of the test in order to simultaneously hear and read the test. Those who fail EFL proficiency tests, however, may need a lengthy period of intensive instruction after entering college, and this instruction may need to supersede their other course work. A few students may be unable fulfil English proficiency requirements, in which case decisions will need to be made about whether or not they should be allowed to waive or substitute the requirement. Just as severity of the language problems exist on a continuum, the support systems in place should reflect a continuum of alternatives. Figure 21.5 presents suggestions for early preparation for proficiency in English and a continuum of accommodations for the EFL requirement for students with dyslexia.

Impact of EFL Requirement

1. How many students with classified learning disabilities apply to the university?
2. How many students leave the university because of failure to meet the EFL requirement?
3. Of those students with learning disabilities, which students are unable to fulfil the proficiency requirement and why?
4. Of those who are able to succeed, what contributes to their success?
5. Is there a disabilities service provider at the university? If not, is the university in a position to hire a person who specialises in learning disabilities?
6. To what extent is the university willing and able to provide compensatory support to students who have difficulty reading and writing English?
7. Which academic faculty might be identified who would be willing to work with the EFL instructor on accommodations? (For information on the role of faculty in working with students with language learning disabilities, see Rose 1993.)
8. What compensatory options is the university willing or able to provide?

Necessity of EFL Requirement

1. How necessary is proficiency in English to the students' overall success at the university? Are there different 'levels' of necessity? Are there different 'kinds' of necessity, such as the need for reading proficiency but not speaking proficiency?
2. Are there differences across programmes of study on the need for English proficiency? Is English proficiency obligatory for some programmes of study (e.g. international studies) and not necessary or as necessary for others (e.g. biology)?
3. Is a support system in place for students with learning disabilities?

Figure 21.3 Impact and necessity of the EFL requirement

1. Who will develop criteria for assessment of language learning difficulties?
2. How will the university determine who is eligible for services?
3. What assessments will be required to determine eligibility for services?
4. Will university staff or outside agencies conduct the assessment? If outside agencies, which agencies or diagnosticians will be acceptable to the university?

Figure 21.4 Diagnostic procedures

I. Preparation prior to entering the university. Instructor should:
  - teach the structure of both native and foreign languages explicitly and directly
  - start this instruction early in the grade school years
  - use visual representations along with speech
  - use computer software to reinforce concepts, not as the focus of instruction
  - be fluent in the language of instruction and not have a 'foreign' accent.

II. Continuum of accommodations after entering the university. University staff should:
A. Consider allowing the student with mild to moderate difficulties
  - extended time to take tests
  - to take tests in distraction-free environment
  - to use assistive technology.
B. Consider allowing student with moderate to severe difficulties (in addition to above accommodations)
  - to take the test in a different format; for example, to listen to a tape as s/he reads along with written copy.
C. Consider advising/allowing student who fails the proficiency test
  - to take a major in which English is not an absolute necessity
  - to take a trial semester of college in the student's native language; if successful, permit student to continue.

Figure 21.5 Preparation for and continuum of accommodations for the English proficiency requirement

Conclusion

Many countries now require the study of EFL for students beginning in grade school. Students with language-learning disabilities often lack a solid firm foundation in their native language, and problems in their mother tongue affect their ability to learn a foreign language. The authors suggest that students with language-learning disabilities who aspire to a university education are likely to need a variety of accommodations in EFL beginning in the early years. Without a continuum of options, these students may find it impossible to succeed at university. Even early, explicit preparation and accommodations in EFL throughout schooling may not be sufficient to enable some students to attain proficiency in EFL. Systematic instruction in both the native and foreign language by instructors trained in teaching the structure of language to students with learning disabilities may be sufficient to enable most students to work within the requirement. Efforts on the part of EFL teachers to address the language-based problems of students with dyslexia early on will certainly be beneficial to later success with English at university. Educators in each country must decide whether or not students with language-learning disabilities should receive the accommodations that may be necessary for them to enter and be successful at university.

Chapter 22

Identifying and Helping Learning-Disabled English as a Second Language (ESL) Students in a College Intensive English Programme

Robin L. Schwarz

This chapter:

- investigates why seemingly bright international students fail English courses in the intensive English programme at the American University, Washington DC
- examines the relationship between this and undiagnosed learning disabilities and
- describes the Learning Skills Programme designed to identify and support ESL students with learning disabilities.

Introduction

Description of the English programme

The English Language Institute (ELI) of the American University in Washington, DC, is a medium-sized intensive English programme of about 500 students, whose purpose is primarily to feed international students into the mainstream of the university. Students can begin academic classes before fully finishing their English requirement, so there is a mixture of non-degree and degree (matriculated) undergraduate students, as well as graduate students and a few English-only students. The skills-based curriculum permits students to study in different levels of reading, writing, listening/speaking and grammar. Students are evaluated separately in the four skills when they arrive and are placed into any of six levels of courses. The first four levels are intensive, with 75-minute classes of all four skills meeting four days per week and the two fifth-level classes also meet four days a week. The credit-bearing sixth-level class, meeting twice a week, is a freshman composition course reserved for international students and is required for graduation. The very minimal entry requirements for ELI – a secondary school diploma of some kind and some previous English study – permit students whose educational backgrounds may be very weak to attempt to gain admission to the university by taking academic courses once they have reached high intermediate English levels. If they can prove they can do university work, they can be admitted.

The ELI students, coming from over 80 countries, with most from Asia and the Arabian Gulf, are taught by 17 full-time teachers in approximately 55 sections.

Since the vast majority have studied English for many years, Level I classes are rarely run and Level II classes may be quite small.

Failing students and learning disabilities

Students who fail despite everyone's best efforts are a source of great frustration in an English programme. This can cause disappointment, and often scholarships or sponsorships, visas and academic hopes are lost. ELI faces a failure rate sometimes as high as 30 per cent of all registrations. One of the causes of failure is the students arriving with poor academic records, while another is the admitted (degree) students who must carry a heavy credit course load and frankly expend minimum effort on their non-credit English classes. A few students have been sent abroad to study by eager parents and are not truly invested in studying. Then there are always some who have been sick or have had family emergencies. However, these reasons do not explain all the failures.

The notion of a learning disability being the cause for problems learning another language was not widely known until fairly recently. In the United States, this idea began to grow in the late 1970s as ESL and bilingual special education specialists became aware that the special education classes in elementary and high schools were filling with limited-English-proficient students. These educators realised that they needed to distinguish the special needs students from those learning English normally. It was not until the 1990s, however, that the existence of learning-disabled college ESL students was considered. Even now, very few post-secondary English programmes and teachers in the United States know much about learning-disabled students. Instead, a common reaction of ESL teachers to their students' failures is a refrain familiar to the parents and others who know learning-disabled students: they are not trying hard enough, they are not concentrating, they are not motivated to do university-level work or they do not have the ability to do university level work (even though some of the failing students already hold undergraduate degrees). Academic faculty and advisors have also been likely to attribute problems to lack of effort or perhaps to lack of English or both, despite clear evidence to the contrary. Somehow the possibility of being a non-native speaker of English and having a learning disability is one that is rarely considered by anyone.

Nonetheless, there obviously are such students. Sheer statistics – the Learning Disabilities Association states that 7–10 per cent of the general population has a learning disability severe enough to cause academic problems – indicate that every English programme will have some learning-disabled students. Moreover, Dinklage (1971) noted years ago at Harvard and Ganschow and Sparks (1993) confirmed that a student can be highly functional in the first language and yet have mild to severe problems when trying to master a second or other language. Recent research indicates that this problem is even more likely to occur when a student already at risk for reading problems learns English (Geva 1999; Goswami 1999b; Spencer 1999). Thus, statistics alone would indicate some learning-disabled students at ELI and the presence of students known from the outset to be academically weak would seem to increase that possibility.

The beginnings of the programme at ELI

Richard Beaubien of Mercer University stated at the 1999 International TESOL Conference in New York that he felt it was the moral responsibility of a school to help its international students who probably had learning disabilities and did not know it. It was this very same sentiment that 12 years earlier had prompted one of the ELI teachers to do something about the students whose failures had no reasonable explanation. Struck by the similarities between the problems she had seen in adult learning-disabled students at the Night School of the Lab School of Washington (a school for the learning disabled) and those of many of the failing ESL students at ELI, the teacher began to look for help in the literature of ESL and of learning disabilities. Though there was little information at that stage, what was there indicated that, just as the teacher had observed, the problems of the learning disabled were the same across languages. With this reassurance, the teacher began asking her colleagues to be aware of students with such problems as poor spelling that persisted despite much correction and instruction, a persistent inability to follow directions contrasting sharply with excellent speaking skills, or reading that did not improve. Gradually the other teachers confirmed these problems in failing students and the students were sent to the interested teacher for in-depth interviews.

Though most students initially denied having any problems in their first language, inevitably some key information would be revealed such as an Arab student having had such a difficult time learning to read that his mother had tied him to her; a Japanese student admitting to never being able to construct very understandable sentences when writing in Japanese; or a Hispanic student saying that he had never been able to spell in Spanish. In this way, students were identified one-by-one as probably having a learning disability. To confirm it so the students could obtain legally mandated accommodations, they were then referred to an outside expert diagnostician with previous experience of non-native speakers of English. The diagnostician, using non-language bound parts of tests plus history from records at ELI and the student's interview, estimated the severity and nature of the specific disability. For the Spanish speaking, who were referred to a Spanish-speaking diagnostician, more could be discovered given the existence of testing instruments in Spanish. Usually, though, the diagnosis could be no more than an accurate guess, since by virtue of being both non-native English speakers and post-adolescent in age, the students did not fit the norming populations of almost any existing tests. Sometimes, for more information, a neurological screening was added, as were hearing and vision examinations.

Once the student had documentation indicating a strong possibility of a learning disability, the ELI teacher assisted her colleagues in understanding what accommodations and adjustments would help the student succeed. Perhaps the student could not clean up the grammar or spelling in the framework of the English courses, and teachers were asked not to penalise the student for these problems. Generally teachers were requested to allow extra time for tests and other tasks, to permit writing students to rewrite before work was graded, to be sure the student received in writing all assignments for homework, or to try alternative assessments. With the cooperation of their ELI teachers, the few students who were helped this way were able to pass the English courses and could get on to their academic courses, where they usually managed fairly well.

Problems

While it was rewarding to see these students gradually having the success they so eagerly sought, this limited system had its problems. First, it was helping only a very few students; many others were failing but were not referred for screening when they ought to have been, often because numerous teachers still did not believe that smart students could be learning disabled, and therefore blamed failure on laziness or simple lack of progress (a circular argument). Second, the at-risk students could not get the direct instruction in phonology which Leonore Ganschow and Richard Sparks (Sparks *et al.* 1991) had recently determined was effective for poor language learners. Similarly, special teaching techniques shown to be helpful for learning-disabled foreign language learners at the University of Colorado at Boulder could not be provided (Downey 1992; Hill *et al.*1995). Also, being unaware of learning disabilities, the ESL students did not understand how learning disabilities affected their lives, especially school, and were not ready to advocate for themselves. Another significant problem was that the teacher initiating the idea had a full teaching load already and lacked time for much more, but the administration of the Institute did not feel that this effort needed any support other than permitting it to happen. Finally, students were not referred for screening until they had already failed more than once and by then, the students were dismayed and their academic record already damaged.

At this point, an academic advisor whose job was to work with the ELI students became deeply interested in the idea of finding out if students had learning disabilities and then providing a support system. In her efforts to counsel students about their problems with classes, teachers and school in general, she had often been puzzled by those whom she could tell were bright and trying hard, but who seemed to make so little progress. She was delighted to have a more constructive response to their difficulties than telling them to work harder. Since she worked closely with the administrators in aspects of running the Institute, the advisor convinced the Director that finding and helping more at-risk students earlier would be beneficial. Consequently, the teacher who had been working with the learning-disabled students was granted release time from one-third of her teaching load to permit her time to work with more students and to screen for problems during ELI's placement test. Students identified this way would be put into one class, called the 'special class' and the teacher would be (unofficially) known as the Learning Skills Advisor (LSA).

Establishing the special class

The academic advisor and the LSA decided that the special class would be a low-level writing class because it was in writing that the students seemed to be at the greatest risk of failure. Also, many of the other elements of the model language classes could easily be included. The low level was chosen so that the LSA could start by re-teaching basic skills and then could move the group as a cohort to the subsequent levels until they had completed level 5 or 6 writing.

Next, a quick way of determining who would be recommended for the class during the placement process was developed. Since students would be placed in writing, their writing samples were the primary focus. After years of experience of evaluating the placement essays in teams, ELI teachers knew that students who wrote a lot, but whose essays were riddled with usage, spelling and mechanical errors were the hardest to place and the most likely to fail in the writing class. The other skill placements of those students whose writing seemed to indicate possible problems were then examined since students with foreign language learning problems generally are somewhat competent in one aspect of language and very weak in another, with oral/aural skills frequently outstripping the writing and grammar (Ganschow and Sparks 1993; Sparks and Ganschow 1995). Most ELI students identified as at risk in writing showed this pattern clearly. The students matching the two criteria – poor control of writing contrasting with strong oral skills – were strongly recommended for the special class.

With this method of screening, approximately 10 per cent, or about 15, of the incoming students in the fall were found to be at risk for problems and recommended for special placement, but some would not accept such a low placement in writing in contrast to their other high placements. For others, the recommendation was overruled because their essays were rated differently by other teachers, or the Director felt the placement was unreasonable. A few other students were recommended for the class who had failed writing the previous semester, and occasionally, a student was identified during diagnostic testing in the first week of classes who had not been caught in the placement screening process. Then, with such limited criteria, inevitably one or two of the students placed in the special class had weak essays merely because of rusty skills or all-out fatigue (many students take the placement test the day after 12–24 hour flights). If these showed sudden improvement in writing, they were immediately moved to regular sections. When the dust finally settled – usually the third week of classes – the special class had anywhere from 12 to 18 students.

Purposes of the special class

Teaching phonological skills

Creating a specialised curriculum designed to meet the needs of the at-risk/learning-disabled students better than the standard writing curriculum of the Institute would was the overarching goal of the special class. One of the first needs the LSA wanted to address was phonological deficits which seemed to be at the root of many language acquisition problems (Ganschow and Sparks 1993; Sparks *et al.* 1991). Thus, one day a week of the schedule was devoted to relearning English phonology and syllable rules. Various commercial materials were used along with many teacher-made ones. Though the students at first felt this was wasting their time in English, once they began to notice the benefits they became very enthusiastic about it. Their spelling improved dramatically and with it, their aural comprehension and their reading. Other teachers corroborated these improvements, which encouraged the students even more.

Providing specialised teaching

Besides the phonological needs of the students, the class was designed to respond to their needs as primarily learning-disabled students. Following the model language classes adapted for learning-disabled students at the University of Colorado at Boulder instruction was multisensory, the pace of instruction was considerably slower than that of a standard ELI writing class, the amount of information that the students were required to learn was limited, an enormous amount of review and re-teaching was planned for, and the class was moulded to have a very supportive atmosphere for the learners (Downey 1992; Hill *et al.* 1995; Sparks *et al.* 1991). Multisensory instruction meant that students not only heard what they needed to learn, but read it, spoke it, wrote it and explained it to each other. Manipulative materials were brought in when learning needed a boost; visual organisers included everything from assignment sheets to 'maps' of composition types to rigidly structured notebooks. Slowing the pace of the class was achieved by following the principle of teaching to mastery, meaning that bad grades resulted in the target lesson being reviewed and re-taught until all students had mastered it. Addressing elements of writing in separate lessons on separate days also guaranteed that the class could not proceed as fast as a regular class, and that students then had plenty of time to absorb one type of lesson before visiting that aspect of writing again. This way of teaching also assured a great deal of review, which in turn provided many opportunities for multisensory activities.

Not only was the amount of information given at any one time reduced, but the way it was talked about was also adjusted. In regular ESL classes and texts, students must learn a 'metalanguage' to talk about grammar and writing and reading. This abstract language was very confusing for the learning-disabled students, so in the special class, terms such as 'major and minor supporting details' would be simplified to 'big ideas' and 'smaller ideas'.

Providing a supportive atmosphere

The students with learning disabilities in the adapted language classes at the University of Colorado could return to regular classes if they chose. Downey reported at the American University's 1992 Conference on Learning Disabilities and Foreign/Second Language Learning that the few students who chose to return to the regular classes quickly left to come back to the special classes. When asked why, the students reported that they felt safer among students with similar problems, and they felt that students in regular classes resented the learning-disabled students' need for repetition and a slower pace. Similarly, the students in the ELI special class had the option of going back into regular writing classes, but none did. They were already in regular classes for their other skills, and found the differences in pace, review time, and psychological comfort quite vivid. Moreover, it was made clear in the special class that all students had trouble with writing and/or English in one way or another, and that part of their responsibilities to the class was to be supportive of their classmates. This was challenging for some who came from cultures where ridicule of weaker students was the norm and not seen as rude. Others were embarrassed that classmates knew they had problems, but seeing their classmates' problems, sometimes worse than their own, they were reassured. Students reported that they especially liked being able to ask 'dumb' questions – that is, questions that seemed obvious to other students or that the teacher had already explained. In this class, such questions were welcomed rather than scoffed at because they indicated that a student had not understood, and were therefore a vital part of the learning process.

Teaching student skills

Although phonological skills were helpful to the students, and the other pedagogical aspects of the course were vital to its success, the third planned element of the class – explicit instruction in study and 'student' skills – undoubtedly met some of the most pressing needs of these students. Many learning-disabled students have trouble with time management, organisation, generalisations, social interactions, and task prioritisation. Add to these difficulties the challenges of a new language and a new culture, especially a new educational culture, and it is easy to understand that the learning-disabled ESL students were at a huge disadvantage in the school culture of a US university. Two aspects of student life gave them particular trouble: accessing the resources of the university, and functioning appropriately in classes. The academic advisor addressed some of these major problem areas in an extra 'lab' session of the class. Later, some of these topics were included in the curriculum of the course, although it was not as effective as the lab had been, largely because not enough time could be devoted to teaching them.

Accessing the resources of the university was addressed first. When they arrive on campus, all international students at the American University are taken in groups through a rapid and information-loaded orientation session given by well-meaning American undergraduates who speak rapidly in highly idiomatic English. The international students are often shy because of language or culture, and therefore do not ask questions that might show they do not understand. Knowing the learning-disabled students were even more likely to have missed a lot, the academic advisor, and later the LSA, first re-presented essential information in small chunks, then personally escorted the students to revisit such places as the International Student Office, the Registrar's Office, the Library Reference desk, the Computer Information Office, and the security building. At these stops, students were introduced to those persons with whom they would need to interact and were permitted to ask questions. Their understanding of what services these places provided was checked and rechecked, and when questions or problems arose during the semester, the students were redirected to these offices. Since much essential information was also on the university website, students were also carefully taught to access it successfully.

The other area of student life, functioning in classes, was also addressed both in the lab and in the special class. These students often did not know what to look for in a syllabus, what attendance policies were, or what happened when they missed deadlines. They tended to apply the rules of their own educational systems instead, but then had problems. In the lab, the academic advisor dealt with time management, teaching students how to make schedule grids so they could see where in their schedules they had time for homework. She also helped them think through problems such as getting to an early class on time, where to go on campus to get help with papers, or what to do if they missed class. Organisation, presentation of work, and following directions were explicitly taught in the class by such methods as using a 3-ring binder to organise handouts and homework. Students were also drilled in details that were often ignored or overlooked such as putting correct headings on papers and formatting papers correctly. Since the learning-disabled students often reported losing points on papers and tests for not paying attention to directions, this behaviour was heavily emphasised in the special class. Homework or essays not done exactly according to directions were returned uncorrected, and had to be done again.

Timeliness, attendance and homework were other aspects of American school culture that the special students found hard to absorb. In the cultures of many of them, attendance is not required, nor is homework. The students take one exam at the end of the term and pass or fail regardless of attendance or homework record. To help them learn attendance and homework discipline, standards in the special class were very strict. Students' homework and attendance improved dramatically, but then they had to be helped to understand that these were lessons to apply to other classes. That idea was reinforced through teaching students to read the course syllabi, which include each professor's attendance requirements, homework policies, format requirements, and so on. Students frequently did not read these first-day handouts, thinking they were just general information, or more likely because they found them linguistically and culturally very challenging.

Teaching self-advocacy skills

According to a recent study by the Frostig Institute of California (Raskind *et al.* 1999) one of the surest guarantees of success for a learning-disabled student in the long run is good self-advocacy skills. Helping the students acquire these skills was another major goal of the special class. First the students needed to recognise what their own strengths and weaknesses were and what was most helpful to them in their weak areas. Then students needed to be explicitly instructed in what accommodations and support was available to them, and when and how they should ask for it. This was a difficult process as the students were wholly unaware of the term 'learning disabled' before coming to the United States and were very wary of a designation that sounded to some like an illness, or at least like a very negative condition. Also, a few preferred what they felt was honourable failure to what they considered unfair intervention.

Another reason for the special class

In addition to being able to adapt the instruction to the needs of the at-risk students, the LSA and the academic counsellor wanted to be able to monitor the students in a way not possible in the regular classes. Because of the nature of language-learning patterns, plus all the cultural variables and issues of adjustment, it was necessary to watch the progress of the at-risk students over a period of time before deciding more firmly that they could have a learning disability. Having them in one class made it easier to watch their progress, their learning styles, and their responses to accommodations, and to gather information from them to pinpoint what was causing difficulty. This information could be passed on to the diagnostician to make the picture of the student more complete.

Referring students for a diagnostic workup

Even after all the screening, observation, accommodation and information gathering, finally obtaining a diagnostic workup was not simple. The primary reason for referring students for further testing was for the student to obtain a legal declaration that s/he was learning disabled. With that designation, the university could extend any accommodation the student might need, just as it did for American students with learning disabilities. Nonetheless, despite that advantage, some students refused to be tested, fearing adverse family reactions; others baulked at the cost; still others were simply not convinced of the need. Usually, however, when faced with the simple fact that without such a designation, they would be dismissed because of low grades, most agreed to testing.

The students in the special class were referred to a psychologist who was bilingual and so was especially sensitive to second language issues that could affect testing results. This diagnostician also used parts of many tests, a long interview, and the history at ELI to prepare a report in which she estimated the learning disability and made recommendations for accommodations. Using the report, the LSA guided the ELI teachers, while the school's Learning Services Office helped the students with accommodations in their academic classes. Generally the ELI teachers helped the students manage in English classes; however, if a student was diagnosed as having severe problems in one area such as grammar or reading and had already failed one of those classes once, s/he would be asked to sit through it again as an auditor; then s/he could proceed to the next level, where full accommodation would be provided (teachers willing). In very rare cases, a full waiver of a class was offered, but only where testing indicated that progress in that skill was highly unlikely. Remediation of skills, except in the special class, was never an option unless the student chose to pursue it outside of the Institute.

The second prong of the Programme

Though the special class was the bigger part of the Programme, screening and helping those students who were failing in other ELI classes was the other. As at the beginning, students continued to be referred by alert teachers, by now more convinced of learning problems. The LSA first checked for visual difficulties which cause problems very much like those of dyslexia and are not usually caught by a traditional eye test. Then the LSA administered a modest test of phonological skills, mostly involving rhyming, and finally conducted the in-depth interview.

The factors governing the referral of these students for further testing were the same as for the students in the special class and the teachers of these students were able to provide work samples, observations and other information that was helpful in making a diagnosis. Since referral and testing was a very time-consuming process, the LSA would advise teachers about measures they could take in their classrooms to help the students in the meantime, especially those students with visual problems. Although some teachers continued to doubt the validity of learning disabilities, many were nonetheless willing to provide some accommodation such as extra time on tests, giving models for homework assignments, or enlarging handouts, that made it easier for the student until a full-blown diagnosis could be obtained.

The efficacy of the Programme

How successful has this Programme been? The informal measures of success have been quite clear: the students in the special class have been devoted to it and they have been able to progress through the Institute. Recently, a 6th-level credit class in freshman composition had 11 students who had been legally identified as learning disabled or having attention deficit problems or both during their stay at ELI, plus three more who had been in the special class for several semesters because they preferred to do the writing in that atmosphere. The teachers of the Institute have been very happy, too. Not only have they had someone to whom to refer their most puzzling students, but they have also been relieved of some of the most difficult students to teach. Where once the Learning Services Office on campus was extremely reluctant to handle non-native English-speaking students, it now serves those students who come to it readily because the LSA and the Programme have shown that ESL students can be diagnosed and can profit from proper accommodation. That office has also appreciated the insight on the students whom the Programme has identified. Similarly, the International Student Office has been enthusiastic about the support that the Learning Skills Programme has offered worthy students who would otherwise have been forced to leave the university.

Certainly the Programme has addressed a clear need at ELI. When the academic advisor was responsible for the ELI students, and when enrolment at ELI was very high, she and the LSA tracked or taught some 30–40 students per year. Of the nearly 200 students the academic counsellor and the LSA identified as at risk and helped during a total of ten years, probably about one-third have already graduated. Every semester, one or two more students contact the advisor or the LSA to announce their graduation. It is tremendously gratifying to hear them say that they would not have continued had they not been helped at ELI. Some are still slowly progressing, but unfortunately, many others have left school, either by choice, or because their grades were low.

It almost goes without saying that the successful at-risk or learning-disabled students have been those who were positively and promptly identified, who agreed to be tested and accepted the diagnosis, and who were willing to learn how to advocate for themselves. In contrast, those who have not been successful were frequently those who were identified after much failure, who did not really want or understand diagnosis. They were unwilling to accept it and unwilling to learn how to advocate for themselves and instead, were often passive and accepting of their fate, a cultural trait that is difficult for Americans to swallow. In fact, the special class was too little too late for a number of students. Though they enjoyed and succeeded in that class, they needed more intervention sooner in their academic experience and much more time to get used to the idea of learning disabilities.

Unfortunately, either they were referred too late, or the failures in other classes were too overwhelming for them to be able to continue.

Of course, a few identified students had needs far too great to be met at the American University. These were referred to colleges in the United States which offer such support as daily supervision and counselling, a faculty highly attuned to the needs of learning disabled students, and a vast array of new technological support. Though reluctant to leave the American University and Washington, these students have admitted that the fit is much better elsewhere.

Conclusion

Because of two profound changes in ELI, the Learning Skills Programme has not been very active in recent semesters. First, the role of the academic advisor changed completely when advising for degree students was moved to academic departments, and second, a large drop in enrolment has meant far fewer students needing special help, so that a special section could not be run. Nonetheless, some important lessons have been learnt from this effort, the most profound of which is that learning disabilities do indeed seem to be at the root of a number of failures in English programmes. Another lesson is that these students can be successfully helped, but to do so all of their needs should be addressed, not just the language problems. In fact, having someone who understands well both learning disabilities and second language learning (in this case ESL) is an essential factor in finding and helping such students. Finally, to achieve the best possible outcome for these students, cooperation of all relevant university offices and services is essential.

Chapter 23

The Neuropsychology of Modern Foreign Language Learning

Jean Robertson

This chapter:

- examines why modern language learning may prove problematic for students with dyslexia
- examines the neuropsychological implications of the task demands of foreign language learning
- examines the role of the cerebral hemispheres in reading and language learning and its implications for teaching.

Introduction

Within mainstream education the student with dyslexia has the right to the 'broad and balanced curriculum' of the National Curriculum (DES 1988). Real access to subjects however may be reduced by the ways in which subjects are presented. One example of this is access to modern foreign languages, which in a survey by the author (Robertson 1991) was cited by 19.2 per cent of a sample of 26 students with dyslexia as being their least favourite subject. The only subject with a higher percentage was mathematics. Such figures, although revealed in a small-scale study, may indicate that having access to subjects does not necessarily mean that pupils are able to learn them. The reasons for this may be varied but may reflect a mismatch between the task demands and the profile of strengths and weaknesses of the student with dyslexia. Modern foreign language learning may prove problematic for students with dyslexia as the requisite skills will include sequencing ability, both short- and long-term memory and phonological skill. Sequencing ability is required for both the sequencing of sounds within words and words within sentences. The complexity will depend on the language, for example German requires the position of the words within the sentence to depend upon (in some instances) the specific verb used. Short- and long-term memory will determine the retention of vocabulary and knowledge of grammatical structures. Phonological skill will determine whether the student can segment words in the second language into phonemic sounds and ultimately reproduce them. The task demands of these will vary with different languages but many of these skills are frequently weak within the profiles of pupils with dyslexia. It may however be possible to modify the teaching approach to increase real access to students with dyslexia. One perspective that can inform this issue is consideration of the neuropsychological implications of second language learning.

The neuropsychological perspective on second language learning

When the task demands of learning a second language are considered, it soon becomes apparent that the challenges presented are similar to those in acquiring a first language. Yet knowledge of the first language may aid acquisition of the second language. Factors may include the knowledge that sounds are represented by letters, which in combination form the word units that comprise the sentences, which communicate meaning. These can be communicated orally via the spoken word or via the medium of written communication. The neuropsychological implications of both processes have been investigated.

The task demands of written language learning

First there is a need to assimilate the physical characteristics of the letters. These may resemble the first language or may be substantially different as in the case of a person accustomed to reading English suddenly being confronted with Greek, Arabic or Chinese symbols. The first challenge is to assimilate the similarities and differences between the symbols. In English the orientation of the letters 'b' and 'd', 'p' and 'q', 'm' and 'w' and 'n' and 'u' need to be acquired. If these are not learnt the words 'bed' or 'man' become indecipherable. In other languages other perceptual differences are important, for example the umlaut in German or the acute or grave accent in French. How does the child first meeting them know they are not simply marks on the paper but are an important part of the symbol?

Once the knowledge of letterforms is established the order of the letters within the words is the next perceptual aspect to be significant. Teachers of students with dyslexia recognise the common difficulties caused for example by the perceptually similar words 'no' and 'on', and 'saw' and 'was'. This perceptual similarity may also occur in other languages. The next aspect of perceptual importance concerns the order of the words within the sentences; for example 'He is at home' requires a different response than 'Is he at home?' yet the elements within the sentences are identical. These perceptual aspects require a slow, careful response to the printed text that gains speed when the letters and words become familiar. During the course of the learning, knowledge of the sounds (phonemes) and the letters that represent them (graphemes) is gained. Response to familiar letters or sequences of letters, for example 'cat' and 'house' become automatic. At this point attention can transfer from the symbols and the sequence of the symbols to the meaning or the syntax of the communication. If words are encountered, which are unfamiliar or complex, letter by letter or syllable by syllable reading can be utilised in an attempt to decode the symbols. For example, the word 'strephosymbolia' will be decoded differently from the word 'dog' or at least until it becomes a familiar part of the lexicon. In another language the Dutch word 'inschrompelen' (meaning shrink) requires a different kind of attention. We are conscious of the process of explicit decoding when faced with unfamiliar languages which may use the same alphabetic symbols as English yet the words may be assembled in very different ways. As knowledge of the written form of English was acquired so must knowledge of the written form of the new language be acquired. Again the emphasis shifts from the perceptual characteristics of the letters and the sounds they represent to the orthography or the written form of the language. As the words become familiar, there is increased use of syntax (grammar) and semantics (meaning).

Contribution of the cerebral hemispheres to reading

There is now evidence that the right and left hemispheres of the brain contribute differentially to these processes. The right hemisphere of the brain is responsible for controlling the left side of the body and the left hemisphere is responsible for controlling the right side of the body. Other specific functions are also found. Generally the right hemisphere is specialist for visuospatial processing, for spatial awareness and for analysing the perceptual aspects of letters and words. In contrast the left cerebral hemisphere is responsible for language (in the majority of right-handed people).

Fries (1963) wrote of the possibility of dual hemispheric involvement in the reading process. During the process of reading one is engaged in a language activity, which activates the left hemisphere. Initially, for the novice reader during the course of reading, letterforms are perceived which are ordered in our culture in a left to right direction. Because of this perceptual load reading also alludes to right hemisphere processing. Thus in skilful reading both hemispheres have a part to play. The Novelty Model of Goldberg and Costa (1981) would support this. This presented evidence that novel information is processed by the right hemisphere and familiar information by the left. The right hemisphere is also more suited to processing material from different modalities such as grapheme–phoneme correspondence tasks, which require use of both the visual and the auditory modalities. Rourke (1982) also supported the involvement of the right hemisphere in the reading process by the initial exploration of surface features. Eventually for reasons of fluency and efficiency these functions are taken over by the left hemisphere. In the light of such theory Bakker (1990) developed the Balance Model of Reading which stated that reading begins in the right hemisphere and transfers to the left hemisphere when the letters and words become familiar. There is thus a developmental process whereby the acquisition of literacy (either for a first or a subsequent language) begins with greater involvement of the right hemisphere and subsequently transfers to the left hemisphere.

Experimental evidence on the dual hemisphere involvement

The theoretical framework of the neuropsychological study of language learning has led to study of the implications of second language learning being investigated and technological advances such as Positron Emission Topography (PET) have added to the knowledge base in this area. (Positron Emission Topography identifies the brain areas that are most involved in certain tasks by measuring their fuel intake and produces clear pictures of the involvement of specific brain regions. The use of a radioactive marker, which is directly injected into the bloodstream, renders its usage being limited to one scanning session of usually 12 scans per year.) Perani *et al.* (1996) utilised PET scans in their study of nine Italian males, all of whom were right-handed. (This is significant as it was presumed that language would be based primarily in the left cerebral hemisphere.) The researchers carried out PET scans while the subjects were listening to their native language. As expected they found language activation in the classic language areas of the left hemisphere including the angular gyrus. Some activity was also found in the right hemisphere in the region of the cerebellum. This pattern confirmed the results of earlier studies in which French and English subjects were scanned while listening to stories in their native language. The areas most active were thought to be those involved in processing extended prose. Differences were found when subjects listened to a foreign language (English) as the set of active language areas was greatly reduced despite the subjects all having a good understanding of English. Brain activity was then investigated while the subjects listened to an unknown language (Japanese). Direct comparison of brain activation during tasks involving listening to both Japanese and English showed equal activation even though the subjects understood only one of the languages (English). The authors suggested that the revealed differences might relate to the age of exposure to the language. The selective response of a network of cerebral areas including the left hemisphere regions to the Italian language as opposed to English or Japanese implied that the organisation had been shaped by exposure to the native language during childhood. The authors concluded that cortical areas are not responsive to a language acquired after the age of seven years and this may represent the 'sensitive period' for language acquisition (Lenneberg 1967). The research design also allowed for investigation into speech processing and when the subjects listened to Japanese played backwards there was increased involvement in the right hemisphere, whereas even the unknown Japanese speech still showed greater activation of the left hemisphere. The authors interpreted this as indicating that some cortical areas distinguish spoken language from non-speech verbal outputs irrespective of any understanding of the language. This study demonstrates the importance of the age of acquisition of the second language and this was supported by a further study by Perani *et al.* (1998). An additional factor revealed in this study was the degree of proficiency attained in the second language. This could be as powerful a factor in determining the pattern of brain activation as age of acquisition. They suggested that in the case of low proficiency individuals various brain regions are recruited to handle the dimensions of L2 which are different from L1. As proficiency increased the highly proficient bilinguals used the same neural mechanisms to deal with both languages. Their data supported the notion that age of acquisition was a main determinant of proficiency and that only late bilinguals who reached high proficiency showed activation patterns similar to native language learners. Thus facility within the language becomes an additional factor in determining the brain regions involved.

The findings of other studies support the notion of differential brain activation for L1 and L2. Klein *et al.* (1994) again using PET scans investigated whether the same neural substrates were involved for both L1 and L2 in normal bilingual subjects who had acquired the second language after the age of five years. The task used was repetition of words in both English and French. They found that speed and accuracy showed equal activation for both languages in all brain regions apart from the left putamen (a nucleus located in the basal ganglia of the forebrain). No other significant increases or decreases were found which suggests that the two languages made demands on almost completely overlapping structures. The activation of the left putamen indicated an additional neural response which was required for the production (as opposed to the comprehension) of L2 rather than L1. They took this as confirmation of the specific contribution of the putamen in articulation, particularly in the precise timing of the motor output required for speech. Differences in language production as opposed to language comprehension was also found by Kim *et al.* (1997). They studied 13 bilingual adults in a functional Magnetic Resonance Imaging study (fMRI). (This technique can reveal the area of greatest brain activity during tasks by revealing those areas which are using most oxygen.) They concentrated on the contribution of the classic language areas of Broca's area and Wernicke's area. (Broca's area is involved in the production of language and Wernicke's area is implicated in the comprehension of language.) Their observations led them to investigate whether age of language acquisition might be a significant factor in determining the functional organisation of the language area of the human brain. When L2 was acquired late the activation site was spatially distinct from the site represented by L1. They found that when both languages were acquired during early childhood (early bilinguals) there was a sharing of activity in Broca's area but this sharing was not evident for those who had acquired L2 late (late bilinguals). This differential activity was only found in Broca's area. The activation of Wernicke's area did not show the same pattern. They suggested that the infant brain which is capable of discriminating phonetically relevant differences may modify the perceptual acoustic space based on early and repeated exposure to the native language. These cortical areas would not be as responsive when the second language is learnt therefore making it necessary for L2 to utilise adjacent cortical areas. This would be in keeping with the findings of Bosch and Sebastian (1997) who showed that in the case of bilingual infants raised in a bilingual environment progress was made in both languages simultaneously, even during the first few months of life. If consistent exposure to both were not maintained then one became dominant.

Other researchers have focused on brain activation patterns of pupils learning a second language. The experimental work of Silverberg *et al.* (1979) also provided support for this initially right hemisphere involvement in foreign language acquisition. They demonstrated different brain activation patterns for foreign languages. Their studies measured the visual field preference of students when reading their first language (Hebrew) against a second language (English). (Due to the crossover brain/body relationship, it is possible to judge which hemisphere is involved in processing visual material.) A left visual field preference (VFP) demonstrates greater involvement of the right hemisphere while a right visual field preference demonstrates greater involvement of the left hemisphere. They found that 7th grade students showed a right visual field preference when reading Hebrew (which demonstrated involvement of the left cerebral hemisphere). However when reading English a left visual field preference was found demonstrating greater involvement of the right cerebral hemisphere. In studies of visual field preference (to demonstrate the involvement of the hemispheres in specific tasks) they found a left visual field preference (VFP) for English words in native Hebrew-speaking adolescents who had just begun to study English (demonstrating the greater involvement of the right hemisphere). This group therefore showed greater involvement of the left hemisphere for their first language yet greater involvement of the right hemisphere for the second language. VFP was then measured in a group of 11th grade students who were more experienced in the language and a right visual field preference was found for both Hebrew and English (showing the involvement of the left hemisphere). The evidence here suggests there will be stronger right hemisphere involvement depending on the complexity of the new orthography. It may also reflect increased competence in the language. Similar findings were reported by Bentin (1981), who also studied native Hebrew-speakers learning English as a second language. He reported that new English words were recognised faster in the left visual field again demonstrating increased involvement of the right hemisphere. An interesting finding from the Bentin study was that when the image was presented in a barely recognisable way, the expected right visual field preference for the first language did not occur. The degraded letterforms had apparently caused the activity to transfer to the right hemisphere. A study by Vaid (1983) also reported increased right hemisphere involvement in processing a non-native unknown alphabet. Others such as Galloway (1982) suggest this is a learning to read effect rather than a learning a second language effect. She considered that the extent of involvement of the right hemisphere might be related not only to age of acquisition but also the orthography of the second language. If the written form of L2 were substantially different from the written form of L1 there would be greater involvement by the right hemisphere. This would be in keeping with the neuropsychological specialisation of the right hemisphere in processing visual shapes and designs. There was also the expected shift to predominantly left hemisphere dominance when the written form of the language became more familiar, which corresponded to the findings of Silverberg, Bentin and Vaid.

There is not universal agreement between workers in this field however. Several studies including Klein *et al.* (1995) found no evidence to support the hypothesis that a second language is represented differently from the native language and is served by different neural substrates. The varied findings were extensively discussed by Paradis (1990) who wrote of the folly of continuing research into the neuropsychology of bilingualism in the light of such conflicting findings. He stated that even if learning a second language involved the right hemisphere we cannot presume it is the most efficient way and may instead reflect individual cognitive style. This would certainly have practical implications for the teacher as it would involve modifying teaching to cater for the range of individual learning preferences within the classroom.

It is possible that the varied findings between studies may reflect differences in the tasks presented, which ranged from word repetition, word and synonym generation tasks (in one or two languages) and listening to connected text in both known and unknown languages. All of these tasks vary greatly in complexity and would show varied cortical activity even in a native language. The range of studies and the varied findings can potentially demonstrate the link between task demand and the cortical regions required to perform the function effectively.

Implications for teaching

Kappers and Dekker (1995) reported an interesting study which utilised neuropsychological teaching methods on a sample of Dutch pupils. The neuropsychological treatments used were Hemisphere Specific Stimulation (HSS), which has been found an effective intervention for dyslexic students by several workers including Bakker (1990), Goldstein and Obrzut (2000) and Robertson (1999, 2000). HSS can be delivered visually via the visual half-fields or via the tactile modality using the hands. HSS visual involves the student being asked to fixate on a central point on a computer screen and reading words flashed either to the right or the left of this central point. HSS tactile involves the student reading unseen words via the fingers of their right or left hand. In this study treatment was given both via the visual and the tactile modality in either Dutch or English and the results showed differences in the two languages. In English improvements were found for both single word and passage reading while in Dutch the improvement was in passage reading only. An interesting finding from this study was that the results were regardless of whether the intervention had been delivered in Dutch or English. The authors concluded that intervention in one language enhances reading in a second untreated language.

Other workers have also reported transfer of skills between languages. Ganschow et al. (1998a) found a similar effect in studies in German, English and Latin and concluded that the effect did not depend heavily on the phonic regularity of the language. Their work also had implications for teaching and supports the idea of there being similar processes at work in the acquisition of both native and modern foreign languages. When they studied pupils who were experiencing failure in the acquisition of a modern foreign language they found the students had experienced similar difficulties in their native language learning. The problems could be in any or all of the aspects of language such as reading, writing, spelling or oral language. Significantly they identified one specific aspect which was more important than either motivation or intelligence and that was auditory ability (specifically grapheme [written] – phoneme [heard sound] conversion). Their studies indicated that poor foreign language learners require direct teaching to acquire the phonological, grammatical and orthographic rule systems. Results from their studies showed three principles that were associated with successful learning: multisensory teaching should be used wherever possible, overhead transparencies (OHTs) should support oral language and that grapho-phonic conversion should be taught explicitly. (These findings have clear implications for the current trends for natural communication as they found this was likely to be unsuccessful for the majority of students.) These findings can also be seen to link to the neuropsychological evidence as OHTs can be designed to maximise the involvement of the right cerebral hemisphere. They also provide a medium whereby the student who learns best via the visual modality has increased opportunities for success.

Conclusions

The varied research evidence can illuminate good practice for the teaching of modern foreign languages. The work of Galloway and Paradis points to the importance of taking individual learning styles into account in the MFL classroom. This will mean the teacher incorporating varied presentation into subject delivery so that pupils have the opportunity to learn in their preferred cognitive style. The classroom will therefore take into account the needs of those who learn best via the visual modality and those who learn best via the auditory modality. Wherever possible multisensory methods should be utilised to increase access for all students but will be especially important to those who are dyslexic.

Following the findings of Ganschow and Sparks the phonology of the second language should be taught explicitly so that the pupils can build up accurate grapheme–phoneme representations of the language. Several studies refer to the importance of age of acquisition and this is one aspect which has relevance for educational policy as English schools usually introduce second languages at secondary school. The neuropsychological evidence suggests that for new and unfamiliar material, the right hemisphere is best suited to the task. Materials should emphasise the perceptual aspects of the letters and words. This could include colours, shapes and the use of highlighter pens to make the symbols more distinct. These may lead to more pupils accessing and retaining the vocabulary of the second language so that a stronger memory trace is established. This should then lead to a speedier progression to the fluent and skilful reading of the left hemisphere.

Ultimately both hemispheres need to be involved in the reading process. However if the material is presented to the pupils according to a developmental model whereby initially there is a greater involvement of the right hemisphere then the evidence suggests that the acquisition of foreign languages is likely to be successful for an increased number of students. This would benefit not only the acquisition of the second language but may also lead to improved skill with the first language also. This may reinforce the need for further study in this area.

Chapter 24

Teaching Modern Foreign Languages to Dyslexic Learners:
A Scottish Perspective

Margaret Crombie and Hilary McColl

This chapter:

- examines the implications of a 'modern language for all' policy in relation to dyslexic students
- provides a detailed analysis of the research in modern languages and dyslexia
- examines the implications of this and the underlying teaching principles for Scottish schools and collaborative staff approaches
- and discusses the practical advantages of a flexible framework of national examination awards.

Features of the Scottish landscape

Policy and practice in Scotland

Modern foreign language learning was established as part of the core examinable curriculum for all students in Scottish secondary schools in 1989. Thereafter, children of all abilities were expected to study at least one foreign language from entry to secondary school at the age of 12 until they reached school leaving age at 16. At the end of the four-year course they would take the Standard Grade examination in Modern Languages administered by the then Scottish Examinations Board (SEB), now replaced by the Scottish Qualifications Authority (SQA). Preparing the whole ability range for a national examination became a new and challenging experience for modern language teachers as well as for that section of the student population which had previously been exempted from foreign language learning.

This 'modern languages for all' policy had political acceptability at a time when Scotland, and indeed Britain, seemed to be lagging seriously behind other European countries in the learning of foreign languages. However, many parents and dyslexic students themselves questioned whether modern languages for all really meant **all**. Clarification was sought concerning the guidance offered in the Secretary of State's Circular 1178 (Scottish Education Department (SED) 1989) which stated that 'all children should be given an opportunity to study foreign languages' while at the same time accepting that some learners 'may have special educational needs which make the learning of a foreign language unrewarding and mainly burdensome'. The circular stated that there 'should be no automatic assumption that pupils with special needs should be excluded from language tuition' (SED 1989). Nevertheless, considerable doubt was expressed as to whether dyslexic children already experiencing difficulties with reading and writing in their first language could benefit from tuition in a second language. In Scotland, the final decision on whether to withdraw a pupil who is experiencing severe difficulties in coming to terms with another language rests with the head teacher, though the decision-making process is a collaborative one, based on the views of SEN or support for learning staff as well as subject teachers, parents and the young person him or herself. Often, the school's educational psychologist is also involved.

Before long it became apparent that the 'exclusion zone' was being interpreted differently in different schools and that whether a dyslexic student was given an opportunity to experience foreign language learning and whether that student found the experience rewarding or not depended more on the school the student happened to attend than on the student's potential for success in the subject. This impression was established in a Scottish Office project (McColl *et al.* 1997) and independent research (Crombie 1995, 1997a) in which the authors suggested that, when suitable courses were offered and teaching strategies employed, dyslexic students could indeed benefit from the experience of learning a foreign language, at least in the early stages. According to these findings, there was, initially at least, no intrinsic reason for denying dyslexic learners access to a core part of the curriculum.

Rough ground

The questions raised

The challenge therefore became a practical one: how could a course which effectively meets the needs of dyslexic students be provided without prejudice to the needs of other learners? How could the principle of entitlement be balanced against practical and logistical considerations? Additional questions were raised about what constituted an appropriate course, what strategies had proved most successful, and how attainment should be assessed.

Finding suitable seeds

Research

Research in Scotland on the subject of modern foreign languages for dyslexic students has been scant, and for a considerable time non-existent. In fact, even in global terms there has been little in the way of thorough, scientifically based study which gives support for any particular model or theory of dyslexia and foreign language learning and teaching. The small amount of research which there is, has come mostly from the United States of America, and any insight which we have gained into teaching strategies likely to benefit those with difficulties is largely founded in the work of Professors Ganschow and Sparks and their colleagues (see for example, Sparks and Ganschow 1993b; Ganschow and Sparks 1995; Ganschow *et al.* 1995). Ganschow and Sparks' research suggests that teaching methodology requires serious consideration if the needs of those who are dyslexic are to be met.

While a core deficit in dyslexic young people appears to be phonological processing, there are often also difficulties in short-term memory, sequencing, word finding, speed of information processing and low self-esteem (Snowling *et al.* 1988; Rack 1994; Crombie 1997b; Goswami 1997). Attitude too is seen by many as a major determinant of success in learning a foreign language. Gardner *et al.* (1976) concludes that motivational variables are as highly related to second language achievement as language aptitude measures. Sparks, Ganschow and colleagues suggest that students who have encountered difficulties with learning their native language are likely to have difficulty with foreign language learning (Sparks and Ganschow 1991). They propose a Linguistic Coding Differences Hypothesis (LCDH) which suggests that the native language skills of phonology/orthography (sound/symbol), syntax (grammar) and semantics (meaning) are a prerequisite for success in foreign language learning. Further it is argued that each of these basic language skills will affect other skills (Sparks *et al.* 1998).

The techniques advocated by Ganschow and Sparks for at-risk learners are those which are generally recommended for dyslexic pupils in first language learning. Specialist teachers of dyslexic children have recognised, for many years, the effectiveness of highly structured multisensory teaching programmes such as the Hickey approach to language training (Hickey 1977; Augur and Briggs 1992). Reading and writing are taught by a technique which stresses overlearning and gaining automaticity (Sparks and Ganschow 1993b). Although Ganschow and Sparks' studies include dyslexic students, those studied had a wider range of difficulties. The techniques referred to however seem to apply to dyslexic learners as well as those with other problems. In fact, advocates of these methods, such as Vail (1992), consider that they work well for the general population.

Studies have indicated that the level of difficulty a young person has with native language learning is often a reasonable indicator of the difficulties which might be anticipated in foreign language learning (Crombie 1997a; Sparks *et al.* 1998). Previous recommendations that students with difficulties should refrain from the reading and writing aspects of foreign language learning have proved disadvantageous to foreign language learners (Javorsky *et al.* 1992), and further studies point towards the success of the multisensory methods. According to Rome and Smith Osman (1993), multisensory techniques enhance awareness skills by encouraging the young person to simultaneously activate the auditory, visual, tactile and kinaesthetic pathways to promote learning. This is confirmed by Ott who considers that 'multisensory learning techniques provide the key to teaching all dyslexic people' (Ott 1997: 290). The teaching programmes are systematic and cumulative with an emphasis on direct instruction with explicit teaching of sound/symbol relationships. Assessment is generally diagnostic in nature, to discover not just what the young person has and has not assimilated, but also to evaluate the methods tried, and to determine how the responses might be varied or altered.

Evaluation of the techniques used have been very positive and results have shown the benefits which can be gained from this type of approach (Ganschow *et al.* 1995; Sparks *et al.* 1998; Miller and Gillis 1999). In addition, the use of dynamic assessment strategies which look at how the young person is approaching learning as well as what is being learnt, combined with a metacognitive approach to teaching and learning advocated by Schneider (1999) has considerable potential. If a general lesson can be drawn from this body of research, it is that dyslexic problems make it considerably more difficult for a dyslexic young person to learn a foreign language. It is therefore essential that appropriate teaching and learning strategies be put in place. The research also suggests that, while what is appropriate for dyslexic learners may not actually be required by many other young people, the strategies and methods which work for dyslexic youngsters may benefit other learners. With this in mind, it should be possible to put in place teaching and learning strategies which will increase the language capability of dyslexic students without prejudice to other learners.

In contrast to the 'natural' communicative approaches to language learning which became prevalent in the 1970s and 1980s, Schneider has taken forward the theory that 'explicitly structured, deductive instruction can lead to successful performance in foreign language' (Schneider 1999: 80) and has developed this into a programme which takes account of the principles of multisensory structured language approaches which were previously discussed. Schneider reports on the work of Kenneweg (1988, 1994) which has been found to be extremely successful for students who are considered to be at risk. At the start of the programme, precise sound–symbol relationships are taught and practised regularly. Students rehearse visual, auditory and blending drills together with board work. The overlearning principle is aided by repetition through tape work at home. Grammar is taught explicitly in a multisensory way. Learning is sequential and cumulative, with instructions being given in the language being studied. New concepts can be introduced inductively through examples to allow students to be directed towards the appropriate conclusions. The multisensory element is further reinforced by the students' holding up representative colour cards to demonstrate their knowledge of sentence structure patterns. Vocabulary is introduced only a few words at a time with visual cues which allow the student to hear the teacher's model pronunciation, see a picture and the word, repeat the word or words several times. The teacher writes the word, and the student emulates the model. There is thus considerable opportunity for overlearning through multisensory methods. Students are then given the opportunity for self-expression using the vocabulary and structures which have just been learnt. Schneider reports the success of this approach, and further develops it through her programme of Multisensory Structured Metacognitive Instruction (1999) which is described fully in her book of the same name.

This type of teaching will present additional challenges to mainstream teachers who are faced with mixed ability pupils in a mainstream setting. It does however suggest how new language might be presented and how children with difficulties might be supported in order to maximise their chances of success. To help them meet these challenges, teachers need a range of structured resources which can be used to present material in an attractive, non-threatening way to ensure that those who require additional opportunities to consolidate their learning are able to achieve overlearning and automatic response. To this effect, language games and practice cards such as those of MLG Publishing (Thomas *et al.* 1991–2000) seem to emulate the Hickey Practice Packs which have proved successful to many in first language learning. The cards present pictures on one side and the words in the target language on the other side. These materials are bright and attractive and can be used by pupils working in pairs or small groups, or sometimes on their own for reinforcement of vocabulary. The addition of language dice allows sentence structures to be built up, manipulated and practised in a concrete fashion capable of infinite variation. To help with pronunciation and intonation, resourceful teachers can add audio input by creating tapes or by using the photocopiable MLG pictures to customise cards for the Drake Language Master. Other resources, such as Stile Trays, can be customised to support second language acquisition.

Fertile soil

The Scottish situation

While the structures recommended in the above approaches are more formal than those currently in place in most Scottish schools, these methods tie in very appropriately with some of the current recommendations being made to Scottish teachers. As in the rest of the UK, efforts are being made at national and whole-school level to improve learning and teaching of modern languages, an area which has given considerable cause for concern (Scottish Council for Research in Education (SCRE) 1999). While some of the approaches described above are more structured and intensive than those in use in most Scottish schools, the underlying *principles* are reflected in some of the advice currently being presented nationally.

A report by Her Majesty's Inspectors of Schools on Standards and Quality in Modern Languages, while expressing concern about many aspects of language teaching in Scottish schools, drew attention to aspects of good practice they had observed in which teachers 'drew pupils' attention to links, similarities and contrast with English' and 'required pupils frequently to memorise text in songs and stories which they also used as teaching contexts' (Scottish Office Education and Industry Department (SOEID) 1998: 13). They expressed approval for courses which 'provided opportunities for memorisation of languages in different forms' (SOEID 1998: 17) and 'teachers who set pupils to memorise words, songs, chunks of text and facts about the language' (SOEID 1998: 21). Good teaching, they maintained, was characterised by lessons in which teachers 'ensured that lessons had a distinct structure; analysed for pupils the foreign language heard by breaking it into component parts, pointing out patterns, encouraging pupils to vary the pattern; drew pupils' attention to pronunciation and intonation rules to help them connect the sound system of the language with the written system; and included imaginative elements to aid learning by using, for example, song, rap, chanting' (SOEID 1998: 21).

At the time of writing, the Scottish Guidelines for Modern Languages 5–14 are being revised, and are still in draft form (Scottish Consultative Council on the Curriculum (SCCC) 1999). It seems clear however that early training in the phonology of the language being learnt and the importance of linking text and sound will be recommended. A new overarching strand called 'Knowing About Language' will encourage teachers and pupils to explore links between and among languages, based on the premise that, 'Embarking on foreign language learning consolidates and builds on skills and capabilities already encountered in the first or second language' (SCCC 1999: 7).

This premise is underpinned by recent work carried out by Professor Richard Johnstone of Stirling University (Johnstone 1994). Restating Cummins'(1984) theory of the interdependence of languages, Johnstone affirms that, 'beneath the surface there is one process of cognition, developed through the first language, that can be transferred to support the additional language' (Johnstone 1994: 37). Johnstone also draws attention to Rose's (1985) work on brain function and describes an integrated and holistic approach which is 'characterised by richness of presentation, by encouragement of learners to engage themselves emotionally in activities, to perform physical actions, to develop techniques for building up a powerful visual memory and to feel secure enough to make mistakes' (Johnstone 1994: 29–30). It is important that teachers take steps to remove stress and fear of failure from the environment, in order to ensure that young people can allow themselves to learn from their mistakes with reassurance and appropriate guidance to consider their responses in a metacognitive way. Johnstone points out that some aspects of the holistic approach are already being applied in primary schools and suggests that such an approach 'holds particular promise for learners with special educational needs' (Johnstone 1994: 30).

These and other features of the educational landscape in Scotland suggest that the classroom environment for dyslexic foreign language learners will be more favourable in the future than it has sometimes been in the past. However, what is needed now, in order for the techniques proposed by research to be adopted in practice, is for the findings to be interpreted in ways which will encourage modern language teachers to experiment with these methods and to consider adding them to their repertoire.

Sowing the seeds

Changing practice

As Johnstone points out in the introduction to his 1994 work, there is much that has been written 'by specialists for other specialists', and there is a need to address a wider and different readership. 'The groups I have in mind include: teachers and student-teachers ... senior school staff, regional officials, and parents. All of these have major responsibilities in providing different sorts of support for children's language learning. Through no fault of their own, such groups may feel unsure as to what the real research evidence is and may therefore feel caught between conflicting claims' (Johnstone 1994: 1). As in the rest of Britain, considerable effort is being expended on whole-school efforts to improve learning and teaching. An influential document *Teaching for Effective Learning* was an explicit attempt 'to encourage teachers to identify and reflect on the nature and processes of teaching and learning' and to bridge the gap between theory and practice (SCCC 1996: iii). The study was generic, but some attempts have been made to customise the process for modern language teachers.

During the Scottish Office project reported previously by McColl *et al.* (1997), the project officers, working in collaboration with the Scottish Dyslexia Association and the Scottish Centre for Specific Learning Difficulties (Dyslexia) published advice to modern language departments which suggested ways in which teaching approaches might be adapted to suit dyslexic learners. The advice was based on observation of techniques which had been shown to work for dyslexic learners in first language acquisition and attempted to translate these into terms which would be meaningful for modern language teachers unfamiliar with the field. Unfortunately the project did not last long enough for the advice to be evaluated in practice. It does, however, provide an additional study text for modern language teachers and others following certificate and diploma courses.

Research has shown that when modern linguists and special needs staff work together to modify courses and adapt teaching methodologies, there is considerable potential for the future of language teaching to dyslexic young people (Downey and Snyder 1999; Crombie 2000). At time of writing, collaborative workshops involving modern language and support for learning teachers are being organised by the Scottish Association for Language Teaching (SALT). This shows considerable flexibility and will to meet the needs of all learners, and responds to growing concerns over the appropriateness of foreign language learning experiences for young people who do not find participation worthwhile.

Looking forward to the harvest

Guidance for the future

In Scotland, the new unitised National Certificate courses offered by SQA provide a flexible framework within which the needs of dyslexic learners can be met. Downey and Snyder (1999), working with American college students, observed that when offered reduced foreign language content and more structured learning approaches, dyslexic students' results compared well with those of their non-dyslexic fellow students. It is possible therefore that, by allowing dyslexic students to study one or two units instead of the usual three which make up a Scottish National Certificate course, some dyslexic learners may be able to achieve levels representative of their ability. While adopting this strategy would mean that students who did not complete the three units would be insufficiently prepared to enter for the final external examination and could not therefore be awarded a National Certificate in Modern Languages, internal assessment of individual units would be recorded on the National Record of Achievement, and would count as individual credits toward a Scottish Group Award. National Certificate units are available at five different levels, so dyslexic students may decide to sacrifice quantity for quality and opt to study a limited number of units in the hope of achieving individual credits at a higher level. Since the new framework is still in the process of adoption, it is too early to say how well it might adapt to the needs of dyslexic young people. Perhaps it will prove to be the key which may open the door to success in modern language learning for youngsters with language learning difficulties.

All of these developments indicate a willingness in the educational community in Scotland to take account of research findings and to embark on new ways of responding to the needs of all learners. Dyslexic learners should benefit. The potential for success is there, and the current climate seems to be propitious.

Resources

Language Master from Scottish Learning Products, Greenacres, Highfield Road, Scone, Perth, PH2 6BR.
MLG Games from MLG Publishing, PO Box 1526, Hanwell, London, W7 1ND.
Stile from LDA, Duke Street, Wisbech, Cambs., PE13 2AE.

Chapter 25

The Language Puzzle: Connecting the Study of Linguistics with a Multisensory Language Instructional Programme in Foreign Language Learning

Stephanie Miller and Marjorie Bussman Gillis

This chapter:

- discusses the structure and sequence of a multisensory language programme
- illustrates the practical application of the programme in relation to theories of learning a foreign language or English as a second language and
- provides a detailed lesson plan for each situation.

Introduction

Dyslexia is a deficit in language processing and knowledge of language structure is the key to successful remediation. At each level of a language's multilevel structured system, smaller units build up into larger units – this is universal to all languages. Each level of language is independent, but all levels depend on one another. Words must have markers on them so that they will make sense within the structure of the sentence. The word parts combine to give the word meaning and each word is a combination of sounds. Teachers must understand how all these parts fit together to form a whole.

Teachers must also understand the speech sound system and have a command of word parts, both spoken and written. This in turn will explain how the orthographic system will represent sounds in spoken words. Many papers discuss the importance of phonological awareness; these discussions have included a rationale and methods for teaching sounds and the ability to segment and blend sounds. However, in order to do a more thorough job of remediating phonological deficits, teachers must understand the principles of co-articulation and the physical properties of sounds. They must also recognise how this understanding forms the foundation for the study of morphology, syntax and semantics.

Background

It has been widely thought that students with dyslexia should be exempted from instruction in a second language. Since dyslexia is often accompanied with deficits in language processing, many ask the question: Why subject these individuals to the difficult job of processing and learning yet another language? This paper will dispel those myths and explain how and why those who exhibit difficulties in learning language should, in fact, be *instructed* in the basics of language both in their native language as well as in their foreign language learning. Research informs us that the individual with dyslexia processes language differently (Adams 1990; Moats 1994; Shaywitz *et al.* 1995). Dyslexics often have difficulty segmenting words into their components. These components or speech sounds are called phonemes. Some individuals have difficulty blending or synthesising these phonemes into words while others have difficulty unblending or analysing these sounds. The synthesis is also called decoding, or reading and the analysis of sounds is encoding, or spelling.

Every alphabetic language is comprised of symbols that represent the sounds of the language. For students with language learning difficulties and for those who are learning a second language, this principle must be taught directly. Since there is rarely a direct one-to-one correspondence between letters and sounds, students must be taught these sound–symbol associations explicitly. Phonology is the essential foundation upon which language is built. Many teachers are uninformed about the various levels of language. In order for their students to understand the foundation of any language, teachers themselves must understand how these parts fit together to form a whole. Once the student is aware of the phonology and has mastered sound–symbol relationships, they are ready to combine them into meaningful units, or morphemes. Morphology is the second level of language. Morphemes not only give clues to meaning, they also serve as markers to fit the words into sentences. Words combine in unique ways to change the meaning of the sentence.

The third level of language, syntax, is the level that dictates word order and sentence structure. The fourth level, semantics, is the ultimate goal of all language learning – meaning. Each of these levels of language, phonology, morphology, syntax and semantics, is independent but all levels depend on one another. This interdependence is universal to all languages. The normal progression of language acquisition begins with a strong emphasis on the sound component of the language. As the ability to hear sound units in words develops, the child will be able to develop the higher levels of language, including the morphology and syntax as well as the meaning of the connected text that s/he hears. Phonology and morphology generate the syntactic and semantic development. Infants may be able to communicate their needs but their communication is primitive and does not have any lexical content. In referring to levels of language it is important to note that the student moves up the pyramid to higher levels of language as soon as s/he learns how to use symbols, a key element of human language. For the child with language-learning disabilities, these higher levels are not acquired unless the foundation of the pyramid is in place. A child's ability to process language fluently is dependent on his/her ability to understand the abstractions of language. In order to communicate effectively, a child must be able to convey a complete message.

Since language is a mechanism for generating ideas and our students have been shown to have deficits in processing many of the foundational elements necessary for understanding language, it is essential that teachers present the structure of the language while helping their students develop their ideas. The structure as shown by the language pyramid is a matter of learning that smaller units combine into larger units at different levels. Meaning is comprised of different components that our students must understand in order to organise their thoughts and ideas. This requires the understanding of the semantic component of language. Once teachers understand what language is comprised of, they can then incorporate the various aspects of language learning into the student's multisensory structured language lesson plan. Remediation must take into account the fact that morphological shape is dependent on phonological shape, that words are made up of meaningful parts, called morphemes, and that certain rules for adding affixes to roots dictate the derivative's orthographic and syntactic representations. The mastery of these principles will help develop the student's ability to manipulate the units of language. This in turn will enable students to practise writing their ideas so that they can realise the fact that language is the mechanism for generating ideas.

Second language acquisition

Miller (1985) proposes that second language acquisition follows the patterns of first language acquisition. During the acquisition period, children progress from inconsistent phonemic shapes to full development of higher-level language. This is the way second language acquisition should be viewed. In the beginning stages, the child can only name things in his own environment. As his language skills develop, he can begin to talk about things out of this context and he can also make inferences. At the last stage of development the child grasps the more abstract principles of higher-level language. At the same time, his knowledge of the structure of language is keeping pace with the development of his ideas. When children start school they bring their oral language experiences to written language. Students with learning disabilities have gaps in their oral language that interfere with acquiring written language. In the same way, second language learners who do not have any oral experience with foreign language will have difficulty acquiring a second language.

All human beings are capable of making certain sounds. However, each language does not use each and every sound. If students are not familiar with certain sounds, these must be taught directly. Phonological awareness activities not only promote an awareness of how sounds are made but in addition, they ensure that children play about with sound structure. Phonological memory provides the codes for storing of verbal material. There is a rate of access for retrieval of word shapes which the second language learner must have in order to put words together in a foreign language. Students who are learning a second language must be given similar practice with the new speech sounds. By playing with the sounds, combining them into words and manipulating these sounds and words, the student gains confidence in the rules of language. This practice is especially important for second language learners who are dyslexic.

Sound–symbol association must also be reinforced. Research has shown that the kinaesthetic reinforcement of auditory pathways is very important. Therefore the association of sound and symbol is key as well as writing and saying the sounds simultaneously. This is what is referred to as multisensory learning. The next step is to combine these sounds into syllables. Syllable instruction is the foundation of the understanding of the structure of language. The syllable unit, *a vowel surrounded by consonants*, is a universal construction. However, the boundaries of the syllable differ from language to language. In order for a student to learn a language and recognise new construction, the dissection of the syllable is key. Morphology, the next rung up from the phonological level on the language pyramid, plays an important role in explaining language differences. Morphemes, the smallest units of meaning, act as cues not only for the meaning of words, but how to place them in sentences. Some languages use morphemes to a higher degree than others. For students with learning disabilities the ability to take a word apart and understand its function provides a bridge that will enable them to proceed from the phonological level to the syntactic level.

Syntax or word order is an important step for arranging words into sentences. This word order is cued by the morphemes and allows the child or second language learner to use syntactic groupings in organising language. This awareness helps the child recognise the relationships between words. A language with a higher degree of inflection relies less heavily on word order to express meaning. The knowledge of a language involves understanding the higher levels of language and these higher levels distinguish animal language from human language. Meaning is often difficult to express in a foreign language. This is especially true for students with learning difficulties who have gaps in semantic knowledge. Many of these students also have problems with sequencing and have difficulty making the association between structure and idea. These skills must be taught explicitly. Vocabulary, an important part of meaning, is an essential piece in learning a second language. Students must be given a lot of practice in recognising and naming common objects while reinforcing the sound system of the language.

The lesson plan

One important technique for advancing students' understanding of foreign vocabulary is to use a hands-on action approach using the appropriate context. Appendix A (p. 226) details a lesson plan designed to teach a foreign language to students with learning disabilities. The lesson plan incorporates the key elements of a multisensory structured language programme (McIntyre and Pickering 1995) as well as the prescribed methodology for such a programme.

The six elements include the following:

- phonology and phonological awareness
- sound–symbol association
- syllable instruction
- morphology
- syntax
- semantics.

The five methods which are part of every lesson are the following:

- simultaneous, multisensory instruction
- systematic and cumulative teaching
- direct instruction
- diagnostic teaching
- synthetic and analytic

The lesson plan includes eight parts as listed below.

Section 1: Oral expression

This section has three goals. First, it is used to teach new vocabulary items using multisensory strategies so the student can learn foreign language vocabulary by hearing, seeing and doing; secondly, the student learns categorisation skills; and finally, it promotes conversation among the students. Part One is designed to give students practice with oral expression. Both students with learning disabilities and students who are learning English as a second language benefit from this experience. In the first case, there are gaps in processing so these students need to be taught vocabulary words explicitly. In the second, these students lack the experience in speaking English and again need to be taught explicitly.

Some of the activities that can be used during this part of the lesson include the following:

Simon Says

This activity can teach the student how to follow directions and how to act out directions. Action verbs are used along with the incorporation of other vocabulary words which need to be taught. For example, the student can be asked to touch clothing, parts of the body, or items that are displayed in the room or on posters.

Step-on posters

This is a very kinaesthetic activity where the student is directed to step on a poster of any vocabulary items you want to teach. *Stepping Stones* is a game where the student has to cross the river by jumping on the poster stepping-stones. They need to name the vocabulary item on the poster to get to the other side without falling in.

Manipulation of concept cards

Students can learn important concepts by going through a sequence of introductory activities such as:

- *My name is* – A puppet is a good tool. Often students are reluctant to ask or answer questions and this is a good way to break the ice.
- *Good morning or good afternoon* – The student can be presented cards with a moon or sun and give appropriate responses.
- *How are you?* Students are given face cards with various expressions on them and they show the card and answer the question.
- *Where do you live?* Not only can students learn to give the correct responses by presenting cards which represent city, country and town, they can also learn vocabulary associated with each response.

Section 2: Phonological awareness

This part of the lesson is used to develop the student's ability to analyse language, an important basis for any foreign language learning. Students with learning disabilities have problems with auditory processing and auditory integration. Many of these students have difficulty learning the sounds and need them to be taught explicitly. They must be taught where and how each sound is made. For students who haven't had previous instruction in multisensory structured language instruction, some time should be spent developing auditory skills in the new language.

There are many hands-on activities that can be used to promote the understanding of language structure. Poker chips are useful for playing with the sounds of language. Students enjoy manipulating them and can use them for representing words in a sentence, syllables in a word or sounds in a syllable. In some cases, students are able to identify sounds in isolation but they have difficulty blending them into sequences. This blending and sequencing is difficult for students with learning disabilities as well as for students learning English as a second language. Other strategies for developing this important awareness of the sound structure of language include the following:

- To begin developing auditory processing, students can be asked to remember a sequence of sounds. The teacher can use classroom objects such as a pencil sharpener, scissors, and a bag of small blocks. The student closes his eyes and first must identify each sound he hears. Once each sound is identified, the teacher can make a series of first two, then three, sounds to strengthen auditory memory.
- To advance to identifying sequences of language sounds, the teacher will say a sequence of sounds such as: /a/ /e/ /ch/. The student will have to state how many sounds have been said without necessarily identifying the sounds. The teacher can then have the students take turns making the sounds in the correct sequence.
- Students change the initial, final or medial sound in a variety of words. Students are given a variety of blocks of different colours. The teacher will then say a word such as *peg*. The student will put a different colour block for each sound /p/, /e/, /g/. The teacher will then say a word with one sound different, e.g. *pet*. The student then replaces the last block with a different colour. The recommended sequence for this activity is to first change the first sound, then the final sound, and finally, the medial vowel sound.
- Another activity that is helpful for developing phonological awareness is to listen for rhyming words. First, students will judge if the words rhyme and they then are asked to supply a rhyming word for a word.

Section 3: Sound review and new concepts

This part of the lesson reviews previously learnt sound–symbol associations and introduces the student to the new sounds of the language. This section is a drill to test the student's knowledge of sounds and is also useful for developing short-term memory. A sound is introduced and the student will copy it, skywrite it or trace it while saying the letter name and sound. Once the previously learnt sounds have been reviewed, the teacher can present a new sound or introduce a new concept. This is best done through discovery teaching, leading the student to discover the sound through a multisensory presentation. First the student listens to a variety of words having a common sound or concept. Then, the teacher writes the words on the board so the student can discover what is similar about all the words.

Section 4: Reading practice

In this section the teacher uses the sounds that have been taught to combine them into sequences of words for practice in accuracy and fluency. It is very important to use multisensory strategies to teach new vocabulary words so the student can have good work attack skills. A study was conducted in a Northeastern US urban school where the students spoke either total Spanish at home or a combination of Spanish and English. Although the students knew the English alphabet and some of the corresponding sounds, many of them were unable to combine these sounds and decode words. A multisensory reading programme, *Preventing Academic Failure* (Bertin and Perlman 1998) was useful for providing a structured format for developing these skills. This programme provided an appropriate sequence of skills, including word lists and context reading for practice.

Section 5: Vocabulary development and oral expression

This next section of the lesson plan is aimed at vocabulary development. Items should be introduced by organising them in certain groups to give students practice in categorisation. Activities are designed to help the student learn the meanings of words, and words from Part One are used for additional reinforcement. For example, when teaching students house vocabulary, students are first asked to label domestic objects. Then they can be given pictures with the names of rooms on them and are then instructed to put the objects in the correct rooms.

Drawing is often a good way for students to start expressing themselves in a foreign language. For example, in the study cited above, the students who were learning household objects were also given a picture of an empty house with four rooms: a bedroom, bathroom, living room and kitchen. They were then asked to draw items that might belong in each of these rooms. After drawing these items, they were asked to discuss what they had drawn. At first the students were reluctant to draw and discuss the pictures. They did not have the oral language skills to express themselves and explain their pictures. However, each week there was improvement noted in this part of the lesson. The students began by repeating one word at a time. Then they progressed to simple sentences; for example, 'This is a bed'.

Section 6: Spelling practice

Once the student learns the sound–symbol associations, practice in writing words and simple sentences can begin. It is important for the student to practise writing sounds and words so that the oral-written language connection is reinforced. Each dictation begins with a review of the sounds. For example, the teacher says: 'What says /a/?' and the student writes the letter 'a'. This continues until all the sounds that the students have learnt are reviewed. Once the sounds are written, the teacher dictates a list of words that include these sounds.

While reinforcing the correct spelling of phonetically regular words, spelling rules should also be taught so that the student has the ability to fully understand foreign language patterns. Word structure is important since students with learning disabilities need to have the means of taking words apart. As the smallest units of meaning, morphemes are not only cues to meaning, they also serve as cues for putting the words into different word order. Students are taught the spelling rules for adding endings to words.

Section 7: Written expression

Syntax plays a key role in teaching the students how to speak and write grammatically correct and meaningful sentences. Many students have difficulty organising and sequencing their ideas. Teachers must teach the parts of speech directly and illustrate how they fit into the sentence. The rules of grammar determine the meaning of the sentence.

Section 8: Higher level language development

This final part of the lesson plan is often ignored in both the teaching of a foreign language as well as in teaching native language. The foundation of the language pyramid must be in place in order to teach the more complex skills. Some of the following activities can be used:

- students make categories and lists; students can either be given a category and asked to list several items in that category or they can be given a list of items and then asked to identify the category
- students identify a given picture and then are asked to describe it using visualising techniques (Bell 1991)
- students sequence cards and retell a story
- students' sequencing skills can be tested by taking away a card and then asking students to say which part of the story sequence is missing
- more advanced students can be asked to read a text, state the main points and then recreate the text based on an outline that they generate from the passage.

Ideally the lesson should last about an hour. In the study mentioned above, the lesson was used with ESL first-graders. These were classified as A or B students, depending on the amount of Spanish spoken at home. These students were mainstreamed and were not identified with learning disabilities. However, several of them exhibited problems with auditory processing. In addition, many of them had short attention spans so the lesson plan was designed to use many kinaesthetic, hands-on activities to keep the students engaged. Additionally, the lesson plan is comprised of many parts so that the student changes gears every 5–10 minutes.

As with all multisensory language-structured, sequential programmes, it is sometimes difficult to complete each part of the lesson plan. To the extent that is possible, the teacher should include at least one activity for each section described above. The progression is also important since the student reviews familiar material first before moving on to the more difficult parts of the lesson plan. Whenever possible, the lesson should end with a listening comprehension activity. This gives students the opportunity to hear English or the foreign language read for pleasure. It also ends the lesson on a more casual note.

Appendix A

Lesson Plan

1. **Vocabulary**
   a. Kinaesthetic activities (Simon Says, Step-on posters)
   b. Manipulation of concept cards (identification of vocabulary on cards; games with cards)

2. **Phonological awareness**
   a. Sentences: Place one poker chip per word in the sentence:
      The dog ate his lunch in the kitchen.
      The cat chased the dog up the hill.
   b. Compound words: Place a poker chip for each part of the word:
      flash light sun rise rain bow mail box mail man cow boy
   c. Syllables: Place a poker chip for each syllable in the multisyllabic word:
      ed it pub lish vel vet den tist in hab it Wis con sin ath let ic
   d. Sounds in words: place a poker chip for each sound; white–consonants, red–vowels
   e. Phonemic awareness activities: identify initial, final and medial sounds in words, change the initial, final or medial sounds in words; manipulate phonemes by deleting, adding, etc.

3. **Review of sounds and presentation of new concepts**
   a. Student gives key word and sound for each sound previously learnt
   b. Student skywrites and names the letter
   c. Present new concepts through discovery teaching (syllable types, spelling rules, etc.)

4. **Reading practice**
   a. Read word lists for accuracy and fluency
   b. Read sentences for context reading
   c. Read passages for comprehension

5. **Vocabulary development and oral expression**
   a. Categorisation activities
   b. Describing hierarchy for labelling and explaining common vocabulary words
   c. Expression of complete sentences

6. **Spelling practice**
   a. What says /a/? A says /a/. Dictate sound, student writes and names the letter
   b. Dictation of phonetic, sight and nonsense words

   c. Dictation of above words in sentences

   d. Review of spelling rules

7. Written expression
   a. Morphology

   b. Grammatical concepts (parts of speech, sentence structure, word order)

8. Development of higher-level language
   a. Categories and associated lists (garden: trees, flowers, shrubs, etc.)

   b. Discovery hierarchy (name an object, give its function, name the category, give the name of other objects within that category)

   c. Visualising and verbalising (read a text and make a picture of it with words or a picture)

   d. Connected language (use vocabulary cards to tell a story)

   e. Reading comprehension and dissection of text for rewriting (read a text, answer questions about text, sentence completion using text)

Appendix B

Multisensory Strategies to Teach Morphology and Syntax

1. Affixes
   a. French subject and verb agreement – Student matches subject and verb ending using matching colours of poker chips (blue–subject; red–verb)

Je donne	*Tu donnes*	*Nous donnons*
I give	*You give*	*We give*

   b. English plurals and past tense – Put root words on index cards and affixes on poker chips

ship + s = ships	*dog + s = dogs*	*bus + es = buses*
jump + ed = jumped	*bang + ed = banged*	*lift + ed = lifted*

2. Grammatical concepts
   a. French masculine and feminine agreement – Student selects different color poker chip for different gender

     le chien noir (masculine – 3 blue chips)

     la maison blanche (feminine – 3 red chips)

   b. Selection of correct object pronoun – Use poker chips to represent various parts of the sentence; blue–subject and verbal unit; white–verb complements; red–pronouns

     Jean donne le devoir au professeur (John gives the homework to the teacher)

     Jean lui le donne   *Jean lui l'a donne*   *Jean veut lui le donner*

     Labelled poker chips can also be used for this exercise – e.g. blue–subject (*Jean*); blue–verb + endings (*donn e*); white–verb complement (*le devoir*); white–verb complement (*au professeur*); red–pronouns (*le lui*). Student lines up poker chips in correct order and replaces nouns with pronouns; also, students move poker chips in front of the correct verbal units.

3. Use of charts to manipulate morphemes

Decoding French Root Word and Suffixes

Root + Suffix	Root Word	Suffix
mangeable	manger	able

Example of Irregular French Verb

Infinitive	Person	Verb Root	Verb+ Ending	Rule
manger	nous (2nd pl)	mang	mangeons	Insert e to keep g soft

English Irregular Verb

Root+Suffix	No change in Root Word	Double the Final Consonant	Drop the Silent e	Change y to i	Root with Suffix
clap+ing		p			clapping

Chapter 26

Dyslexia and Modern Foreign Language Learning – Strategies for Success

Melanie Jameson

This chapter:

- examines the nature of the difficulties experienced by dyslexic students in foreign language learning
- considers a range of possible approaches and practical strategies
- examines specifically the role of visual stress in reading and language learning and
- discusses how to enable adult learners to learn a foreign language.

Introduction

The study of foreign languages is generally challenging for children with dyslexia (Miles 1993). Research from Scotland and overseas (Crombie 1997a; Ganschow *et al.* 1995) has shed light on unexpected areas of difficulty and shown how dyslexic difficulties can transfer into the learning of foreign languages. We have also discovered that the initial experience of modern foreign language learning is often positive (Crombie 1996) and it has been observed that dyslexic children, living abroad, seem able to pick up a new language verbally through social interaction – a 'hands-on' stress-free approach that is well suited to their haptic learning style.

Students with dyslexia rarely choose to study foreign languages in further and higher education. Clearly dyslexic learners are 'voting with their feet' and abandoning subjects in which they feel success is unattainable. Whether they have experienced the more traditional grammar-based course or the more lively 'target language teaching' approach, success has eluded them. Both methodologies – especially in their more extreme versions – impinge on key dyslexic areas of difficulty. In the former, there is the burden of rote learning, the lack of oral expression, the prominence of sequences of conjugations and declensions and a focus on the written word. In the contemporary 'target language' style of teaching, set phrases are heard first and seen later; the structured framework, which was fundamental in the grammar-based approach, now seems completely absent. The well-documented dyslexic difficulties with phoneme/morpheme segmentation (Pollock and Waller 1994) prevent the learner from separating a piece of language into meaningful units – this is especially pertinent in the two most frequently taught foreign languages, French and German.

It is unfortunate that dyslexic strengths are rarely brought into play in the foreign language classroom, since there undoubtedly are ways in which the informed teacher/tutor can build on dyslexic strengths and minimise many of the difficulties in order to promote success. Of course many talented foreign language teachers moderate their teaching and provide elements of support. However lack of awareness of the specific problems faced by dyslexic learners (and there will be at least one dyslexic child on average in a typical class of 30) means that they are not optimising their efforts.

One important factor is the visual quality of the textbook/study materials. Care should be taken that routine classroom testing does not discriminate against the dyslexic student; creative approaches to differentiation may well be required (Griffiths and Hardman 1994). Alternative syllabi will be discussed together with the merits and disadvantages of 'disapplication' of the National Curriculum requirement to study a language at Key Stage 4 (England and Wales). Further considerations arise with adult dyslexic learners who will often have failed to gain competence in modern languages at school. Protection of self-esteem and the building up of confidence are essential components of success for this group.

Reducing 'visual stress' in study

The visual quality and layout of the foreign languages textbook should be noted. Teachers may not know that a proportion of the population, which includes epileptics, migraine sufferers and dyslexics, is not particularly good at perceiving patterns of small symbols on white paper. Their symptoms, referred to variously as visual stress, visual discomfort, or Meares-Irlen Syndrome (formerly known as Scotopic Sensitivity Syndrome), include the following:

- perceiving a glare from white paper, which makes it hard to decipher the text
- struggling as print appears to lose its focus or move on the page
- frequently losing the place
- headaches or eye strain when reading.

The cause of these symptoms may be undetected eye problems which require treatment from an optometrist or orthoptist, preferably one specialising in the visual correlates of dyslexia (Evans 1996). It should be stressed that these are problems which are not picked up in routine school eye tests. Sometimes intuitive coloured overlays or tinted spectacles can help (Wilkins 1996). However there is no doubt that reading difficulties can be exacerbated by reading matter that contains the following features: glossy paper, printing in either red or green, small fonts (below size 12) and inadequate spacing. In addition, capitalisation of whole words and phrases and the use of fancy or unusual fonts mean that words lose their distinctive features and become harder to recognise.

Several of the most common foreign language textbooks are characterised by overcrowded 'busy' pages where the words themselves seem lost in the overwhelming effect of jazzy presentation. When selecting a textbook or producing learning materials the principal criterion should be clear text on an uncluttered page. The features listed below are also helpful (Jameson 1998):

- Pictograms and graphics which assist with meaning and can speed up the location of information.
- Left justification only (i.e. leaving a ragged right margin) which makes it easier to keep the place.
- Consistent colour coding, to distinguish between regular categories of information, such as masculine, feminine (and neuter) nouns and to highlight patterns of endings. The visual impact of the colour then serves as reinforcement.
- Shaded boxes of key points for emphasis.

Valuing dyslexic strengths

Let us now proceed to the key question: how can dyslexic strengths be brought into play when learning a language? The answer is: only when the methodology used allows them to be expressed. Education seems to draw principally on those talents associated with the left side of the brain, namely the ability to categorise, sequence, retain facts and formulae, produce well-structured arguments and analyse information. By contrast, many dyslexics excel in 'right-brained' skills; unfortunately these talents are seldom required or acknowledged in the way the majority of school subjects are taught (West 1997). This categorisation of left and right hemispheric skills, although somewhat crude and oversimplified, is nevertheless helpful in gaining an insight into a more balanced teaching methodology that would greatly benefit many of our learners.

Features of 'right-brained' thinking, often noted in dyslexic people, are:

- the ability to gain an overview and see the overall pattern
- a talent for making unexpected links and associations
- artistic talent, originality and creativity
- an affinity for fantasy and visualisation/pictorial representations
- a feel for colour
- lateral thinking and troubleshooting skills
- a natural rhythmic sense
- learning by doing. (Vitale 1982)

It must be stressed that, as with dyslexic difficulties, dyslexic skills vary greatly from individual to individual but the outline above encompasses many areas of strength associated with the condition.

Recommended approaches

The following section reports on strategies for teaching foreign languages to dyslexic pupils. Structured multisensory approaches as expounded by Hornsby and Sheer (1980) and Crombie (1992) are foremost in any review of successful methodology. The structured element comprises:

- teaching one thing at a time, then combining the steps in a cumulative way
- being aware of the skills and sub-skills involved
- fostering motivation by achievable 'bite size' targets which are clearly defined.

The multisensory dimension entails reinforcement of the same item(s) in different ways, using different senses. The following sequence is helpful:

See – Hear – Trace – Locate/match – Speak – Insert – Use in context – Adapt

The following elements should also be incorporated where possible:

- Linking and expanding units of language. Once taught, each structure should be expanded into key phrases which, in turn, should be highlighted in worksheets and spotted by students in short audio tape or video extracts.
- Visual images.
- Use of rhythm. The chanting of set phrases is helpful so that the rhythm itself can serve as a reinforcement tool and aid to recall.
- Provision of reference materials. Dyslexic children should be supplied with reference materials of various types, such as charts containing grammatical information; bilingual lists of sequences such as months of the year since they may not be secure with these in English; bilingual spellcheckers, if available.
- Support for a weak short-term memory. Lists of random vocabulary should not be given for homework. Children should be urged to think of ways of remembering new words by association – the wackier, the better. The use of a dictaphone should be allowed (where appropriate) to assist with organisation and to dictate vocabulary. The use of our own voice is acknowledged to be a prime method of retaining information.
- Personal choice. Many dyslexic people find it very hard to be motivated unless there is an element of personal interest and choice in what they study.
- Drama. Active participation through drama or role-play can bring language lessons to life and provide scope for those with creative, dramatic and improvisation skills. The language is thus internalised and reinforced through rehearsal.

It should be evident that none of the above suggestions disadvantage the majority of non-dyslexic learners in the class. In the matter of catering for dyslexic pupils, I must underline that subject staff are not expected to be in a position to identify the strengths and difficulties of these children. It is up to the Special Needs Coordinator (SENCO) to circulate a profile of any child on the Special Educational Needs Register (DfEE Code of Practice 1994). It is, however, incumbent on all staff to have a general understanding of dyslexia, given the prevalence of the condition (Peer 1995).

Alternatives and disapplication

Since September 1998, it has become possible for certain pupils who have opted for a work-related curriculum at Key Stage 4 to drop certain subjects including foreign languages (Circular QCA /98/215). This seems a better alternative for those non-academic pupils who wish their education to have a strong vocational component and will be following an NVQ route. The issue of disapplication of the National Curriculum can arise leading to the suspension of a core National Curriculum subject for up to six months. Although it is stressed that reintegration should be approached carefully, this is clearly almost impossible when much work has been missed. Understandably, most schools keep 'reapplying' the exemption. Disapplication has two obvious advantages, namely leaving more time for specific dyslexia support or private study and removing certain children from the study of a subject in which they seem unable to succeed. The advantages of persisting in the language classroom include a consideration of the effect of further exclusion on self-esteem, full participation in school trips and the chance to acquire a skill which may be of benefit later.

Enabling adult learners to succeed

Because the study of modern foreign languages is generally so fraught with hazards for dyslexic children, it is a wonder that many adults with dyslexia decide to study languages for interest; it is vitally important that success is achieved the second time round. A key factor is sensitivity to the dyslexic adult without patronising or drawing attention to them in class. The most successful approach is one that combines skilful encouragement and perception.

Tutors teaching foreign languages to adults should bear the following points in mind in order to minimise dyslexic difficulties. Study problems mentioned by students in their 'Learner Agreements' should be followed up by tutors, preferably in a confidential tutorial session.

- All students should have the chance to complete administrative forms at home, regarding anything filled out in class as a personal rough copy.
- Always ask for a volunteer rather than 'pouncing' on individuals.
- When selecting a textbook or compiling handouts, avoid the following: bright white or glossy paper; visual 'clutter' due to overprinting in different colours and/or different font sizes and text styles (this issue is covered in detail in the section on Reducing Visual Stress).
- Unmediated use of the target language is hard to follow: it is far more helpful to set the scene, provide visual aids or clues and allow the use of written back-up or reference materials. One suggestion is speaking at normal speed the first time (for the benefit of advanced students) then repeating more slowly with breaks between words or, in the case of German, between the components of compound words.
- Tutors who are native speakers of the foreign language often seem particularly unaware of the difficulties faced by those to whom language study does not come easily and often teach in an academic traditional way, or plunge the class into language immersion – either way school failure is likely to be reinforced. Comprehensive staff development is probably the way forward here.

Dyslexic people tend to think in pictures rather than words. They may have abilities to make links and associations and pictorial or diagrammatic ways of recording information should be encouraged. New vocabulary can be linked with English equivalents e.g. the French word for beach – *plage* – with the English *plague* (the resulting image is a 'plague on the beach'). It is best if students make up their own associations; a good way of compensating for a poor short-term memory is by drawing on a skill.

Using technology

Another approach, often suitable for adults and children with dyslexia, is to use technology. A range of language courses are now available on CD-ROM, an interactive medium which can adapt to the pace and learning preferences of the individual. In this private environment, the student does not feel 'shown up' in front of others; if a word is slow in coming the program will usually 'wait'; there is the option, well suited to the majority of dyslexic learners, of hearing/seeing the answer first, understanding why it is right then having a go yourself. The reinforcement of sound, picture and word clearly illustrates the multisensory approach. Audio tapes and video materials linked to the chosen textbook are helpful particularly if captions are used.

Conclusion

Best practice for dyslexic learners of any age arises out of an informed understanding of potential dyslexic weaknesses and strengths, a readiness to differentiate language activities and the key aim of building up confidence by introducing strategies for success.

Chapter 27

Structured Multisensory Teaching for Second Language Learning in Israel

Susan Secemski, Rika Deutsch and Carmel Adoram

This chapter:

- highlights the use of structured multisensory teaching with pupils studying English as a foreign language and specifically the Jerusalem Reading Recovery Programme
- provides guidance on developing and implementing similar programmes
- and provides examples of assessment procedures to evaluate such programmes.

Introduction

In Israel pupils are required to study English as a foreign language from the 4th year of school (age 10). A high level of proficiency in English is a prerequisite for any higher education; yet many intelligent pupils fail to acquire the necessary skills in English, and as a result, are barred from pursuing higher education and prevented from realising their own potential.

Purpose

The Jerusalem Reading Recovery Programme (no connection with the American namesake, henceforth RR) is designed to give a second chance to pupils in 7th grade who have been studying English as a foreign language for 3–4 years but have not acquired sufficient literacy skills in English to function in a regular, heterogeneous EFL classroom. The aim is to give enough remediation to enable pupils to return to the mainstream classroom as soon as possible and to provide basic skills in English for very weak pupils.

Population

Since many of these pupils come from culturally and financially disadvantaged backgrounds, only a small percentage (approximately 20 per cent) have actually been diagnosed as learning disabled (LD). Fortunately, the Ministry of Education, in conjunction with the Jerusalem Municipality, has taken a position in line with Ganschow *et al.*'s claim (1998b) that it is 'unproductive to identify foreign language learners simply by labelling them LD or by examining achievement discrepancies; rather, it is productive to focus on the precise nature of the difficulties learners face in that language and develop a continuum of strategies for addressing their problem area(s)'.

It was found that within the identified 'non-reader' population, there were at least three sub-groups:

- those who literally did not know an 'a' from a 'b'
- pupils with gaps in basic decoding skills
- those who were borderline, but whose weak vocabulary and reading comprehension skills did not enable them to benefit from regular lessons.

Screening process

Pupils are chosen for participation in the Programme according to achievement on a standardised written test administered to all students in the 7th grade. This test is designed to determine the degree and nature of their difficulties. Those who fall below 50 per cent are classified as 'non-readers', considered to have special needs and given remediation in small groups whether or not they have been formally diagnosed as dyslexic. Borderline cases (50–70 per cent) are tested individually in order to make a final decision regarding inclusion in the Programme.

Teaching methods and materials

In 1993, Lindsay Peer adapted Kathleen Hickey's Multisensory Language Course to meet the needs of teaching English as a foreign language for dyslexic Israeli pupils. Since then, teachers in the field have been creating and adapting materials, incorporating Orton methods as well (Gillingham and Stillman 1956). The teachers meet throughout the year in order to improve teaching methods, share materials, and discuss problems, under the guidance of a supervisor appointed by the Ministry of Education and Jerusalem Municipality.

For the past three years, structured, multisensory methods have been used in conjunction with whole language (Vail 1997). Simple readers are used, sometimes with accompanying tapes, for exposure to a whole-language experience that is within the limited proficiency levels of the students. Special methods for teaching basic literacy skills in English have been developed, taking into account mother tongue interference and the differing structures of the two languages. For instance, in Hebrew, by 3rd grade, vowels are removed from the printed page, but understood via knowledge of the root, and contextual clues. Thus, Israeli pupils often write and read words without regard to vowels. 'The auditory-visual match for vowels alone drives our dyslexic youngsters to despair' (Weingrod 1990). Thus, great stress is placed on teaching vowels which are introduced very gradually with much reinforcement. Similarly, in Hebrew, sentences can exist without a verb (the verb 'to be' is understood), so the concept that every English sentence contains a verb requires considerable reinforcement (see Kahn-Horowitz et al. 1998, for a description of problems and suggested methodology specific to teaching English to Hebrew speakers).

The methods previously used for individual remediation had to be adapted to teaching groups. In order to answer a growing need for appropriate materials for group use, new textbooks for reading recovery programmes have been published in Israel, including Ready, Steady, Read (Barzilay *et al.* 1997), which was chosen for use in this RR Programme. This book is based on a structured, multisensory, phonics-based approach and is tailored to the needs of Israeli pupils with special needs. Reading is taught in conjunction with writing, spelling, listening and spoken language. The skills of decoding, vocabulary, and reading comprehension are dealt with systematically. Alphabet letters, letter cards and rule cards are included for multisensory instruction. Reading rules are taught explicitly in a structured, sequential manner and reinforced by accompanying texts.

Teachers use this book in conjunction with individually prepared materials. The book introduces seven letters in the first lesson, and four to five letters or digraphs in subsequent lessons. For some foreign language learners, the material must be broken down further into smaller, more manageable chunks. Some pupils can only add one letter per lesson, especially where there is mother tongue interference.

Structured, multisensory instruction in each lesson

The 45-minute class is generally divided into smaller units, in which the teacher switches from one modality to another. Sequencing activities include: alphabetising of letter cards, letter tracking, and subsequently alphabetising simple words. Dictation generally follows – reviewing spelling rules previously taught. Initially pupils 'spell' the words using letter cards and only later actually begin writing in a notebook. Thus, pupils connect the sounds heard to the letter on the card and eventually to the kinaesthetic movements required to produce the whole words on the page. The main part of the class period is devoted to introducing new letters, new sight words, new reading rules, and vocabulary.

Reading comprehension skills are introduced by having pupils read a story based only on the sounds and common whole words that have been taught explicitly. (Some untrained teachers misuse the book by reading the passages to pupils. As a result, pupils learn listening comprehension skills or how to memorise a text, but not how to read.) Reading comprehension exercises after each passage include yes/no questions, matching pictures and words, multiple choice questions, and sentence completion. Crossword puzzles or word searches provide additional reinforcement.

Games are used extensively to reinforce new material learnt. In addition, they are used as a vehicle to introduce or review basic vocabulary which these pupils generally fail to acquire in their early exposure to English. Thus, numbers, colours, basic classroom equipment, and names of animals are introduced via charts, posters and games, such as bingo. Although vocabulary recall is of utmost importance for the comprehension skills required for reintegration into the mainstream classroom, it remains a weak area for many RR pupils. Behaviour modification has been found very useful for overcoming serious behaviour problems and establishing basic work habits. Immediate reinforcement in the form of rewards, such as stickers, is used consistently for completion of classwork in the book. Upon accumulation of ten stickers, a larger prize is offered. Learning strategies and metacognition are incorporated into the lesson. For instance, pupils are taught scanning techniques in order to locate information in a text. Furthermore, mnemonic devices are utilised in order to make new vocabulary more meaningful, thus improving retention. Periodically, pupils are asked to evaluate their own performance in order to increase self-awareness.

Procedures for setting up the Programme

The Ministry of Education appoints a supervisor who is responsible for setting up the Programme and ensuring that the following procedures are followed well in advance:

1. Preparatory meetings with school administration and teachers

It is essential to explain to school administrators the purpose of the Programme, the methods used, and the importance of meticulous planning in order to enable the Programme to maximise efficiency. Although teachers are generally aware of the need for remediation in foreign language instruction, many administrators are not articulate in the causes and solutions to management problems in EFL classes. Meetings with the English Department heads take place before school starts in order to introduce schools to the Programme guidelines. This ensures that the logistics of scheduling parallel classes and the creation of suitable groups is anticipated and planned carefully. Thus, this special programme is established as a priority within the school.

2. Appointment of a liaison

The schools have sometimes felt threatened by having experts come in from the 'outside'. In order to decentralise supervision of the Programme, one English teacher within the school was appointed as liaison person. All negotiating was done through the liaison, so that the 'specialists' could keep a low profile. As the schools learn to appreciate the quality and special skills of the specialists, the administration gradually values them as an asset to the school rather than a threat. In fact, the Programme usually becomes an integral part of the school's educational system.

3. Planning regarding co-teaching

Often, RR specialists trained in learning differences co-teach with regular teachers. Teachers are carefully selected, begin special training, and meet their partners prior to the school year in order to avoid problems and misunderstandings. Proper planning has enabled the teachers to clarify their roles and responsibilities on a basis of equal status, and collaborate on teaching materials and methods, behaviour modification and pupil evaluation. Thus, students benefit from the strengths of both teachers.

4. Allocation of rooms

Children with special difficulties need appropriate permanent settings for study. Schools do not always consider it a priority to place these students in appropriate settings. Thus, schools are required to set aside a regular, enclosed, permanent classroom as a condition for funding. Shelters, balconies, and hallways are totally inappropriate for children with learning and attention problems.

5. Orientation for parents and pupils prior to entry into the Programme

In some cases, pupils resist being removed from regular classes because they are concerned about being stigmatised. Meetings with parents and pupils, in order to explain the purpose of the Programme and previous success rates of reintegration, have a salutary effect. Problem behaviours have been addressed by having pupils and their parents sign a contract before entering the Programme. The contract emphasises that only pupils who comply with certain standards of behaviour, class participation and work habits will be allowed to remain in the Programme. In certain cases, pupils have been removed because of breach of contract.

Assessment of student progress

Teachers in the Programme provide ongoing assessment in conjunction with self-evaluation by pupils. Furthermore, it was essential to document student progress in a scientific manner to determine the success of the Reading Recovery Programme as a basis for making further recommendations.

Discussion of the Israeli Reading Recovery Programme

The basic premise of the Israeli Reading Recovery Programme is that learning English as a foreign language in a relatively small group using special methods enables special needs pupils to receive the attention they need to overcome their problems. In research conducted by the authors, at-risk pupils were found to exhibit multiple behaviour problems as well as problems in speaking, listening and writing. This resulted in their inability to function in a regular class, while also interfering with the progress of other pupils. Thus, the existence of this Programme enables the heterogeneous class teacher to meet the needs of the 'readers' at grade level.

Inclusion and the heterogeneous English class

Nevertheless, some teachers and administrators continue to believe firmly, that all pupils must be included in the heterogeneous classroom, even if they cannot read. An article published in the Israeli *English Teachers' Journal* (Rabbe *et al.* 1998) describes the attempt, in one school that had been selected to participate in the project, to keep 'non-readers' in the heterogeneous classroom. When a diagnostic test was administered, the results revealed a surprisingly high number of 'non-readers' – 33 per cent, as well as a large group of weak learners. The RR Programme supervisor suggested that these non-readers must receive remediation individually or in small groups. However, this suggestion went unheeded in the name of true inclusion. The article describes how after three months of attempts to integrate these children into the heterogeneous class, the administration and staff admitted that this was no solution to the non-reader problem. Neither the non-readers, nor the other pupils were making satisfactory progress.

Subsequently, the school administration urgently requested professional help with the 'non-readers' from the Ministry Inspectorate; however, it was too late in the year to form special non-reader classes, so an expert remedial teacher screened at-risk pupils and began pull-out instruction with very small groups of pupils that were not functioning in the regular classes at all. These pupils were usually weak all round, and their need to catch up on other lessons missed constituted a burden for them. The weak pupils did make some headway through the remedial lessons, but many of them felt dislocated at being taken out of the regular class in the middle of the year. They were not able to close the gap with the homeroom class, and this created a high level of frustration and anxiety among them, resulting in low motivation (Rabbe *et al.* 1998).

Evaluation was complicated by the fact that pupils were taught by two different teachers, a specialist and regular classroom teacher, using different material and activities. In one learning environment, their chances of success were very high; in the other, their 'previous failures were perpetuated' (Rabbe *et al.* 1998). The article attests to the fact that the administration and staff eventually recognised the importance of the Programme as an absolute necessity. The following year, this school scheduled English classes so that non-reader groups could be formed at the very beginning of the year.

Change of attitude to learning difficulties

The existence of the Programme in a school tends to change the attitude of staff and administration to create 'non-reader friendly schools'. The participants' return to the mainstream class, as bonafide, functioning members of the group, becomes a more realistic possibility. It creates a more friendly environment for learning difficulties and differences within the heterogeneous class.

Self-esteem

The benefits in self-esteem for the pupils participating in the Programme are considerable, but need to be researched further. At the beginning of the year, a pupil handed the specialist teacher a note stating: 'Dear teacher, I just want you to know that I can't learn English. Please keep this a secret.' Even this pupil gained sufficient literacy skills in English to return to the heterogeneous class at the end of the year. The above quote contrasts strikingly with the following comments received at the end of the year when participants view themselves as potential readers and learners in English: 'I now feel good in English.' 'I'm not as stupid as I thought.' 'Can I really return to a regular class?'

Degree of success

Because the Programme is expensive to maintain, the question arose as to its cost efficiency. It was considered essential to show that students benefited. An attempt was made to measure gains in ability to decode and comprehend as a result of participation in the RR Programme by comparing the pre- and post-test scores for each student. A defined statistical improvement was shown on the basis of t-test results.

In our research 41 per cent of the pupils required a second year in the Programme on the basis of teacher recommendations. Although they had learnt how to decode, these pupils still lacked the reading comprehension skills needed for the regular class. Many of them needed further reinforcement of basic vocabulary and development of study skills within the small group setting. Of the 59 per cent who were recommended for reintegration to the heterogeneous class having acquired basic literacy skills in English, 25 per cent could return only with the assistance of learning support specialists. Since no such arrangement is currently available, we advocate allocation of funds to provide this essential service.

A follow-up study of a sample of 43 pupils in one large school was conducted to trace what happens to RR pupils in the 8th and 9th grades. Of 20 pupils, 60 per cent continued in the Program, 30 per cent were mainstreamed into level three (the lowest level), 5 per cent to level two and 5 per cent left the school. In 9th grade, out of 23 pupils, 26 per cent were in level three, 52 per cent in level two (middle level!), and 22 per cent left the school. This shows that, where streaming into levels still exists, RR pupils are not doomed to continuing their English studies in the lowest group. There is a need for longitudinal studies to determine long-term success. The results of testing and teacher reports on reintegration show that a small percentage will probably not be reintegrated into the mainstream classroom; they must be provided for in secondary education in special classes.

In spite of successes with the use of behaviour modification, many serious behaviour problems persist. Schools need to accept the fact that the RR Programme is not a dumping ground for pupils who disrupt the regular class. In spite of the use of behaviour contracts described above, there is a constant struggle, because when a child has been thrown out of the Programme, the regular teacher is loath to permit re-entry into the mainstream class. As a result, there is nowhere for him/her to go within the system. Adequate provision must be made by schools for this population in order to ensure the success of the Programme for those who remain.

Teacher training

Teacher-training courses must continue to provide teachers with the tools for creating multisensory materials which meet the specific needs of their pupils. (Unfortunately there is still a shortage of trained teachers in this specialised EFL field.) Some pupils have to unlearn mistakes that have been ingrained by incorrect teaching of vowel correspondences using cognates which are not accurately matched to the English sounds. Thus the importance of having a specially trained co-teacher in the classroom cannot be overemphasised. Actually, all English teachers need training in explicit, structured teaching of phonological awareness, particularly the troublesome vowel sounds. In-service training becomes essential for both experienced classroom teachers who lack fundamental knowledge in this area, as well as specialist teachers in order to keep abreast of the latest methods and materials in the field. A library of materials, available at centres for teacher training, would be most helpful.

Recommendations regarding methodology

The success rate demonstrates that structured, multisensory, phonics-based instruction in conjunction with whole language works for this at-risk population.

These approaches must be combined in a balanced manner from the outset of EFL instruction. The large numbers of 'non-readers' reaching 7th grade suggests that current second language teaching methodologies are not proving successful for at-risk pupils, both dyslexic and weak learners. Hopefully, expansion of RR programmes and their inception in the younger grades will improve the situation.

Expansion of the Programme

The 7th grade Reading Recovery Programme, which began three years ago as an experimental pilot project in three extremely large junior high schools, has now expanded to serve 15 schools. This expansion enables more pupils who have not been able to acquire literacy in English in regular heterogeneous classrooms to benefit from remediation in small groups until such time as they can be integrated into the regular classroom.

There are other programmes already in existence in 5th and 6th grade, especially a very successful, long-standing programme. Discussions are now being held as to the possibility of expanding to include more 5th graders at the very early stages of reading in order to lower the number of pupils who cannot read at all at the beginning of 7th grade. Thus, it would reserve the 7th grade Programme as an opportunity to use limited funding more intensively on fewer pupils, enabling a faster and larger percentage of success.

There is an ongoing dialogue among teachers of 'non-readers' in other parts of Jerusalem and throughout Israel (via conferences and the internet) in order to adopt the more successful models and constantly introduce improvements. We anticipate that this paper will contribute to the international dialogue on this subject.

Conclusion

As the Reading Recovery Programme expands, it is becoming an integral part of the Israeli educational system. Hopefully, the successes recorded herewithin will encourage schools to consider implementing reading recovery programmes with the aim of reintegrating pupils into the heterogeneous classroom only when they have acquired basic literacy skills in English and can therefore benefit from instruction. We believe that this study amply demonstrates the value of the Programme and makes a valuable contribution in enabling more accurate planning and budgeting in the future. We hope that language teachers, learning support specialists and policy makers will collaborate to find appropriate solutions which will meet the needs of all both in Israel and in the international community, where similar difficulties may be encountered (Crombie 1997a).

Acknowledgements

The Jerusalem Education Authority, Avi Sela, Tzviah Ariel, Ellen Serfaty.

Chapter 28

Application of the GAME Approach to Dyslexic Learners in Israel

Shlomit Ilan

This chapter:

- provides an overview of the teaching approach known as GAME which has been developed to provide essential ingredients for a second language learning programme.

What is GAME?

GAME is the Global Analytical Method of teaching the reading of English. Global means learning to read whole meaningful sentences within a meaningful context before having to analyse them into their components – the words. Analytical means analysing the words into their components – the syllables – and then analysing the syllables into their components – the letters.

Based on the assumption that reading is actually a global process, this course is a combination of the global and the analytical approaches. This means that when reading is taught, the learner is led to read whole words within sentences that convey messages, rather than building them up from letters. Then, after having grasped a sufficient number of words in context, the learner is introduced to the analytical approach. This occurs through analysing whole words and eventually applying the rules discovered in the process into new combinations of letters and syllables. At this point decoding takes place. For example, after learners have been taught to read the word 'ten', they are expected to be able to read 'tent'. After learning 'measure' they should be able to read 'pleasure'. In order to help the learner memorise the new forms, the introduction of letters is gradual. The alphabet is not taught as a consecutive ABC. Rather the material for teaching the 26 letters of the English alphabet, with their 44 sounds (and hundreds of different spelling clusters to those very same sounds), is carefully graded and divided into three stages.

GAME is a method for teaching English as a second, or foreign language. Thus, while learning to read, the students learn English or, while learning English, they also learn to read. All languages can be taught along the underlying principles of GAME, but for English it is especially apt. This is because English is not a phonetic language. For example, a person who learns to read 'ear' will find it difficult to read 'earth' without making a mistake. It is obvious that after learning to read 'is' and 'land' the reading of 'island' can still only be facilitated with the aid of a teacher.

In order to bring home the message that English is not a phonetic language, the famous English playwright George Bernard Shaw made the following jest. He wrote the word 'fish' as follows: 'GHOTI': The 'gh' produces the same sound as in 'tough'; the 'o' as in 'women' and the 'ti' as in 'nation'. 'Fish', unlike many other words in English, complies with supposedly phonetic rules, but when looking at all the letters in the word 'tough' one can see how complicated English spelling is. By adding an 'h' after the 't' ('though'), both the 't' and the 'ou' no longer sound as they sounded in 'tough'. All in all 'ou' has six different sounds in the following words: 'tough', 'though', 'thought', 'through', 'journey' and 'house'. The combination 'ea' has nine different sounds in the following words and names: 'read', 'head', 'heart', 'great', 'ocean', 'idea', 'beautiful', 'Sean' and 'Mediterranean', and the letter 'o' has no less than nine sounds: 'one', 'on', 'so', 'some', 'room', 'book', 'door', 'women', 'onion', with about three times as many spelling possibilities.

Reading and the dyslexic

Dyslexics, who are unable to remember a cluster before they have seen it many times, find it extremely hard to blend the three aspects of the word. They may find decoding almost impossible. Most remedial teaching methods for dyslexics concentrate on decoding, believing that after the dyslexics have mastered this skill they will become literate. Such methods force dyslexics to do what they find most difficult. When they have learnt to decode, and are eventually considered 'readers', they become slow readers for the rest of their lives.

Breznitz (1997) established that dyslexics' comprehension could be improved by accelerating their reading rates. Her research has also shown that, while the visual recognition of the symbol is a short process, the auditory one is a rather lengthy one. In spite of this, 'normal readers' are able to synchronise the two processes, thus gaining automaticity in reading. Dyslexics, however, are unable to synchronise the two channels of recognition and therefore reading is extremely difficult for them and remains a difficult process even when they have mastered reading. Therefore the goal of the teacher is not to teach dyslexics how to read, but rather to enable them to become automatic readers who need not struggle with the visual and auditory symbols, but recognise the word in context. GAME helps achieve automaticity as well as an accelerated reading rate.

Davis (1994) claims that in many aspects dyslexia is a gift. The dyslexic person is able to think in pictures, which is a thousand times faster than thinking verbally. There is a fair chance that in the process of learning to read – which is often a linear activity – as opposed to nonverbal conceptualisation – which is not – the dyslexic will lose the gift. He suggests that written words cause the dyslexic disorientation and confusion. This occurs mainly with words he calls 'empty', i.e. they have no corresponding picture. This problem is bypassed with the help of GAME because, when reading, the learner does not encounter individual words. The smallest unit taught in GAME is neither a letter nor a word but a full sentence. The learner actually skips the difficult stage of having to cope with 'empty words'. When s/he sees a picture of the earth and has to read the sentence: 'This is the earth' – a sentence which contains three empty words and only one word which has a corresponding picture – s/he grasps the whole sentence as one meaningful entity. By constant repetition, but also by substituting one word for another, forming a new sentence like 'This is the sea', reading remains a meaningful activity and empty words, such as 'This is the' can stick in the learner's mind without causing confusion.

The four principles of GAME are; Repetition, Structure, Variation and Interest. Repetition is well integrated in the material. The structure of GAME is based on gradual introduction of both letters and of new material. The variation is provided through playing games, singing songs and by using the computer program *GAME for Windows* and interest is maintained through the variation and structure of the program. Students are also introduced to general concepts which expand their knowledge of the world.

GAME and the teaching of reading

Reading is taught through meaningful sentences which are accompanied by simple drawings. Thus, the learner need not resort to his/her mother tongue in order to comprehend. Though the drawings are self-explanatory, it is recommended that new language items be taught orally first – using gestures, body language and the objects themselves.

A description of the course

The course consists of four books, a booklet of songs, six cassettes, computer software and scores of games. Stages are colour-coded and each stage represented by a different colour.

- Stage 1 introduces only ten letters t, h, i, s, e, a, r, l, n, d.
- Stage 2 introduces the letters m, o, w.
- Stage 3 introduces thirteen more letters f, g, b, y, x, u, q, k, c, p, v, j, z.

There are four components in every stage:

1. The Teacher's Input Material
2. The Pupil's Workbook
3. The Reader
4. The Reinforcement Reader.

A cassette recording is available for components 1 and 3.

First component: The Teacher's Input Material

This constitutes the global stage. We suggest it be taught by a teacher with the aid of an audio-cassette. Because English is not a phonetic language, the students should not be encouraged to attempt reading this section of the book on their own. Even a student who recognises the letters and the sounds they are supposed to make, may fail in decoding this material.

Second component: The Pupil's Workbook

These are exercises based entirely on what has been taught in the Teacher's Input Material and in the readers (see below). It demands reading comprehension as well as knowledge of the material that has been taught. The students should do the exercises independently.

Third component: The Reader

This is the analytical section. In it all the words that appeared in the first stage reappear, while new words are added to comply with the anticipated phonetic rules of the English language. The students can read this part with little assistance. They may need the cassette rather than the teacher. In order to demonstrate comprehension the student is asked to draw lines from the sentences to the relevant picture.

Fourth component: The Reinforcement Reader

This is provided in order to reinforce students' reading and decoding ability. The reinforcement should improve their fluency and help them become efficient readers. 'Efficiency is speed, accuracy and being at ease' (R. Feuerstein, personal communication).

In addition there is a fourth book – *The Book of Animals* – which is also for reinforcement. Students are expected to cope with it on their own with the aid of a cassette. This helps them acquire silent reading habits. Another form of reinforcement is the software *GAME for Windows*. The main activity in it is that of the Interactive Reader. Here the user reads a text, illustrated by a photograph, digests its meaning and responds according to the instructions. There are also some matching and spelling games.

Conclusion

GAME can make the learning of reading easier. Its structure and the use of repetition are important for every lesson as some new material is introduced even if the previous material has not yet been mastered, because of the constant recycling of elements. Every word or subject which has been mentioned once will reappear, each time on a higher level, using words which have already been taught together with new ones; introducing new letters and concepts while using old familiar words and structures. GAME is also an attempt to wed elements of both the whole-word global method and the phonic analytical method. It does so in an elegantly simple manner: it reduces the number of letters that are used to create words and ensures that every single word used has a clear meaning. Clarity of meaning is achieved by using words and sentences that can be illustrated and every sentence is illustrated. The number of words and pictures on a page are also limited which adds to the clarity. Moreover, most of the sentences are themselves intrinsically interesting because of this match between word and picture. Thus, reading in GAME is always a meaningful activity. It is especially meaningful when it is preceded by interactive activities with objects so that these objects are already familiar to the pupil before s/he comes across them in the written text.

Recent research on learning and memory has brought to light the efficacy of stimulating both hemispheres of the brain. As school learning tends to overemphasise the left, analytical side, many of the innovative approaches stress the importance of the subconscious, synthetic abilities of the mind. Much of the impact of GAME is synthetic. The term *global* does in fact refer to this 'gestalt' character. Having global and analytical elements enables the mind/brain to learn both in a focused and a defocused manner, which is maximally effective. The same research on memory that stresses the subconscious aspects of learning also shows that a multisensory, multimodal presentation of material enhances learning and remembering (Zimin 1992).

Chapter 29

Dyslexia – Does it Mean Anything to a Foreign Language Teacher?

Joanna Nijakowska

This chapter:

- examines the results of a Polish survey involving language teachers in relation to their awareness of dyslexia and
- discusses the implications of this for the identification and supporting of dyslexic learners in school.

Introduction

Dyslexia is not widely recognised by teachers in Poland. This is very likely due to lack of appropriate training and knowledge of the most recent advances in the field as has been revealed in a survey conducted by the author (Nijakowska 1999). Additionally it has been indicated by several authors that dyslexic students may encounter difficulties in EFL learning (Bogdanowicz 1994; Brejnak and Zablocki 1999; Ott 1997; Ganschow *et al.* 1998a; Sparks 1995; Sparks and Ganschow 1993b; Sparks *et al.* 1989, 1992, 1998; Mickiewicz 1995). The Linguistic Coding Differences Hypothesis (LCDH) developed by Ganschow and Sparks suggests that dyslexic learners may experience difficulties in three components of linguistic coding – phonological, syntactic and semantic.

In LCDH it is suggested that EFL learning problems are based on either overt or subtle difficulties with native language (NL) learning. This means that an individual's skill in the NL components constitutes the foundation for successful EFL learning. Students with difficulties in the phonological component of their NL are likely to experience immediate difficulty in the EFL classroom. The most noticeable deficit concerns phonemic awareness, which refers to the ability to isolate and manipulate consciously the sounds of the language and relate them to the appropriate written letters or letter combinations, whereas students with intact phonological processing skills but weaker semantic ability often experience difficulty at later stages of EFL learning. It is also hypothesised that both NL and EFL learning depends on basic language learning mechanisms and that problems with one language skill – for example, phonological processing – are likely to have negative effects on both language systems. The authors of LCDH believe that most students who exhibit difficulty with EFL learning generally have academic problems specific to EFL rather than with all academic courses.

The results of the research conducted by Sparks *et al.* (1989, 1992, 1998), Sparks and Ganschow (1993b) and Ganschow *et al.* (1998a) provide evidence for the effectiveness of MSL – multisensory structured learning on both NL and EFL performance. According to Gillingham and Stillman (Ott 1997) multisensory teaching is based upon the constant use of all of the following: how a letter or word looks, how it sounds, how the speech organs or the hand in writing feels when producing it. The pupil uses the visual channel (eyes), auditory channel (ears), kinaesthetic (motor memory), and tactile (hands) to learn. It has been shown by Ganschow and Sparks that teaching an EFL with the MSL approach produces greater gains in EFL aptitude than does teaching with non-MSL methods in students with dyslexia. Adaptations of MSL approach to EFL instruction emphasises the direct, explicit and systematic teaching of the spelling–sound relations, grammar and morphology of an EFL. Without explicit teaching of these systems, students with weaker NL skills and EFL aptitude are unlikely to learn a system of a new language as easily as students with stronger NL and EFL aptitude. Small amounts of material should be presented at one time, ensuring complete mastery by repetition and using MSL techniques. Lessons should be carefully sequenced from simple to complex. EFL instruction in both NL and EFL is more effective than instruction in an EFL only.

It has been admitted that, even though phonological/orthographic skills and EFL aptitude of students with specific learning difficulties who receive MSL instruction in an EFL improve significantly on standardised tests, they still lag behind other learners in some NL skills and on the Modern Language Aptitude Test (MLAT).

Results of the Polish survey

In January 1999 the survey of teachers' awareness and experience with dyslexia was conducted among primary and secondary school teachers in the author's home town. The survey was originally addressed to teachers of different subjects (Nijakowska 1999). The author decided to concentrate only on language teachers and analyse their answers to the survey questions. Thirty-eight language teachers answered the survey questions, 22 of whom were English teachers plus teachers of Polish (12), German (3) and French (1). All qualified teachers, 23 taught in secondary and 15 in primary schools. Four had graduated from teacher training college, 20 from higher pedagogical school and 14 from university. The teachers were aged from 25 to 50, and most of them (33) were women. Twenty-two had taken part in various courses to widen their professional knowledge.

Pupils taught in primary school were aged from 7 to 15, secondary school students were 15 to 19 years old. The number of students each of the teachers had varied considerably, from 70 to 200. EFL teachers usually taught classes divided into two groups consisting of about 15 pupils each, whereas teachers of Polish taught classes of 30 students. Twenty (53 per cent) of all of the teachers were class tutors. Of these, four were not aware of the number of dyslexic students in their classes while the others had numbers that varied from 0 to 9. No fewer than 10 per cent of their pupils were said to encounter specific difficulties in reading and writing. These figures are consistent with previous research in which it was stated that 10–15 per cent of children in Poland are stated to have these problems (Bogdanowicz 1994, 1997a, 1999; Brejnak and Zablocki 1999). What is more, on average, there could be about three or more such children in each class, and, in fact, 89.5 per cent of the teachers agreed that dyslexia is not a sporadic phenomenon, whereas only 10.5 per cent claimed the opposite (see Figure 29.1). Still, even though there seems to be quite a high level of awareness of the existence of this disorder, it does not go with the ability to define and understand it. Very few teachers could explain the nature of dyslexia; only 7.9 per cent of them were able to provide an accurate explanation.

Teacher training

The level of dyslexia awareness among language teachers depended upon whether they were familiarised with this notion during their training or during special courses. According to the results of the survey, the more teachers knew about dyslexia the easier they recognised and understood dyslexic students' problems and were ready to adjust their teaching to their learners' needs (see Figures 29.2 and 29.3). What seems to be worrying is the fact that only 39.5 per cent of the teachers were familiar with the notion of dyslexia during their training, while as many as 60.5 per cent had not heard about it before they started their teaching career or they had not heard of it at all (Figures 29.1 and 29.4). It might be suggested that if they had undergone dyslexia training during their studies, their attitude towards children with dyslexia would have been different. Around 20 per cent of the teachers were familiar with the notion of multisensory teaching and only 15 per cent claimed that they had applied special methods and techniques as far as work with dyslexic students was concerned.

Working with dyslexic students

Nevertheless, regardless of how much they knew about dyslexia, 76.3 per cent of the teachers claimed they worked with dyslexic students, the number of such students varying from 1 to 48 per teacher. Only 23 per cent of the teachers claimed there were no children with dyslexia among their pupils and as most of these knew very little about the difficulty they were unable to identify it.

Most of the teachers (63 per cent) agreed that their dyslexic students experienced problems in mastering compulsory teaching contents, and that they could not cope with the school requirements. That is why individualised requirements were introduced for these students but they were misinterpreted by the teachers. Even though 76 per cent admitted that such children usually need more time for performing a given activity than other students, surprisingly, not more then 66 per cent of the teachers allowed their dyslexic students to work longer when they needed more time for completing a given task (see Figure 29.5). Even fewer teachers (around half) agreed to do it during written tests. Furthermore, only 40 per cent of the teachers did not judge the whole work on the basis of its low orthographic level – for them orthographic and spelling mistakes were not the reason for disqualifying a dyslexic child's written work or for lowering his/her school marks. Constant access to dictionaries during lessons was allowed by 60 per cent of the teachers, and as many as 44 per cent not only issued grades from 1 to 6 but also provided their students with dyslexia with a descriptive mark, stressing good, strong points of a given student's work.

	Some of the survey questions the language teachers answered	No. / % of teachers who answered 'yes'	No. / % of teachers who answered 'no'
1	Were you familiarised with the notion of developmental dyslexia during your training?	15 / 39.5	23 / 60.5
2	Are there any children with developmental dyslexia among your students?	29 / 76.3	9 / 23.7
3	Is developmental dyslexia a common phenomenon among your students?	34 / 89.5	4 / 10.5
4	Do students with developmental dyslexia encounter problems in mastering compulsory teaching contents?	24 / 63.2	14 / 36.8
5	Do you introduce individualised requirements towards students with developmental dyslexia?	24 / 63.2	14 / 36.8
6	Do you apply any special methods of work with students with developmental dyslexia?	6 / 15.8	32 / 84.2
7	Are you familiar with the notion of multisensory teaching?	7 / 18.4	31 / 81.6
8	Do you lower marks for written tasks of students with developmental dyslexia because of their low orthographic level?	23 / 60.5	15 / 39.5
9	Do children with developmental dyslexia need more time for performing a given activity than other students?	29 / 76.3	9 / 23.7
10	Do you usually give more time to students with developmental dyslexia for completing a given activity when they need it?	25 / 65.8	13 / 34.2
11	Do you give more time to students with dyslexia for completing tasks during written tests?	21 / 55.3	17 / 44.7
12	Do students with developmental dyslexia have constant access to dictionaries during your lessons?	23 / 60.5	15 / 39.5
13	Do you provide students with developmental dyslexia with descriptive marks?	17 / 44.7	21 / 55.3

	1	2	3	4	5	6	7	8	9	10	11	12	13
Series2	60.5	23.7	10.5	36.8	36.8	84.2	81.6	39.5	23.7	34.2	44.7	39.5	55.3
Series1	39.5	76.3	89.5	63.2	63.2	15.8	18.4	60.5	76.3	65.8	55.3	60.5	44.7

Question number

☐ Series1   ▣ Series2

% of teachers who answered 'yes'   % of teachers who answered 'no'

Figure 29.1 Questionnaire responses

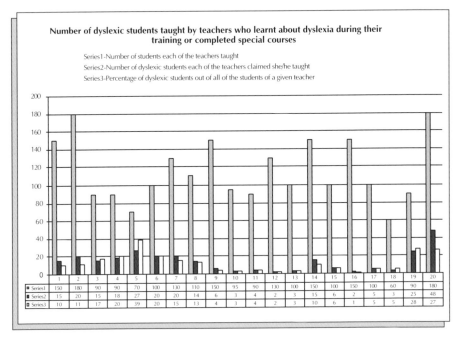

Number of dyslexic students taught by teachers who learnt about dyslexia during their training or completed special courses

Series1-Number of students each of the teachers taught
Series2-Number of dyslexic students each of the teachers claimed she/he taught
Series3-Percentage of dyslexic students out of all of the students of a given teacher

	1	2	3	4	5	6	7	8	9	10	11	12	13	14	15	16	17	18	19	20
Series1	150	180	90	90	70	100	130	110	150	95	90	130	100	150	100	150	100	60	90	180
Series2	15	20	15	18	27	20	20	14	6	3	4	2	3	15	6	2	5	3	25	48
Series3	10	11	17	20	39	20	15	13	4	3	4	2	3	10	6	1	5	5	28	27

Figure 29.2

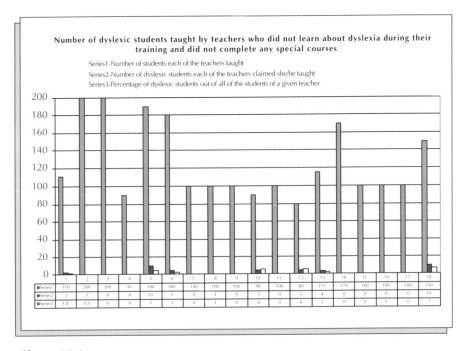

Number of dyslexic students taught by teachers who did not learn about dyslexia during their training and did not complete any special courses

Series1-Number of students each of the teachers taught
Series2-Number of dyslexic students each of the teachers claimed she/he taught
Series3-Percentage of dyslexic students out of all of the students of a given teacher

	1	2	3	4	5	6	7	8	9	10	11	12	13	14	15	16	17	18
Series1	110	200	200	90	190	180	100	100	100	90	100	80	115	170	100	100	100	150
Series2	2	1	0	0	10	5	0	1	0	5	0	5	4	0	0	0	0	10
Series3	1.8	0.5	0	0	5	3	0	1	0	6	0	6	3	0	0	0	0	7

Figure 29.3

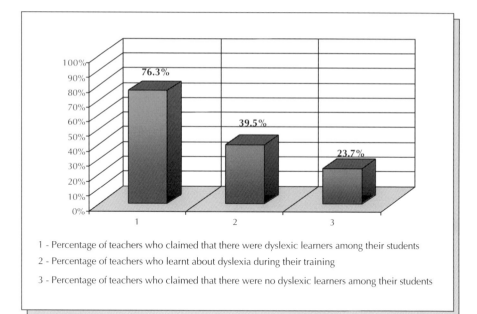

1 - Percentage of teachers who claimed that there were dyslexic learners among their students

2 - Percentage of teachers who learnt about dyslexia during their training

3 - Percentage of teachers who claimed that there were no dyslexic learners among their students

Figure 29.4

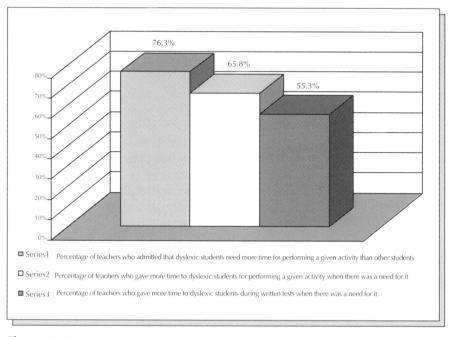

☐ Series1 Percentage of teachers who admitted that dyslexic students need more time for performing a given activity than other students

☐ Series2 Percentage of teachers who gave more time to dyslexic students for performing a given activity when there was a need for it

■ Series3 Percentage of teachers who gave more time to dyslexic students during written tests when there was a need for it

Figure 29.5

Interviews and observations of students with dyslexia during their English lessons

In order to see the problem of dyslexia from a wider perspective and from a different point of view, the author conducted several interviews and observations of dyslexic students during their English classes. These interviews and observations took place in two primary and two secondary schools during the second semester of the school year 1998/99. Eleven students (six girls and five boys) aged from 7 to 19 were chosen – six of them attended primary schools while the remaining five were secondary school students. Three of the children from primary school were only children (i.e. did not have siblings). Usually it was a parent or a teacher of Polish from primary school who noticed the difficulties and had the children examined and diagnosed by a psychologist.

It is worth noting that in the cases of eight of the students, family members had also encountered dyslexia which accords with the hypothesis of a hereditary link to the problems mentioned. Furthermore, in seven cases the affected relatives were male (fathers or brothers), which seems to reflect the fact that men are more likely than women to be dyslexic (Bogdanowicz 1994; Brejnak and Zablocki 1999; Krasowicz 1997; Selikowitz 1999).

When the attitude of other members of the class towards dyslexic pupils is taken into consideration, seven students claimed that their classmates were indifferent to their problems, three of the students could usually count on their peers' help, whereas only one admitted he had been teased by his collegues because of his difficulties. Three students used to have regular meetings with a psychologist and all of them had attended remedial classes, at least for some time. However, these classes were only concerned with the Polish language; such classes were not organised for dyslexic students having problems in learning EFL. However, nine students took part in such classes organised at school, the aim of which was to practise spelling and orthogrphic rules of Polish. Unfortunately, they did not work on development of such skills as reading for comprehension, planning and organising written work, note-taking, learning and revising vocabulary, not to mention strategies for poor memory and organisational skills or training in relaxation techniques (very useful during examinations and tests). The time each of the students devoted to attending correction and compensation classes in Polish varied considerably, from six months to eight years, usually one hour per week. According to their Polish language teachers, despite their great effort and commitment, in the cases of six students no progress or improvement was observed; the remaining five seemed to get better and better.

The number of compulsory English lessons each of the students had at school varied from two to five hours per week. Seven of the students attended additional, private lessons of English, from one to four hours per week. The number of years each of the students spent learning English as a foreign language varied from one to eight years. The time spent on preparing for English lessons by each student varied from half an hour to eight hours per week. Five of them admitted that they had to spend much more time on learning English than other subjects. It has been observed that most of the students had difficulties in learning English; they could not easily cope with the school requirements as far as learning English as a foreign language was concerned. Learning vocabulary, both spelling and pronunciation, constituted a great problem as well as learning grammatical rules and terms. They encountered considerable difficulties in mastering the relationship between speech sounds and written language, a phoneme–grapheme relation. The inability to write what is heard and to read what is written was very apparent. Unfortunately, in the cases of six students low orthographic level of their written work was a cause of lowered school marks. Only six of the students had constant access to dictionaries during English lessons but nobody was allowed to use them during written tests. Moreover, four students had never been given a chance to answer orally instead of in writing, whereas seven pupils in some cases were allowed on occasion to choose an oral answer instead of a written one.

Another important observation concerned slow information processing by children with dyslexia – much slower than in the cases of other students in the class – so that more time was required for performing some tasks. This was particularly evident during tests when the time for completing the work was limited. Nine of the students usually needed more time for performing a given activity during a lesson than other students in the class, as well as more time for completing written tests. Primary school teachers usually gave more time to their pupils when there was a need for it, unlike secondary school teachers, among whom only one allowed his student to work longer than other students in the class. Learning new words and accessing them from memory seemed to be difficult and time-consuming. What is more, severe impairment of speaking skill was experienced by those students as well.

Despite the problems the dyslexic students had in acquiring English as a foreign language, neither individualised requirements nor any forms of individual work or special teaching methods were introduced by the teachers and the school in the cases of ten students. The requirements were the same as towards the rest of the students in a class. However, as many as three of the students believed that their problems in learning English were minor, and, in fact, they were limited to spelling difficulties, sometimes connected with low graphic level of their writing. Most of the students were very motivated and claimed that they enjoyed learning English despite the difficulties they had been encountering. They also recognised the importance of English in international communication, its usefulness for making friends with people from abroad, travelling or computing. Some of them said they just had fun learning a new language. However, as many as four of the students claimed they hated learning English and were strongly convinced that if English was not a compulsory subject at school, they would not have chosen to learn it at all. An interesting fact here is that some of the students had great achievements in other fields of knowledge and were considered to be good or very good students. On the other hand, for nine students learning other subjects – not only Polish or other EFLs but also history (dates), mathematics and physics, biology or geography (reading maps) – posed some problems.

As far as their school marks in English were concerned, they were diversified from unsatisfactory to very good. The majority of those good learners were from primary school. Unfortunately, the older the student and the higher the level of

English they were supposed to acquire, the poorer the result and, at the same time, the lower school marks. Only one student from secondary school felt successful in learning English.

The range of difficulties the observed students showed in learning EFL was wide, depending on the intensity of the disorder. Each of the students was different from the others, both in relation to problems in acquiring an EFL and the ways in which they dealt with them. It needs stressing that much depended upon the personality of the given student. Most of them were very well aware of the kind of problems they were (and still are) encountering and were ready to deal with them. They were motivated, persistant and very hard working. In order to follow up the pace in the classroom they were supposed to work at home repeating and drilling language material. Most of them also attended private lessons in English. They seemed to strongly believe that knowledge of English would be of great importance in the future, and despite their difficulties, they were determined to work much harder than the others in order to achieve a reasonable command of English.

On the other hand, there were students who could not come to terms with the situation they found themselves in and were constantly depressed, embarrassed, angry and frustrated. They were not as determined as the others and gave up hope of achieving any academic success in English. They gave in because no matter how hard they tried, the effects of their efforts were very poor.

Conclusion

Dyslexic students are different due to the fact that dyslexia is not a homogeneous phenomenon but it is characterised by inconsistency, a wide spectrum of difficulties and various symptoms (Bogdanowicz 1994, 1997a, 1997b, 1999; Brejnak and Zablocki 1999; Krasowicz 1997; Ott 1997; Reid 1998; Selikowitz 1999).

One of the greatest problems that dyslexic children may encounter is their teachers' indifference, lack of knowledge and failure in understanding the dyslexic difficulties. It has been observed that the teachers' familiarity with the notion of dyslexia as well as the introduction of individualised requirements towards students with dyslexia was very poor, in addition to the lack of application of multisensory techniques in teaching such children. It is evident that the better informed teachers are, the more they can do to help dyslexic students to be successful in EFL learning. Teachers' sensitivity and readiness to cooperate and help, as well as to appreciate a lot of effort in spite of poor results, is of paramount importance as far as scholastic success of dyslexic children is concerned.

Great changes and improvements are needed concerning not only the use of appropriate teaching methods but also teachers' attitudes, not simply to identify the needs and limitations but also to recognise the talents and positive points of children with dyslexia.

Chapter 30

Using the Internet as a Multimedia Method of Teaching a Modern Foreign Language to People with Dyslexia

Mary Scully

This chapter:

- explores the use of the internet as a resource for teaching a modern foreign language to people with Dyslexia
- focuses on key issues such as accessibility, motivation, and style of presentation and
- provides examples of possible uses of the internet for language learners and teachers.

Accessibility and style of presentation

Having accessibility to the internet via school, home or college is only the beginning of the issue. There is no doubt that the majority of students enjoy having opportunities to 'surf the net' and will happily do so for hours at a stretch. Having studied a group of students who were either dyslexic or had specific learning difficulties at school using the internet, I discovered some interesting results. For the average dyslexic student the speed of delivery of instructions from the teacher on how to use the internet was too quick. Those with language-processing problems were also not able to process the instructions at the same speed as the delivery. Because of the desire to maintain the appearance of the same level of activity as their peers the students with language difficulties did not ask for further clarification from the teacher or technician. Instead they copied from their friend or asked for some guidance from an adjacent student. This has implications for teachers and learners alike. The teacher must be prepared to adjust their instructions so that they are accessible to all and must take note of what they can do to help the dyslexic.

The following is offered as friendly advice: firstly teachers should 'chunk' the information so that each portion can be digested before the next piece is given; secondly they need to check that the information has been received and understood; and thirdly they need to provide a visual back-up for the information. This could be in the form of a guide which the teacher has prepared. If it is a series of instructions which is regularly issued the teacher could look into producing the guidelines on card, laminating them and placing them in prominent positions in the room where the work is to be carried out. This is just one area of difficulty which the dyslexic student has in terms of accessibility.

The student, once connected to the internet, is faced with further problems. Firstly in connection with his own search. If the dyslexic student using a search engine spells a word incorrectly he may not realise he has done so because he may not be able to recognise whether a word is correctly spelled or not. The result of a misspelling could be twofold, either the search engine may not be able to process the request if the word is not recognisable in its memory, or it may process it if the word is recognisable but is not the intended word of the student. This leads to frustration on the part of the student who cannot then proceed with his work. It would be advantageous to the dyslexic student if web designers and programmers were to create a facility in which possible matches for the incorrect word formed a part of the overall design. This can be accomplished by putting the incorrect spellings in the META Tag keywords (this is where many search engines look to index the pages). This would lead to the student being able to access the information he required in a higher proportion of cases.

When the student connects correctly to the internet the amazing array of sites and information he is presented with often prove overwhelming. If the student has difficulty in processing written text he may not be able to gain the information he requires because he will not be able to sift through the data presented. When this is the case the average student will down load material indiscriminately 'to work through later'. This approach reflects an inefficient use of the student's time and an ineffective use of the internet as a resource. It would be in the dyslexic student's interest if there were dialogue between teachers, dyslexics and web designers. If this were the case then a number of pitfalls could be avoided when a web page was being designed. I am including a few helpful guidelines of which all web designers should take note. I mention 'all web designers' because there are an increasing number of teachers and technicians in schools who are creating their own websites.

Research has shown that dyslexics:

1. Find a text which uses a single font easier to read.
2. Find small amounts of text on a page easier to read.
3. Find it easier to access text if a standard format is applied; this allows them to become familiar with the text and so find their way around it more successfully.
4. Find it more accessible if there is not a lot of bold and italics used to highlight text.
5. People read more slowly from computer screens so therefore the amount of text should be less than in an equivalent textbook.
6. Find it easier to read if the text is adjusted to the left.

When accessing a commercially designed web page dyslexic readers can find themselves submerged in a rich sea of images, flashing symbols and words, a myriad of font styles and sizes. These are designed to stimulate but all too often have the opposite effect. Designers often compete to enhance pages with tickers, animations and multimedia splash screens. Consistency and simplicity are bywords for the producer of the web page designed with the dyslexic in mind. According to some dyslexic users of the internet 'Possibly the most difficult part about using the Net is actually gaining access to a specific piece of information' (Care and Lisgarten 1998: 233–4). Each website has a unique address which is called a URL. It is essential to get this address correct in order to access the site you want. There are several ways around the problem for the dyslexic:

1. Get someone else to take note of the correct address, especially if it is given on a television or radio programme.
2. Ask someone else to type in the address.
3. Make sure that the address is written down and available to copy before beginning to type it.
4. Try looking at the address as small groups or components between the dots and the slashes of the web address.

The government is taking a step in the right direction in order to improve commercial websites; perhaps web designers in general should follow suit. 'Plans to improve the quality of its websites as it puts more public services on the internet have been announced by the Government. E-envoy Alex Allan has announced guidelines for building public sector websites which aim to improve the sites' design, access and navigation. The government is also establishing a new media team to monitor its websites' (*Computing Magazine* February 2000).

Issues of motivation

A familiar but nevertheless illuminating quote from Einstein:

> I can never teach my students anything. I can only attempt to create the conditions in which they learn

is poignant when discussed in conjunction with the use of the internet as a language resource. The constraints of the traditional language classroom have been well documented and I do not propose to do so at length here. However there are some which need to be reiterated, particularly when discussing students' needs and motivation.

A student who because of learning difficulties or who is too 'socially minded' to sit still in a classroom setting can sit still for at least an hour if s/he can work 'on the computer' thereby creating conditions in which s/he can learn. It behoves all of us as language teachers to create the conditions in which students can learn. Sometimes because of constraints in the classroom and as a result of the nature of teaching a language, which is different from teaching other subjects, we cannot create the best learning conditions. If we think we are powerless in this respect then we need to be introduced to a powerful motivational tool which already exists to help us move out of the classroom and access the world outside – the internet.

I am aware that 'moving out of the classroom' is only in a virtual sense as to access the internet the student must at least be in front of a computer wherever that computer might be. Below is a table comparing the motivational aspects of a student who is a traditional text book learner with a student who has access to the internet as a resource. This shows the results of an informal study carried out in two schools in which I worked.

Learner with access to the internet	Traditional textbook-based learner
Is in control of his/her pace of learning	Teacher is in control of the pace of learning
Has access to a wide range of resources	Has access to a limited range of resources
Has to be proactive in his/her language learning	Can remain a passive learner and in some circumstances a silent one
Is less affected by environment	Is more affected by environment
Has access to more multisensory resources	Can be disadvantaged by lack of multisensory input
Can still learn if not at school provided there is internet access at home or other location	Learning is greatly affected by absenteeism, lateness or truancy

Figure 30.1 Motivation issues

Research has shown that students who learn languages in an open access way are more in control of their learning. They learn more because axiomatically they are more in control of their own learning. The choice of being passive does not exist. There is another issue here: students who have the facility to learn through using the internet because they cannot attend school can learn and minimise the deficit in their learning as a result of not attending school. It is not an option yet to learn in a remote way for the mainstream student but it may well be a reality in the future.

When the information highway is in operation, the texts of millions of books will be available. A reader will be able to ask questions, print the text, read it on screen, or even have it read in his choice of voices. He'll be able to ask questions. It will be his tutor. (Gates 1995: 195)

The internet will not bring about the demise of teachers but it can and should be incorporated into our teaching and embraced as readily as books, tapes and videos were ten years ago.

I include another quote from Bill Gates because of its reference to the very students I am concerned about in this article.

Different learning rates will be accommodated, because computers will be able to pay individual attention to independent learners. Children with learning disabilities will be particularly well served. Regardless of his or her ability or disability, every student will be able to work at an individual pace. (Gates 1995: 195)

This was the vision of five years ago and while it is not yet perfect, it offers another route to explore in the teaching of foreign languages to the dyslexic student. I am pleased that in the above quotation both the able and the less able student have been mentioned because using the internet offers a challenging resource to both.

Possible uses of the internet in teaching a modern foreign language to dyslexics

There are advantages and disadvantages to using the internet as a resource for teaching students with dyslexia. However, if the sub-skills of accessing the internet are taught first then we eliminate the first and major hurdle; that of being disorientated by the layouts and design of web pages. Let us not forget that the best practices in teaching students with dyslexia are also unquestionably those for teaching the non-dyslexic.

Taking the viewpoint that teachers need to know how to integrate new media resources into lessons so that they complement the teaching objectives, I will explore possible ways of doing just that. There are two ways initially of using the internet as a resource:

1. The teacher provides the material.
2. The teacher accesses and uses what is already available.

To provide one's own material is of course a time-consuming task and requires dedication and innovation on the part of the teacher, but that is nothing new as any well-resourced language teacher will testify. Many teachers have already put authentic materials into web-accessible formats. It is the new media version of realia which all language teachers collect on trips abroad. Equipped with their own knowledge or the knowledge of someone who can do it for them, teachers can scan in text such as menus or graphics such as maps, and digitise sound or video. It brings a whole new perspective to the home movies or slides of yesteryear. In addition if you use your own materials you do not have to worry about copyright clearance. In conjunction with establishing your own materials for the internet, if you have access to a web server you can restrict access to your materials and to your web pages. It is not only a question of putting authentic materials on a web page for the student to look at; that would just be a different version of reading or looking in the classroom. It is not only desirable but also essential that there be some degree of interaction involved. This removes the passivity which I have mentioned before as a feature of the classroom. As language teachers, and particularly as language providers to students with dyslexia, we have to be mindful of our teaching objectives. We want our students, who find foreign language learning more difficult than the non-dyslexic, to use the language as much as possible both inside and outside the classroom through speaking and writing. We want them to use the language for real communication and to learn from other students. This is possible to one degree or another using the internet, through establishing links with other schools, e-mail partners and working collaboratively with other language teachers and learners.

The second route is to avail oneself of what is already published. Any foreign language teacher who has 'surfed the net' in search of suitable material can attest to the vast quantities of material available. Much of the material is intriguing, some of it puzzling, some useless and some is unfortunately not updated and therefore by default falls in to the latter category. It can take hours or even days to search through for suitable material. As the average teacher does not have a lot of time available it is necessary to be selective and have a clear idea of the purpose of the search in order to make the most effective use of valuable time. One of the best ways to begin a search is to browse through web pages which have already been created.

The Centre for Information on Language Teaching (CILT) has a large number of addresses which are available for consultation. They are not in any particular order and they do not provide a recommended list. However, it is a good place to start if you have not made any previous searches. Teachers must not lose sight of the fact that we should be using the new technologies to enhance the curriculum and not to drive it. The aim of making the internet accessible to our students is also to empower them to become better independent language learners.

Teachers can initially search for materials to support a specific lesson or topic. They can look for specific materials to reinforce or extend a particular topic or ideas. For example, if the topic is transport the teacher can search for sites which have maps of the Paris underground, timetables for trains from Sacre Coeur to the Louvre and have a lot of fun on the way. There are a number of websites provided by schools explaining how they set up and brought to conclusion projects related to their curriculum.

Finding useful sources is a time-consuming task. Happily there are tools available on the internet itself which help to search for specific topics by performing keyword searches. These are called search engines and some of the most commonly known ones are, AltaVista, Yahoo and WebCrawler. Some search words are too general – a word such as school or dyslexia will be found in so many documents that the search results will be next to useless. Several searches are often necessary to access the information required. We should keep to the forefront our objective to improve foreign language instruction and learning by using the internet when we begin our searches. As one educator says 'The possibilities for obtaining and using authentic materials and information on a myriad of Target Language topics are multiplying exponentially with an increasing number of websites, interest in other cultures, and Foreign Language educator technological acumen' (LeLoup and Ponterio 1996).

This valuable resource brings together an interest in foreign language learning and an exploration of other cultures, which is supported by the National Curriculum for Modern Foreign Languages.

The students we teach today, whether dyslexic or not, are increasingly visually orientated. Students who have grown up with computer games and video are not as excited by textbooks as we as teachers might like them to be. Many students are also computer literate and think it is cool to admit to 'being good on computers' rather than admit that they are good at 'reading'. Using technology is an accepted component of their education. Using the multimedia resource of the internet allows students the freedom to read and speak in real time to people all over the world. The net allows them to be interactive and productive. The benefit to the dyslexic student is that the interchange is spontaneous, the feedback is immediate and the situation is completely real and not simulated. However, we must take note also that 'While use of such programmes is probably not feasible in the classroom on a regular basis due to a number of concerns such as time zones, bandwidth, sufficient available hardware for all students and appropriateness of conversation topics), exposure to these language possibilities may encourage students to become lifelong learners of language and other cultures' (LeLoup and Ponterio 1996).

Conclusion

I have explored the areas of accessibility, motivation and possible uses for enhancing foreign language learning and teaching by exploiting the internet as a multimedia resource. Although at first many people are put off using the internet through what might be described as a form of technophobia, once they have come to terms with accessing the new medium they almost all become converts. While the computer will never replace the human resource in teaching it is providing us with a teaching and learning tool that can enhance our teaching and empower our students and teachers.

References

Adams, M. J. (1990) *Beginning to Read. Thinking and Learning about Print*. Cambridge, MA: MIT Press.

Akamatsu, N. (1999) 'The effects of first language orthographic features on word recognition processing in English as a second language', *Reading and Writing* **11**, 381–403.

Al-Sulaimani, A. (1990) *Reading problems in Arab learners of English*. Unpublished Ph.D. thesis, Birkbeck College, University of London.

Anstrom, K. (1996) What are the defining characteristics of effective instructional programs for language minority students?
http://www.ncbe.gwu.edu/pathways/effective/slides.htm

Appell, R. and Muysken, P. (1987) *Language Contact and Bilingualism*. London: Edward Arnold.

Ashman, A. and Elkins, J. (eds) (1998) *Educating children with special needs*, 3rd edn. Sydney: Prentice Hall.

Association on Higher Education and Disability (AHEAD) (1997) *Guidelines for Documentation of a Learning Disability in Adolescents and Adults*. Columbus, OH: AHEAD.

Augur, J. and Briggs, S. (1992) *The Hickey Multisensory Language Course,* 2nd edn. London: Whurr Publishers Limited.

Avery, P. and Ehrlich, S. (1987) 'Specific Pronunciation Problems', *TESL-Talk* **17**, 81–116.

Baca, L. M. and Cervantes, H. T. (1984) *The Bilingual Special Education Interface*. St Louis, Toronto and Santa Clara: Times Mirror/Mosby College Publishing.

Bain, A. M. *et al.* (eds) (1991) *Written Language Disorders: Theory into Practice*. Austin, TX: PRO-ED.

Baker, C. (1996) *Foundations of Bilingual Education and Bilingualism*, 2nd edn. Clevedon: Multilingual Matters Limited.

Bakker, D. J. (1990) *Neuropsychological Treatment of Dyslexia*. New York: Oxford University Press.

Banks, J. (1997) *Teaching Strategies for Ethnic Studies*, 6th edn. Needham Heights, MA: Allyn and Bacon.

Bartlett v. New York State Board of Law Examiners, 1-131 (1997) United States District Court, Southern District of New York.

Barton, D. (1994) *Literacy: An Introduction to the Ecology of Written Language*. Oxford: Blackwell.

Barzilay, P. *et al.* (1997) *Ready, Steady, Read!* (book and teacher's guide): Ra,anana, Israel: Onda Publications Ltd.

Beard, J. (1994) *Basic Study Skills*. Buckingham: University of Buckingham.

Beaubien, R. (1999) *Adult learning disabilities in intensive English programs: A call for action*. Paper presented at the International TESOL Conference, New York, NY, March.

Beech, J. R. and Keys, A. (1997) 'Reading, vocabulary and language preference in 7- to 8-year-old bilingual Asian children', *British Journal of Educational Psychology* **67**, 405–14.

Bell, N. (1991) 'Gestalt imagery: A critical factor in language comprehension', *Annals of Dyslexia* **41**, 246–60.

Bensoussan, M. (1993) *Materials for Dyslexia Courses*. EFL dyslexia Committee, Haifa University, Israel.

Bentin, S. (1981) 'On the representation of a second language in the cerebral hemispheres of right-handed people', *Neuropsychologia* **19**, 599–603.

Berman, P. *et al.* (1995) School reform and student diversity: Case studies of exemplary practices for LEP students.
http://www.ncbe.gwu.edu/mispubs/schoolreform/9haroldwiggs.htm

Bertin, P. and Perlman, E. (1998) *Preventing Academic Failure: A Multisensory Curriculum for Teaching Reading, Writing and Spelling in the Elementary Classroom*. Cambridge, MA: Educators Publishing Service.

Bishop, D. (1989) *Test for Reception of Grammar*. Manchester: University of Manchester, Department of Psychology.

Bishop, R. and Glynn, T. (1999) *Culture Counts: Changing Power Relations in Education*. Palmerston North, NZ: Dunmore.

Boder, E. (1973) 'Developmental Dyslexia: A diagnostic approach based on three atypical reading patterns', *Developmental Medicine and Child Neurology* **15**, 663–87.

Bogdanowicz, M. (1994) *O Dysleksji czyli Specyficznych Trudnościach w Czytaniu i Pisaniu – Odpowiedzi na Pytania Rodziców i Nauczycieli*. Lubin: Wydawnictwo Popularnonaukowe LINEA.

Bogdanowicz, M. (1997a) *Integracja Percepcyjno-motoryczna: Teoria – Diagnoza – Terapia*. Warszawa: Centrum Metodyczne Pomocy Psychologiczno-Pedagogicznej Ministerstwa Edukacji Narodowej.

Bogdanowicz, M. (1997b) 'Specyficzne trudności w czytaniu i pisaniu w świetle klasyfikacji medycznych, psychologicznych i pedagogicznych', *Audiofonologia* **10**, 145–57.

Bogdanowicz, M. (1999) 'Specyficzne trudności w czytaniu i pisaniu – dysleksja rozwojowa', in Jastrębowska G. and Gałkowski T. (eds) *Logopedia – Pytania i Odpowiedzi*, 815–59. Opole: Wydawnictwo Uniwersytetu Opolskiego.

Bolton, T. and M'gadzah, H. (1999) 'Challenging racism and inequality', *Educational and Child Psychology* **16**(3).

Bosch, L. and Sebastian, G. (1997) 'Native language recognition abilities in four month-old infants from monolingual and bilingual environments', *Cognition* **65**, 33–69.

Bose, R. (2000) 'Families in transition', in Lau, A. (ed.) *South Asian Children and Adolescents in Britain*, 47–60. London: Whurr Publishers Limited.

Boulton-Lewis, G. M. (1993) 'Young children's representations and strategies for subtraction', *British Journal of Educational Psychology* **63**(3), 441–56.

Bowers, P. G. and Wolf, M. (1993) 'Theoretical links among naming speed, precise timing mechanisms and orthographic skill in dyslexia', *Reading and Writing: An Interdisciplinary Journal* **5,** 69–85.

Brady, S. and Shankweiler, D. (1991) *Phonological Processes in Literacy: A Tribute to Isabelle Y. Liberman.* Hillsdale, NJ: Lawrence Erlbaum Associates.

Breinburg, P. (1986) 'Language Attitudes: The Case of Caribbean Language', in Sutcliffe, D. and Wong, A. (eds) *The Language of the Black Experience.* Oxford: Blackwell.

Brejnak, W. and Zabłocki K. J. (1999) *Dysleksja w Teorii i Praktyce.* Warszawa: Oficyna Wydawniczo - Poligraficzna 'ADAM'.

Breznitz, Z. (1997) 'Enhancing the Reading of Dyslexic Children by Reading Acceleration and Audiory Masking', *Journal of Educational Psychology* **89**(1).

Brisk, M. (2000) Portraits of success. Portraits@lab.brown.edu.

British Dyslexia Association (2000) *The Dyslexia Handbook 2000.* Reading: British Dyslexia Association.

British Psychological Society (1999) *Dyslexia, Literacy and Psychological Assessment.* Report by a Working Party of the Division of Educational and Child Psychology. Leicester: British Psychological Society.

Bruder, I. (1992) 'Multicultural education: Responding to the demographics of change', *Electronic Learning* **12**(2), 20–27.

Bruner, J. S. (1986) *Actual Minds, Possible Worlds.* Cambridge, Mass.: Harvard University Press.

Cain, K. and Oakhill, J. (1998) 'Comprehension Skill and Inference-Making Ability: Issues of Causality', in Hulme, C. and Joshi, R. M. (eds) *Reading and Spelling: Development and Disorders*, 329–42. London: Lawrence Erlbaum Associates.

Caldwell, E. (1999) *'Byte your Tongue'*, *TES Online*, 12 November, 30–31.

Care, H. and Lisgarten, K. (1998) *The Dyslexia Handbook.* Reading: British Dyslexia Association.

Carpenter, P. A. *et al.* (1990) 'What one intelligence test measures: a theoretical account of the processing in the Raven Progressive Matrices test', *Psychological Review* **97**(3), 404–31.

Carrell, P. L. (1988) 'Some causes of text-boundedness and schema interference in ESL reading', in Carrell, P. L. *et al.* (eds) *Interactive Approaches to Second Language Reading*, 101–13. Cambridge: Cambridge University Press.

Carter, T. and Coussins, J. (1986) *Shattering Illusions: West Indians in British Politics.* London: Lawrence and Wishart.

Catts, H. W. (1989) 'Defining dyslexia as a developmental language disorder', *Annals of Dyslexia* **39**, 50–64.

Chamot, A. Uhl and O'Malley, J. M. (1994) *The CALLA Handbook: implementing the cognitive academic language learning approach.* Reading, MA: Addison-Wesley.

Charles, C. (1999) *Building classroom discipline.* New York: Longman.

Chiappe, P. and Siegel, L. S. (1999) 'Phonological Awareness and Reading Acquisition in English and Punjabi-Speaking Canadian Children', *Journal of Educational Psychology* **91**(1), 20–28.

Cline, T. (1998) 'The assessment of special educational needs for bilingual children', *British Journal of Special Education* **25**(4), 159–63.

Cline, T. (1999a) 'Training to reduce racism in the practice of educational psychology', *Educational and Child Psychology* **16**(3), 127–35.

Cline, T. (1999b) *Multilingualism and dyslexia: Challenges for research and practice.* Paper presented at the First International Conference on Multilingualism and Dyslexia, Manchester, 17–19 June.

Cline, T. and Cozens, B. (1998) Miscues and response to text of bilingual and monolingual pupils when reading aloud in English. Personal communication.

Cline, A. and Frederickson, N. (1991) *Bilingual pupils and the National Curriculum: Overcoming difficulties in teaching and learning.* London: University College.

Cline, T. and Reason, R. (1993) 'Specific learning difficulties (dyslexia): Equal opportunities issues', *British Journal of Special Education* **20**(1), 30–34.

Cline, T. and Shamsi, T. (2000) *Language Needs or Special Needs? The Assessment of Learning Difficulties in Literacy among Children Learning English as an Additional Language: A Literature Review.* London: DfEE Publications.

Coady, J. (1979) 'A psycholinguistic model of the ESL reader', in R. Mackay *et al.* (eds) *Reading in a second language.* New York: Newbury House.

Coard, B. (1971) *How the West Indian Child is Made Educationally Sub-normal in the British School System.* London: New Beacon Books (reprinted by Karia Press, 1991).

Collier, V. P. (1992) 'A synthesis of studies examining long-term language minority student data on academic achievement', *Bilingual Research Journal* **1–2**, 187–212.

Collier, V. P. (1995a) *The education of language minority students: United States policies, practices and assessment of academic achievement.* Paper presented at the Invitational Conference on Teaching and Learning English as an Additional Language, 27–28 April. London: Commission for Racial Equality.

Collier, V. P. (1995b) *Promoting Academic success for ESL Students.* New Jersey: NJTESOL –BE.

Collins, K. (1999) *Supporting emergent bilingual learners to literacy.* Keynote presentation to the First International Conference on Multilingualism and Dyslexia, Manchester, 17–19 June.

Coltheart, M. D. *et al.* (1979) 'Phonological encoding in the lexical decision task', *Quarterly Journal of Experimental Psychology* **31**, 489–507.

Commission for Racial Equality (1992) *Set to fail? Setting and banding in secondary schools.* London: CRE Publications.

Commission for Racial Equality (1996) *Special Educational Needs Assessment in Strathclyde: Report of a Formal Investigation.* London: CRE publications.

Commission for Racial Equality (2000) *Learning for All: Standards for Racial Equality in Schools – for Schools in England and Wales.* London: CRE publications.

Cook, V. (1991) *Second Language Learning and Language Teaching.* London: Edward Arnold.

Cooke, A. (1994) *Dealing with dyslexia the Bangor way.* London: Whurr Publishers Limited.

Cornwall, K. and France, N. (1997) *Group Reading Test (Second Edition 6–14).* Windsor: NFER-Nelson.

Corson, D. (1995) *Using English words.* Dordrecht: Kluwer Academic Publisher.

Cossu, G. *et al.* (1988) 'Awareness of phonological segments and reading ability in Italian children', *Applied Psycholinguistics* **9**, 1–16.

Council for Exceptional Children (1996) *What Every Special Educator Must Know: The International Standards for the Preparation and Certification of Special Educational Teachers.* Reston, VA: CEC.

Crombie, M. (1992) *Specific Learning Difficulties: Dyslexia – A Teacher's Guide.* Glasgow: Jordanhill College.

Crombie, M. (1995) 'It's all Double Dutch: Teaching foreign languages to dyslexic pupils', *Special Children* **82**, 9–12.

Crombie, M. (1996) *Modern Foreign Languages.* BDA Information Sheet T06. Reading: British Dyslexia Association.

Crombie, M. A. (1997a) 'The effects of specific learning difficulties (dyslexia) on the learning of a foreign language in school', *Dyslexia: An International Journal of Research and Practice* **3**(1), 27–47.

Crombie, M. (1997b) *Specific Learning Difficulties: Dyslexia – A Teachers' Guide,* 2nd edn. Belford: Ann Arbor Publishers.

Crombie, M. A. (2000) 'Dyslexia and the Learning of a Foreign Language in School: Where Are We Going?' *Dyslexia: An International Journal of Research and Practice* **6** (awaiting publication).

Cummins, J. (1976) 'The Influence of Bilingualism on Cognitive Growth: A Synthesis of Research Findings and Explanatory Hypotheses', *Working Papers on Bilingualism* **9**, 1–43

Cummins, J. (1979) 'Linguistic Interdependence and the Educational Development of Bilingual Children', *Review of Educational Research* **49**, 222–51.

Cummins, J. (1981a) 'Age on Arrival and Immigrant Second Language Learning in Canada: A Reassessment', *Applied Linguistics* **2**, 132–49 (as mentioned in Hvenekilde *et al.* 1996).

Cummins, J. (1981b) *The Role of Primary Language Development in Promoting Educational Success for Language Minority Students* (as mentioned in Hamers J. F. and Blanc M. J. (1989), *California State Department of Education Schooling and Language Minority Students: A Theoretical Framework* **53**. Los Angeles: Los Angeles Evaluation, Assessment and Dissemination Centre).

Cummins, J. (1981c) *Bilingualism and Minority Language Children.* Ontario: Ontario Institute for Studies in Education.

Cummins, J. (1984) *Bilingualism and Special Education: Issues in Assessment and Pedagogy.* Clevedon: Multilingual Matters.

Cummins, J. and McNeely, S. N. (1987) 'Language development, academic learning and empowering minority students', in Fradd, S. H. and Tikunoff, W. J. (eds) *Bilingual Education And Bilingual Special Education: A Guide For Administrators.* Boston, Mass.: College Hill Press.

Curnyn, J. C. *et al.* (1991) *Special Educational Need and Ethnic Minority Pupils.* Edinburgh: Scottish Office Education Department.

Curtis, S. (1990) *Peer tutoring – Integrating 'bilingual' pupils into the mainstream classroom.* Northampton: Support Service, Northamptonshire LEA Ethnic Minority.

Da Fontoura, H. A. and Siegel, L. (1995) 'Reading, syntactic and working memory skills of bilingual Portuguese-English Canadian Children', *Reading and Writing: An Interdisciplinary Journal* **7**, 139–53.

Davis, R. (1994) *The Gift of Dyslexia*. USA: Ability Publishers.

Day, S. L. and Edwards, B. J. (1996) 'Assistive technology for postsecondary students with learning disabilities', *Journal of Learning Disabilities* **29**, 486–92, 503.

DeFrancis, J. (1984) *The Chinese Language: Fact and Fantasy*. Honolulu: University of Hawaii Press.

Department for Education and Employment (1994) *Code of Practice on the Identification and Assessment of Special Educational Needs*. London: DfEE.

Department for Education and Employment (1998) *The National Literacy Strategy*. Sudbury: DfEE Publications.

Department for Education and Employment (2000) *Removing the Barriers. Raising Achievement Levels for Minority Ethnic Pupils*. Sudbury: DfEE Publications.

Department of Education and Science (1978) *Special Educational Needs*. Report of the Committee of Enquiry into Education of Handicapped Children (Warnock Report). London: HMSO.

Department of Education and Science (1988) *The Education Reform Act*. London: HMSO.

Deponio, P. *et al.* (2000) 'An audit of the processes involved in identifying and assessing bilingual learners suspected of being dyslexic: a Scottish study', *Dyslexia: An International Journal of Research and Practice* **6**(1).

Dewsbury, A. (1999) 'First steps: making the links – assessment, teaching and learning', in Watson, A. J. and Giorcelli, L. R. (eds) *Accepting the Literacy Challenge*, 133–56. Gosford, Australia: Scholastic Publications.

Dimitriadi, P. (1999) *Multimedia Authoring and Specific Learning Difficulties (Dyslexia): A Single Case Study*. Paper delivered at CAL99, Institute of Education, London, 29–31 March.

Diniz, F. Almeida (1997) 'Working with families in a multi-ethnic European context', in Carpenter, B. (ed.) *Families in Context: Emerging Trends in Family Support*, 107–20. London: David Fulton Publishers.

Dinklage, K. T. (1971) 'Inability to learn a foreign language', in Blaine, G. and MacArthur, C. (eds) *Emotional Problems of the Student*. New York: Appleton-Century-Crofts.

Downey, D. (1992) *Accommodating the foreign language learning disabled student*. Paper presented at the American University Foreign Language Learning and Learning Disabilities Conference, Washington, DC, April.

Downey, D. and Snyder, L. (1999) *College students with dyslexia: Persistent linguistic deficits and foreign learning*. Presentation made at the First International Multilingualism and Dyslexia Conference, Manchester, 17–19 June.

Duane, D. D. (ed.) (1991) *The Reading Brain: the Biological Basis of Dyslexia*. Parkton, MD: York Press.

Dunn, Ll. M. *et al.* (1997) *British Picture Vocabulary Scale*, 2nd edn (BPVS-II). Windsor: NFER-Nelson.

Dunn, R. and Dunn, K. (1994) *Teaching Young Children through their Individual Learning Styles: Practical Approaches for Grades K-2*. Needham Heights, MA: Allyn and Bacon.

Dunn, R. and Milgram, R. M. (1993) 'Learning styles of gifted students in diverse cultures', in Milgram R. M. *et al.* (eds) *Teaching and Counseling Gifted and Talented Adolescents: An International Learning Style Perspective*, 3–23. Westport, CT: Praeger Publishers.

Dunn, R. (1993) 'Educating diversity', *American Demographics*, April, 38–43.

Duran, E. (1988) *Teaching the moderately and severely handicapped student and autistic adolescent: With particular attention to bilingual special education.* Springfield, IL: Charles C. Thomas Publisher.

Durie, M. (1995) 'Tino Rangatiratanga: Self-Determination', *He Pukenga Korero* **1**(1), 44–53.

Edwards, (1986) *Language in a Black Community*. Clevedon: Multilingual Matters.

Edwards, J. (1994) *The Scars of Dyslexia*. London: Cassell.

Edwards, V. (1998) *The Power of Babel*. Staffordshire: Trentham Books.

Elbro, C. (1989) 'Morphological awareness in dyslexia', in Von Euler, C. *et al.* (eds) *The Brain and Reading*. London: Macmillan.

Elbro, C. and Arnbak, E. (1996) 'The role of morpheme recognition and morphological awareness in dyslexia', *Annals of Dyslexia* **46**, 209–40.

Elley, W. B. (1992) *How in the world do students read?* Netherlands: IEA.

Elley, W. B. (ed.) (1994) *The IEA study of reading literacy: Achievement and instruction in thirty two school systems*. Oxford: Pergamon.

Elliott, C. D. (1990) *Differential Ability Scales*. New York: Harcourt Brace Jovanovitch, Psychological Corporation.

Elliott, C. D. *et al.* (1983) *British Ability Scales*. Windsor: NFER-Nelson.

Elliott, C. D. *et al.* (1996) *British Ability Scales Second Edition* (BAS-II). Windsor: NFER-Nelson.

Ellis, R. (1989) 'Classroom learning rules and their effect on second language acquisition: a study of two learners', *System* **17**(4), 249–62.

Ellis, R. (1997) *The Study of Second Language Acquisition*, 5th impression (first published in 1994). Oxford: Oxford University Press.

Ellis, R. and Rathbone, M. (1987) *The Acquisition of German in a Classroom Context*. Mimeograph. London: Ealing College of Higher Education.

Evans, B. (1996) 'Visual problems and dyslexia', *Dyslexia Review* **8**(1), 4–7.

Edwards, S. (1998) *Modern Foreign Languages for all: Success for Pupils with SEN*. Tamworth: National Association for Special Educational Needs.

Everatt, J. *et al.* (1999) 'Motor aspects of dyslexia', in Everatt, J. (ed.) *Reading and Dyslexia: Visual and Attentional Processes*, 122–36. London: Routledge.

Everatt, J. *et al.* (2000) 'Dyslexia screening measures and bilingualism', *Dyslexia: An International Journal of Research and Practice* **6**(1).

Faas, L. A. and D'Alonzo, B. J. (1990) 'WAIS-R Scores as Predictors of Employment Success and Failure Among Adults with Learning Disabilities', *Journal of Learning Disabilities* **23**(5), 311–16.

Fawcett, A. and Nicolson, R. (eds) (1994) *Dyslexia in Children*. London: Harvester Wheatsheaf.

Fawcett, A. J. and Nicolson, R. I. (1996) *The Dyslexia Screening Test Manual*. London: Psychological Corporation.

Fawcett, A. and Nicolson, R. (1998) *Dyslexia Adult Screening Test*. London: Psychological Corporation.

Feldman, L. B. (ed.) (1995) *Morphological Aspects of Language Processing*. Hillsdale, NJ: Lawrence Erlbaum Associates.

Fish, J. (1985) *Educational Opportunities for All? The Report of the Committee Reviewing Provision to meet Special Educational Needs*. London: ILEA Publications.

Fletcher, J. M. *et al.* (1997) 'Subtypes of Dyslexia: An old problem revisited', in Blachman, B. A. (ed.) *Foundations of Reading Acquisition and Dyslexia.* Mahwah, NJ: Lawrence Erlbaum Associates.

Frederickson, N. and Frith, U. (1997) *The Phonological Assessment Battery: findings from the British standardisation.* Paper presented at the 4th International Conference of the British Dyslexia Association, York, 1–4 April.

Frederickson, N. and Frith, U. (1998) 'Identifying dyslexia in bilingual children: A phonological approach with inner London Sylheti speakers', *Dyslexia: An International Journal of Research and Practice* **4**(3), 119–31.

Frederickson, N. *et al.* (1997) *Phonological Assessment Battery Manual and Test Materials.* Windsor: NFER-Nelson.

Fries, C. C. (1963) *Linguistics and Reading.* New York : Holt, Rinehart & Winston.

Frith, U. (1995) 'Dyslexia: can we have a shared theoretical framework?' in Frederickson, N. and Reason, R. (eds) 'Phonological Assessment of Specific Learning Difficulties', *Educational and Child Psychology* **12**(1), 6–17.

Frith, U. (1997) 'Brain, mind and behaviour in dyslexia', in Hulme, C. and Snowling, M. (eds) *Dyslexia: Biology, Cognition and Intervention.* London: Whurr Publishers Limited.

Frith, U. (1999) 'Paradoxes in the definition of dyslexia', *Dyslexia: An International Journal of Research and Practice* **5**(4), 192–214.

Galloway, L. M. (1982) 'Bilingualism: Neuropsychological considerations', *Journal of Research and Development in Education* **15**, 12–28.

Ganschow, L. and Sparks, R. (1993) '"Foreign" language learning disabilities: Issues research, and teaching implications', in Vogel, S. and Adleman, P. (eds) *Success for college students with learning disabilities*, 283–320. New York: Springer-Verlag.

Ganschow, L. and Sparks, R. (1995) 'Effects of direct instruction in Spanish phonology on the native-language skills and foreign-language aptitude of at-risk foreign-language learners', *Journal of Learning Disabilities* **28**(2), 107–20.

Ganschow, L. and Sparks, R. (in press) 'Reflections on foreign language study for students with language learning problems: research, issues, and challenges', *Dyslexia: An International Journal of Research and Practice.*

Ganschow, L. *et al.* (1989) 'Foreign language policies and procedures for students with specific learning disabilities', *Learning Disabilities Focus* **5**, 50–58.

Ganschow, L. *et al.* (1991) 'Identifying native language deficits among foreign language learners in college: A "foreign" language learning disability?' *Journal of Learning Disabilities* **24**, 530–41.

Ganschow, L. *et al.* (1995) 'Learning a foreign language: Challenges for students with language learning difficulties', *Dyslexia: An International Journal of Research and Practice* **1**, 75–95.

Ganschow, L. *et al.* (1998a) 'Foreign language learning difficulties: an historical perspective', *Journal of Learning Disabilities* **31**(3), 248–58.

Ganschow, L. *et al.* (1998b) 'Commentary on 'Facing the Challenges of Learning English as a Foreign Language in Israel: in Response to Ganschow, Sparks and Schneider', *Dyslexia* **4**, 175–9.

Ganschow, L. *et al.* (1999) 'A 10-year follow-up survey of programs and services for students with learning disabilities in graduate and professional schools', *Journal of Learning Disabilities* **32**, 82–4.

Garcia, E. (1991) The education of linguistically and culturally diverse students: Effective instructional practices. http://www.ncbe.gwu.edu/miscpubs/ncrcdsll/eprl/index.htm

Garcia, J. and Pugh, S. L. (1992) 'Multicultural education in teacher preparation programs: A political or an educational concept?' *Phi Delta Kapan*, November, 214–19.

Gardner, R. *et al.* (1976) 'Second language learning: a social psychological perspective', *Canadian Modern Language Review* **32**, 198–213.

Gates, Bill (1995) *The Road Ahead*. London: Viking.

Gathercole, S. E. and Baddeley, A. D. (1989) 'Evaluation of the role of phonological STM in the development of vocabulary in children: A longitudinal study', *Journal of Memory and Language* **28**(2), 200–13.

Gathercole, S. E. and Baddeley, A. D. (1993) 'Phonological working memory: a critical building block for reading development and vocabulary acquisition?', *European Journal of Psychology of Education* **8**(3), 259–72.

Gathercole, S. E. *et al.* (1992) 'Phonological memory and vocabulary development during the early school years: a longitudinal study', *Developmental Psychology* **28**(5), 887–98.

Geva. E. (1999) *Issues in the assessment of reading disabilities in children who are working in their second language – beliefs and research evidence.* Paper presented at the First International Conference on Multilingualism and Dyslexia, Manchester, 17–19 June.

Gillborn, D. and Gipps, C. (1996) *Recent Research on the Achievements of Ethnic Minority Pupils: OFSTED Review of Research*. London: HMSO.

Gillingham, A. and Stillman, B. (1956) *Remedial Training for Children with Specific Disability in Reading, Spelling and Penmanship*, 5th edn. New York: Sackelt and Wilhelms.

Gilroy, D. and Miles, T. (1986) *Dyslexia at college*. London: Routledge.

Given, B. and Reid, G. (1999) *Learning Styles: a guide for teachers and parents*. St Annes on Sea: Red Rose Publications.

Glynn, T. (1998) *A collaborative approach to teacher development: new initiatives in special education.* Paper presented at the Symposium for Australian Teacher Education Association, 28th Annual Conference, Melbourne, Australia.

Glynn, T. and Bishop, R. (1995) 'Cultural Issues in Educational Research: A New Zealand Perspective', *He Pukenga Korero* **1**(1), 37–43.

Glynn, T. and McNaughton, S. S. (1985) 'The Mangere Home and School Remedial Reading Procedures: continuing research on their effectiveness', *New Zealand Journal of Psychology* **15**(2), 66–77.

Glynn, T. *et al.* (1992) *Remedial reading at home. Helping you to help your child*. Wellington: New Zealand Council for Educational Research.

Glynn, T. *et al.* (1993) *Tatari Tautoko Tauawhi: He awhina tamariki ki te panui pukapuka*. Some preliminary findings. Cultural Justice and Ethics Symposium Report, New Zealand Psychological Society, Wellington.

Glynn, T. *et al.* (1997) *Research, training and indigenous rights to self-determination: Challenges arising from a New Zealand bicultural journey.* Paper presented at the International School Psychology XXth Annual Colloquium, School Psychology-Making Links: Making the Difference, Melbourne, Australia.

Goldberg, E. and Costa, L. D. (1981) 'Hemisphere differences in the acquisition and use of descriptive systems', *Brain and Language* **14,** 144–73.

Goldstein, B. and Obrzut, J. (2000) *Neuropsychological Treatment of Dyslexia.* Paper presented at the 28th Annual Meeting of the International Neuropsychological Society. Denver.

Goodman, Y. M. *et al.* (1987) *Reading miscue inventory: Alternative procedures.* New York: Richard C. Owen.

Goswami, U. (1997) 'Learning to read in different orthographies: phonological awareness, orthographic representations and dyslexia', in Hulme, C. and Snowling, M. (eds) *Dyslexia: Biology, Cognition and Intervention*, 131–52. London: Whurr Publishers Limited.

Goswami, U. (1999a) *Phonological Representations, Reading Development and Dyslexia: Towards a Cross-Linguistic Theoretical Framework.* Paper presented at the First International Conference on Multilingualism and Dyslexia, Manchester, 17–19 June.

Goswami, U. (1999b) *Towards a theoretical framework for understanding reading development and dyslexia in different orthographies.* Paper presented at the First International Conference on Multilingualism and Dyslexia, Manchester, 17–19 June.

Goswami, U. and Bryant, P. (1990) *Phonological Skills and Learning to Read.* Hove: Lawrence Erlbaum Associates.

Gregory, E. (1996) *Making Sense of a New World: learning to read in a second language.* London: Paul Chapman.

Griffiths, D. and Hardman, M. (1994) 'Specific Learning Difficulties (Dyslexia) and Modern Foreign Languages in Language Learning', *Journal of the Association for Language Learning* **10**, 84–5.

Grosjean, F. (1982) *Life with Two Languages.* Harvard, Mass.: Harvard University Press.

Guckenberger v. Trustees of Boston University (1997) Case No. 96-11426-PBSD. Mass.

Gupta, A. and Garg, A. (1996) 'Visuo-Perceptual and Phonological Processing in Dyslexic Children', *Journal of Personality and Clinical Studies* **12**(1–2), 67–73.

Hakuta, K. and D'Andrea (1992) 'Some properties of bilingual maintenance and loss in Mexican background high-school students', *Applied Linguistics* **13**(1), 72–99.

Hall, D. (1995) *Assessing the Needs of Bilingual Pupils: Living in two languages.* London: David Fulton Publishers.

Halliday, M. A. K. (1978) *Language as a social semiotic: The social interpretation of language and meaning.* London: Arnold.

Hamers, J. F. and Blanc, M. J. (1989) *Bilinguality and Bilingualism.* Cambridge: Cambridge University Press.

Harmer, J. (1987) *The practice of English Language Teaching.* London: Longman.

Hatcher, P. J. *et al.* (1994) 'Ameliorating early reading failure by integrating the teaching of reading and phonological skills: The phonological linkage hypothesis', *Child Development* **65**, 41–57.

Heath, S. B. (1983) *Ways with Words.* Cambridge: Cambridge University Press.

Henderson, C. (1995) *College Freshmen with Disabilities: a Triennial Statistical Profile.* Washington, DC: American Council on Education, HEATH Resource Center.

Heyward, S. (1992) *Access to Education for the Disabled: A Guide to Compliance with Section 504 of the Rehabilitation Act of 1973*. Jefferson, NC: McFarland.

Hickey, K. (1977) *Dyslexia: A Language Training Course for Teachers and Learners*. London: Kathleen Hickey.

Higgins, E. L. and Raskin, M. H. (1997) 'The compensatory effectiveness of optical character recognition/speech synthesis on the reading comprehension of postsecondary students with learning disabilities', *Learning Disabilities: a Multidisciplinary Journal* **8**, 75–87.

Hill, B. *et al.* (1995) 'Accommodating the needs of students with severe language learning difficulties in modified foreign language classes', in Grouse, G. (ed.) *Broadening the Frontiers of Foreign Language Education*, 45–56. Lincolnwood, IL: National Textbook Co.

Ho, CS-H. and Bryant, P. (1997) 'Phonological skills are important in learning to read Chinese', *Developmental Psychology* **33**(6), 946–51.

Ho, CS-H. and Lai, DN-C. (in press) *Naming-speed deficits and phonological memory deficits in Chinese developmental dyslexia. Learning and Individual Differences.*

Hohepa, M. *et al.* (1992) 'Te Kohanga Reo. Hei Tikanga Ako i Te Reo Maori: Te Kohanga Reo as a context for language learning', *Educational Psychology* **12**(3, 4), 333–46.

Höien, T. and Lundberg, I. (1997) Dysleksi: Fra teori til praksis (*Dyslexia: From theory to practice*). Oslo: Ad Notam Gyldendal.

Honey, J. (1997) *Language Is Power: The Story Of Standard English And Its Enemies*. London: Faber.

Hornby, P. (1977) *Bilingualism: Psychological, Social and Educational Implications*. New York: Academic Press (as mentioned in Baca and Cervantes 1984: 23).

Hornsby, B. (1996) *Overcoming Dyslexia*, 3rd edn. London: Random House.

Hornsby, B. and Sheer, F. (1980) *Alpha to Omega*, 3rd edn. Oxford: Heinemann.

Horwitz, E. (1987) 'Surveying student beliefs about language learning', in Wenden, A. and Rubin, J. (eds) *Learning Strategies in Language Learning*. Englewood Cliffs, NJ: Prentice Hall.

Horwitz, E. and Young, D. (1991) *Language Learning Anxiety: from Theory and Research to Classroom Implications*. Englewood Cliffs, NJ: Prentice Hall.

Houghton, S. and Bain, A. (1993) 'Peer Tutoring with ESL and Below-Average Readers', *Journal of Behavioural Education* **3**(2), 125–42.

Houghton, S. and Glynn, T. (1993) 'Peer tutoring of below-average secondary school readers with Pause Prompt and Praise: Successive introductions of tutoring components', *Behaviour Change* **10**(2), 86–92.

Hudelson, S. (1994) 'Literacy development of second language children', in Hvenekilde, A. (ed.) *Veier til Kunnskap og Deltakelse* (*Ways to Knowledge and Participation*), 54. Oslo: Novus Forlag.

Hvenekilde, A. *et al.* (1994) 'Spraktilegnelse og tospraklighet (Language Acquisition and Bilingualism)', in Hvenekilde, A. *et al. Minoritetselever og Sprakopplaering* (*Minority Pupils and Language Learning*), 55. Vallset: Oplandske Bokforlag.

Idowu, A (1985) 'Counselling Nigerian Students in United States Colleges and Universities', *Journal of Counselling and Development* **63**, 506–9.

Jakobsen, H. A. (1997) 'Morsmalslaererens undervurderte rolle (The Undervalued Role of the Mother Tongue Teacher)', *Skolefokus* (Focus on School) **17**, 30.

James, H. (1995) *Bilingualism and Special Educational Needs*. MA dissertation, Roehampton Institute, London (now University of Surrey, Roehampton). (Unpublished manuscript.)

Jameson, M (1998) *Visual Aspects of Dyslexia + Information Sheet on Visual Discomfort and Reading*. London: Adult Dyslexia Organisation.

Jameson, M. (1999) 'Dyslexic gifts – the good news', *Dyslexia Contact*, **18**(1), 24.

Javorsky, J. *et al.* (1992) 'Perceptions of college students with and without specific learning disabilities about foreign language courses', *Learning Disabilities Research and Practice* **7**, 31–44.

Jensen, A. R. (1998) *The G Factor*. New York: Praeger.

Jerram, H. *et al.* (1988) 'Responding to the message; providing a social context for children learning to write', *Educational Psychology* **8**(1, 2), 31–40.

Johnstone, R. (1994) *Teaching Modern Languages in Primary School: Approaches and Implications*. Edinburgh: Scottish Council for Research in Education.

Kahn-Horowitz, J. *et al.* (1998) 'Facing the challenges of learning English as a foreign language in Israel: in response to Ganschow, Sparks and Schneider', *Dyslexia: An International Journal of Research and Practice* **4**, 169–74.

Kappers, E. J. and Dekker, M. (1995) 'Bilingual effects of unilingual neuropsychological treatment of dyslexic adults: A pilot study', *Journal of the International Neuropsychological Society* **1**, 494–500.

Kenner, C. (1998) 'Keeping the Door Open for Biliteracy: How can Schools Support Parents and Children?', *Language Issues* **10**(1), 4–7.

Kenneweg, S. (1988) 'Meeting special learning needs in the Spanish curriculum of a college preparatory school', in Snyder, B. (ed.) *Get Ready, Get Set, Go! Action in the foreign language classroom*, 16–18. Columbus, OH: Ohio Foreign Language Association.

Kenneweg, S. (1994) *The Spanish solution to non-achievers in the foreign language classroom*. Unpublished video referred to in Schneider (1999).

Khoo, P. L. S. *et al.* (1994) 'Counselling foreign students: A Review of Strategies', *Counselling Psychology* **7**(2), 117–31.

Kibel, M. and Miles, T. R. (1994) 'Phonological errors in the spelling of taught dyslexic children', in Hulme C. and Snowling M. (eds) *Reading Development and Dyslexia*, 105–27. London: Whurr Publishers Limited.

Kidde, Anne Marie (ed.) (1997a) *Dansk i Multikulturelle Klasser. Sammenfattende rapport*. København: Københavns skolevæsen.

Kidde, Anne Marie (ed.) (1997b) *Dansk i Multikulturelle Klasser. Tre idekataloger med beskrivelse af danskfaglige undervisningsforløb*. København: Københavns Skolevæsen.

Kidde, Anne Marie (1999) *PPR's arbejde med tosprogede elever*. Vejledning for PPR-medarbejdere, en kortfattet oversigt over vigtige temaer. København: Skolepsykologi.

Kim, K. H. S. *et al.* (1997) 'Distinct cortical areas associated with native and second languages', *Nature* **388**, 10 July, 171–4.

Kimbrough Oller, D. *et al.* (1998) 'Phonological translation in bilingual and monolingual children', *Applied Psycholinguistics* **19**, 259–78.

Kirk, J. (2000) *Dyslexia and University Students: News and Views*. Edinburgh: Scottish Dyslexia Trust.

Kirk, L. and Pearson, H. (1996) 'Genres and learning to read', *Reading* **30**(1), 37–41.

Klein, C. (1993) *Diagnosing Dyslexia*. London: Basic Skills Agency.

Klein, D. *et al.* (1994) 'Left putaminal activation when speaking a second language: evidence from PET', *NeuroReport* **5**, 2295–7.

Klein, D. *et al.* (1995) 'The neural substrates underlying word generation: A bilingual functional-imaging study', *Proceedings of the National Academy of Science, USA* **99**, 2899–903.

Krasowicz, G. (1997) *Jzyk, Czytanie i Dysleksja*. Lublin: Agencja Wydawniczo – Handlowa AD.

Kress, G. R. (1994) *Learning to write*, 2nd edn. London and New York: Routledge.

Kress, G. (1997) *Before Writing: Rethinking the Paths to Literacy*. London: Routledge and Kegan Paul.

Krupska, M. and Klein, C. (1995) *Demystifying Dyslexia*. London: London Language and Literacy Unit.

Lambert, W. E. (1974) 'Culture and Language as Factors in Learning and Education', in Abode, F. E. and Mead, R. D. (eds) *Cultural Factors in Learning*. Bellingham: Western Washington State College.

Lambert, W. E. (1977) 'Effects of Bilingualism on the Individual', in Hornby, P. A. (ed.) *Bilingualism: Psychological, Social and Educational Implications*. New York: Academic Press (as mentioned in Hamers and Blanc 1989, 56).

Landon, J. (1999) 'Early intervention with bilingual learners: towards a research agenda', in South, H. (ed.) *Literacies in Community and School*, 84–96. Watford: National Association for Language Development in the Curriculum (NALDIC).

LeLoup, J. W. and Ponterio, R. (1996) 'Choosing and using materials for a "net" gain in FL instruction', in Levine, E. D. *Reaching Out to the Communities We Serve*. NYSAFLT Annual Meeting Series **13**, 23–32.

Lenneberg, E. H. (1967) *Biological Foundations of Language*. New York: Wiley.

Liow, S. R. (1999) 'Reading skill development in bilingual Singaporean children', in Harris, M. and Hatano, G. (eds) *Learning to read and write: A cross-linguistic Perspective*. Cambridge: Cambridge University Press.

Littlefair, A. (1991) *Reading all types of writing: The importance of genre and register for reading development*. Milton Keynes: Open University Press.

Littlefair, A. (1992) 'Let's be positive about genre', *Reading* **26**(3), 2–6.

Lovett, M. W. *et al.* (1990) 'Training the word recognition skills of reading disabled children: treatment and transfer effects', *Journal of Educational Psychology* **82**(4), 769–80.

Lundberg, I. (1999a) 'Learning to read in Scandinavia', in Harris, M. and Hatano, G. (eds) *Learning to read and write: A cross-linguistic Perspective*. Cambridge: Cambridge University Press.

Lundberg, I. (1999b) *Bilingualism: Psychological Perspectives*. Unpublished position paper, Dept. of Psychology, Göteborg University, Sweden.

Lyon, G. R. and Moats, L. C. (1997) 'Critical Conceptual and Methodological Considerations in Reading Intervention Research', *Journal of Learning Disabilities* **30**(6), 578–88.

Macfarlane, A. (1998) *Piki Ake Te Tikanga: Culture counts in special education.* Paper presented at the Teacher Education: Challenge and Creativity. 28th Annual Conference, Australian Teacher Education Association, Melbourne, Australia.

Macfarlane, A. and Glynn, T. (1998) *Mana Maori in the professional development programme for Resource teachers: Learning and Behaviour.* Paper presented at the NZARE 20th Annual Conference, Dunedin, 3–6 December, University of Waikato, Hamilton.

MacIntyre, P. and Gardner, R. (1991) 'Methods and results in the study of foreign language anxiety: a review of the literature', *Language Learning* **41**(1), 25–57.

Macpherson, W. (1999) *The Stephen Lawrence Inquiry Report.* London: HMSO.

Marshall, J. C. and Newcombe, F. (1973) 'Patterns of paralexia', *Journal of Psycholinguistic Research* **2**, 175–99.

Martin, D. *et al.* (1997) 'Phonological awareness in Panjabi/English children with phonological difficulties', *Child Language Teaching and Therapy* **12**, 59–72.

Masterson, J. (1983) *Surface dyslexia and the operation of the phonological route in reading.* Unpublished Ph.D. thesis, Birkbeck College, University of London.

Masterson, J. M. *et al.* (1985) 'Surface dyslexia in a language without irregularly spelled words', in Patterson, K. *et al.* (eds) *Surface Dyslexia: neuropsychological and cognitive studies of phonological reading.* London: Lawrence Erlbaum Associates.

McBride-Chang, C. and Ho, C. (in press) 'Naming Speed and Phonological Awareness in Chinese Children: Relations to Reading Skills', *Journal of Psychology in Chinese Studies.*

McColl, H. *et al.* (1997) *Europe, Language Learning and Special Educational Needs.* Edinburgh: Scottish Office Education and Industry Department.

McCormick-Piestrup in Simons, H. D. and Johnson, K. R. (1974) 'Black English Syntax and Reading Interference', *Research into the Reading of English* **8**, 339–58.

McCrum, R. *et al.* (1992) *The Story Of English,* 2nd edn. London: Faber and Faber.

McIntyre, C. W. and Pickering, J. S. (eds) (1995) *Clinical Studies of Multisensory Structured Language Instruction for Students with Dyslexia and Related Disorders.* Salem, OR: International Multisensory Structured Language Education Council.

McKeown, S. (2000) *Dyslexia and ICT. Building on Success.* Coventry: BECTa.

McLaughlin, B. (1978) *Second-language Acquisition in Childhood.* Hillsdale, N J: Lawrence Erlbaum Associates (as mentioned in Grosjean 1982, 226).

McLoughlin, D. *et al.* (1994) *Adult Dyslexia: Assessment, Counselling and Training.* London: Whurr Publishers Limited.

McNaughton, S. (1995) *Patterns of emerging literacy: processes of development and transition.* Auckland: Oxford University Press.

McPherson, W. (1999) *The Stephen Lawrence Enquiry.* London: HMSO.

McWilliam, N. (1998) *What's in a Word? Vocabulary Development in Multilingual Classrooms.* Stoke on Trent: Trentham Books Ltd.

Meadows, S. (1998) 'Children learning to think: Learning from others? Vygotskian theory and educational psychology', *Educational and Child Psychology* **15**(2), 6–13.

Medcalf, J. and Glynn, T. (1987) 'Assisting teachers to implement peer-tutored remedial reading using Pause, Prompt and Praise procedures', *Queensland Journal of Guidance and Counselling* **1**(1), 11–23.

Mehler, J. and Dupoux, E., tr. Southgate, P. (19940 *What Infants Know.* Oxford: Blackwell.

Metge, J. (1984) *Learning and Teaching: He Tikanga Maori.* Wellington, NZ: Maori and Islands Division, Dept. of Education.

M'gadzah, S. H. *et al.* (1999) 'Black and Asian consultants – working together to meet the cultural, linguistic and special educational needs of all children within a multicultural community: bridging the divide between the LEA and the community', *Educational and Child Psychology* **16**(3), 68–88.

Mickiewicz, J. (1995) *Jedynka z Ortografii? – Rozpoznawanie Dysleksji w Starszym Wieku Szkolnym.* Toru: Dom Organizatora.

Miles, T. R. (1993) *Dyslexia: The Pattern of Difficulties*, 2nd edn. London: Whurr Publishers Limited.

Miles, T. R. (1997) *Bangor Dyslexia Test*, 2nd edn. Cambridge: Learning Development Aids.

Miles, T. R. and Miles, E. (1999) *Dyslexia: A hundred years on*, 2nd edn. Buckingham: Open University Press.

Miles, T. R. and Varma, V. (eds) (1995) *Dyslexia and Stress.* London: Whurr Publishers Limited.

Milgram, R. M. *et al.* (1993) *Teaching and counseling gifted and talented adolescents: an international learning style perspective.* Westport, CT: Praeger Publishers.

Miller, S. (1985) *A Generative Model of an Interlanguage System.* Paper presented at the Boston Language Development Conference. Eric Reports. Alexandria, VA.

Miller, S. and Gillis, M. (1999) *The Language Puzzle: Connecting the Study of Linguistics with a Multisensory Language Instructional Program.* Presentation made at the First International Multilingualism and Dyslexia Conference. Manchester, 17–19 June.

Milton, J. L. (1985) *The development of English consonant pronunciation and related perceptual and imitative skills among native Arabic speakers learning English as a foreign. language.* Unpublished Ph.D. thesis, University of Wales.

Ministry of Education (1993) *The New Zealand curriculum framework.* Wellington, NZ: Learning Media.

Ministry of Education (1997) *Governing and managing New Zealand schools: A guide for boards of trustees.* Wellington, NZ: Learning Media.

Ministry of Education (1999) *Report of the Literacy Taskforce.* Wellington, NZ: Ministry of Education.

Moats, L. C. (1994) 'The Missing Foundation in Teacher Education: Knowledge of the Structure of Spoken and Written Language', *Annals of Dyslexia* **44**, 81–104.

Monarez, P. (1992) 'I'm not a Scatterbrain', *Providence Journal–Bulletin*, P. F3.

Moore, B. J. (1982) 'English reading skills of multilingual pupils in Singapore', *The Reading Teacher* March, 696–701.

Morais, J. (1991) 'Constraints on the development of phonemic awareness', in Brady, S. A. and Shankweiler, D. P. (eds) *Phonological Processes in Literacy.* Hillsdale, NJ: Lawrence Erlbaum Associates.

Morais, J. *et al.* (1979) 'Does awareness of speech as a sequence of phonemes arise spontaneously?', *Cognition* **7**, 323–31.

Morais, J. *et al.* (1986) 'Literacy training and speech segmentation', *Cognition* **24**(1–2), 45–64.

Morais, J. *et al.* (1998) 'Why and how phoneme awareness helps learning to read', in Hulme, C. and Joshi, R. M. (eds) *Reading and Spelling: Development and Disorders*. Hillsdale, NJ: Lawrence Erlbaum Associates.

Morfidi, E. and Pumfrey, P. D. (1998) 'Text genre and miscue analysis: A pilot study in a primary school', *Psychology of Education Review* **22**(1), 27–31.

Moseley, D. (1997) 'Assessment of spelling and related aspects of written expression', in Beech, J. R. and Singleton, C. (eds) *The Psychological Assessment of Reading*, 204–23. London: Routledge.

Muter, V. *et al.* (1997a) 'Segmentation, not rhyming, predicts early progress in learning to read', *Journal of Experimental Child Psychology* **65**, 370–96.

Muter, V. *et al.* (1997b) *Phonological Abilities Test*. London: Psychological Corporation Limited.

Myrberg, M. (1996) Grunden för fortsatt lärande: En internationell jämförande studie av vuxnas förmåga att förstå och använda tryckt och skriven information. (*Grounds for continued education: An international comparative study of adults' ability to understand and use written information.*) Skolverkets rapport 115. Stockholm: Skolverket.

Myrberg, M. *et al.* (2000) International Adult Literacy Survey: Invandrares läs-, skriv- och räkneförmåga på svenska. (*Immigrants' reading, writing and numerical abilities in Swedish.*) Skolverket: Stockholm.

National Joint Committee on Learning Disabilities (1997) 'Operationalizing the NJCLD definition of learning disabilities for ongoing assessment in schools: a report from the National Joint Committee on Learning Disabilities, Feb. 1, 1997', *Perspectives* (a publication of the International Dyslexia Association) **23**(4), 29–33.

National Working Party on Dyslexia in Higher Education (1999) *Dyslexia in Higher Education*. Hull: University of Hull.

Neale, M. D. (1997) *Neale Analysis of Reading Ability (Second Revised British Edition)*. Windsor: NFER-Nelson.

Newton, M. and Thomson, M. E. (1976) *The Aston Index*. Wisbech: Learning Development Aids.

Nicholson, T. (1997) 'Closing the gap on reading failure: social background, phonemic awareness, and learning to read', in Blachman, B. (ed.) *Foundations of Reading Acquisition and Dyslexia*. Hillsdale, NJ: Lawrence Erlbaum Associates.

Nicolson, R. and Siegel, L. (eds) (1996) Special Issue: Dyslexia and Intelligence. *Dyslexia: An International Journal of Research and Practice* **2**(3).

Nielsen, Jørgen Chr. (1997) *Læseundervisning i klasser med tosprogede elever*. København: Danmarks Pædagogiske Institut.

Nijakowska, J. (1999) 'Aixelsyd – dyslexia – should a foreign language teacher be interested in it?' *Network – a Journal for English Language Teacher Education* **1**(2), 9–14.

Oakhill, J. V. and Patel, S. (1991) 'Can imagery training help children who have comprehension problems?', *Journal of Research in Reading* **14**, 106–15.

Oakhill, J. *et al.* (1998) 'Individual Differences in Children's Comprehension Skill: Towards an Integrated Model', in Hulme, C. and Joshi, R. M. (eds) *Reading and Spelling: Development and Disorders*, 343–67. London: Lawrence Erlbaum Associates.

Office for Standards in Education (1999) *Raising the Attainment of Minority Ethnic Pupils* (Ref. HMI 170). London: HMSO.

Ogilvy, C. M. (1992) 'Staff-child interaction styles in multi-ethnic nursery schools', *British Journal of Developmental Psychology* **10**, 85–97.

Omark, D. R. and Erickson, J.G. (1983) *The bilingual exceptional child.* San Diego, CA: College Hill Press.

Oney, B. *et al.* (1997) 'Phonological processing in printed word recognition: Effects of age and writing system', *Scientific Studies of Reading* **1**(1), 65–83.

Ortiz, A. and Ramirez, B. A. (1988) *Schools and the culturally diverse exceptional student: Promising practices and future directions.* Reston, VA: Council for Exceptional Children – ERIC Clearinghouse on Handicapped and Gifted Children.

Orton, S. T. (1937) *Reading, writing and speech problems in children.* London: Chapman Hall.

Ott, P. (1997) *How to Detect and Manage Dyslexia.* Oxford: Heinemann.

Oxford, R. (1992) 'Who are our students? A synthesis of foreign and second language research on individual differences with implications for instructional practice', *TESL Canada Journal* **9**(1), 30–49.

Pallas, A. M. *et al.* (1989) 'The changing nature of the disadvantaged population: Current dimensions and future trends', *Educational Researcher* **18**, 16–22.

Paradis, M. (1990) 'Language Lateralization in Bilinguals: Enough already', *Brain and Language* **39**, 576–86.

Paulesu, E. *et al.* (1996) 'Is developmental dyslexia a disconnection syndrome? Evidence from PET scanning', *Brain* **119**, 143–57.

Peer, L. (1995) *Dyslexia: The Training and Awareness of Teachers*, 2nd edn. Reading: British Dyslexia Association.

Peer, L. (1996) *Winning with Dyslexia in Secondary School.* Reading: British Dyslexia Association.

Peer, L. (1997) 'Dyslexic and Bi/multilingual: In a Class of their Own', in Salter, R. and Smythe, I. (eds) *The International Book of Dyslexia*, 212–15. London: World Dyslexia Network Foundation.

Peer, L. (2000) *Winning with Dyslexia: a guide for secondary schools*, 3rd edn. Reading: British Dyslexia Association.

Perani, D. *et al.* (1996) 'Brain processing of native and foreign languages', *NeuroReport* **7**, 2439–44.

Perani, D. *et al.* (1998) 'The bilingual brain: proficiency and age of acquisition of the second language', *Brain* **121**,1841–52.

Perfetti, C. A. *et al.* (1996) 'Sources of Comprehension Failure: Theoretical Perspectives and Case Studies', in Cornoldi, C. and Oakhill, J. (eds) *Reading Comprehension Difficulties: Processes and Intervention*, 137–65. Hillsdale, NJ: Lawrence Erlbaum Associates.

Philips, L. *et al.* (1991) 'The college foreign language requirement: An action plan for Alternatives', *NACADA (National Academic Advising Association) Journal* **11**, 51–6.

Phillips, C. J. and Birrell, H. V. (1990) 'Learning to be literate: A study of young Asian pupils in English schools', *Education and Child Psychology* **7**, 55–66.

Pinker, S. (1995) *The Language Instinct.* Harmondsworth: Penguin Books.

Pinter, R. and Keller, R. (1922) 'Intelligence Tests for Foreign Children', *Journal of Educational Psychology* **13**, 214–22 (as mentioned in Hamers and Blanc 1989, 48).

Pollock, J. and Waller, E. (1994) *Day-to-Day Dyslexia in the Classroom.* London: Routledge.

Pumfrey, P. D. (1994) 'Sources and lists of recent education and curriculum-related publications', in Verma, G. K. and Pumfrey, P. D. (eds) *Cultural diversity and the curriculum: Cross-curricular contexts, themes and dimensions in primary schools* (vol. 4), 251–60. London: Falmer Press.

Pumfrey, P. D. (1996) *Specific Developmental Dyslexia: Basics to Back?* Leicester: British Psychological Society.

Rabbe, L. *et al.* (1998) 'Do What I Say … Not What I Did!' *English Teachers' Journal* **52**, 73–7.

Race Relations Act (1976) Halsbury's Statutes (4th edn, vol. 7) (1999 Reissue) *Civil Rights and Liberties* 115–192. London: Butterworths.

Race Relations (Amendment) Bill [H.L.] Session 1999–2000. Internet Publications. http://www.publications.parliament.uk/pa/cm199900/cmbills/060/00060-a.htm

Rack, J. P. (1994) 'Dyslexia: The Phonological Deficit Hypothesis', in Fawcett, A. and Nicolson, R. (eds) *Dyslexia in Children – Multidisciplinary Perspectives*, 5–37. London: Harvester Wheatsheaf.

Rack, J. P. (1997) 'Issues in the assessment of developmental dyslexia in adults: theoretical perspectives', *Journal of Research in Reading* **20**(1), 66–76.

Rack, J. P. *et al.* (1992) 'The non-word reading deficit in developmental dyslexia: a review', *Reading Research Quarterly* **27**(1), 28–53.

Raskind, M. H. *et al.* (1999) 'Patterns of change and predictors of success in individuals with learning disabilities: Results from a twenty-year longitudinal study', *Learning Disabilities Research and Practice* **14**(1), 35–49.

Raven, J. C. (1962) *Coloured Progressive Matrices.* London: H. K. Lewis and Co.

Raven, J. C. *et al.* (1990) *Coloured Progressive Matrices.* Windsor: NFER-Nelson.

Reason, R. and Boote, R. (1994) *Helping children with reading and spelling.* London: Routledge.

Reed, T. (1999) 'The millennium objective: give our minority communities a good deal by eliminating white yardsticks and institutional racism', *Educational and Child Psychology* **16**(3), 89–100.

Reid, G. (ed.) (1996) *Dimensions of Dyslexia (vol. 1) Assessment, Teaching and the Curriculum.* Edinburgh: Moray House Publications.

Reid, G. (1998) *Dyslexia: A practitioner's handbook.* Chichester: John Wiley and Sons.

Riddick, B. (1996) *Living with Dyslexia.* London: Routledge.

Riding, R. and Rayner, S. (1998) *Cognitive Styles and Learning Strategies: understanding style differences in learning and behaviour.* London: David Fulton Publishers.

Robertson, J. (1991) *Locus of control belief and pupils with specific learning difficulties.* Unpublished Master's thesis. Victoria University, Manchester.

Robertson, J. (1999) *Dyslexia and reading: a neuropsychological approach.* London: Whurr Publishers Limited.

Robertson, J. (2000) 'Neuropsychological intervention in dyslexia: two studies on British pupils' (to appear in) *Journal of Learning Disabilities* **33** (2).

Robertson, J. (in press) 'Teaching modern foreign languages to pupils with dyslexia: A neuropsychological perspective' (to appear in) *Support for Learning.*

Robertson, J. and Bakker, D. (1999) 'Classification of Developmental Dyslexia', in Fabbro, F. (ed.) *Concise Encyclopedia of Language Pathology.* Oxford: Pergamon and Elsevier Science.

Rome, P. and Smith Osman, J. (1993) *Language Tool Kit.* Cambridge, MA: Educators' Publishing Service.

Rose, E. (1993) 'Faculty development: Changing attitudes and enhancing knowledge about LD', in Vogel, S. and Adelman, P. (eds) *Success for College Students with Learning Disabilities*, 131–50. NY: Springer-Verlag.

Rose, C. (1985) *Accelerated Learning.* Aylesbury: Accelerated Learning Systems.

Roseberry-McKibbin, C. (1995) 'Distinguishing language differences from language disorders in linguistically and culturally diverse students', in Fieiberg, K. (ed.) (2000) *Educating exceptional children*, 78–81. Guilford, CT: Dushkin/McGraw-Hill.

Rourke, B. P. (1982) 'Central processing deficiencies in children: Towards a developmental neuropsychological model', *Journal of Child Neuropsychology* **4**, 1–18.

Ryan, A. (1993) *'Vowel Blindness' in Arabic learners of English.* Unpublished Ph.D. thesis, University of Wales, Swansea.

Ryan, A. (1997) 'Learning the form', in McCarthy, M. and Schmitt, N. (eds) *Second language vocabulary.* Cambridge: Cambridge University Press.

Salter, R. and Smythe, I. (eds) (1997) *The International Book of Dyslexia.* London: World Dyslexia Network Foundation.

Saunders, G. (1988) *Bilingual children: From birth to teens.* Clevedon: Multilingual Matters.

Schneider, E. (1999) *Multisensory Structured Metacognitive Instruction: an Approach to Teaching a Foreign Language to At-risk Students at an American College.* Frankfurt am Main: Peter Lang Verlag.

Schneider, E. *et al.* (1999) *Impact of English as a foreign language on dyslexics: cross-cultural perspectives.* Paper presented at the International Dyslexia Association, Chicago, November.

Scottish Consultative Committee on the Curriculum (1996) *Teaching for Effective Learning.* Dundee: SCCC.

Scottish Consultative Council on the Curriculum (1999) *Modern Languages 5–14 National Guidelines.* Consultation Draft. Dundee: SCCC.

Scottish Council for Research in Education (1999) *Foreign languages in the Upper Secondary School: A Study of the Causes of Decline.* Edinburgh: SCRE.

Scottish Education Department (1989) *The Teaching of Languages other than English in Scottish Schools.* SED Circular No 1178, 16. Edinburgh: SED.

Scottish Office Education and Industry Department (1998) *Standards and Quality in Primary and Secondary Schools 1994–98: Modern Languages: A Report by Her Majesty's Inspectors of Schools.* Edinburgh: SOEID.

Scottish Office Education Department (1991) *Special education needs and ethnic minority pupils*. Edinburgh: Scottish Office.

Selikowitz, M. (1999) *Dysleksja*. Warszawa: Prószyski i S-ka.

Service, E. (1989) *Phonological coding in working memory and foreign language learning*. Helsinki: University of Helsinki General Psychology Monographs no. B9.

Service, E. (1992) 'Phonology, working memory and foreign language learning', *Quarterly Journal of Experimental Psychology* **45a**(1), 21–50.

Service, E. and Craik, F. I. M. (1993) 'Differences between young and older adults in learning a foreign vocabulary', *Journal of Memory and Language* **32**, 608–23.

Service, E. and Kohonen, V. (1995) 'Is the relation between phonological memory and foreign language learning accounted for by vocabulary acquisition?', *Applied Psycholinguistics* **16**, 155–72.

Shah, R. (1995) *The Silent Minority: children with disabilities in Asian families* (revised edition). London: National Children's Bureau.

Shaywitz, B. A. *et al.* (1995) 'Defining and classifying learning disabilities and attention-deficit/hyperactivity disorder', *Journal of Child Neurology* **10**, 550–57.

Sleeter, C. E. (1992) 'Restructuring schools for multicultural education', *Journal of Teacher Education* **43**, 141–8.

Silverberg, R. *et al.* (1979) 'Shift of visual field preference for English words in native Hebrew speakers', *Brain and Language* **8**, 184–90.

Smythe, I. and Everatt, J. (in preparation) *The International Dyslexia Test*.

Snowling, M. J. (1995) 'Phonological processing and developmental dyslexia', *Journal of Research in Reading* **18**, 132–8.

Snowling, M. J. and Nation, K. A. (1997) 'Language, phonology and learning to read', in Hulme, C. and Snowling, M. J. (eds) *Dyslexia: Biology Cognition and Intervention*. London: Whurr Publishers Limited.

Snowling, M. J. *et al.* (1996) *Graded nonword reading test*. Bury St Edmunds: Thames Valley Test Company.

Snowling, M. *et al.* (1988) 'Object-naming deficits in developmental dyslexia', *Journal of Research in Reading* **11**, 67–85.

Solity, J. (1996) 'Discrepancy definitions of dyslexia: an assessment-through-teaching perspective', *Educational Psychology in Practice* **12**(3), 141–51.

Spadafore, G. J. (1983) *Spadafore Diagnostic Reading Test*. Novato, CA: Academic Therapy Publications.

Sparks, R. (1995) 'Examining the Linguistic Coding Differences Hypothesis to Explain Individual Differences in Foreign Language Learning', *Annals of Dyslexia* **45**, 187–214.

Sparks, R. and Ganschow, L. (1991) 'Foreign language learning difficulties: Affective or native language aptitude differences?' *Modern Language Journal* **75**, 3–16.

Sparks, R. and Ganschow, L. (1993a) 'Identifying and instructing at-risk foreign language learners in college', in Benseler, D. (ed.) *The Dynamics of Language Program Direction*, 173–99. Boston, Mass.: Heinle and Heinle.

Sparks, R. and Ganschow, L. (1993b) 'The effects of multisensory structured language instruction on native language and foreign language aptitude skills of at-risk high school foreign language learners: A replication and follow-up study', *Annals of Dyslexia* **43**, 194–216.

Sparks, R. and Ganschow, L. (1995) 'Searching for the cognitive locus of foreign language learning difficulties: Linking first and second language learning', *Modern Language Journal* **77**(3), 289–302.

Sparks, R. *et al.* (1989) 'Linguistic Coding Deficits in Foreign Language Learners', *Annals of Dyslexia* **39**, 179–94.

Sparks, R. *et al.* (1991) 'Use of an Orton-Gillingham approach to a foreign language to dyslexic/learning disabled students: Explicit teaching of phonology in a language', *Annals of Dyslexia* **41**, 96–118.

Sparks, R. *et al.* (1992) 'The Effects of Multisensory Structured Language Instruction on Native Language and Foreign Language Aptitude Skills of At-Risk High School Foreign Language Learners', *Annals of Dyslexia* **42**, 25–53.

Sparks, R. *et al.* (1997) 'Foreign language proficiency of at-risk and not-at-risk foreign language learners over two years of foreign language instruction', *Journal of Learning Disabilities* **30**, 92–8.

Sparks, R. *et al.* (1998) 'Benefits of multisensory structured language instruction for at-risk foreign language learners: A comparison study of high school Spanish students', *Annals of Dyslexia* **48**, 239–70.

Spencer, K. (1999) *Is English a dyslexic language?* Paper presented at the First International Conference on Multilingualism and Dyslexia, Manchester, June.

Spolsky, B. (1989) *Conditions for second language learning.* Oxford: Oxford University Press.

Spreen, O. (1988) 'Prognosis of learning disability', *Journal of Consulting and Clinical Psychology* **56**, 836–42.

Stackhouse, J. and Wells, B. (1997) *Children's Speech and Literacy Difficulties.* London: Whurr Publishers Limited.

Stamboltzis, A. (1997) *Text genre, reading miscues and comprehension of pupils of similar reading attainment at National Curriculum Years 3 and 5.* Unpublished M.Phil. dissertation, University of Manchester.

Stanovich, K. E. (1986) 'Matthew effects in reading: Some consequences of individual differences in the acquisition of literacy', *Reading Research Quarterly* **21**, 360–407.

Stanovich, K. E. (1988) 'Explaining the differences between the dyslexic and the garden variety poor reader: the phonological core variable difference model', *Journal of Learning Disabilities* **21**(10), 590–612.

Stanovich, K. E. (1991) 'Discrepancy definitions of reading disability: Has intelligence led us astray?', *Reading Research Quarterly* **26**(1), 7–29.

Stanovich, K. *et al.* (1997) 'Progress in the search for dyslexia sub-types', in Hulme, C. and Snowling, M. (1997) *Dyslexia: Biology, Cognition and Intervention.* London: Whurr Publishers Limited.

Steffensen, M. S. *et al.* (1979) 'A cross-cultural perspective on reading comprehension', *Reading Research Quarterly* **15**(1), 10–29.

Sunderland, H. *et al.* (1997) *Dyslexia and the Bilingual Learner: assessing and teaching young people who speak English as an additional language.* London Borough of Southwark: Language and Literacy Unit.

Svensson, I. *et al.* (in press) *The prevalence of reading and spelling difficulties among inmates of institutions for compulsory care of juvenile delinquents.*

Swan, M. and Smith, B. (1987) *Learner English.* Cambridge: Cambridge University Press.

Tapine, V. and Waiti, D. (1997) *Visions for Maori Education*. Wellington, NZ: New Zealand Council for Educational Research.

Tarnpole, L. and Tarnpole, M. (eds) (1976) *Reading Disabilities: An International Perspective*. Baltimore, MD: University Park Press.

Taube, K. (1995) *Hur läser invandrarelever I Sverige? (How do immigrant pupils read in Sweden?)* Skolverket report no. 79. Stockholm: Skolverket.

Taylor, D. (1983) *Family Literacy*. London: Heinemann.

Thomas, S. *et al.* (1991–2000) *MLG Games*. London: MLG Publishing.

Thomas, W. and Collier, V. (1997) *School Effectiveness for Language Minority Students*. Washington, DC: National Clearinghouse for Bilingual Education, the George Washington University Center for the Study of Language and Education.

Thomson, M. E. (1990) *Developmental Dyslexia*, 3rd edn. London: Whurr Publishers Limited.

Tomlinson, S. (1989) 'Asian pupils and special issues', *British Journal of Special Education* **6**(3), 119–22.

Topping, K. (1996) 'Parents and Peers as Tutors for Dyslexic Children', in Reid, G., *Dimensions of Dyslexia*, vol. 2, Literacy, Language and Learning. Edinburgh: Moray House Publications.

Tucker, B. P. (1996) 'Application of the Americans with Disabilities Act (ADA) on Section 504 to colleges and universities: an overview and discussion of special issues relating to students', *Journal of College and University Law* **23**, 1–41.

Turner, M. (1993) 'More Testing Times', *Special Children* **66**, 12–13.

Turner, M. (1997) *Psychological Assessment of Dyslexia*. London: Whurr Publishers Limited.

Usmani, K. (1999) 'The influence of racism and cultural bias in the assessment of bilingual children', *Educational and Child Psychology* **16**(3), 44–54.

Vaid, J. (1983) 'Bilingualism and brain lateralization', in Segalowitz, S. J. (ed.) *Language functions and brain organization*. New York: Academic Press.

Vail, P. (1992) *Learning Styles*. New York: Modern Learning Press.

Vail, P. (1997) 'Watch Out for the Hole in Whole Language: Keep the Wonder, the Work, and the Welcome', *ETAI Forum* **VII**(3), 24–7.

Vik, G. H. (1976) 'Reading Disabilities in Norwegian Elementary Grades' in Tarnpole, J. and Tarnpole, M. (eds) *Reading Disabilities: An International Perspective*, 252. Baltimore, MD: University Park Press.

Vitale, B. M. (1982) *Unicorns are Real: A Right-Brained Approach to Learning*. Calif.: Jalmar Press.

Vogel, S. (1975) *Syntactic Abilities in Normal and Dyslexic Children*. Baltimore, MD: University Park Press.

Vogel, S. (1998) 'Introduction to the special series (Adults with Learning Disabilities)', *Journal of Learning Disabilities* **31**, 210–11.

Vogel, S. *et al.* (1998) 'The national learning disabilities postsecondary data bank: an Overview', *Journal of Learning Disabilities* **31**, 234–47.

Wagner, D. A. *et al.* (1989) 'Does learning to read in a second language always put the child at a disadvantage? Some counter-evidence from Morocco', *Applied Psycholinguistics* **10**, 31–8.

Wagner, R. K. and Torgesen, J. K. (1987) 'The nature of phonological processing and its causal role in the acquisition of reading skills', *Psychological Bulletin* **101**(2), 192–212.

Walker, R. (1990) *Struggle without end: Ka whawhai tonu matou*. Auckland, NZ: Penguin.

Wallace, C. (1988) *Learning to Read in a Multicultural Society: The Social Context of Second Language Literacy*. Hemel Hempstead: Prentice Hall.

Watson, C. and Willows, D. M. (1993) 'Evidence for a visual processing deficit subtype among disabled readers', in Willows, D. M. *et al.* (eds) *Visual Processes in Reading and Reading Disabilities*, 287–309. Hillsdale, N J: Lawrence Erlbaum Associates.

Wechsler, D. (1981) *The Wechsler Adult Intelligence Scale (Revised)*. New York: Psychological Corporation.

Wechsler, D. (1992) *Wechsler Intelligence Scale For Children – Third Edition UK* (WISC-III). New York: Harcourt Brace Jovanovitch, Psychological Corporation.

Wechsler, D. (1998) *Wechsler Memory Scale – Third Edition*. London: Psychological Corporation.

Weingrod, B. (1990) 'Aspects of Dyslexia Among and Between English and Hebrew Speakers', *English Teacher's Journal* **40**, 25–33.

Weinreich, H. (1978) 'Sex-role Socialisation', in Chetwynd, J. (ed.) *The Sex Role System: Psychological and Sociological Perspectives*, 18–27. London: Routledge and Kegan Paul.

Wenden, A. (1987) 'How to be a successful learner: insights and prescriptions form L2 learners', in Wenden, A. and Rubin, J. (eds) *Learner Strategies in Language Learning*. Englewood Cliffs, NJ: Prentice Hall.

West, T. G. (1991) *In the mind's eye. Visual thinkers, gifted people with learning difficulties, computer images and the irony of creativity*, 3rd edn. Buffalo, NY: Prometheus Books.

Westwood, P. *et al.* (1974) 'One minute addition test – one minute subtraction test', *Remedial Education* **9**(2), 71–2.

Wheldall, K. and Mettem, P. (1985) 'Behavioural peer tutoring: Training 16 year old tutors to employ the "pause, prompt and praise" method with 12 year old remedial readers', *Educational Psychology* **5**, 27–44.

Wiig, E. H. and Secord, W. (1992) *Test of Word Knowledge*. London: Psychological Corporation Limited.

Wilkins, A. (1996) 'Dyslexia Helping Reading with Colour', *Dyslexia Review* **7**(3), 4–7.

Wilkinson, G. S. (1993) *Wide Range Achievement Test 3*. London: Psychological Corporation Limited.

Wilson, J. (1997) *Phonological Awareness Training*. London: UCL Educational Psychology Publishing.

Wimmer, H. (1993) 'Characteristics of developmental dyslexia in a regular writing system', *Applied Psycholinguistics* **14**(1), 1–33.

Wimmer, H. and Goswami, U. (1994) 'The influence of orthographic consistency on reading development: Word recognition in English and German children', *Cognition* **51**, 91–103.

Wolf, M. (1999) 'What time may tell: towards a new conceptualization of developmental dyslexia', *Annals of Dyslexia* **49**, 3–28.

Working Party of the Division of Educational and Child Psychology of the British Psychological Society (1999) *Dyslexia, literacy and psychological assessment*. Leicester: British Psychological Society.

Wright, S. *et al.* (1996) 'Dyslexia: stability of definition over a five year period', *Journal of Research in Reading* **19**, 46–60.

Yamada, J. (1998) 'Script makes a difference: The induction of deep dyslexic errors in logograph reading', *Dyslexia: An International Journal of Research and Practice* **4**, 197–211.

Yang, L. and Givon, T. (1993) *Tracking the acquisition of L2 vocabulary: the Keki language experiment.* University of Oregon, Institute of Cognitive and Decision Strategies: Technical report No. 93–11.

Yuill, N. M. and Oakhill, J. V. (1988) 'Effects of inference awareness training on poor reading comprehension', *Applied Cognitive Psychology* **2**, 33–45.

Zimin, S. (1992) *Teacher's Guide of the GAME Books.* Tel Aviv: Uriel Ilan.

Index